Data Recovery Techniques for Computer Forensics

Edited by

Alex Khang

Faculty of AI and Data Science
Global Research Institute of Technology and Engineering
Raleigh, North Carolina
USA

Sanchit Dhankhar

Chitkara College of Pharmacy
Chitkara University, Rajpura-140401, Punjab
India

Sandeep Bhardwaj

DRP Education Centre, Chennai
Tamil Nadu 600021, India

Avnesh Verma

Department of Instrumentation
Engg Kurukshetra University
Kurukshetra, India

&

Satish Kumar Sharma

Glocal School of Pharmacy, Glocal University
Mirzapur Pole, Uttar Pradesh 247121, India

Data Recovery Techniques for Computer Forensics

Editors: Alex Khang, Sanchit Dhankhar, Sandeep Bhardwaj, Avnesh Verma & Satish Kumar Sharma

ISBN (Online): 978-981-5274-67-7

ISBN (Print): 978-981-5274-68-4

ISBN (Paperback): 978-981-5274-69-1

need for a court order if at any point you breach any terms of this License Agreement. In no event will any delay or failure by Bentham Science Publishers in enforcing your compliance with this License Agreement constitute a waiver of any of its rights.

3. You acknowledge that you have read this License Agreement, and agree to be bound by its terms and conditions. To the extent that any other terms and conditions presented on any website of Bentham Science Publishers conflict with, or are inconsistent with, the terms and conditions set out in this License Agreement, you acknowledge that the terms and conditions set out in this License Agreement shall prevail.

Bentham Science Publishers Pte. Ltd.
80 Robinson Road #02-00
Singapore 068898
Singapore
Email: subscriptions@benthamscience.net

**BENTHAM
SCIENCE**

CONTENTS

Heena Dhiman, Rajneesh Gujral, Rajesh Khanna, Neelam Oberoi, Sachin Dhiman,
Rohini Tewatia and Manni Rohilla

PREFACE

This technical book will provoke a lot of debate as it covers an interesting topic. We feel compelled to share our knowledge, analyses, and conclusions after working for numerous years in the field of pharmacy. We have written many papers and book chapters on various facets. Perhaps this description will increase knowledge of the issue and initiate a discussion that could result in significant ideological transformations. There are two reading categories for this book. First off, it can be read by regular individuals with little to no prior knowledge of science. Professionals from academia and government organizations will be represented by the second set of readers. It is hard to believe that all members of the scientific community will comply with the concepts and ideas presented in this work. But we do hope that the knowledge and information provided will serve as a guide for all the sections of society. In this introductory volume, we embark on a journey into the realm of data recovery, a critical aspect of any forensic investigation. In the digital age, evidence often resides not on physical documents, but within the intricate labyrinth of storage devices. The deleted files, hidden partitions, and encrypted data – these are the challenges computer forensics professionals face, tasked with recovering the hidden pieces of the digital puzzle. There are eleven chapters in the book. The introduction to elementary knowledge of data recovery is introduced in chapter 1 of this book. The reasons for data loss are discussed in Chapter 2, which also provides a detailed knowledge of hardware and software reasons for data loss. The data protecting technologies, elementary knowledge of hard disk, hard disk organization, common cases of partition recovery, FAT16 file system check, management of FAT32 file system, management of NTFS file system, and dynamic disk introduction were introduced in chapters 3 to 10 respectively, along with introduction of data security software in chapter 11. We wish a lot of people read this book. In order to escape the mistakes of the past, we must alter course and begin utilising knowledge built up by scientists.

Happy reading!

Alex Khang
AFaculty of AI and Data Science
Global Research Institute of Technology and Engineering
Raleigh, North Carolina
USA

Sanchit Dhankhar
Chitkara College of Pharmacy
Chitkara University, Rajpura-140401, Punjab
India

Sandeep Bhardwaj
DRP Education Centre, Chennai
Tamil Nadu 600021, India

Avnesh Verma
Department of Instrumentation
Engg Kurukshetra University
Kurukshetra, India

&
Satish Kumar Sharma
Glocal School of Pharmacy, Glocal University
Mirzapur Pole, Uttar Pradesh 247121, India

List of Contributors

Anjali Garg	Chitkara College of Pharmacy, Chitkara University, Rajpura, Punjab, India Swami Devi Dyal College of Pharmacy, Golpura Barwala, Panchkula, Haryana, India
Ankush	Ganpati Institute of Pharmacy, Bilaspur 135102, Haryana, India
Abhinav Singhal	Guru Gobind Singh College of Pharmacy, Yamuna Nagar, Haryana, India
Ankit Kumar	Ganpati Institute of Pharmacy, Bilaspur, Haryana, Yamuna Nagar, India
Heena Dhiman	M.M. College of Engineering, Maharishi Markandeshwar (Deemed to be University), Mullana, Ambala, Haryana, India
Himanshu Sharma	Ganpati Institute of Pharmacy, Bilaspur 135102, Haryana, India Chitkara College of Pharmacy, Chitkara University, Rajpura 140401, Punjab, India
Manni Rohilla	Chitkara College of Pharmacy, Chitkara University, Rajpura, Punjab, India Swami Vivekanand College of Pharmacy, Ram Nagar, Banur, Punjab, India
Monika Saini	Swami Vivekanand College of Pharmacy, Ram Nagar, Banur, Punjab, India M.M. College of Pharmacy, Maharishi Markandeshwar (Deemed to be University), Mullana, Ambala, Haryana, India
Mani Goyal	M.M. College of Engineering, Maharishi Markandeshwar (Deemed to be University), Mullana, Ambala, Haryana, India
Nitika Garg	Chitkara College of Pharmacy, Chitkara University, Rajpura, Punjab, India
Neelam Oberoi	M.M. College of Engineering, Maharishi Markandeshwar (Deemed to be University), Mullana, Ambala, Haryana, India
Pooja Mittal	Chitkara College of Pharmacy, Chitkara University, Rajpura, Punjab, India
Rishabh Chaudhary	M.M. College of Pharmacy, Maharishi Markandeshwar (Deemed to be University), Mullana, Ambala, Haryana, India
Rajneesh Gujral	M.M. College of Engineering, Maharishi Markandeshwar (Deemed to be University), Mullana, Ambala, Haryana, India
Rajesh Khanna	M.M. College of Engineering, Maharishi Markandeshwar (Deemed to be University), Mullana, Ambala, Haryana, India
Rohini Tewatia	Mahamaya Government Polytechnic of Information Technology, Hariharpur, Khajani, Gorakhpur, Uttar Pradesh, India
Sachin Dhiman	Chitkara College of Pharmacy, Chitkara University, Rajpura, Punjab, India
Sanchit Dhankhar	Chitkara College of Pharmacy, Chitkara University, Rajpura, Punjab, India
Samrat Chauhan	Chitkara College of Pharmacy, Chitkara University, Rajpura, Punjab, India
Shivam	Ganpati Institute of Pharmacy, Bilaspur 135102, Haryana, India
Shushank Mahajan	Chitkara College of Pharmacy, Chitkara University, Rajpura 140401, Punjab, India
Vishnu Mittal	Guru Gobind Singh College of Pharmacy, Yamuna Nagar, Haryana, India
Wasswa Shafik	School of Digital Science, Universiti Brunei Darussalam, Jalan Tungku Link, Gadong, BE1410, Bandar Seri Begawan, Brunei Darussalam Dig Connectivity Research Laboratory (DCRLab), Kampala, Uganda

CHAPTER 1

Elementary Knowledge of Data Recovery

Heena Dhiman[1,*], Sachin Dhiman[2], Manni Rohilla[2,3], Rishabh Chaudhary[5], Anjali Garg[2,4], Sanchit Dhankhar[2], Nitika Garg[2], Monika Saini[3,5] and Samrat Chauhan[2]

[1] *M.M. College of Engineering, Maharishi Markandeshwar (Deemed to be University), Mullana, Ambala, Haryana, India*

[2] *Chitkara College of Pharmacy, Chitkara University, Rajpura, Punjab, India*

[3] *Swami Vivekanand College of Pharmacy, Ram Nagar, Banur, Punjab, India*

[4] *Swami Devi Dyal College of Pharmacy, Golpura Barwala, Panchkula, Haryana, India*

[5] *M.M. College of Pharmacy, Maharishi Markandeshwar (Deemed to be University), Mullana, Ambala, Haryana, India*

Abstract: Data recovery is the process of recuperating deleted, formatted, corrupted, damaged, or inaccessible data from storage media or obtaining files that have no backups. In forensics, data recovery is a crucial stage that aids in extracting digital evidence from devices under suspicion. As cybercrime continues to rise daily, IT enterprises must develop strategies and resources to manage these criminal activities. Logical recovery and physical recovery are the two types of attempts to damage data. Physical damage refers to the act of permanently deleting evidence, which requires specialized tools to fix broken components of the storage device, such as burnt chips, halted spindles, and scratched or smashed plates. In contrast, logical damage occurs when the device's internal data is corrupted by virus attacks, but its physical components remain operational. Software-based techniques can restore data from a storage device that has experienced an operating system logical error or unintentional user deletion. Cybervandals cause damage or destruction in digital form. Digital vandalism seeks to damage, destroy, or disable data, computers, or networks. Various methods are used to retrieve and examine data, even when the file structure has been destroyed or damaged. This chapter addresses many tools and methods available for data recovery from a forensic standpoint.

Keywords: Data, Digital, Hardware, Recovery, Software.

INTRODUCTION

Data recovery in computer forensics involves the retrieval of lost, erased, or corrupted digital information from storage media such as hard disks, solid-state

* **Corresponding author Heena Dhiman:** M.M. College of Engineering, Maharishi Markandeshwar (Deemed to be University), Mullana, Ambala, Haryana, India; E-mail: dhimanheena001@gmail.com

Alex Khang, Sanchit Dhankhar, Sandeep Bhardwaj, Avnesh Verma & Satish Kumar Sharma (Eds.)

drives, USB drives, and other digital storage devices. The objective of data recovery is to reconstruct and restore data in a functional format for investigative or legal objectives. Data recovery in computer forensics is a crucial procedure that entails retrieving lost, destroyed, or corrupted digital information from storage devices. The goal is to reconstruct and restore data in a functional manner to aid in investigative, legal, or security-related tasks. Data recovery is crucial when digital evidence is endangered by inadvertent deletion [1]. Data loss is the inadvertent or deliberate destruction, alteration, or unavailability of digital data. Data loss in a forensic setting can provide substantial obstacles when investigators attempt to retrieve and examine evidence. Understanding the primary causes of data loss is crucial for forensic investigators and cybersecurity professionals, as it can occur in many situations. Users might unintentionally remove files, directories, or complete partitions, resulting in the loss of crucial data. Furthermore, malfunctions in storage devices such as hard drives, solid-state drives (SSDs), or external drives can also lead to data loss [2].

Common failures may involve disk crashes, faulty sectors, or controller malfunctions. Corruption of file systems or software can occur owing to faults, malfunctions, or malware infections, resulting in files becoming inaccessible or unreadable. Malicious software such as viruses, ransomware, or other malware can infect a system and either destroy or encrypt data, rendering it unusable. Physical damage to storage media, such as fire, water, or impact damage, can result in irreversible data loss. Abrupt power outages or electrical surges can lead to erroneous shutdowns [3].

IMPORTANCE OF DATA RECOVERY

- Data recovery is crucial in cybersecurity, law enforcement, litigation, company operations, and personal data management. It aids in recovering lost or deleted data, assisting in investigations, assuring responsibility, and maintaining the authenticity of digital material. Data recovery is essential for various reasons, particularly in the fields of computer forensics and digital investigations.
- Data recovery allows for the preservation of vital evidence in criminal investigations, civil lawsuits, or cybersecurity incidents. Recovering erased or missing data might offer crucial insights for identifying suspects, establishing timeframes, or demonstrating intent.
- Analyzing recovered data can help recreate events, reveal trends, and discover linkages between individuals or groups involved in illicit acts or security breaches. This analysis can be crucial for constructing a case or comprehending the modus operandi of cybercriminals.
- Data recovery safeguards individuals' rights by enabling access to information that could be pertinent to their defense in legal matters. It helps to preserve

evidence that could prove someone's innocence and guarantees a just trial [4].

- Corporate business continuity depends heavily on data recovery to maintain operations in the face of data loss. Recovering critical corporate data, like customer records, financial information, or intellectual property, minimizes disruptions and financial losses.
- Data recovery helps reduce financial losses caused by data breaches, system failures, or inadvertent deletions. Organizations can prevent the expenses of recreating lost information or compensating affected parties by retrieving vital data [27].
- Many sectors must adhere to stringent regulatory standards for data retention and protection. Data recovery helps enterprises comply with rules by allowing them to recover and store data as required by law.
- Data recovery is essential for individuals to retrieve personal or sentimental data, including family photos, documents, and other digital assets. Data loss due to hardware failure or accidental deletion can be devastating, but data recovery offers a chance to recover these irreplaceable items [2].

COMMON CAUSES OF DATA LOSS

Common reasons of data loss include:

- Preservation of Evidence: If the storage device containing evidence suffers a hardware failure, such as a hard drive crash or corruption, data loss can occur.
- Investigative Analysis: Software errors in forensic equipment might result in data loss. For instance, a flaw in a data recovery tool could accidentally replace or erase crucial evidence.
- Human Error: Errors committed by forensic investigators, like unintentionally deleting files or mishandling evidence, can lead to data loss.
- Malicious Actions: Deliberate alteration or destruction of evidence by attackers or insiders can result in data loss in computer forensics investigations.
- Loss of evidence: Data loss can lead to the destruction of important digital evidence needed for investigations. Compromised investigations can be hindered by incomplete or insufficient data, impacting the ability to recreate events [5].
- Business Continuity: Businesses may experience intellectual property loss, which can affect their competitiveness and security by compromising sensitive information.
- Mitigation of Financial Losses: Failure to safeguard or retrieve essential data might result in legal consequences and non-compliance with regulations.
- Compliance and Regulatory Requirements: Overwriting occurs when investigators neglect to employ appropriate write-blocking methods, leading to the potential loss of valuable evidence by writing over data on the storage medium.

- Recovery of Personal Data: Media degradation occurs when storage media deteriorates over time, resulting in data loss. This is particularly accurate for aging or inadequately kept storage devices [3].

BASICS OF FILE SYSTEMS

File systems are essential in computer forensics as they determine the methods of storing, organizing, and accessing data on storage devices. Forensic investigators handling digital evidence must have a thorough understanding of file systems. A file system is a method or structure utilized by an operating system to arrange and store files on storage media. It offers a hierarchical framework for structuring data. Understanding the fundamentals of file systems is crucial for forensic investigators to analyze digital evidence, reconstruct events, and present results in judicial processes. It requires understanding various file system types, their structures, and the tools and methods employed in file system analysis [6].

Overview of File Systems

- A file system is an essential element of a computer system that oversees the storage, organization, and retrieval of data on storage media. Comprehending different file systems is crucial in computer forensics for investigators to assess digital evidence efficiently. File systems are essential for forensic investigators to effectively evaluate digital evidence, reconstruct events, and present results in court processes. Various file systems have distinct architectures, characteristics, and difficulties, necessitating forensic experts to adjust their analysis techniques accordingly. Below are essential components and principles associated with file systems: File: A file is a compilation of data or information saved with a designated name on a storage device. Files can store text, photos, videos, programs, or any form of data.
- Directory: A directory, usually referred to as a folder, is a container utilized to categorize and group interconnected files and other directories within a file system. Directories can consist of files and subdirectories, forming a hierarchical arrangement.
- File Path: A file path is a distinct identifier that indicates the precise location of a file in the file system. The file path usually consists of directory and subdirectory names leading to the file, separated by slashes or backslashes, depending on the operating system.
- Metadata: Metadata encompasses supplementary details linked to files, including file size, creation date, and modification date, file permissions, file type, and file attributes. File systems utilize metadata to monitor and control files, encompassing their arrangement, accessibility, and security configurations.
- The File Allocation Table (FAT): The File Allocation Table (FAT) is a file system structure that stores information on file allocation on a storage medium.

The system logs the positions of files and their respective data clusters (blocks) on the disk.

- Master File Table (MFT): The Master File Table (MFT) is a component of the NTFS file system specifically utilized by Windows operating systems. The NTFS volume holds metadata and attributes for each file and directory, creating a centralized index of file system objects.
- Inode: An inode, short for "index node," is a data structure used by Unix-like file systems like EXT2, EXT3, and EXT4. It stores metadata about files, including permissions, ownership, timestamps, and pointers to data blocks.
- Journaling: Journaling is a method employed by certain file systems to enhance data integrity and facilitate recovery in case of system crashes or power outages. It requires keeping a log of file system transactions to enable rapid recovery and consistency testing when the system reboots.
- Cluster: A cluster, usually referred to as a block, is the smallest unit of storage allocation in a file system. Files are kept in clusters, with the cluster size subject to variation based on the file system and disk formatting configurations.
- File System Fragmentation: Fragmentation is the result of files being stored in a non-contiguous manner on a storage medium, causing reduced performance and efficiency. File systems may employ defragmentation to rearrange and consolidate fragmented files in order to enhance access performance [7].

How File Systems Manage Data

File systems are fundamental to managing data on storage devices in computer forensics. They provide a structured approach to storing, accessing, and organizing files and folders. Understanding how file systems manage data is crucial for forensic investigators examining digital evidence. Files are named collections of data, such as documents, photos, or programs. Directories, on the other hand, are containers that store files and other directories, creating a hierarchical structure for organizing data [6]. File systems reserve storage space on storage devices for files. They oversee clusters or blocks, which are the most basic pieces of storage. When a file is erased, the file system typically designates the space as free, although the data can still be retrieved until it is overwritten. Forensic investigators utilize methods such as file carving and recovery tools to recover deleted material. Data management by file systems is crucial for digital forensics. It allows investigators to effectively understand and analyze digital evidence, ensuring the accuracy and integrity of conclusions in judicial processes. Forensic professionals need to adjust their approaches according to the distinct characteristics of each file system found in an investigation [8].

STORAGE MEDIA AND DATA RETRIEVAL

Storage media and data retrieval play a crucial role in the investigation and analysis of digital evidence in computer forensics. Comprehending various storage media types and data retrieval procedures is essential for forensic investigators. Diverse storage media like Hard Disk Drives (HDD), Solid-State Drives (SSD), External Drives, *etc.*, have distinct characteristics. Understanding these characteristics, utilizing suitable data retrieval techniques, and effectively employing forensic tools are essential for successful computer forensics investigations. Forensic professionals must adjust their methods according to the type of storage media they uncover and the focus of the investigation [28].

Storage Media Types

Computer forensics investigators come across many forms of storage media containing digital information. Comprehending various storage media types is essential for efficient data retrieval and analysis. Various forms of storage media include Hard Disk Drives (HDD), Solid-State Drives (SSD), External Drives, and more.

Different types of storage media, such as Hard Disk Drives (HDDs), Solid-State Drives (SSDs), and external drives, require specific data retrieval methods and forensic tools. Successful computer forensic investigations depend on understanding the characteristics of these media and adapting techniques accordingly.

Types of Storage Media

Computer forensic investigations involve examining various types of storage media, such as Hard Disk Drives (HDDs), Solid-State Drives (SSDs), and external drives. Understanding these media is essential for effective data retrieval and analysis.

1. *Hard Disk Drives (HDDs)* are traditional magnetic storage devices that use rotating disks. They are commonly used as primary storage in desktops, laptops, and servers. In computer forensics, HDDs are significant because they often contain the operating system, applications, and user data.

2. *Solid-State Drives (SSDs)* use NAND flash memory for storage. They are commonly found in laptops, ultra-books, and high-performance devices. In computer forensics, SSDs are significant due to their faster access times and their use as primary storage [9].

3. External Drives, such as USB drives, external hard disk drives, and external SSDs, are portable storage devices used for backup, data transfer, and data preservation. They are commonly used in computer forensics to store and transport digital evidence.

4. Optical discs, such as CDs, DVDs, and Blu-ray discs, are used for data storage, software distribution, and multimedia. Forensic significance includes installation media or backup files.

It is essential for investigators to comprehend the features and forensic significance of different storage media in order to properly manage, examine, and retrieve digital evidence in computer forensic investigations. Every storage media type poses distinct challenges and factors for forensic experts [5].

Impact of Storage Media on Data Recovery

The choice of storage medium significantly affects data recovery procedures in computer forensics. Different storage media have unique characteristics that influence the complexity and effectiveness of data retrieval.

- Recovering data from physically damaged hard disk drives typically necessitates specialized gear and experience.
- Components like the read/write heads, platters, and spindle motor may be damaged, resulting in data loss.
- SD cards utilize NAND flash memory cells to store data, which have a finite number of write cycles before they degrade.
- Data retrieval from malfunctioning SSDs frequently requires addressing intricate firmware problems, wear-leveling techniques, and encryption systems.
- Data retrieval from RAID arrays can be intricate because of the array's setup, parity data, and interconnections among drives.
- Failures like repeated disk failures, controller problems, or misconfigurations can complicate the recovery.

Best Practices for Handling Storage Media

Properly managing storage media in computer forensics involves following established guidelines to guarantee the integrity, conservation, and acceptability of digital evidence. One aspect of chain custody is known as maintenance, which involves documenting and monitoring the possession, transfer, and treatment of storage media from seizure to its presentation in court. Chain of custody documents must contain dates, times, individuals, and acts carried out.

To prevent accidental damage or contamination, it is crucial to minimize physical handling of storage media. Forensic duplicates or photos should be used instead of modifying or saving data on the original device. When creating a forensic image, reliable imaging tools must be used to ensure an exact copy of the original data, preserving its integrity. Detailed records should be kept of all steps involved in handling, imaging, and examining storage media. This includes documenting the software and hardware used, settings applied, and any deviations from standard procedures. By following these best practices, we can ensure that storage media is handled with care and professionalism, maintaining the integrity of digital evidence for legal purposes. This also promotes transparency, accountability, and the credibility of forensic findings [10].

DATA RECOVERY TOOLS AND TECHNIQUES

Data recovery in computer forensics involves using specialized tools and techniques to retrieve, reconstruct, and analyze digital evidence from storage media. The choice of tools and techniques depends on the investigation's nature, the storage media involved, and the specific data recovery goals. Forensic investigators must follow proper procedures, maintain documentation, and adhere to legal and ethical standards throughout the process. Fundamental retrieval is a concept used to recover deleted, lost, or inaccessible files from storage media.

Most data recovery software offers a user-friendly interface, making it accessible to both novice and experienced users. These tools support a wide range of file types, including documents, images, videos, archives, and more. Users can also selectively recover specific files or folders, rather than recovering the entire storage medium [11].

Introduction to Data Recovery Software

Data recovery software is created to assist users in retrieving lost, erased, or inaccessible data from storage devices such as hard disks, SSDs, USB drives, memory cards, and RAID arrays. The software tools employ many methods to scan storage media for missing data, reconstitute file systems, and aid in the recovery process. Below are some commonly used data recovery software choices:

- EaseUS Data Recovery Wizard: EaseUS Data Recovery Wizard is a versatile data recovery tool for Windows and Mac. It can recover different file types like documents, photos, videos, and emails. The software has a user-friendly interface with clear instructions, suitable for users with different technical skills. It can retrieve data from various storage devices such as hard drives, SSDs, USB drives, memory cards, and RAID array.

- Recuva: Recuva is a data recovery program created by Piriform, a company owned by Avast, known for its lightweight design. Recuva can retrieve deleted files from Windows-based computers, both from internal and external storage devices. It features a user-friendly interface with quick and thorough scanning options to find and restore lost files. The program is capable of recovering files from damaged or formatted drives and includes a feature to securely delete confidential data [6].
- Stellar Data Recovery: Stellar Data Recovery is a versatile data recovery software compatible with Windows, Mac, and Linux systems. It can recover a wide range of file types like documents, photos, videos, audio files, and email archives. The software includes advanced features like RAW file recovery, disk imaging, and RAID recovery for intricate data loss situations. It has a user-friendly interface.
- Disk Drill: Disk Drill is a data recovery tool for Windows and Mac that can recover deleted files, lost partitions, and formatted drives. It includes data protection features to prevent future data loss and offers various scanning algorithms like quick scan, deep scan, and partition search. The software has a user-friendly interface with file preview options.
- R-Studio: R-Studio is a robust data recovery software tailored for experienced users and experts. It enables data recovery from a range of file systems such as NTFS, FAT, exFAT, HFS+, APFS, and others. R-Studio includes a wide range of features for disk imaging, file carving, and RAID reconstruction, making it ideal for intricate data recovery operations. It offers a customized interface with scripting support and command-line tools for automation and batch processing [7].

Hardware-Based Data Recovery

Hardware-based data recovery in computer forensics employs specialized equipment and techniques to retrieve data from physically damaged, corrupted, or mechanically faulty storage media. This method is particularly useful when software-based techniques are insufficient due to hardware issues. Common targets for hardware-based recovery include hard disk drives (HDDs) and solid-state drives (SSDs). Experts assess the extent of physical damage to determine the appropriate recovery method. Severe damage may necessitate recovery in a clean room environment to prevent contamination [12]. Cleanrooms reduce the likelihood of airborne particles causing harm to delicate components during the recovery process [13].

Hardware-based recovery utilizes specialized tools and equipment specifically created for physical repair and recovery. Examples include head stack replacement tools for HDDs and soldering stations for fixing electronic components. Defective parts on storage devices, including read/write heads on HDDs, could require replacement. Professionals utilize appropriate spare parts that are compatible with the particular make and model of the storage device. Professionals may perform platter transplanting in severe cases of damage to the magnetic disks inside HDDs. This process entails moving the platters from the impaired drive to a donor drive in order to retrieve data. Hardware-based recovery may entail the repair or reprogramming of the firmware in the storage device. Firmware problems can lead to data becoming inaccessible, and it is crucial to address them promptly for a successful recovery. Hardware-based data recovery is used as a final option when physical damage hinders the application of conventional software-based recovery techniques. A high level of knowledge, adherence to best practices, and a complete understanding of the unique hardware are necessary. This method is usually used by specialized data recovery labs or forensic professionals who have the required expertise and equipment due to its complexity and potential hazards [14].

Software-Based Data Recovery

Software-based data recovery in computer forensics utilizes specialized tools to retrieve, restore, and analyze digital evidence from storage media that may be damaged, corrupted, or accidentally deleted. This method is frequently used when the loss of data is caused by logical concerns rather than physical harm. Software-based recovery is appropriate for instances of data loss caused by logical errors such as unintentional deletion, formatting, or file system damage. Data recovery software is compatible with many file systems such as FAT, NTFS, exFAT, HFS+, and others, allowing it to work with varied storage media. Software tools often have user-friendly interfaces, making them accessible to both forensic professionals and non-experts. Many tools offer quick scan options for rapid detection of recoverable files and deep scans for a thorough investigation of storage media. Users can selectively recover individual files or folders, enabling precise retrieval of relevant digital data. File carving techniques are used to locate and recover files from unallocated space or fragmented sections of storage media. Additionally, software programs often include preview functions that allow users to examine recoverable files before finalizing the recovery process [13].

To ensure data integrity, recovered files are authenticated using checksums (MD5, SHA-1, and SHA-256). Software solutions with search and filter functions allow users to easily locate specific files based on criteria like file name, size, or date. Software data recovery technologies are essential for forensic investigators, providing effective solutions for retrieving digital evidence from logically damaged storage devices. These tools are versatile, user-friendly, and capable of handling various logical data loss scenarios [29].

Choosing the Right Tools for the Job

It is essential to select appropriate tools for computer forensics to conduct thorough investigations and ensure precise analysis of digital evidence. There are important factors to consider when choosing tools for different phases of a computer forensics investigation:

- Identify the Type of Data Loss: Identify the type of data loss by determining the nature of the data loss you are experiencing. Was the data loss caused by unintentional deletion, formatting, logical corruption, or physical damage to the storage device? Comprehending the reason for data loss can assist in selecting suitable recovery tools.
- Assess the Storage Media: Determine the storage media type for data recovery, including hard disks, SSDs, USB drives, memory cards, or RAID arrays. Various recovery tools may excel at retrieving data from particular kinds of storage
- Consider Your Technical Expertise: Determine your skill level and knowledge of data recovery processes. Some solutions provide intuitive interfaces and guided wizards for novices, while others demand a higher level of technical expertise for optimal utilization.
- Evaluate Features and Functionality: Look for data recovery tools that offer the features and functionality you need to address your specific data loss scenario.
- File Type Support: Verify if the tool can recover the specific file formats required, such as documents, photographs, videos, emails, *etc*.
- Scan Options: Verify if the utility has adjustable scanning choices like quick scan, deep scan, or specialized file system scans.
- Preview Capabilities: Seek tools that let you preview recoverable files prior to restoration to confirm their integrity and quality.
- Additional Features: Take into account any extra functions you might need, including disk imaging, RAID recovery, safe deletion, *etc*. Read Reviews and Recommendations: Research and read reviews from other users or experts to get insights into the performance, reliability, and effectiveness of different data recovery tools. Look for recommendations from reputable sources or online communities specializing in data recovery.
- Trial and Testing: Whenever possible, try out the data recovery tools using their trial versions or free versions to evaluate their performance and compatibility with your system. Test the tools on a sample storage device or data set to see how well they recover lost or deleted files.
- Consider Professional Services: Examine feedback from users and professionals to get an understanding of the performance, dependability, and efficacy of various data recovery programs. Seek advice from credible sources or online communities that focus on data recovery.

Investigators can choose appropriate tools for forensic investigations by analyzing the requirements and features of the digital evidence. Forensic practitioners must consistently update their toolsets and keep abreast of developing innovations in the field [15].

Common Data Recovery Scenarios

Data recovery in computer forensics is a crucial procedure that entails recovering lost, destroyed, or corrupted digital data for analysis. It is essential for forensic investigators to comprehend prevalent scenarios that can result in data loss or inaccessibility.

- Accidental deletion frequently occurs in computer forensics when users unintentionally delete files or directories from storage media.
- Recovery procedure utilizes specialized tools and approaches to retrieve deleted data for forensic investigation. An overview of unintentional deletion and the recovery method in computer forensics is provided here.
- A user accidentally deletes files or directories. Deletion can be done by different methods, including the operating system's file manager, command-line interface, or third-party apps.
- When a file is removed, the file system usually designates the space taken up by the file as available for future use [13].
- The directory structure of the file system is modified to show the deletion, but the data is retained on the storage media until it is replaced.
- It is essential to cease writing any new data to the storage media as soon as accidental loss is detected in order to increase the likelihood of successful recovery.
- Using the storage device more can increase the chances of accidentally replacing the erased data [16].

Formatted Drives and Recovery

Formatted drives in computer forensics refer to situations where the file system on a storage device is destroyed, leading to data loss. The recovery method entails utilizing specialized tools and techniques to extract data from the formatted drive for forensic investigation. Users may deliberately format a drive to delete all data, typically for routine maintenance or to reuse the storage device. Accidental formatting may result from human errors, including choosing the incorrect drive while formatting.

- Formatting is typically carried out while installing a new operating system, which involves deleting all data on the drive.

- Malicious software or cyberattacks may format drives as part of destructive actions, resulting in data loss.
- Stop using the formatted drive immediately to avoid data overwriting. Prolonged use raises the likelihood of permanent data loss.
- Choose a dependable data recovery tool that is compatible with the file system and format of the storage device.
- Commonly used software applications for data recovery are EaseUS Data Recovery Wizard, R-Studio, and TestDisk. Install the chosen data recovery software on a different PC or external drive to prevent adding new data to the formatted drive [17].

Corrupted Files and Data Reconstruction

Corrupted files are a frequent obstacle in computer forensics, where data integrity can be compromised by software failures, hardware problems, malware attacks, or sudden system shutdowns. Data reconstruction is the procedure of recovering and fixing damaged data to their initial condition, enabling forensic investigators to retrieve and examine important digital evidence. Software flaws in programs or operating systems can result in file corruption. Instances such as system failures while saving files or errors in programs that handle data. Hardware failures can lead to data corruption due to problems in storage devices or other hardware components. Common hardware-related causes include sudden power outages, bad RAM, and disk issues. Malware and cyber-attacks involve the deliberate corruption of files to disrupt operations or block access to important information. Data reconstruction in computer forensics is a meticulous procedure that necessitates a blend of technical proficiency, specialized tools, and thorough documentation. Forensic investigators can retrieve crucial evidence and aid in resolving digital investigations by proficiently restoring corrupted files [13].

Preventive Measures and Backup Strategies

Preventive measures and backup techniques are crucial in computer forensics to protect digital data, maintain data integrity, and enable effective recovery in case of data loss or corruption. Regular updates to operating systems, software, and security software are essential to address vulnerabilities and prevent exploitation. Continuous security awareness training for users helps reduce the risk of social engineering attacks, phishing, and other user-related security issues. Strong access controls and authentication methods are implemented to limit unauthorized access to critical data and systems. Firewalls, intrusion detection systems, and other network security protocols are deployed to protect against external threats.

Antivirus software, endpoint security solutions, and anti-malware technologies are used to detect and prevent malicious software [18]. Regular security audits and assessments help identify system vulnerabilities and weaknesses. Encryption is used to protect sensitive data from unauthorized access during storage and transmission. A well-defined incident response plan is essential to guide actions in case of a security incident or data breach.

Securely configure systems by adhering to best practices for system hardening to minimize the attack surface. Establish strong monitoring and logging systems to identify and address any questionable behaviors effectively [10].

Importance of Regular Backups

- Regular backups are essential in computer forensics for various reasons. These backups are crucial for protecting digital data, maintaining data integrity, and aiding in forensic investigations.
- Regular backups safeguard important digital data by duplicating files, configurations, and system states. This guarantees that important data is preserved in case of unintentional removal, corruption, or unexpected events.
- Backups are a dependable resource for recovering and reconstructing data in case of data loss, corruption, or a security incident.
- Forensic investigators utilize backups to recover systems to a verified secure condition and extract crucial evidence for examination.
- Backups serve as a foundation for forensic analysis. Investigators can analyze the present state of a system by comparing it to a known backup to detect alterations, irregularities, or unauthorized adjustments.
- This comparison is useful for identifying harmful activity and comprehending the sequence of events.
- Having current backups facilitates quick incident response in the event of security problems or breaches.
- Investigators can promptly recover impacted systems, reducing downtime and lessening the incident's effects [7].
- Regular backups serve as a preventative step to mitigate data loss. Regularly backing up important data helps organizations minimize the risk of unintentional deletion, system failures, software mistakes, and other unexpected events.

Implementing Effective Backup Strategies

Implementing robust backup solutions in computer forensics is essential for protecting digital data, maintaining data integrity, and enabling swift recovery in the event of data loss or corruption.

Identify the crucial data that needs to be backed up regularly. This may consist of case files, evidence repositories, system configurations, and any other essential information for forensic investigations.

Determine a backup schedule according to the importance of the data and how frequently it is updated. Choose between daily, weekly, or incremental backups based on the type of data being stored. Select dependable and esteemed backup products that are compatible with the file systems and data kinds used in your forensic setting. Commonly used tools are Veeam, Acronis, and Backup Exec. Utilize a mix of full, incremental, and differential backups to enhance storage efficiency and backup speed. Full backups encompass the complete dataset, whereas incremental and differential backups concentrate on modifications made since the previous backup. Automate the backup procedure to guarantee uniformity and dependability. Automated backups scheduled in advance minimize the chance of human error and guarantee regular backup performance [19].

Keep backups in an alternative location to safeguard against physical disasters, theft, or other localized issues. Cloud storage solutions are efficient for storing backup data remotely. Introduce encryption for backup data to safeguard sensitive information while it is stored and transferred. Encryption guarantees data security even if backups are breached. Regularly verify the integrity of backups by recovering data in a distinct environment. Verify that the recovered data is precise, comprehensive, and functional. Consistent testing boosts trust in the backup plan.

Data Security and Risk Mitigation

Ensuring data security and minimizing risks are crucial in computer forensics to safeguard sensitive information, preserve the integrity of digital evidence, and reduce potential investigation risks. Enforce robust access restrictions to limit access to critical forensic data and tools. Implement role-based access control and authentication techniques to restrict access to forensic resources to authorized workers. Secure confidential forensic data by encrypting it while at rest and in transit. Encryption prevents illegal access and ensures the secrecy of digital evidence. Guarantee the physical protection of forensic workstations, servers, and storage systems. Restrict access to these resources and use physical security measures to deter manipulation or theft.

Secure digital evidence in tamper-evident storage. Utilize dedicated servers, encrypted drives, or hardware security modules to improve the security of stored forensic data. Create and maintain a computer forensics-specific incident response plan and update it periodically [3]. Provide detailed protocols for managing security events, breaches, or illegal access to forensic data. Furthermore, categorize digital evidence according to its sensitivity and significance. Implement varying security protocols and access restrictions according to the classification level to emphasize safeguarding. By incorporating these factors into computer forensics procedures, experts can improve data security, reduce hazards, and maintain the integrity of digital evidence. Success and credibility of forensic investigations require a comprehensive approach that considers physical, technical, and procedural security factors [12].

CASE STUDIES AND EXAMPLES

Real-Life Data Recovery Scenarios

Corporate Data Theft

Scenario: An employee from a major firm commits intellectual property theft before quitting. The corporation suspects theft and engages a computer forensic specialist.

Forensic Procedures

- Perform imaging of the employee's computer and examine email correspondence.
- Inspect external storage devices for unwanted data transfers.
- Retrieve erased files and analyze timestamps to create a chronological sequence.

Result

- The forensic analysis determines the employee's participation.
- The evidence is utilized in court proceedings to retrieve stolen data and take legal action against the employee.

Cyber Extortion

Situation: A small business owner is targeted by a ransomware assault and is asked to pay a sum of money to unlock important business data.

Forensic Procedures

- Quarantine impacted systems and examine the ransomware code.
- Analyze network records to identify the origin of the malware.
- Try to identify the culprits by tracing digital footprints.

Result

- Forensic analysis aids in decrypting data without ransom payment.
- Attacker information is shared with law enforcement for additional investigation.

Employee Misconduct

Situation: An organization suspects an employee of engaging in illicit internet usage and disclosing confidential information.

Forensic Procedures

• Supervise the employee's computer activities live.
• Analyze internet browsing history, email correspondence, and file access habits.
• Retrieve deleted files and analyze their content.

Result

• Evidence of misconduct is collected.
• Disciplinary action is taken by the organization according to the forensic results.

Child Exploitation Case

Scenario: Law enforcement finds a suspect engaged in disseminating illegal content related to kids online.

Forensic Procedures

• Confiscate the suspect's gadgets and conduct a forensic examination.
• Retrieve erased files, chat logs, and encrypted data.
• Analyze metadata to determine the source and dissemination of illicit content.

Result

• Forensic evidence is essential for apprehending and convicting the culprit.
• The investigation results in identifying and rescuing victims.

Step-by-Step Recovery Processes

Computer forensics recovery technique entails a methodical and meticulous strategy to recover lost or inaccessible digital data. Here is a detailed instruction describing a typical recuperation procedure.

• *Step 1*. Identification of resources and devices used in the investigation:
• Determine possible sources of digital evidence such as PCs, mobile devices, external storage media, cloud services, and network logs. Record the whereabouts and state of each device or storage medium.
• *Step 2*: Preserve the essential data by securely storing it in a controlled environment to maintain its integrity and confidentiality. Implement security

protocols to prevent unauthorized access, alteration, or tampering of the evidence.

- *Step 3*: Analyze the obtained digital evidence to extract pertinent information concerning the investigation. This process may require analyzing file information, system logs, internet history, email correspondence, deleted files, and other evidence using specialist forensic tools and methods.
- *Step 4*. Document the forensic analysis process, detailing the methodologies, tools, findings, and conclusions. Keep thorough documentation to substantiate the accuracy and dependability of the inquiry results in legal settings.
- *Step 5*: Deliver the forensic results to appropriate parties, like law enforcement, legal advisors, or company leadership. Articulate the importance of the evidence and its consequences for the inquiry or legal case [13].

Lessons Learned from Successful Recoveries

Effective outcomes in computer forensics frequently provide valuable insights that can help refine procedures and readiness for future events.

Proactive and regular backup strategies are quite important. Organizations that have well-established backup strategies are more likely to successfully restore data. Lessons cover the importance of regular backups, offsite storage, and periodic testing of backup restoration processes. Comprehensive documentation of the rehabilitation process is essential. Comprehensive documentation helps in comprehending the occurrence, promoting teamwork, and creating a thorough report for legal or investigative needs. Responding promptly to a data loss situation is crucial. Quickly isolating affected systems, determining the main cause, and starting recovery procedures can reduce the impact of the incident and improve the likelihood of successful data recovery [20].

Testing data recovery processes routinely is crucial. Effective recoveries are frequently credited to thoroughly practiced and validated recovery strategies. Lessons encompass the importance of scenario-based testing, assuring compatibility with advancing technologies, and adjusting procedures accordingly.

CHALLENGES AND FUTURE TRENDS

Challenges

- The growing utilization of encryption technology presents a substantial obstacle to computer forensics. Encrypted data can be unavailable if decryption keys are not available, which can impede investigations.
- The increasing use of cloud services and virtualized environments creates difficulties in maintaining and gathering evidence kept off-site or in virtual

computers, necessitating the development of new forensic techniques.

- New storage technologies like solid-state drives (SSDs) and hybrid storage solutions might affect data recovery and forensic analysis because of wear leveling and intricate storage architectures.
- Perpetrators use anti-forensic methods to delete digital traces, alter timestamps, or obscure data.
- Detecting and countering these strategies necessitate sophisticated forensic methods. The increasing amount of network data and the use of encryption in communication pose difficulties in analyzing network behavior, which hampers the detection of hostile operations [13].
- Balancing the requirement for digital proof with privacy concerns presents difficulties. Legal frameworks and privacy restrictions can influence the extent and techniques used in computer forensic investigations.
- Digital evidence is susceptible to being volatile, which means it can be easily altered or deleted. Quick reaction and accurate evidence storage are crucial for upholding the integrity of forensic discoveries.

Future Trends

Forensic tools and procedures are advancing to analyze cryptocurrency transactions, smart contracts, and blockchain-based systems as blockchain technology becomes more prominent. With the increasing importance of blockchain technology, forensic tools and procedures are developing to analyze bitcoin transactions, smart contracts, and blockchain systems. Utilizing automated threat hunting technologies to actively seek for signs of compromise, improving the capability to identify and address cyber threats.

With the progress of quantum computing, computer forensics encounters obstacles in creating new cryptography techniques and adjusting to the possible decryption skills of quantum computers [21].

Evolving Threats to Data

Data in digital forensics faces growing dangers due to technological advancements and the development of new strategies by hackers. Below are some emerging risks to data in forensic investigations:

Encryption and Data Protection

Encryption technologies provide difficulties for digital forensic investigators. Failure to decrypt encrypted data may impede or block access to crucial evidence stored on devices or transferred *via* networks.

Anti-Forensic Techniques

Cybercriminals use different anti-forensic methods to obscure or alter digital evidence, complicating the task for investigators to identify, retrieve, and examine pertinent material. These methods may involve file wiping, data concealment, file fragmentation, and altering timestamps [22].

Cloud Storage and Virtualization

The growing use of cloud storage services and virtualization technology complicates digital forensic investigations. Data kept in the cloud or virtual environments can be spread out in several locations and overseen by third-party providers, necessitating specific methods to retrieve, gather, and examine evidence.

IoT Devices and Wearables

The increasing number of Internet of Things (IoT) devices and wearable technologies broadens the potential targets for cybercriminals and introduces fresh obstacles for digital forensic investigators. These devices frequently gather and retain sensitive data, like personal health information or location data, which could be the focus of cyberattacks or privacy breaches.

Data Fragmentation and Data Compression

Operating systems and storage systems utilize data fragmentation and compression techniques that might hinder data recovery and reconstruction in digital forensic investigations. Dispersed data stored in several locations on storage devices or compressed files may necessitate specific tools and skills for successful recovery and analysis.

Steganography and Steganalysis

Steganography is the act of hiding information within different digital items like photos, audio files, or papers to avoid being detected. Cybercriminals utilize steganography methods to conceal malicious code, sensitive data, or communication pathways, which complicates the task of forensic analysts in detecting and retrieving covert information using steganalysis.

Memory Forensics

Memory forensics is crucial for identifying and examining volatile data contained in system memory due to the rising complexity of malware and other harmful applications [23]. Advanced threats such as memory-resident malware and rootkits can avoid typical disk-based forensic methods, requiring the application of specialist memory forensics tools and approaches.

Mobile Device Forensics

The prevalent utilization of mobile devices, like smartphones and tablets, poses distinctive obstacles in digital forensic inquiries. Mobile devices include a significant amount of confidential information such as call logs, text messages, images, and app data, which could be the focus of criminal activity. Examining mobile devices necessitates specialized tools and methodologies to retrieve, scrutinize, and construe digital evidence from diverse mobile operating systems and device models.

Blockchain and Cryptocurrencies

Blockchain technology and cryptocurrencies complicate the process of tracing financial transactions and digital assets in forensic investigations. Transactions made with cryptocurrency on decentralized networks can be anonymous or pseudonymous, making it difficult for investigators to trace them back to specific individuals or entities without specialist forensic techniques and knowledge.

Artificial Intelligence and Machine Learning

Cybercriminals are using artificial intelligence and machine learning to improve their attacks by creating advanced software, avoiding detection, and organizing specific social engineering strategies. Digital forensic investigators must keep up with the latest AI and ML technologies to successfully combat advancing threats [20].

Emerging Technologies in Data Recovery

Machine Learning and Artificial Intelligence

ML and AI systems can automate the identification and categorization of digital evidence by classifying file types, finding abnormalities in data patterns, and anticipating areas of interest for future research.

Blockchain Forensics

Sophisticated methods and instruments are created to scrutinize blockchain transactions, track the movement of digital assets, and detect illegal activities like money laundering, fraud, or criminal trade carried out using cryptocurrencies.

Memory Forensics

Modern memory forensics technologies use sophisticated methods to collect and examine memory dumps from active systems or forensic images, allowing investigators to discover important data that may not be obtainable through conventional disk-based forensics.

Cloud Forensics

Cloud forensics tools and procedures are created to gather, examine, and safeguard digital evidence found in cloud infrastructures, including virtual machines, storage buckets, and application logs. They ensure the integrity of evidence and adherence to legal standards.

Internet of Things (IoT) Forensics

Investigators can now utilize advanced IoT forensics methods to gather and scrutinize digital evidence from various IoT environments, including as network traffic, device logs, firmware images, and cloud-based telemetry data [3].

Quantum Forensics

Quantum forensics research focuses on developing new methods to identify and address vulnerabilities to digital evidence that stem from quantum technology, including encryption algorithms that are resistant to quantum attacks and cryptographic protocols that are secure against quantum threats.

Augmented Reality (AR) and Virtual Reality (VR) Visualization

AR/VR visualization tools allow investigators to explore virtual crime scenes, reconstruct digital artifacts in 3D, and work with colleagues in real-time, improving the efficiency and efficacy of forensic analysis and case presentation [11].

Continuous Learning and Skill Development

Below are some tactics for ongoing learning and skill enhancement in forensic investigations:

• Participate in training sessions provided by professional organizations, government agencies, and private training providers. The programs encompass many subjects such as digital forensics, crime scene investigation, evidence processing, and courtroom testifying.

- Utilize internet resources like webinars, tutorials, blogs, and forums to be informed on the most recent trends, methods, and optimal approaches in forensic investigation.
- Participate in professional associations and business groups like the International Association of Computer Investigative Specialists (IACIS) and the American Academy of Forensic Sciences (AAFS).
- Stay updated on the latest research, case studies, and articles in forensic science journals, academic conferences, and industry publications [24].
- Acquire practical experience by participating in internships, apprenticeships, or entry-level roles in forensic laboratories, law enforcement organizations, or private investigation firms.
- Collaborate with professionals from several fields including law enforcement, legal, cybersecurity, psychiatry, and forensic anthropology to get diverse views and insights for complicated forensic investigations.
- Seek feedback and peer review from colleagues, mentors, and subject matter experts to assess your work, pinpoint areas for enhancement, and enhance your forensic procedures and methodology [25].

CONCLUSION

Data recovery is a crucial aspect of forensic investigations as it allows investigators to recover, analyze, and interpret digital evidence from different sources such computers, mobile devices, and storage media. The successful recovery of digital evidence plays a vital role in revealing facts, reconstructing events, and assisting legal proceedings in criminal investigations, civil litigation, and cybersecurity issues.

RECAP OF KEY CONCEPTS

Forensic investigations use a comprehensive method for data recovery that includes technological expertise, specialized instruments, and compliance with legal and ethical standards. Forensic examiners need to use reliable procedures to collect, preserve, and assess digital evidence while preserving the chain of custody and guaranteeing the integrity and admissibility of the evidence in court.

Forensic examiners must engage in continuous learning and skill development to be updated on advancing technology, changing hazards, and optimal methods in data recovery and forensic analysis. Forensic examiners can enhance their abilities in performing thorough and dependable data recovery in forensic investigations by obtaining formal education, acquiring essential certifications, participating in training programs, and engaging with professional networks.

Data recovery in forensic investigations ultimately aims to reveal the truth, ensure justice, and uphold the integrity of digital data in a world that is becoming more linked and digital. Forensic examiners play a crucial role in safeguarding the integrity of digital evidence and upholding the rule of law in today's dynamic forensic environment through the application of new technology, sound processes, and ethical standards.

ENCOURAGEMENT FOR FURTHER EXPLORATION

Individuals interested in data recovery, either professionally or as a personal interest, have several reasons to explore this subject in more depth. Data recovery is an intriguing journey filled with chances for acquiring knowledge, development, and making a meaningful impact [22]. Exploring the subject of data recovery can be a rewarding pursuit for those motivated by academic curiosity, career aspirations, or a desire to create an impact. Embrace the challenge, delve into the complexity, and allow your curiosity lead you on this thrilling voyage of discovery.

Data recovery is a complex area that overlaps with fields like computer science, cybersecurity, forensic investigation, and information technology. As you go further into data recovery, you will come across a wide range of subjects to investigate, including file systems, disk structures, advanced forensic techniques, and developing technologies. Recovering and analyzing digital evidence is a valuable competence desired by firms in several industries in the current digital era. Proficiency in data recovery is valuable for anyone working in law enforcement, cybersecurity, legal compliance, or IT forensics, as it can lead to rewarding job prospects and enhance professional development [26]. Data recovery frequently requires solving intricate riddles and surmounting technical obstacles to retrieve lost or corrupted data. Navigating through obstacles and recovering useful information necessitates a blend of analytical thinking, inventiveness, and technological expertise. Every data recovery situation is distinct, providing a new and gratifying task.

REFERENCES

[1]   S. Tomer, "Data recovery in Forensics", *2017 International Conference on Computing and Communication Technologies for Smart Nation (IC3TSN),* IEEE., 2017. [http://dx.doi.org/10.1109/IC3TSN.2017.8284474]

[2]   B.P. Battula, B.K. Rani, R.S. Prasad, and T. Sudha, "Techniques in computer forensics: A recovery perspective", *International Journal of Security,* vol. 3, no. 2, pp. 27-35, 2009.

[3]   S.N. Varayogula, K. Dodiya, P. Lakhalani, and A. Chawla, "Computer Forensics Data Recovery Software: A Comparative Study", *International Journal of Innovative Research in Computer Science & Technology,* vol. 10, no. 2, pp. 513-518, 2022.

[4]   D.G. Revathi Jagarlamudi, "A Novel tool for Data Recovery in cyber forensics", *Ann. Rom. Soc. Cell*

Biol., pp. 19600-19611, 2021.

[5]   S. Bui, M. Enyeart, and J. Luong, *Issues in computer forensics.* Santa Clara University Computer Engineering: USA, 2003.

[6]   B. Carrier, *File system forensic analysis.* Addison-Wesley Professional, 2005.

[7]   V. Roussev, Y. Chen, T. Bourg, and G.G. Richard, "md5bloom: Forensic filesystem hashing revisited", *Digital Investigation,* vol. 3, pp. 82-90, 2006.

[8]   F. Buchholz, and E. Spafford, "On the role of file system metadata in digital forensics", *Digit. Invest.,* vol. 1, no. 4, pp. 298-309, 2004.
[http://dx.doi.org/10.1016/j.diin.2004.10.002]

[9]   I.P.A.E. Pratama, "Computer forensic using photorec for secure data recovery between storage media: A proof of concept. International Journal of Science", *Technology & Management,* vol. 2, no. 4, pp. 1189-1196, 2021.

[10]   B. Aziz, P. Massonet, and C. Ponsard, "A formal model for forensic storage media preparation tools", *in 2014 11ᵗʰ International Conference on Security and Cryptography (SECRYPT),* IEEE., 2014.
[http://dx.doi.org/10.5220/0004996001650170]

[11]   K.K. Sindhu, and B.B. Meshram, "Digital forensic investigation tools and procedures", *International Journal of Computer Network and Information Security,* vol. 4, no. 4, pp. 39-48, 2012.
[http://dx.doi.org/10.5815/ijcnis.2012.04.05]

[12]   H. Suthar, and P. Sharma, *An Approach to Data Recovery from Solid State Drive: Cyber Forensics* Apple Academic Press, 2023, pp. 185-204.
[http://dx.doi.org/10.1201/9781003369479-9]

[13]   X. Lin, and X. Lin, "and Lagerstrom-Fife", In: *Introductory Computer Forensics.* Springer, 2018.

[14]   M. Breeuwsma, "Forensic data recovery from flash memory", *Small Scale Digital Device Forensics Journal,* vol. 1, no. 1, pp. 1-17, 2007.

[15]   P. Mayer, *Data Recovery: Choosing the Right Technologies.* Datalink White Paper, 2003.

[16]   S. Yulianto, and B. Soewito, "Investigating the Impact on Data Recovery in Computer Forensics", *2023 IEEE International Conference on Cryptography, Informatics, and Cybersecurity (ICoCICs),* IEEE., 2023.
[http://dx.doi.org/10.1109/ICoCICs58778.2023.10276573]

[17]   P. Nabity, and B. Landry, *Recovering deleted and wiped files: A digital forensic comparison of FAT32 and NTFS file systems using evidence eliminator.* SWDSI, 2013.

[18]   Y. Onoda, K. Kurisaka, and T. Sakai, "Fundamental safety strategy against severe accidents on prototype sodium-cooled fast reactor", *J. Nucl. Sci. Technol.,* vol. 53, no. 11, pp. 1774-1786, 2016.
[http://dx.doi.org/10.1080/00223131.2016.1159532]

[19]   G. Tsakalidis, K. Vergidis, S. Petridou, and M. Vlachopoulou, "A cybercrime incident architecture with adaptive response policy", *Comput. Secur.,* vol. 83, pp. 22-37, 2019.
[http://dx.doi.org/10.1016/j.cose.2019.01.011]

[20]   H.F. Mueller, L. Piemontese, and A. Tapsoba, *Recovery from conflict: lessons of success.* World Bank Policy Research Working Paper, 2017, p. (7970).
[http://dx.doi.org/10.1596/1813-9450-7970]

[21]   C.B. Tan, M.H.A. Hijazi, Y. Lim, and A. Gani, "A survey on Proof of Retrievability for cloud data integrity and availability: Cloud storage state-of-the-art, issues, solutions and future trends", *J. Netw. Comput. Appl.,* vol. 110, pp. 75-86, 2018.
[http://dx.doi.org/10.1016/j.jnca.2018.03.017]

[22]   A.A. Mughal, "A comprehensive study of practical techniques and methodologies in incident-based approaches for cyber forensics", *Tensorgate Journal of Sustainable Technology and Infrastructure for*

Developing Countries, vol. 2, no. 1, pp. 1-18, 2019.

[23]   D. Quick, and K.K.R. Choo, "Impacts of increasing volume of digital forensic data: A survey and future research challenges", *Digit. Invest.,* vol. 11, no. 4, pp. 273-294, 2014.
[http://dx.doi.org/10.1016/j.diin.2014.09.002]

[24]   A. Fukami, R. Stoykova, and Z. Geradts, "A new model for forensic data extraction from encrypted mobile devices", *Forensic Science International: Digital Investigation,* vol. 38, p. 301169, 2021.

[25]   M.S. Zareen, A. Waqar, and B. Aslam, "Digital forensics: Latest challenges and response", *in 2013 2nd National Conference on Information Assurance (NCIA).,* IEEE., 2013.
[http://dx.doi.org/10.1109/NCIA.2013.6725320]

[26]   B.K. Sharma, M.A. Joseph, B. Jacob, and B. Miranda, "Emerging trends in digital forensic and cyber security-an overview", *Sixth HCT Information Technology Trends,* vol. 2019, pp. 309-313, 2019. [ITT].
[http://dx.doi.org/10.1109/ITT48889.2019.9075101]

[27]   H. H. Khanh, and A. Khang, "The Role of Artificial Intelligence in Blockchain Applications", *Reinventing Manufacturing and Business Processes through Artificial Intelligence,* vol. 2, In Rana G, Khang A., Sharma R., Goel A. K., Dubey A. K. CRC Press., pp. 20-40, 2021.
[http://dx.doi.org/10.1201/9781003145011-2]

[28]   A. Khang, K.C. Rath, S.K. Satapathy, A. Kumar, S.R. Das, and M.R. Panda, "Enabling the Future of Manufacturing: Integration of Robotics and IoT to Smart Factory Infrastructure in Industry 4.0", In: *Handbook of Research on AI-Based Technologies and Applications in the Era of the Metaverse.,* A. Khang, V. Shah, S. Rani, Eds., IGI Global, 2023, pp. 25-50.
[http://dx.doi.org/10.4018/978-1-6684-8851-5.ch002]

[29]   A. Khang, "Semenets-Orlova Inna, Klochko Alla, Shchokin Rostyslav, Mykola Rudenko, Romanova Lidia, Bratchykova Kristina, "Management Model 6.0 and Business Recovery Strategy of Enterprises in the Era of Digital Economy", In: *Khang, A., Gujrati, R., Uygun, H., Tailor, R.K., & Gaur, S., Data-driven Modelling and Predictive Analytics in Business and Finance.* 1st ed. CRC Press, 2024.
[http://dx.doi.org/10.1201/9781032618845-16]

CHAPTER 2

Data Loss Software Reason and Hardware Reason

Wasswa Shafik[1,*]

[1] *School of Digital Science, Universiti Brunei Darussalam, Jalan Tungku Link, Gadong, BE1410, Bandar Seri Begawan, Brunei Darussalam Dig Connectivity Research Laboratory (DCRLab), Kampala, Uganda*

Abstract: Data loss (DL) is a detrimental state that occurs inside information systems when data is deleted due to failures or negligence during the processes of storage, transfer, or processing. To minimize the potential for DL or expedite the retrieval of lost data, it is necessary to implement measures like disaster recovery, backup mechanisms, and protocols. Due to the dynamic nature of digital information, the potential threat of DL is a critical concern, highlighting the need for a thorough comprehension of its various underlying factors and the implementation of effective measures to minimize its impact. This study explores the complex domain overview of software and hardware, elucidating the intricate fabric of data vulnerabilities. Human errors, encompassing unintentional deletions and formatting errors, constitute a critical vulnerability in maintaining data integrity. Simultaneously, malicious software and viruses present an ongoing risk by encrypting or destroying crucial data. In addition to the inherent risks, the presence of software faults, malfunctions, and file system corruption exacerbates the situation. In terms of hardware, potential challenges include hard drive failures, degradation of storage media, physical damage, and the unpredictable impact of natural disasters is examined. This research delves into the intricate relationship between software compatibility and firmware difficulties, aiming to get insight into the multifaceted factors contributing to DL. It offers a framework for enhancing resilience by implementing proactive steps, including periodic data backups, selecting safe hardware options, and educating users. Furthermore, it underscores the significance of comprehensive data recovery strategies. Finally, the study argues for a full examination of these aspects, promoting a holistic strategy to protect data at a time when its loss has significant consequences for both individuals and organizations.

Keywords: Data loss, Data recovery, Emerging technologies, Hardware reason, Hardware reason.

* **Corresponding author Wasswa Shafik:** School of Digital Science, Universiti Brunei Darussalam, Jalan Tungku Link, Gadong, BE1410, Bandar Seri Begawan, Brunei Darussalam Dig Connectivity Research Laboratory (DCRLab), Kampala, Uganda; E-mail: wasswashafik@ieee.org

INTRODUCTION

Within the complex realm of data integrity, a multitude of software and hardware vulnerabilities create opportunities for potential loss of data. Human errors, which are frequently disregarded, pose a substantial risk [1]. Accidental deletions and formatting errors serve as examples of how vital data can be easily lost. Simultaneously, the surreptitious intrusion of malicious software and computer viruses presents an incessant peril, as it encrypts or corrupts data without exhibiting any remorse. Hardware, despite being commonly considered reliable, also possesses weaknesses [2]. These vulnerabilities include mechanical breakdowns in storage devices and the slow degradation of storage media. These issues might potentially lead to catastrophic data loss incidents. The diverse nature of vulnerabilities necessitates a nuanced approach to prevention and recovery techniques, as highlighted in a research study [3].

In the midst of a complex network of vulnerabilities, the concept of readiness emerges as a crucial and indispensable factor. Proactive data recovery strategies serve as a proactive measure to mitigate the impact of unforeseen data loss incidents, enabling prompt and efficient actions in the face of unexpected occurrences [4]. By acknowledging the inescapable presence of vulnerabilities, these strategies provide a protective mechanism, allowing both organizations and individuals to recover from the verge of data loss. Acknowledging the interconnected nature of software and hardware vulnerabilities, it becomes crucial to adopt an integrated approach that combines preventive measures with strong recovery tactics [5]. The imperative does not solely involve the identification of vulnerabilities but rather encompasses the reinforcement of defenses and the establishment of a resilient infrastructure that can effectively withstand the future onslaught of attacks.

The quantity and diversity of this phenomenon serve as catalysts for pioneering developments across several industries. Data analytics plays a crucial role in the operations of businesses by enabling them to analyze consumer behavior, forecast market trends, and enhance operational efficiency [6]. In the domains of technology like machine learning and artificial intelligence, data plays a fundamental role in providing the basis for advancements in autonomous systems, natural language processing, and predictive analytics [7]. The utilization of data-driven innovation extends beyond the realm of business, as it facilitates progress in scientific research, hence facilitating the exploration of solutions to global concerns such as climate change and healthcare developments [8]. The integration of data with technical advancements has emerged as a crucial catalyst for societal advancement and economic expansion, consistently transforming various sectors and unlocking unparalleled opportunities [9].

Data serves as the medium by which our global society maintains its interconnectedness. Social media platforms, communication networks, and worldwide systems are highly dependent on the efficient flow and processing of data [10]. The phenomenon of interconnection surpasses the limitations imposed by geographical boundaries, hence promoting the formation of global communities, facilitating instantaneous communication, and enabling collaboration on an unprecedented magnitude. The utilization of data-driven communication has fundamentally transformed the processes of information dissemination, sharing, and consumption, leading to significant changes in several domains, such as personal relationships, economic transactions, and diplomatic relations [11]. The efficient functioning of contemporary civilization heavily depends on extensive networks that facilitate the uninterrupted transmission of data, hence enabling a global environment characterized by easy access to information and immediate communication.

The inherent worth of data is in its capacity to furnish actionable insights. Fig. (**1**) presents the top causes of data loss. The emergence of advanced data analytics and big data approaches has provided firms with unparalleled access to useful patterns, trends, and predictions. The utilization of data-driven decision-making has emerged as a fundamental aspect of successful strategies in various industries [12]. Business enterprises utilize data in order to optimize operational procedures, improve customer satisfaction, and foster innovation. Governments utilize data analytics to enhance policy-making processes and the quality of public services. The utilization of data-derived insights enables executives to make well-informed decisions based on evidence, thus promoting efficiency, productivity, and growth [13]. The utilization of data analytics enables the conversion of unprocessed data into practical knowledge, thereby unleashing the capacity for well-informed choices that significantly impact our society.

The acquisition, examination, and application of healthcare data have brought about a transformative impact on the provision of patient care, advancements in medical research, and the enhancement of treatment outcomes [4]. The utilization of electronic health records, medical imaging, and genomic data has facilitated the implementation of personalized medicine, allowing for the customization of therapies based on the distinctive attributes of individual patients. The utilization of data-driven research expedites the process of uncovering novel therapeutic interventions, diagnostic instruments, and techniques for disease prevention [15]. Furthermore, the utilization of data analytics in the healthcare sector has been shown to promote operational efficiency, streamline processes, and improve patient outcomes through the identification of patterns and the prediction of potential health hazards [16]. The integration of data and healthcare has facilitated the advent of precision medicine and significant advancements in medical research, ultimately enhancing the standard of treatment and resulting in life-saving outcomes.

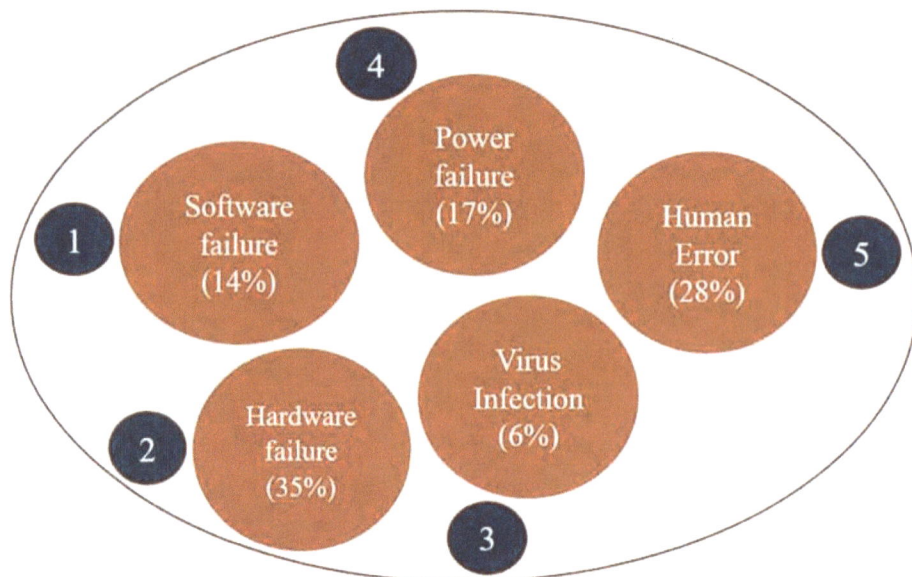

Fig. (1). Top five Causes of Data Loss.

In the context of the increasing abundance of data, ensuring the protection of security and privacy has emerged as a matter of utmost importance. The facilitation of interconnection through data also poses issues in safeguarding sensitive information [15]. The implementation of cybersecurity measures is of utmost importance in order to effectively prevent data breaches, instances of identity theft, and harmful assaults. Maintaining confidence in the digital environment necessitates the careful management of data accessibility and privacy rights, ensuring a delicate equilibrium [14]. Regulations and standards are implemented with the objective of promoting ethical data practices, with a particular focus on openness, user permission, and responsible data stewardship. In the current era characterized by the abundance and vulnerability of data, the implementation of robust security measures, encryption techniques, and compliance standards is crucial for ensuring data integrity and maintaining individuals' privacy [19].

THE STUDY MOTIVATION

The comprehension and mitigation of data loss risks are of paramount importance in preserving the integrity, continuity, and trust within our society that heavily relies on digital technologies. The imperative to understand potential vulnerabilities, including human errors, malicious cyber threats, and hardware failures, is underscored by the exponential rise and increasing reliance on data [2]. Efficient mitigation solutions effectively address the detrimental outcomes associated with data loss, thereby safeguarding essential information that holds significant importance for enterprises, institutions, and individuals [3]. In addition to the adverse effects on finances and operations, the loss of data has the potential to undermine trust, threaten the security of sensitive information, and damage reputations. Implementing proactive measures to mitigate these risks is crucial in maintaining resilience against unforeseen events [5]. These measures include the establishment of robust backup systems, the implementation of stringent security protocols, and the development of comprehensive disaster recovery plans. By adopting these measures, organizations not only enhance their ability to withstand potential threats but also uphold the fundamental principles of confidentiality, integrity, and availability in the digital domain [6]. This, in turn, ensures the ongoing functionality and trustworthiness of our data-driven world.

THE CHAPTER CONTRIBUTIONS

This study presents the following contribution as summarized.

- The study explores and analyzes the various causes of data loss software and hardware factors related to data loss and prevention strategies in the dynamic nature of technology and an accelerated smart online application.
- Unraveling the complexities behind software and hardware factors contributing to data loss vulnerability.
- Analytically presents a specific vulnerability like human errors, malware, and hardware failures for targeted prevention.
- Examine the measures identical to regular backups, secure hardware choices, and user education for resilience.
- The study highlights the importance of disaster data recovery plans in mitigating the impact of unforeseen events.
- The study emphasizes the need for software compatibility and robust firmware management to prevent data compromise.
- Finally, it accentuates the significance of proactive data recovery plans to swiftly counter unexpected data loss events.

THE CHAPTER ORGANIZATION

The remainder of this chapter is structured as follows. Section 2 presents software factors relating to data loss, including human error, malware and viruses, software bugs and glitches, and File System Corruption, among others. Section 3 details the hardware factors like hard drive or storage device failures, data storage media degradation, accidental physical damage, natural disasters, theft or loss, and corrupted firmware. Section 4 illustrates data prevention approaches demonstrating the importance of regular backups, using reliable hardware and storage solutions, security measures to prevent malware and unauthorized access, and educating users on safe computing practices. Section 5 presents data recovery plans depicting the significance of having data recovery plans in place, steps to be taken in the event of data loss, and regular testing and updating of data recovery plans. Finally, Section 6 presents the study conclusion.

DATA LOSS SOFTWARE FACTORS

Software factors comprise a wide range of components that contribute to vulnerabilities resulting in data loss. Human error is a significant contributing component, including unintentional deletions or formatting mistakes, hence underscoring the vulnerability of data to inadvertent actions [7]. Malicious software and computer viruses, which are both covert and widespread, provide substantial risks by encrypting or modifying data, jeopardizing its integrity and availability. Software bugs and glitches, which are inherent in intricate systems, have the potential to result in data corruption or loss, hence affecting the functionality of both applications and operating systems [8].

File system corruption is a significant contributing factor that can result in errors that leave data inaccessible or compromised. The utilization of incompatible software might aggravate hazards, hence potentially leading to data corruption or system instability. Improper shutdowns, which can occur due to power failures or sudden system closures, offer a risk of data corruption and highlight the significance of maintaining reliable computing environments [9]. In aggregate, the elements pertaining to software serve to magnify the vulnerabilities present and underscore the imperative nature of implementing proactive steps in order to protect the integrity of data.

Human Error

Human error is a notable risk factor that contributes to the loss of data, primarily occurring as a result of unintentional deletion and formatting errors. Accidental deletion refers to the inadvertent removal of essential files, folders, or complete directories by users [10]. Frequently, the inadvertent selection and deletion of crucial material by users can lead to its irrevocable destruction, stemming from a lack of attention or oversight. One prevalent mistake made by users is the inadvertent formatting of storage devices, such as hard disks or external drives, which can result in the unintended deletion of all data stored on the device [11]. These errors may occur as a result of drive confusion, triggered by system prompts, or when attempting to execute a different activity, resulting in the accidental formatting of an incorrect storage unit. Both inadvertent deletion and errors in formatting underscore the vulnerability of data to human error, underscoring the importance of exercising caution, maintaining regular backups, and cultivating awareness to mitigate such instances of data loss [12].

Accidental Deletion

Software interfaces, including those related to file management systems, offer users a range of choices for the purpose of manipulating and organizing files and folders. Instances of accidental deletion can occur inside these interfaces when users, with the intention of executing an alternative action such as relocating or arranging files, inadvertently select the delete option [13]. The execution of this operation prompts the software to permanently delete the data that has been selected. User interfaces sometimes lack robust safeguards to prevent accidental deletion, generally relying on confirmation prompts or discard bins as their primary means of protection [14]. Nevertheless, it is important to note that these procedures may not be entirely effective in mitigating unintended deletions in every possible situation. Occasionally, users may circumvent or fail to acknowledge these safety protocols, leading to the involuntary loss of vital data as a consequence of the software's promptness in executing user instructions [9].

Formatting Mistakes

Formatting is the procedure by which a storage device, such as a hard drive or USB, is prepared for data storage. This involves establishing the requisite file system structure to facilitate the storage of data [10]. Formatting errors can arise when users unintentionally commence the formatting procedure on a storage device, often as a result of misunderstanding prompts, conflating several drives, or misinterpreting the intended purpose of the action they are doing inside the program interface. The ramifications of formatting are significant as it results in the complete removal of all data stored on the device, hence rendering data recovery efforts arduous, if not unattainable [12]. Software interfaces commonly provide users with formatting options that, if selected or executed incorrectly, may result in the unintentional deletion or corruption of data saved on the respective device.

Accidental deletion and formatting errors arise as a result of user engagement with software interfaces and the inherent responsiveness of these interfaces to user commands. Software systems contain safety measures such as confirmation dialogs or recycling bins in order to limit potential hazards. However, it is important to note that these systems ultimately depend on users' cautious and accurate interactions to prevent unintentional data loss effectively [14]. Hence, it is imperative to possess a comprehensive comprehension of software interfaces, exercise constant attention, and establish backup mechanisms to effectively minimize the consequences of software-related failures on data loss [15].

Malware and Viruses

Malware, often known as malicious software, comprises a variety of dangerous programs that are intentionally built with malicious intent. These applications gain unauthorized access to systems by exploiting software flaws or deceiving users into unintentionally installing them. Various forms of malicious software, commonly referred to as malware, encompass a range of such malware, such as viruses, worms, trojans, ransomware, spyware, and adware [16]. After gaining unauthorized access to a computer system, malware has the potential to compromise the integrity, confidentiality, and availability of data by corrupting, pilfering, erasing, or encrypting data, resulting in either inaccessibility or irreparable harm. One example of malicious software known as ransomware involves the encryption of files, followed by a demand for payment in exchange for the decryption key [17]. This act of keeping data hostage might result in irreversible loss if not promptly addressed. Similarly, viruses are a distinct form of malicious software that exhibits the ability to self-replicate and propagate by attaching itself to various files or programs. Upon activation, viruses carry out vicious acts, including the deletion or corruption of data, the disruption of system functions, or the propagation to other systems within a network [18]. As an illustration, a file virus affixes itself to executable files and initiates its payload upon the opening of those files, resulting in potential data loss or compromised system stability.

Malware and viruses exhibit covert behavior, frequently eluding detection by security mechanisms, hence posing significant risks to the security of data. Cyber attackers utilize several methods to gain unauthorized access to computer systems and compromise the integrity of data [19]. These methods include exploiting software vulnerabilities, targeting flaws in network setups, and taking advantage of human error, such as engaging with questionable links or downloading infected files [20]. Mitigating the risks associated with malware and viruses, as well as protecting against data loss and system compromise, necessitates the implementation of preventive measures. These measures include utilizing reputable antivirus software, regularly updating software and security patches, adhering to safe browsing habits, and establishing robust cybersecurity protocols [21].

Malware Types Affecting Data

It is imperative to possess a comprehensive comprehension of the unique attributes and ramifications associated with various forms of malware to successfully establish robust security protocols that may effectively deter infestations and minimize the potential consequences of data loss and system vulnerability, as presented.

Ransomware

Ransomware functions as a highly advanced type of malicious software that uses encryption techniques to render data or entire computer systems inaccessible, thereby coercing victims into paying a ransom in exchange for decryption [2]. The encryption techniques employed are specifically designed to render data inaccessible in the absence of the decryption key, which potential attackers hold. The aforementioned malicious software specifically focuses on compromising the integrity of data by encrypting crucial files that are essential to individuals or businesses. The consequences of data loss are substantial, as encrypted information becomes unattainable unless a ransom is sent, and there is no guarantee of retrieval even following payment [3]. Organizations encounter a daunting predicament whereby they must decide whether to comply with ransom demands, potentially incentivizing future assaults, or decline and potentially suffer irreversible data loss. Ransomware attacks have the potential to cause significant disruptions to organizational operations, threaten the security of critical information, and undermine the faith that stakeholders have in the affected entity [5].

Viruses

Viruses are a type of malicious software that affixes themselves to executable files, thereby reproducing and disseminating throughout computer systems. Malicious software possesses the capability to compromise the integrity of data by either corrupting or deleting information contained within infected files [7]. The exponential propagation of these entities within networks increases the potential for data loss or corruption on a larger scope. Viruses are frequently disseminated *via* infected files, emails, or external storage devices, capitalizing on vulnerabilities in order to infiltrate computer systems. Comprehending the behavior of viruses is of utmost importance in order to apply antivirus solutions, ensure regular system updates, and establish user education programs that effectively reduce their adverse effects on data security [4]. The quick infectivity and destructive potential of these entities highlight the significance of implementing proactive cybersecurity measures to mitigate the risk of data loss and uphold the integrity of digital assets.

Worms

Worms are a type of self-replicating malware that autonomously propagates *via* networks without requiring any user intervention. These creatures leverage weaknesses in software or network setups, allowing them to spread quickly [1]. Worms use substantial network resources, resulting in disruptions and impairments to system performance. The influence of worms on data integrity is significant, as they remove or compromise data while proliferating over networked systems, resulting in extensive data loss or corruption. The mitigation of hazards associated with worms entails the implementation of comprehensive network security measures, the regular upgrading of software and security patches, and the frequent execution of security audits to detect and resolve vulnerabilities [2]. The possibility for rapid proliferation heightens the urgency to develop effective cybersecurity solutions, as it greatly amplifies the impact of worms on data integrity and system operation.

Trojans

Trojans are a type of harmful software that employs deceptive tactics by masquerading as normal programs, thereby deceiving users into unwittingly initiating their execution. These deceitful entities frequently necessitate user engagement in order to commence their operations, such as the downloading and execution of a file or application [4]. Trojans possess the capability to illicitly acquire sensitive data, bestow illegal access to computer systems, or assist in the installation of supplementary malicious software. The consequences of their actions on data loss are significant, as they possess the ability to alter or remove information, damage the security of systems, or result in data breaches [6]. The prevention of Trojan infections necessitates the provision of user education regarding safe browsing practices, the implementation of robust cybersecurity measures such as firewalls and antivirus software, and the regular updating of system software to address vulnerabilities [7]. Gaining a comprehensive comprehension of the misleading characteristics inherent in Trojan assaults is of utmost importance in effectively countering such threats and ensuring the preservation of data integrity inside digital realms.

Spyware

Spyware functions surreptitiously, gathering user data without obtaining their explicit agreement or awareness. Although spyware does not generally result in data loss, it presents a substantial risk to the privacy and confidentiality of data [8]. This software possesses the capability to record keystrokes, observe surfing patterns, and acquire confidential data, hence potentially resulting in the compromise of data security and violations of privacy. The pervasive characteristics of spyware underscore the significance of using resilient antivirus and anti-spyware measures, regularly performing system scans, and adopting vigilant surfing practices in order to avert infections [10]. The prevention of spyware entails the consistent exercise of caution and the implementation of rigorous security protocols to protect confidential information and uphold the integrity of personal and institutional data [51].

Adware

Adware is a form of malicious software that interferes with the user's experience by presenting undesired advertisements or diverting them to advertising websites. Adware predominantly affects the user's experience and the performance of their system, hence indirectly increasing the vulnerability of data leakage or breach [11]. In certain instances of severity, the adware can prompt users to interact with malevolent links embedded within adverts, hence potentially leading to the compromise of sensitive data or unintentional installations of more pernicious malware [10]. The process of mitigating adware dangers encompasses the utilization of ad-blocking software from trusted sources, exercising caution during internet surfing activities, and providing users with education on the identification and avoidance of potentially hazardous advertisements [12]. While adware itself may not be directly responsible for data loss, its existence serves as a reminder of the wider dangers linked to malware outbreaks. It emphasizes the significance of taking proactive steps to safeguard against possible data breaches [15].

Rootkits

Rootkits function covertly, enabling assailants to acquire unauthorized entry to computers and change data without being detected. The capacity to effectively conceal their presence and provide continuous access presents a notable risk to the integrity of data and the security of systems. Rootkits alter or erase files, jeopardize confidential data, and elude detection by antivirus software or security protocols [22]. The prevention of rootkit infections necessitates the implementation of solid security measures, conducting frequent system scans utilizing reputable antivirus solutions, and the incorporation of intrusion detection systems to detect any potentially suspicious actions. Gaining comprehension of the elusive characteristics exhibited by rootkit attacks and adopting rigorous security protocols is imperative in the identification and mitigation of such attacks [23]. These steps are essential for preserving the integrity of data and ensuring the resilience of systems operating inside digital environments.

Software Bugs and Glitches

Software defects and anomalies pose substantial hazards to the integrity and availability of data. The issues arise as a result of coding faults or deficiencies in software design, resulting in unforeseen behaviors or breakdowns inside the system [24]. In the realm of computer systems, insects possess the capability to induce data corruption or modification through the disruption of application behavior, hence leading to the undesirable consequences of data loss or corruption. Glitches, which are frequently characterized by their temporary and intermittent nature, have the potential to disturb the regular operations of software [25]. This disruption can have an impact on the accessibility of data since it may briefly leave data or applications inaccessible. Although bugs and glitches may not directly alter data, their effect on the performance of software might indirectly jeopardize the integrity and accessibility of data. To effectively tackle these concerns, it is imperative to conduct comprehensive software testing, engage in ongoing debugging efforts, and promptly address found vulnerabilities through patching [26]. This approach aims to mitigate the potential consequences on both data security and system stability.

Application Failures

Instances when software programs experience a loss of correct functionality or terminate suddenly during the execution of tasks. These failures may arise due to a multitude of circumstances, encompassing software defects, memory leaks, compatibility concerns, or insufficient allocation of system resources [26]. In instances where programs experience failure, they disrupt concurrent functions, hence posing a risk of data loss or corruption, particularly if the software was engaged in data modification or handling activities. The effect on data integrity is contingent upon the type of failure encountered. For instance, a sudden system crash during a file save procedure has the potential to result in file corruption [27]. The occurrence of program failures can have a detrimental impact on the accessibility of data, as it hinders users from effectively utilizing certain capabilities or accessing specific files within the application. The implementation of robust error-handling mechanisms, regular software updates, and effective system resource management is crucial in order to minimize the potential risks associated with program failures and ensure the preservation of data integrity and accessibility [28, 29].

Operating System Errors

Operating system faults comprise a diverse array of difficulties that arise inside the fundamental program responsible for managing a computer's hardware and software resources. These problems may arise due to software defects, compatibility challenges, conflicts between drivers, or failures in hardware components [30]. When the operating system encounters problems, it can result in system crashes, freezes, or the inability to execute critical functions. The potential consequences for data integrity can be significant, as faults inside the operating system have the potential to result in data corruption or loss, particularly if essential system files or data structures are impacted [31]. Furthermore, these errors have the potential to adversely affect the accessibility of data by rendering specific files or directories inaccessible or leading to malfunctions in applications. To mitigate the potential dangers associated with operating system failures and preserve the integrity and accessibility of data, it is imperative to adhere to certain practices [32]. These include keeping operating systems up to date, regularly backing up data, and implementing effective security measures.

File System Corruption

The term points to the degradation of the structure or arrangement of a storage system, resulting in the inability to access, damage, or make use of the data stored inside it. System failures can arise from a multitude of sources, including hardware malfunctions, software glitches, unexpected power disruptions, or inadequate system shutdown procedures [33]. The occurrence of file system corruption can result in data storage failures, rendering files or directories unavailable or resulting in data loss. Corruption has the potential to disturb the coherent arrangement of data on storage media, leading to mistakes during file access or modification. Consequently, this can have adverse effects on the integrity and accessibility of the data [34]. The mitigation of file system corruption necessitates the regular conduct of system checks, the utilization of reliable hardware, the implementation of backup techniques, and the utilization of file system repair tools. These measures are essential for preventing or recovering from potential instances of data loss or inaccessibility resulting from file system corruption [35].

Common Causes of File System Errors

This subsection presents some of the common causes of the file system errors.

Hardware Failures

File system faults often arise due to hardware failures, including problems with hard drives, solid-state drives (SSDs), or storage media. The integrity of stored data can be compromised due to physical damage to storage devices, such as the presence of bad sectors or disk read/write errors [36]. Hardware flaws can arise due to various factors, including manufacturing mistakes, gradual deterioration from usage, or abrupt mechanical failures. The failure of these physical components has the potential to result in data corruption or loss within the file system [37]. Implementing robust hardware maintenance practices, conducting regular monitoring of storage devices, and promptly addressing any problematic hardware components through replacement or repair are crucial steps in mitigating the potential hazards associated with file system failures caused by hardware issues [38]. These actions are critical for ensuring the integrity of data.

Software Glitches and Bugs

File system problems can be caused by software faults or glitches present in the operating system or file system software. Unexpected behaviors in handling file systems might arise due to coding flaws, programming faults, or compatibility issues between software components. These faults can be observed in the form of inadequate data handling, inaccurate file allocation, or irregularities in the maintenance of file structures [39]. As a result, faults in the file system, such as the absence of files, corrupted directories, or the inability to access data, may manifest. Ensuring the integrity of file systems and the accessibility of data necessitates the implementation of routine software updates, the application of patches to address identified vulnerabilities, and the utilization of dependable file system utilities or repair tools [40].

Improper Shutdowns or Sudden Power Outages

The occurrence of sudden power outages or incorrect shutdown procedures can lead to file system failures. This is mostly due to the interruption of current data write operations or the creation of inconsistent file structures [41]. In the event of an abrupt shutdown of a system, there is a possibility that the ongoing process of writing data to storage may be interrupted, resulting in the creation of incomplete or corrupted files. Moreover, the abrupt interruption has the potential to render the file system in an unstable condition, hence resulting in faults upon system reboot [42]. The implementation of uninterruptible power supplies (UPS), the utilization of systems equipped with journaling or file system consistency checks, and the adherence to appropriate shutdown protocols are crucial preventive steps in mitigating file system faults that may arise due to power-related problems [43].

Malware or Virus Attacks

The presence of malware or viruses presents substantial risks to the integrity of the file system. Malicious programs possess the capability to specifically target file systems, thereby engaging in activities such as file corruption or encryption, alteration of file properties, or the removal of vital data [44]. After gaining unauthorized access to a computer system, malware exploits weaknesses present in the file system, hence enabling the manipulation or compromise of data that is stored within. To mitigate the risk of malware-related file system failures and safeguard data from compromise or loss, it is imperative to employ preventive measures such as the utilization of renowned antivirus software, the implementation of solid cybersecurity policies, and the regular conduction of system scans [45].

Effects on Data Reliability

File system mistakes can have significant ramifications on the reliability of data, ultimately undermining the trustworthiness and consistency of stored information. Data corruption, loss, or inaccessibility can occur as a result of several factors, such as device failures, software faults, power outages, or hostile attacks [41]. Data integrity or completeness may be compromised due to file system faults, resulting in corrupted files or directories. This can lead to untrustworthy data. The reliability of data is compromised when files become inaccessible or when errors introduce inaccuracies to the stored information, hence affecting its credibility for crucial activities or decision-making processes [31]. The lack of reliability in data poses a significant challenge to the credibility of systems, as it can lead to a series of negative consequences in subsequent processes. This can have far-reaching implications for various aspects, such as business operations, the integrity of research, and the trust placed by users in the system [21]. Ensuring data reliability in the face of file system faults necessitates the implementation of preventive measures such as regular backups, strong system maintenance, and diligent cybersecurity policies.

Incompatible Software

The occurrence of this mismatch frequently stems from the utilization of software versions that lack smooth compatibility, resulting in conflicts pertaining to functionality, data formats, or system resources. The consequential effects of incompatible software on the reliability of data are substantial, perhaps resulting in data corruption, processing errors, or system instability [4]. The presence of incompatibility concerns can lead to the inability to access or accurately interpret specific files or data formats, hence compromising the dependability and integrity of the stored information [9]. Conflicts of this nature have the potential to interrupt the smooth functioning of workflows, impede collaborative endeavors, and compromise the appropriate interpretation and utilization of data, thereby impacting decision-making processes and overall operational efficiency [7]. The resolution of incompatible software difficulties frequently entails updating software versions, employing intermediary tools for data conversion, or exploring compatible alternatives to guarantee the dependability and uniformity of data across diverse applications or systems.

Risks Associated with using Incompatible Software

Initially, it is important to acknowledge that the danger of data loss or corruption is widespread. This risk arises due to the potential mishandling of file formats or inaccurate interpretation of data by incompatible software [28]. Consequently, this might result in errors or the presence of missing information. Another significant issue to consider is the potential for system instability, which can arise due to conflicts in software features. This can lead to various disruptions like crashes, freezes, or malfunctions, ultimately impeding the smooth running of the system [39].

The presence of compatibility concerns poses a significant obstacle to the efficient execution of workflows and collaborative efforts, hence hindering the seamless interchange or interpretation of data across diverse applications or platforms. Furthermore, the presence of security vulnerabilities frequently arises as a result of obsolete or incompatible software versions that lack crucial updates or patches, rendering systems vulnerable to possible breaches or cyber threats [33]. The hazards collectively erode the dependability of data, jeopardize operational continuity, and pose substantial obstacles in upholding a secure and efficient working environment.

Strategies for Preventing Software-Related Data Loss

The prevention of data loss caused by software-related issues necessitates the implementation of robust techniques aimed at safeguarding data integrity and mitigating the risks associated with vulnerabilities in software systems. Below are a few productive tactics.

Regular Software Updates and Patch Management

The prompt highlights the significance of timely updates and patch management in effectively resolving vulnerabilities present in software systems. Maintaining up-to-date software components, such as applications, operating systems, and security tools, enhances resilience against potential cyber threats [15]. The implementation of a proactive approach serves to mitigate the potential for exploitation of identified vulnerabilities, hence decreasing the probability of data loss resulting from security breaches or software deficiencies.

Data Backup and Redundancy

The implementation of a comprehensive backup strategy necessitates the consistent and automatic execution of backups for critical data, which are then stored in secure off-site locations or cloud storage. The presence of redundancy guarantees that data may be easily restored in the event of software failures, system crashes, or cyber-attacks [21]. Organizations employ the strategy of duplicating data to effectively limit the consequences of data loss incidents, hence ensuring the continuity of operations and minimizing periods of inactivity.

Implementing Robust Security Measures

The use of a wide range of cybersecurity measures, including firewalls, antivirus software, intrusion detection systems, and access controls, enhances the resilience of security systems against the threats posed by malware, viruses, and unwanted access attempts [35]. The implementation of security protocols serves as a protective measure against potential breaches that undermine the integrity of data, hence ensuring the safeguarding of sensitive information.

Regular System Maintenance and Monitoring

Regular system inspections, audits, and maintenance chores are essential in identifying and resolving software issues before they escalate into incidents resulting in data loss [39]. The use of proactive monitoring of system health and performance enables the timely detection and repair of software bugs, glitches, or compatibility issues that have the potential to undermine data integrity or system stability.

User Training and Awareness

The dissemination of knowledge regarding cybersecurity best practices, the proper handling of data to ensure its safety, and the ability to identify possible dangers enable users to reduce the risks associated with human errors effectively [40]. Organizations can mitigate the risk of data loss and enhance their overall security posture by cultivating a culture that prioritizes security awareness and vigilance, hence minimizing the occurrence of unintentional actions.

Implementing Data Loss Prevention (DLP) Solutions

The utilization of DLP tools facilitates the ability of companies to effectively monitor, exercise control over, and ensure the security of sensitive data within their network infrastructure [37]. These solutions contribute to the prevention of unwanted access, data leakage, and unintended data loss situations, thus improving overall data protection and ensuring compliance with regulatory requirements. Conducting regular integrity assessments on stored data guarantees the precision and coherence of the information [39]. These checks serve the purpose of identifying and resolving any inconsistencies or possible data corruption problems, hence ensuring the dependability of the data and mitigating the likelihood of data loss resulting from undetected integrity concerns, as Fig. (**2**) presents.

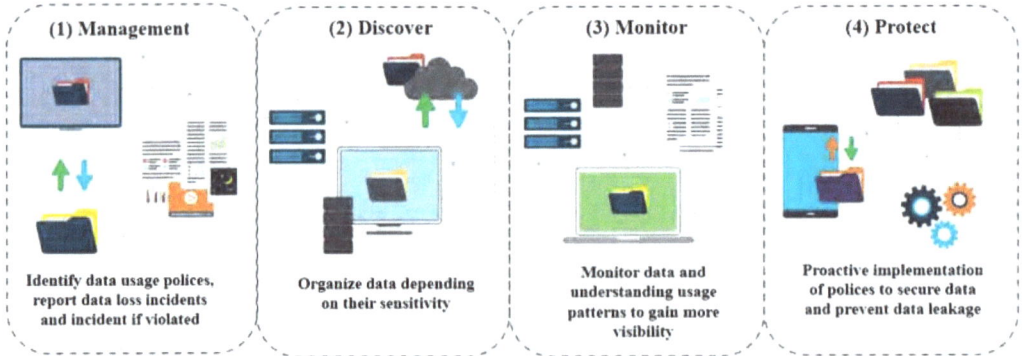

Fig. (2). Essential Components of data loss prevention.

Improper Shutdowns

Improper shutdown events, such as power failures, system breakdowns, or sudden closures, present a substantial threat to the integrity of data and the stability of computer systems. In the event of an unforeseen system shutdown, there is a possibility that ongoing write operations or system processes may be interrupted, resulting in the potential for incomplete or corrupted files. These potential consequences include the loss of data, faults in the file system, and discrepancies in the stored information [17].

In addition, abrupt terminations might result in the file system or operating system being left in an unstable condition, which may lead to errors or harm to essential system data. To address the potential hazards linked to inadequate shutdowns, it is imperative to implement uninterrupted power supplies (UPS), configure systems with journaling or file system consistency checks, and ensure adherence to appropriate shutdown protocols [38]. These endeavors aid in the reduction of the likelihood of data corruption, preservation of file system integrity, and mitigation of the consequences of abrupt shutdowns on data dependability.

Power Failures and Data Corruption

Power outages that occur suddenly while data is being written or system operations are in progress can be the consequence of files being incomplete or partially written, which can ultimately lead to data corruption or loss [24]. The abrupt cessation of electrical power can lead to the disruption of the systematic organization of data, which has the potential to result in harm to file structures or the introduction of discrepancies within recorded information. In addition, it is worth noting that power fluctuations or surges occurring during operational processes have the potential to cause harm to storage media, resulting in the corruption of stored data and rendering it unattainable [37]. The implementation of uninterruptible power supplies (UPS), surge protectors, or backup power sources serves to mitigate the risks associated with power failures. These measures protect against data corruption by enabling systems to undergo a controlled shutdown or sustain temporary operations during power outages [28]. As a result, the potential impact on data integrity is reduced.

Importance of Proper Shutdown Procedures

Ensuring appropriate shutdown protocols is of utmost importance in order to uphold system stability, uphold the integrity of data, and mitigate the risk of potential data loss or corruption. The act of initiating a systematic shutdown guarantees the completion of ongoing processes, write operations, and file alterations prior to the powering down of the system, thereby ensuring their safety [28]. The implementation of an organized termination process serves to mitigate the occurrence of sudden disruptions, which have the potential to result in file system malfunctions, unfinished write operations, or data corruption [16]. By adhering to appropriate shutdown procedures, the operating system is able to effectively end applications, transfer data from memory to storage, and conclude activities in a controlled manner, thereby reducing the likelihood of data loss or system instability. By following these processes, the risk of hardware damage is minimized, and the system is prepared for future startups, hence enhancing the system's overall reliability and lifespan [52].

Data Interference

The act of unlawful or intentional modification, manipulation, or tampering with stored information with the intention of disrupting its accuracy, integrity, or reliability. Interference can manifest in diverse forms, including cyberattacks, malware infiltrations, or human fallibility, leading to alterations, removals, or impairments of data. The consequences of data interference are significant since they degrade the quality of information, result in erroneous decision-making, and disrupt vital activities [11]. The interference of data has a detrimental impact on the level of confidence associated with stored information, hence compromising its usability and credibility in several domains, such as company operations, research initiatives, and decision-making procedures. The implementation of comprehensive cybersecurity measures, including access limits, encryption methods, and regular integrity checks, plays a critical role in safeguarding against data interference [20]. These measures are essential for maintaining the resilience and reliability of stored information inside digital ecosystems.

Instances where other Applications may Interfere with Data Integrity

Interference with data integrity by other applications frequently arises as a result of concurrent file access, software defects, conflicts in resource allocation, challenges in interoperability, and deliberate hostile actions [13]. The occurrence of conflicts and data corruption can arise from the simultaneous access of files by many applications, while unintended modification of data may result from software defects. Resource conflicts can lead to mistakes or unfinished operations due to the struggle for system resources [27]. The presence of incompatible apps or versions can potentially result in the misreading of data formats, hence compromising the integrity of data during exchanges. Furthermore, deliberate interference from malicious software change or corrupt data compromises its integrity [36]. It is necessary to utilize programs that are compatible with each other, establish appropriate access restrictions, guarantee data isolation, and implement strong cybersecurity measures to protect against hostile intervention.

Mitigation Strategies

The implementation of stringent access controls and permissions serves to govern the interactions between applications and sensitive data effectively, hence mitigating the potential for unwanted modifications [27]. By utilizing suitable and well-designed apps, as well as implementing thorough testing and quality assurance measures, the probability of unintentional data modifications caused by software bugs or interoperability problems is significantly reduced [37]. The implementation of data isolation or separation between applications serves to restrict the extent of potential interference, hence mitigating the ability of one application to impact unrelated data. In addition, the implementation of consistent data backups and the utilization of strong cybersecurity protocols, such as firewalls, antivirus software, and intrusion detection systems, enhances the resilience of protective measures against harmful disruptions [48]. The dissemination of knowledge regarding secure computing practices and the cultivation of a security-conscious environment also play a crucial role in a complete approach to reducing the potential dangers connected with data integrity breaches caused by other apps.

HARDWARE FACTORS

Hardware factors refer to essential components found in computer systems that have a direct impact on the integrity and accessibility of data [26]. The security of stored data against corruption or loss is significantly influenced by the dependability of storage devices, such as hard disk drives (HDDs), solid-state drives (SSDs), and external storage solutions. The occurrence of hardware failures, which can be attributed to causes such as aging, flaws, or environmental conditions, presents substantial hazards that have the potential to result in data corruption or difficulties in accessing data [27]. The establishment of compatibility and interoperability between hardware components and software applications is of paramount importance in ensuring the preservation of data integrity during the process of data transfers or activities.

Hardware performance can be compromised by environmental conditions, such as fluctuations in temperature or occurrences of electrical surges, which in turn can have an impact on the reliability of data [34]. The implementation of redundancy, backup systems, robust data recovery methods, and adherence to regular maintenance practices are crucial in mitigating the risks associated with hardware elements. These measures are essential for guaranteeing data resilience and shielding against potential threats to data integrity and accessibility.

Hard Drive or Storage Device Failures

Both categories of failures have the potential to have a substantial influence on the integrity and accessibility of data, hence requiring the implementation of data recovery techniques or the involvement of professionals to extract information from storage devices that have been affected [42]. Implementing regular backup procedures, engaging in preventive maintenance activities, and taking precautions to minimize physical shocks or power surges can effectively reduce the potential dangers connected with hard drive failures, as demonstrated.

Mechanical Failure

Instances of this particular form of failure frequently entail the malfunctioning of tangible constituents present in the storage device, like the read/write heads, spindle motor, or disk platters. Mechanical failures can arise as a consequence of gradual deterioration caused by wear and tear, resulting in the degeneration of components involved in motion. Frequent occurrences encompass head collisions, motor failures leading to disk immobilization, and damage to disk platters caused by physical shock or vibration [36]. The occurrence of mechanical malfunctions has the potential to render the drive non-functional, hence leading to the possibility of data loss or corruption. Consequently, this can pose significant difficulties in accessing the information stored within the drive.

Electronic Failure

Electronic failures are associated with problems that arise in the circuitry or electronic components of the drive. These failures may be due to power surges, electrical problems, or the degradation of components. Electronic failures can present themselves in several ways, such as the malfunctioning of the control board, the incapability of the drive to power up, or the occurrence of communication issues between the drive and the system [29]. Although electronic failures may not cause physical harm to the data storage components, they might impede the computer's ability to detect or use the drive, resulting in potential data inaccessibility or loss.

Data Storage Media Degradation

Data storage media degradation pertains to the progressive decline of physical storage mediums, such as hard disk drives, optical discs, or flash drives, which may result in the eventual loss or corruption of stored information as time passes [7]. Various factors, including exposure to environmental elements, fluctuations in temperature, changes in humidity, and prolonged usage, are known to contribute to the degradation of the subject in question. As storage media undergoes aging, the magnetic characteristics of disks can deteriorate, resulting in potential data corruption or loss within magnetic storage systems [39]. Optical discs are susceptible to many forms of damage, such as scratches, oxidation, and delamination, which can adversely impact their capacity to be read and compromise the integrity of the stored data. The degradation of flash memory is a consequence of its finite write cycles, resulting in the deterioration of memory cells and the possibility of data inaccuracies [14]. The significance of maintaining the longevity and dependability of stored information is highlighted by the deterioration of media, emphasizing the necessity of regular data movement, refreshing storage media, and adopting appropriate storage conditions.

Wear and Tear Over Time

Data storage mediums, like HDDs or SSDs, are subject to degradation as a result of prolonged usage and the natural process of aging. During the operation of HDDs, the moving components, for example, the read/write heads and spindle motor, undergo friction and mechanical stress, resulting in the occurrence of wear [26]. Over a prolonged duration, the process of wear and tear can result in the deterioration of components, affecting the performance of the drive and potentially resulting in malfunctions. SSDs, despite their absence of mechanical components, possess a finite quantity of write cycles per memory cell. The constant writing and erasing of data on cells leads to wear and tear, which diminishes their dependability and may result in data inaccuracies or malfunctions [39]. The inevitable outcome of extended usage is the occurrence of wear and tear, which has a significant impact on the durability and overall quality of the storage medium.

Signs of Media Degradation

The phenomenon of media deterioration is evident through a range of indicators, which suggest possible concerns with the dependability of storage media. Signs of potential issues with HDDs can manifest in various ways. These may include heightened levels of noise during operation, decreased read or write speeds, frequent occurrences of system freezes or crashes, or the inability to access files [34]. Symptoms commonly observed in SSDs encompass a decline in storage capacity, a progressive rise in the number of bad sectors, the occurrence of mistakes during data write operations and a deterioration in overall performance. Optical discs may exhibit observable indications such as scratches, warping, or discoloration, which can impact their legibility and compromise the integrity of stored data [37]. Engaging in proactive monitoring of these indicators aids in the early detection of possible media deterioration, hence facilitating rapid intervention such as data movement or replacement to mitigate the risk of data loss or corruption.

Accidental Physical Damage

Unintentional physical harm to data storage devices presents a notable risk to the integrity and availability of data. The potential for damage exists as a result of multiple circumstances, including drops, impacts, spills, or improper handling, which can lead to detrimental effects on HDDs, SSDs, or other forms of storage media [39]. The occurrence of head crashes in HDDs can be attributed to physical shocks, wherein the read/write heads come into contact with the disk surface, resulting in potential harm to the platters and subsequent loss of data. SSDs exhibit vulnerability to physical impact, as the application of extreme force or pressure can result in detrimental effects on the intricate electrical components, hence causing data inaccessibility or corruption [48].

Furthermore, it should be noted that external storage devices, such as USB drives or external hard disks, are susceptible to potential physical damage resulting from accidental accidents or exposure to water. This vulnerability poses a significant risk of data loss for the stored information [49]. The prevention of unintended physical harm entails the careful handling of storage devices, the use of protective containers, and the implementation of backup mechanisms to limit the potential hazards of data loss.

Impact of Physical Damage on Data Storage Devices

As an illustration, the inadvertent dropping or mishandling of a hard disk drive (HDD) can lead to occurrences of head crashes when the read/write heads come into contact with the rotating platters, resulting in the formation of scratches or physical harm [42]. The impact has the potential to result in sectors becoming illegible, hence causing the loss or corruption of data. In a similar vein, solid-state drives (SSDs) may be susceptible to harm inflicted upon their fragile electrical components as a consequence of excessive force or pressure, leading to data that is either inaccessible or substantially impaired [26]. In all circumstances, physical damage undermines the reliability of the storage device, potentially leading to irreversible data loss or diminished functionality.

Preventive Measures to avoid Physical Damage

The implementation of preventive measures is of utmost importance in order to protect data storage devices from potential physical harm. The utilization of shock-resistant casings or enclosures for portable storage devices, such as external HDDs or SSDs, serves to safeguard these devices against inadvertent drops or impacts [43]. Adhering to appropriate handling protocols, such as refraining from sudden movements during the operation of a storage device or properly ejecting removable media, mitigates the potential for physical harm. Furthermore, the act of storing equipment in stable and secure areas, which are isolated from potential environmental threats such as liquids, high heat, or humidity, serves to reduce the likelihood of unintentional harm [39]. Implementing regular backups of essential data to distinct and secure locations offers an additional level of safeguarding against potential data loss that may arise from physical harm to storage devices.

Natural Disasters

Natural disasters provide significant hazards to the integrity and availability of data, frequently leading to massive loss of data and periods of system inoperability. Natural disasters such as earthquakes, floods, hurricanes, fires, or power outages have the potential to cause significant disruptions to data centers and physical storage infrastructure, resulting in irreversible harm to hardware components and storage media [31]. The destructive potential of floodwaters or fires can lead to irreparable damage to servers and storage devices, resulting in the inaccessibility or permanent loss of stored data [38].

Hardware damage and data corruption can occur as a result of power surges or electrical disturbances that take place during natural disasters. Furthermore, the destruction of infrastructure or outages in connectivity might impede remote access to backup systems or cloud storage, thus increasing the loss of data [46]. The process of mitigating these risks entails the implementation of disaster recovery plans, the establishment of off-site backups, and the utilization of a robust data center infrastructure that incorporates sufficient precautions against environmental hazards. These measures are aimed at minimizing the potential consequences of natural disasters on the integrity of data and the uninterrupted functioning of activities.

How Natural Disasters can Lead to Hardware Damage

Natural catastrophes have the potential to cause hardware damage through a variety of mechanisms. Water-related calamities, like floods, have the potential to inundate data centers and infrastructure, resulting in irreversible harm to servers, storage devices, and networking equipment [20]. Hardware can be directly affected by fires that arise from natural disasters, leading to the melting of components or inflicting physical harm [17]. The occurrence of earthquakes or intense vibrations has the potential to induce structural deterioration and failing infrastructure and hardware. Furthermore, it is important to note that power surges or electrical interruptions that occur during these occurrences have the potential to cause circuitry malfunctions, resulting in detrimental effects on hardware components [37]. The confluence of these variables frequently leads to extensive hardware impairment, causing systems and storage devices to become non-functional and posing a danger of data loss or corruption.

Importance of off-site Backups

The implementation of off-site backups is important in order to reduce the potential hazards associated with natural disasters effectively. The practice of storing data backups in geographically remote places serves to safeguard the integrity of the backup data in the case of a disaster that may compromise the primary data center or infrastructure [37]. The use of redundancy serves as a protective measure against the possibility of hardware damage or data loss resulting from natural disasters, thereby enabling prompt recovery and uninterrupted continuation of activities. Off-site backups play a crucial role in guaranteeing the resilience of data, reducing the amount of time during which systems are unavailable, and facilitating the recovery of essential information following a catastrophic event [45]. By preserving business continuity and mitigating the adverse effects of hardware impairment on the integrity of data, off-site backups serve as an indispensable safeguard.

Theft or Loss

The loss or theft of devices such as laptops, cellphones, or external drives exposes the data held on these devices to the risk of illegal access or misuse. The scope of this threat extends beyond the mere physical loss of the device. It involves the possibility of unauthorized individuals gaining access to proprietary information, sensitive papers, or personal data [28]. The potential consequences of such instances might be significant, encompassing identity theft, financial fraud, and violations of business or personal privacy. The use of sophisticated security features, including encryption, remote wiping capabilities, and password protection, serves to limit the potential dangers that arise from theft or loss. These methods effectively guarantee the confidentiality and integrity of the data contained on these devices [36]. Regularly backing up critical data to secure places or cloud storage is essential for ensuring data recovery in the event of device loss or theft. This practice helps to minimize the negative effects on data accessibility and continuity.

Risks Associated with Stolen or Lost Devices

The potential dangers associated with the theft or loss of electronics are diverse, spanning both real and intangible problems [36]. Concretely, the material misplacement of technological equipment such as computers, smartphones, or portable drives can give rise to the compromising of sensitive data, hence increasing the likelihood of breaches in the confidentiality of information, instances of identity theft, or occurrences of financial fraud. The loss or theft of such devices can have intangible consequences since it poses hazards to both personal and business privacy. This, in turn, can jeopardize trust and reputation [19]. The violation of data protection regulations might result in regulatory compliance concerns. Additionally, the possibility of unwanted entry into corporate networks or systems *via* the misplaced device might compound security vulnerabilities to a greater extent [16]. The concerns underscore the imperative of implementing strong security protocols and proactive initiatives to minimize the impact of device theft or loss on data security, privacy, and organizational integrity.

Encryption and Remote Wiping as Protective Measures

Encryption and remote wiping are essential security techniques that effectively mitigate the potential hazards connected with the loss or theft of equipment [29]. Encryption serves as a strong protective measure by employing encoding techniques to render stored data unintelligible without the corresponding decryption key. Consequently, this ensures the security of critical information, even *in situ*ations when unauthorized individuals get access to the device [30]. This measure guarantees the preservation of data confidentiality and serves as a deterrent against unauthorized access or breaches of data security. In addition to encryption, the implementation of remote wiping provides users or administrators with the capability to erase data from a device that is lost or stolen, thereby mitigating the risk of unauthorized access or disclosure of confidential data [31]. These procedures effectively reduce the likelihood of data compromise, identity theft, and privacy breaches. They provide a proactive strategy to safeguard against the negative consequences of device loss or theft, thereby ensuring data security and maintaining confidentiality [19].

Corrupted Firmware

This damage can be caused by a variety of sources, such as software defects, malware infections, or interruptions during the updating process. When the firmware becomes corrupted, it can lead to several undesirable outcomes, for example, erratic behavior, failure to initiate, or functional difficulties, which can negatively affect both the performance and security of the devices [32]. The presence of corruption undermines the stability of the gadget and hampers its capacity to perform essential functions. The process of restoring corrupted firmware typically requires the utilization of specialist processes or tools provided by the device manufacturer in order to re-flash or reinstall the firmware [33]. The objective of this procedure is to address the compromised code, thereby ensuring the appropriate operation of the system and minimizing the potential hazards associated with data loss or security vulnerabilities resulting from the compromised firmware.

Understanding Firmware Issues

Firmware concerns involve a range of challenges associated with embedded software that govern the functionalities of a device. These issues can originate from various factors, including software defects, insufficient updates, viruses, or hardware faults, resulting in firmware corruption or instability [34]. Comprehending firmware issues is crucial due to their direct influence on the fundamental functionalities, stability, and security of a device. The presence of corrupted firmware has the potential to induce malfunctions, manifest erratic behavior, or render equipment completely non-functional [35]. The resolution of firmware issues frequently necessitates the involvement of individuals with specialist knowledge, access to certain tools, or assistance from device manufacturers in order to re-flash or reinstall the firmware, with the objective of addressing the fundamental problems at hand [36]. Timely resolution of firmware issues is of utmost importance in guaranteeing the dependability and operational effectiveness of devices while also minimizing the possible hazards of data loss or security vulnerabilities that may arise from corrupted firmware.

Measures to Prevent and Address Firmware-related Data Loss

The prevention and mitigation of data loss caused by firmware-related issues necessitates the implementation of a comprehensive strategy. The implementation of periodic firmware upgrades from reputable sources serves to address identified vulnerabilities, hence diminishing the potential for data loss arising from firmware-related complications [37]. The utilization of manufacturer-approved routes for getting firmware guarantees both the validity and integrity of the firmware, hence reducing the likelihood of compromised data security resulting from damaged firmware (38).

The use of robust backup procedures serves to protect against potential occurrences of data loss, while the validation of firmware integrity prior to installation effectively reduces the risks associated with modified or malicious firmware. Timely correction of firmware anomalies can be achieved by promptly engaging with manufacturer support channels [39]. This proactive approach effectively mitigates the impact of firmware-related issues on both data integrity and system stability. These solutions jointly enhance protection against data loss caused by firmware issues, hence safeguarding data integrity and assuring continuous operations.

DATA LOSS PREVENTION STRATEGIES

DLP methods involve a variety of procedures that are used to protect against both unintentional and deliberate data loss. These measures are put in place to ensure the confidentiality, integrity, and availability of sensitive information [40]. By incorporating these tactics into a complete data loss prevention program, organizations substantially diminish the likelihood of data breaches, alleviate the consequences of prospective incidents, and maintain the security and integrity of vital information, as depicted.

Importance of Regular Backups

Regular backups play a crucial role in mitigating the risk of data loss incidents resulting from a range of circumstances, including hardware malfunctions, cyber intrusions, or inadvertent deletions [41]. These backup measures guarantee that in the occurrence of system malfunctions or data deterioration, businesses may promptly recover lost data, thereby reducing downtime and preserving business continuity [27]. They serve as an essential element within disaster recovery strategies, facilitating the retrieval of crucial information and mitigating the risk of irretrievable data loss.

Using Reliable Hardware and Storage Solutions

Ensuring the integrity and accessibility of data is contingent upon the utilization of dependable hardware components and storage systems. The utilization of high-quality hardware, such as durable hard drives or solid-state drives, serves to minimize the potential for hardware failures that may result in the loss of data [42]. Reliable storage solutions, such as redundant storage systems or cloud-based storage with robust data redundancy mechanisms, contribute to the preservation of data accessibility even in the presence of hardware malfunctions or failures, hence augmenting data resilience and dependability [43, 44].

Educating Users on Safe Computing Practices

The dissemination of knowledge to users regarding secure computing practices, such as the identification of phishing efforts, the implementation of robust password management, and the adherence to data handling standards, plays a crucial role in limiting human errors that may result in data loss [43]. Through the promotion of cybersecurity awareness and the cultivation of a security-conscious environment among users, companies effectively mitigate the potential for unintentional actions that may jeopardize data security [44]. As a result, they make a substantial contribution to the broader endeavors aimed at preventing data loss.

DATA RECOVERY PLANS

This section identifies some identified data recovery plans, entailing the significance of having them in place, steps to be taken in the event of data loss, and regular testing and updating of data recovery plans as presented.

Risk Assessment and Data Inventory

The process of performing a thorough risk assessment entails the identification of potential risks to the integrity of data, the comprehension of vulnerabilities, and the prioritization of crucial information. Conducting a comprehensive assessment of data assets facilitates the classification of information according to its significance and level of sensitivity [45]. The purpose of this evaluation is to guide the formulation of recovery strategies. It accomplishes this by identifying crucial data sets and potential dangers that necessitate the implementation of targeted protection measures or contingency plans.

Backup Strategies

The establishment of efficient backup methods entails the identification of the appropriate frequency and nature of backups required for distinct categories of data. This encompasses the process of carefully choosing suitable storage sites, implementing redundancy measures, and conducting periodical integrity checks to validate the effectiveness of backups [46]. The synchronization of backup procedures with the operational requirements of an organization guarantees the dependable preservation and accessibility of crucial data in the event of data loss occurrences.

Recovery Time Objectives (RTOs) and Recovery Point Objectives (RPOs)

The establishment of RPOs and RTOs provides a fundamental framework for data recovery by defining the acceptable level of data loss and the prescribed timeframe for the recovery of systems or data [47]. These objectives serve to enable the selection of appropriate backup systems and the development of recovery procedures, ensuring that the organization can efficiently resume its operations within acceptable limitations.

Incident Response Protocols

The establishment of incident response protocols entails the development of explicit procedures aimed at the identification, reporting, and handling of situations involving data loss. The process of incident management is enhanced by designating specific roles, providing clear escalation processes, and defining effective communication channels [48]. These measures contribute to the efficient and coordinated response to data loss incidents, ultimately minimizing their impact.

Continuous Updates and Maintenance

Regular, ongoing evaluation and revisions of the data recovery plan guarantee its congruence with shifting organizational requirements, improvements in technology, and emerging security risks [49]. Consistent maintenance activities are crucial in ensuring the ongoing relevance, currency, and efficacy of the strategy, hence enhancing the organization's ability to withstand and recover from data loss disasters.

Data Recovery Procedures

The comprehensive documentation of meticulous, sequential data recovery techniques serves as a valuable resource for information technology staff, facilitating their navigation through the intricate process of data restoration [50]. The following procedures delineate the steps involved in retrieving and validating backed-up data. These methods are designed to guarantee the accuracy and completeness of the data during the restoration process, hence expediting the recovery of vital systems and information.

CONCLUSION

The establishment of effective data loss prevention techniques is contingent upon several key elements, namely risk assessment, backup strategies, clearly stated recovery targets, structured incident response protocols, thorough data recovery procedures, regular testing, and ongoing plan maintenance. The need to highlight the imperative nature of adopting a comprehensive strategy for mitigating data loss cannot be overstated. This entails integrating technology measures, educating employees, and implementing organizational protocols. This approach acknowledges that the issue of data protection extends beyond technical considerations and involves various aspects, including human behavior, system resilience, and strategic planning [53].

Future studies should investigate the potential of AI in detecting threats to enable proactive risk mitigation. There is a need for further exploration of improved encryption approaches to enhance the security of data both when it is stored and when it is being sent. Developments in user-centric training programs should be pursued to strengthen awareness and compliance among users. The integration of nascent technologies such as blockchain and secure multi-party computation has the potential to fundamentally transform the field of data privacy, ushering in a novel era of secure data sharing. Ongoing research and advancements play a crucial role in the development of data protection frameworks, enabling them to remain adaptable in the face of constantly emerging threats.

REFERENCES

[1]   M. Themessl, K. Enigl, S. Reisenhofer, J. Köberl, D. Kortschak, and S. Reichel, "Collection, Standardization and Attribution of Robust Disaster Event Information—A Demonstrator of a National Event-Based Loss and Damage Database in Austria", *Geosciences (Switzerland),* vol. 12, no. 8, 2022.

[2]   L.A. Herrera, "Challenges of acquiring mobile devices while minimizing the loss of usable forensics data", *8th International Symposium on Digital Forensics and Security, ISDFS 2020,* 2020. [http://dx.doi.org/10.1109/ISDFS49300.2020.9116458]

[3]   K. Moser, K.K.R. Choo, and N.A. Le-Khac, "Database Forensics for Analyzing Data Loss in Delayed Extraction Cases", In: *Studies in Big Data* vol. 116. Springer, Cham, 2022, pp. 175-232. [http://dx.doi.org/10.1007/978-3-031-16127-8_6]

[4]   A. Arfeen, M. Asim Khan, O. Zafar, and U. Ahsan, "Process based volatile memory forensics for ransomware detection", *Concurr. Comput.,* vol. 34, no. 4, p. e6672, 2022. [http://dx.doi.org/10.1002/cpe.6672]

[5]   V. Balajichandrasekhar M, T.S. Rao, and G. Srinivas, "An improvised methodology to unbar android mobile phone for forensic examination", *International Journal of Electrical and Computer Engineering (IJECE),* vol. 8, no. 4, p. 2239, 2018. [http://dx.doi.org/10.11591/ijece.v8i4.pp2239-2246]

[6]   M.V.B. Chandrasekhar, and T. Srinivasa Rao, "CS pattern cracker algorithm: To unlock an android mobile phone pattern lock without data loss for forensic examination", *J. Adv. Res. Dyn. Control Syst,* vol. 11, no. 2, pp. 363-374, 2019.

[7]   R. Adee, and H. Mouratidis, "A Dynamic Four-Step Data Security Model for Data in Cloud Computing Based on Cryptography and Steganography", *Sensors (Basel),* vol. 22, no. 3, p. 1109, 2022. [http://dx.doi.org/10.3390/s22031109] [PMID: 35161853]

[8]   B.A.F. Jarah, M.A.A.L. Jarrah, S.N. Almomani, E. AlJarrah, and M. Al-Rashdan, "The effect of reliable data transfer and efficient computer network features in Jordanian banks accounting information systems performance based on hardware and software, database and number of hosts", *International Journal of Data and Network Science,* vol. 7, no. 1, pp. 357-362, 2023.

[http://dx.doi.org/10.5267/j.ijdns.2022.9.012]

[9]   IPAE Pratama, "Computer Forensic Using Photorec for Secure Data Recovery Between Storage Media: a Proof of Concept. International Journal of Science, Technology & Management", *2021,* vol. 2, p. 4, 2021.
[http://dx.doi.org/10.46729/ijstm.v2i4.256]

[10]   TH Lenhard, "Data Security: Technical and Organizational Protection Measures against Data Loss and Computer Crime", *Data Security: Technical and Organizational Protection Measures against Data Loss and Computer Crime.,* 2022.

[11]   Y. Zhao, X. Wang, Y. Fang, and C. Xu, "Depth Recovery With Large-Area Data Loss Guided by Polarization Cues for Time-of-Flight Imaging", *IEEE Access,* vol. 11, pp. 38840-38849, 2023.
[http://dx.doi.org/10.1109/ACCESS.2023.3267814]

[12]   B. Aziz, "Analysing potential data security losses in organisations based on subsequent users logins", *PLoS One.,* vol. 18, p. 8, 2023.

[13]   S. Li, H. Zhong, L. Wang, J. Cui, J. Han, and Z. Ying, "SecuCar: Data Loss Prevention for Cloud assisted VSS based on Public Auditing Technique", *IEEE Trans. Vehicular Technol.,* pp. 1-12, 2023.
[http://dx.doi.org/10.1109/TVT.2023.3281728]

[14]   Y. Yu, G.P. Liu, and W. Hu, "Coordinated Distributed Predictive Control for Voltage Regulation of DC Microgrids With Communication Delays and Data Loss", *IEEE Trans. Smart Grid,* vol. 14, no. 3, pp. 1708-1722, 2023.
[http://dx.doi.org/10.1109/TSG.2022.3208946]

[15]   L. Daubner, and A. Považanec, "Data Loss Prevention Solution for Linux Endpoint Devices", *ACM International Conference Proceeding Series,* 2023.
[http://dx.doi.org/10.1145/3600160.3605036]

[16]   S. Canu, and D. Fourdrinier, "Data based loss estimation of the mean of a spherical distribution with a residual vector", *Metrika,* vol. 86, no. 8, pp. 851-878, 2023.
[http://dx.doi.org/10.1007/s00184-023-00895-4]

[17]   S. Roy, K. Bhalla, and R. Patel, "Mathematical analysis of histogram equalization techniques for medical image enhancement: a tutorial from the perspective of data loss", *Multimed Tools Appl,* vol. 83, no. 5, pp. 1-30, 2023.

[18]   F.I. Villenas, F.J. Vargas, and A.A. Peters, "A Kalman-Based Compensation Strategy for Platoons Subject to Data Loss: Numerical and Empirical Study", *Mathematics,* vol. 11, no. 5, p. 1228, 2023.
[http://dx.doi.org/10.3390/math11051228]

[19]   Y. Zhou, and W. Song, "DDLDroid: A Static Analyzer for Automatically Detecting Data Loss Issues in Android Applications", *In: ISSTA 2023 - Proceedings of the 32nd ACM SIGSOFT International Symposium on Software Testing and Analysis,* 2023.
[http://dx.doi.org/10.1145/3597926.3604916]

[20]   F. Zhang, M. Hua, and M. Gao, "Dynamic Output Feedback Quantization Control of a Networked Control System with Dual-Channel Data Packet Loss", *Mathematics,* vol. 11, no. 11, p. 2544, 2023.
[http://dx.doi.org/10.3390/math11112544]

[21]   B. Li, Q. Pan, J. Zhong, and W. Xu, "Long-Run Behavior Estimation of Temporal Boolean Networks With Multiple Data Losses", *IEEE Trans. Neural Netw. Learn. Syst.,* vol. 35, no. 10, pp. 15004-15011, 2024.
[PMID: 37224348]

[22]   F. Heldmann, S. Berkhahn, M. Ehrhardt, and K. Klamroth, "PINN training using biobjective optimization: The trade-off between data loss and residual loss", *J. Comput. Phys.,* vol. 488, p. 112211, 2023.
[http://dx.doi.org/10.1016/j.jcp.2023.112211]

[23]   W. Zhang, Y. Zeng, Y. Li, and Z. Zhang, "Prediction of dissolved gas concentration in transformer oil

considering data loss scenarios in power system", *Energy Rep.,* vol. 9, pp. 186-193, 2023.
[http://dx.doi.org/10.1016/j.egyr.2022.10.389]

[24]   M. Klaes, J. Zwartscholten, A. Narayan, S. Lehnhoff, and C. Rehtanz, "Impact of ICT Latency, Data Loss and Data Corruption on Active Distribution Network Control", *IEEE Access,* vol. 11, pp. 14693-14701, 2023.
[http://dx.doi.org/10.1109/ACCESS.2023.3243255]

[25]   Y. Wang, W. Shafik, J.T. Seong, A. Al Mutairi, M. SidAhmed Mustafa, and M.R. Mouhamed, "Service delay and optimization of the energy efficiency of a system in fog-enabled smart cities", *Alex. Eng. J.,* vol. 84, pp. 112-125, 2023.
[http://dx.doi.org/10.1016/j.aej.2023.10.034]

[26]   D.M. Smith, "The cost of lost data", *J. Contemp. Bussiness. Pract,* vol. 6, no. 3, pp. 1-9, 2003.

[27]   S. Petale, and J. Thangaraj, "Link failure recovery mechanism in software defined networks", *IEEE J. Sel. Areas Comm.,* vol. 38, no. 7, pp. 1285-1292, 2020.
[http://dx.doi.org/10.1109/JSAC.2020.2986668]

[28]   M. Tahmasbi, "Chaos control in networked permanent magnet synchronous motor using Lyapunov-based model predictive subject to data loss", *Eng. Rep.,* vol. 6, no. 5, p. e12765, 2024.

[29]   W. Shafik, *A Comprehensive Cybersecurity Framework for Present and Future Global Information Technology Organizations. InEffective Cybersecurity Operations for Enterprise-Wide Systems.* IGI Global, 2023, pp. 56-79.

[30]   C. Manthiramoorthy, K.M.S. Khan, and N.A. A, "Comparing Several Encrypted Cloud Storage Platforms", *International Journal of Mathematics, Statistics, and Computer Science,* vol. 2, pp. 44-62, 2023.
[http://dx.doi.org/10.59543/ijmscs.v2i.7971]

[31]   B Murugeshwari, D Selvaraj, K Sudharson, and S. Radhika, "Data Mining with Privacy Protection Using Precise Elliptical Curve Cryptography", *Intelligent Automation & Soft Computing.,* vol. 1:35, no. 1, 2023.
[http://dx.doi.org/10.32604/iasc.2023.028548]

[32]   Q. Zhao, D. Zheng, Y. Zhang, and Y. Ren, "Fine-Grained Forward Secure Firmware Update in Smart Home", *Mathematics,* vol. 11, no. 14, p. 3084, 2023.
[http://dx.doi.org/10.3390/math11143084]

[33]   W. Shafik, *Making Cities Smarter: IoT and SDN Applications, Challenges, and Future Trends. InOpportunities and Challenges of Industrial IoT in 5G and 6G Networks.* IGI Global, 2023, pp. 73-94.
[http://dx.doi.org/10.4018/978-1-7998-9266-3.ch004]

[34]   R. Akkaoui, A. Stefanov, P. Palensky, and D.H. Epema, "Resilient, Auditable and Secure IoT-Enabled Smart Inverter Firmware Amendments With Blockchain", *IEEE Internet Things J.,* vol. 11, no. 5, pp. 8945-8960, 2024.

[35]   W. Shafik, "Blockchain-Based Internet of Things (B-IoT): Challenges, Solutions, Opportunities, Open Research Questions, and Future Trends", In: *Blockchain-based Internet of Things* vol. 8. Talyor and Franscis., 2024, pp. 35-58.

[36]   L. Seidel, D. Maier, and M. Muench, "Forming faster firmware fuzzers", *InProceedings of the 32nd USENIX Conference on Security Symposium,* pp. 2903-2920, 2023.

[37]   Z. Lokmic-Tomkins, D. Bhandari, C. Bain, A. Borda, T.C. Kariotis, and D. Reser, "Lessons learned from natural disasters around digital health technologies and delivering quality healthcare", *Int. J. Environ. Res. Public Health,* vol. 20, no. 5, p. 4542, 2023.
[http://dx.doi.org/10.3390/ijerph20054542] [PMID: 36901559]

[38]   A. Khang, S.K. Gupta, C.K. Dixit, and P. Somani, "Data-driven application of human capital management databases, big data, and data mining", *InDesigning Workforce Management Systems for*

Industry, vol. 4, no. 0, pp. 105-120, 2023. [CRC Press.].
[http://dx.doi.org/10.1201/9781003357070-7]

[39]   A. Al-Harrasi, A.K. Shaikh, and A. Al-Badi, "Towards protecting organisations' data by preventing data theft by malicious insiders", *Int. J. Organ. Anal.,* vol. 31, no. 3, pp. 875-888, 2023.
[http://dx.doi.org/10.1108/IJOA-01-2021-2598]

[40]   GK Lockwood, D Hazen, Q Koziol, RS Canon, K Antypas, J Balewski, N Balthaser, W Bhimji, J Botts, J Broughton, and TL Butler, *Storage: A vision for the future of hpc storage.,* 2020.

[41]   A. Mishra, T.S. Jabar, Y.I. Alzoubi, and K.N. Mishra, "Enhancing privacy☐preserving mechanisms in Cloud storage: A novel conceptual framework", *Concurr. Comput.,* vol. 35, no. 26, p. e7831, 2023.
[http://dx.doi.org/10.1002/cpe.7831]

[42]   G. Ramesh, J. Logeshwaran, and V. Aravindarajan, "A Secured Database Monitoring Method to Improve Data Backup and Recovery Operations in Cloud Computing", *BOHR International Journal of Computer Science,* vol. 2, no. 1, pp. 1-7, 2023.
[http://dx.doi.org/10.54646/bijcs.019]

[43]   A.J. Lynch, A.A. Hyman, S.J. Cooke, S.J. Capon, P.A. Franklin, S.C. Jähnig, M. McCartney, N.P. Hòa, M.A. Owuor, J. Pittock, and M.J. Samways, "Future-proofing the Emergency Recovery Plan for freshwater biodiversity", *Environ. Rev.,* vol. 32, no. 3, pp. 350-365, 2024.

[44]   G.J. O'Reilly, A.M.B. Nafeh, and D. Shahnazaryan, "Simplified tools for the risk assessment and classification of existing buildings", *Procedia Struct. Integr.,* vol. 44, pp. 1744-1751, 2023.
[http://dx.doi.org/10.1016/j.prostr.2023.01.223]

[45]   S. Tekin, K. Bicakci, O. Mersin, G.N. Erdem, A. Canbay, and Y. Uzunay, "Optimal data backup policies for information systems subject to sudden failure", *J. Qual. Mainten. Eng.,* vol. 29, no. 2, pp. 338-355, 2023.
[http://dx.doi.org/10.1108/JQME-01-2022-0009]

[46]   S. Flowers, *Implement Backup and Restore. InDesigning and Implementing Cloud-native Applications Using Microsoft Azure Cosmos DB: Study Companion for the DP-420 Exam,* Berkeley, CA: Apress., pp. 149-157, 2023.
[http://dx.doi.org/10.1007/978-1-4842-9547-2_16]

[47]   M. Ivanov, and R. Ravanliyski, "Copy Services: A Client's Shield Against Data Loss", *2023 Eight Junior Conference on Lighting (Lighting),* IEEE., pp. 1-4, 2023.
[http://dx.doi.org/10.1109/Lighting59819.2023.10299430]

[48]   PM Maniscalco, CP Holstege, and SB Cormier, "Operations Security, Site Security, and Incident Response", *InCiottone's Disaster Medicine 2024,* Elsevier., pp. 573-581, 2024.

[49]   L. Zhuang, A. Xu, and X.L. Wang, "A prognostic driven predictive maintenance framework based on Bayesian deep learning", *Reliab. Eng. Syst. Saf.,* vol. 234, p. 109181, 2023.
[http://dx.doi.org/10.1016/j.ress.2023.109181]

[50]   M. Chiesa, A. Kamisiński, J. Rak, G. Retvari, and S. Schmid, "A survey of fast recovery mechanisms in the data plane", *Authorea Preprints,* 2023.

[51]   A. Khang, K.C. Rath, P.T. Anh, S.K. Rath, and S. Bhattacharya, "Quantum-Based Robotics in the High-Tech Healthcare Industry: Innovations and Applications", In: *Medical Robotics and AI-Assisted Diagnostics for a High-Tech Healthcare Industry.,* A. Khang, Ed., IGI Global, 2024, pp. 1-27.
[http://dx.doi.org/10.4018/979-8-3693-2105-8.ch001]

[52]   A. Khang, A.V. Hajimahmud, T. Triwiyanto, V.A. Abuzarova, and R.N. Ali, "Cloud Platform and Data Storage Systems in the Healthcare Ecosystem", In: *Medical Robotics and AI-Assisted Diagnostics for a High-Tech Healthcare Industry.,* A. Khang, Ed., IGI Global, 2024, pp. 343-356.
[http://dx.doi.org/10.4018/979-8-3693-2105-8.ch021]

[53]   A. Khang, Y. Singh, and D. Barak, "Review of the Literature on Using Machine and Deep Learning Techniques to Improve IoT Security", In: *Revolutionizing Automated Waste Treatment Systems: IoT*

and Bioelectronics. In Khang A., Hajimahmud V. A., Litvinova E., Musrat G. L., Avramovic Z. (Ed.). IGI Global, 2024.
[http://dx.doi.org/10.4018/979-8-3693-6016-3.ch018]

CHAPTER 3

Data Protection Technologies

Ankush[1], Shivam[1], Sanchit Dhankhar[2,*], Nitika Garg[2], Himanshu Sharma[1,2], Samrat Chauhan[2], Monika Saini[3] and Shushank Mahajan[2]

[1] *Ganpati Institute of Pharmacy, Bilaspur 135102, Haryana, India*

[2] *Chitkara College of Pharmacy, Chitkara University, Rajpura 140401, Punjab, India*

[3] *M.M. College of Pharmacy, Maharishi Markandeshwar (Deemed to be University), Mullana 133-207, Ambala, Haryana, India*

Abstract: The digital age, which can be defined as a collection of various technological solutions such as virtual environments, digital services, intelligent applications, machine learning, knowledge-based systems, *etc.*, is responsible for determining the particulars of e-communications, virtualization, information sharing, intelligent applications, and other aspects of the modern world. These particulars are determined by the digital age. The uncontrolled access to information and personal data that is stored at various nodes of the global network poses a possible danger to some fundamental principles of information security and privacy, which may be violated by the technology that is prevalent in the digital era. The purpose of this article is to investigate the factors that distinguish information and personal data protection from other forms of protection, as well as to provide a summary of the most significant dangers to user privacy and security in the digital era. This chapter goes over the fundamentals of data protection architecture, as well as the components of information security that help ward off attacks and threats. In conclusion, the chapter concludes by presenting data protection as an endeavor that is constantly evolving and necessitates continuous adjustments in order to stay up with the ever-changing technical and risk landscape. In order to assist businesses in navigating the complexities of the digital age, this chapter provides insights and recommendations for the development of trustworthy data protection plans.

Keywords: Data, Hardware, Information security.Protection, Software.

INTRODUCTION

The hardware, software, and communications are the three basic components that makeup information systems [1]. This is done with the purpose of developing and executing information security industry standards as protection and prevention

---

* **Corresponding author Sanchit Dhankhar:** Chitkara College of Pharmacy, Chitkara University, Rajpura 140401, Punjab, India; E-mail: sanchitdhankhar@gmail.com

Alex Khang, Sanchit Dhankhar, Sandeep Bhardwaj, Avnesh Verma & Satish Kumar Sharma (Eds.)

measures at three separate levels or layers: physical, personal, and organizational. The implementation of procedures or policies is essentially the process of instructing individuals (administrators, users, and operators) on how to utilize goods in order to guarantee the confidentiality of information within the companies [2]. Throughout the subsequent sections of this paper, we will examine various aspects of information technology security, and lastly, we will examine the technologies that are now associated with IT security.

The demand for sophisticated data protection systems has become of the utmost importance in light of the growing incidence of cyber threats such as ransomware attacks, phishing efforts, and threats initiated by insiders [3]. To ensure that data is protected during its entire lifecycle, these technologies not only serve as a defense mechanism against external dangers, but they also address weaknesses that exist within the organization [4]. In the realm of data protection technologies, encryption is considered to be one of the fundamental components. Information security refers to the measures taken to prevent unauthorized individuals from gaining access to, using, disclosing, interfering with, altering, or destroying data or information systems.

Commonly, people will use the words information assurance, computer security, and information security interchangeably [5]. While there are some subtle differences between these areas, they are often interconnected and work toward the same goal of protecting information in three ways: availability, integrity, and secrecy. Despite this, they do share a few commonalities [6]. The main elements that cause these variations are the methodologies used, the regions of concentration, and the overall perspective on the topic. The fundamental goals of information security are to ensure the privacy, authenticity, and accessibility of data. This holds true irrespective of the format the data is in, be it digital, printed, or any other form. Computer security does not necessarily have to worry about the data stored or processed by a computer; it might focus on keeping the system up and running smoothly.

Governments, militaries, corporations, banks, hospitals, and private companies all gather vast amounts of sensitive information on their personnel, clients, goods, studies, and financial situation [7]. Many computers now collect, process, and store this data before sending it on to other computers *via* networks. A loss of revenue, legal action, or even bankruptcy may occur if a competitor gets their hands on sensitive information about a company's consumers, finances, or new product line. In many cases, both ethical and legal considerations make it imperative that firms take reasonable precautions to protect customers' personal information.

Individually, privacy, which varies from culture to culture and is perceived in diverse ways, is significantly impacted by information security. Much progress and growth have been achieved in the realm of information security since the turn of the century. There are a number of entry points into the field, which makes it a viable career option. Among the many subfields covered by this site are digital forensics science, business continuity planning, information systems auditing, security testing, application and database security, and network and related infrastructure safeguarding [8]. Lastly, data protection solutions are crucial due to the increasing number of cybersecurity risks and digital data. Data loss prevention (DLP), data encryption, access controls, data masking, and other security measures prevent unauthorized access, data breaches, and privacy violations. Information is better protected with cloud security and better threat detection [52].

Organizations must invest in comprehensive data protection technology as they navigate the digital landscape. This is crucial for keeping the trust of customers, partners, and stakeholders, as well as for meeting compliance requirements. To stay ahead of risks and issues, businesses must continually update and alter their data protection procedures in response to changing technology and cyber threats [9]. Data security and its underlying principles are thoroughly discussed in this chapter.

CRYPTOGRAPHY AND ENCRYPTION

Fundamentals of Cryptography

"Secret communication" is the definition of cryptography. Important for keeping networks safe, this is an outgoing technology [10]. Disclosing private information securely is the goal of cryptography. Conferences marked by divergent opinions, alignment, information, non-denial, and informational objectivity can be usefully examined in this way. Secure computer systems and networks must be safeguarded from such unwanted access in order to process and communicate sensitive or important information. Cryptography is the study of secret codes for communication. To take a larger view, it is all about creating and evaluating rules that thwart attackers. In order to transmit muddled information efficiently, testing is necessary.

One promising approach to achieving robust security in sensor systems is to encrypt messages using a secret key that is known only during transmission and by the recipient [11]. In asset compulsory sensor arrangement, there are a lot of nagging messages about secure key deals between the sender and the receiver. Before clients send their data to a remote distributed storage service, they should encrypt it. This will ensure the data's security. The distributed storage architecture will make the information available without knowing the exact nature of the encoded segment returned to the client when they request partial realization of the entire data rather than full realization [12].

Types of Encryption Algorithms

In the realm of cryptography, the two basic classifications are symmetric cryptography and asymmetric cryptography [13]. In the case of symmetric cryptography, the encryption and decryption processes are carried out with the same key. When both the sender and the recipient of a message have access to the same secret key, this method functions very effectively. Within the realm of asymmetric cryptography, which is more widely known as public key cryptography, the process of encryption and decryption is carried out with distinct keys [14]. Because this makes it possible to exchange secure messages without requiring the sender and the receiver to share a secret key, it is suitable for situations in which the sender and the recipient do not in fact share a secret key.

Data Encryption Techniques

Many different encryption methods differ in terms of the key that is used (symmetric or asymmetric), the length of the key, the size of the data blocks that are encrypted, and other factors [15]. Within the scope of this post, we have provided an overview of several of the most widely used encryption tools. Only a limited number of tools are now available for use with encryption methods. All of them include

- Triple DES is a method that disorganized the Data Encryption Standard (DES) algorithm. It plays with three separate keys that are each 56 bits in length [16]. The Triple DES algorithm is an improved variation of the DES algorithm that uses the DES cipher method three times for each and every data block. You can use them to encrypt ATM passcode and different information.
- RSA is a personal encryption algorithm that is used to safeguard data while it is being transmitted over the internet [17]. Utilizing both public and private keys, this algorithm for encrypting data is known as an asymmetric key encryption algorithm.

It is the Blowfish. It does this by dividing the message into 64 bits and then encrypting those bits, which is a technique that is utilized by certain payment gateways [18]. It is lightning-quick, very efficient, and adaptable. There is a use for Blowfish in embedded systems, and it has been evaluated as having a level of security that is satisfactory.

- The Twofish algorithm is a symmetric key encryption technique that uses keys that are 256 bits in length. The algorithm is also known as the Two-fish algorithm [19]. The encryption software solution known as Twofish is still utilized in a great number of file and folder formats. The encryption of 128 bits in a data block is a technique that does not require a license. Additionally, it always encrypts data in rounds of 16, which makes it slower.

- Advanced Encryption Standard (AES) is a leading encryption standard that is trusted by numerous standard organizations. 128bit, 192bit, and 256bit encryption are all within its capabilities [20]. The Advanced Encryption Standard (AES) is a symmetric encryption technique that is in widespread use today. The AES algorithm is utilized for both data at rest and data while it is in transit.

Access Control and Authentication

The term "authentication" describes the steps used to confirm the identity of a user before granting them access to a resource (such as a server, application, website, or system) [21]. A person's claimed identity must be confirmed in order for authentication to be effective.

USER AUTHENTICATION METHODS

Password Based Login

When you use an online service on a daily basis, you will most likely utilize a password-based login approach because it is the most common and extensively used regular login authentication method [22]. In order to use the Password-Based Authentication method, you are required to input not only a password but also a combination of your username and mobile number. Only after the confirmation of both of these components has been made is the individual allowed to proceed [51].

Multi-Factor Authentication

An authentication mechanism known as Multi-Factor Authentication (MFA) requires users to provide more than one piece of information before granting them access to a service or network [22]. In addition to the usual login process that involves a password, this adds another level of protection. Along with their username and password, users are also required to provide a one-time password which can be sent *via* email or phone as an additional security measure. You can add an additional safeguard to your resources by rapidly configuring multiple Multi-Factor Authentication (MFA) methods. Some examples of multi-factor authentication systems include one-time passwords (OTPs) sent by text message or email, hardware tokens, push notifications, and mobile authenticators (Google, Microsoft, Authy, *etc.*).

Biometric Authentication

In this process, personal characteristics such as fingerprints, palms, retinas, voice, face, and speech recognition are utilized [23]. The following is an explanation of how biometric authentication operates: The first step is to enter the physical attributes of individuals into a database. When a user wants to go inside the premises or utilize any equipment, the database is compared to the data that is stored in the database, and the physical characteristics of the individual are checked against the data.

Two Factor Authentication

As the name suggests, in order for a person to gain access to a certain resource, they are required to successfully complete two separate authentication processes. "Two-factor authentication" is the name given to this particular technique. Just take into consideration the following scenario: In order to protect your website, app, or collection of apps from contemporary cyberattacks such as phishing, data breaches, and key logger usage, you should work to improve the security of your website, app, or collection of applications. Additional two-factor authentication (two-factor authentication) alternatives are available through MiniOrange. These options include One-Time Passwords (OTP *via* SMS/Email), Push Notifications, Biometrics, Authenticators (Google, Microsoft, and Authy), and Hardware Tokens, along with Yubikey [24].

According to the findings of one of the most recent security surveys, two-factor authentication has the potential to prevent eighty percent of data breaches. With miniOrange, you are able to configure two-factor authentication for any website or application that is developed on any platform. Additional two-factor authentication (two-factor authentication) alternatives are available through MiniOrange. These options include One-Time Passwords (OTP *via* SMS/Email), Push Notifications, Biometrics, Authenticators (Google, Microsoft, and Authy), and Hardware Tokens, along with Yubikey [24]. According to the findings of one of the most recent security surveys, two-factor authentication has the potential to prevent eighty percent of data breaches.

The Fundamentals of Network Security

- Data loss prevention (DLP): Preventing employees from sharing data outside of an approved network is one way to prevent data loss. It guarantees the secure transmission of all data. Example: An organization should have a high-security level if it gathers and maintains data, including sensitive personal information and data that is considered intellectual property or trade secrets. DLP adds an additional layer of security by flagging unusual activity surrounding data and assisting in its secure classification and tagging [25].

- Email security: Security breaches frequently originate from email gateways, which are brittle points in the network. Emails are the main source of phishing attacks that are enhanced with social engineering techniques. These kinds of attacks can be reduced with email security. Such malicious emails can be stopped from arriving by installing a secure email gateway on-site or in the cloud [26]. Solutions for email encryption provide defense against legal infractions and data loss. For instance: Consider a scenario where a company routinely sends emails containing social security numbers, bank account information, name, and address, among other personally identifiable information [27]. In that scenario, the business ought to use an email security network from an external network, like the internet, is called firewall. They control inbound and outbound network traffic using a set of established protocols.

- Firewall:- The walls that separate an internal network from an external network, like the internet, are called firewalls [28]. They control inbound and outbound network traffic using a set of established protocols. The first line of defense is a firewall. Firewalls stop data from entering an organization if it is received that does not follow its defined set of protocols. For instance: At a computer's ports, which are points of entry where data is exchanged with external devices, firewalls monitor traffic [29]. For instance, *via* port 22, a source address of 165.12.2.1 is permitted to reach a destination of 171.14.2.2. In this case, the destination address (171.14.2.2) will only be accessible to trusted packets with source addresses (165.12.2.1). In addition, firewalls can hide your computer and stop illegal access to a system.

- VPN: VPN builds a secure tunnel over the internet to allow information to pass through. From the point of origin to the point of destination, the tunnel is encrypted, guaranteeing the security of all data sent and received [30]. Employees who work from home or telecommute frequently rely on insecure networks to access the internet, which exposes company data to security breaches. Employees can work from anywhere in the world with a secure network that protects corporate information thanks to VPNs.

Other types of network security include:

- Antivirus and anti-malware software: Antivirus software protects a network from a wide range of dangerous applications, including viruses, worms, Trojan horses, ransomware, spyware, and ransomware [31]. Due to the fact that malicious software can infiltrate a system and remain dormant for an extended period of time, the program is able to monitor access, eliminate it, identify and fix any issues that it may have created, and carry out routine anomaly checks.

- Behavioral analytics: This technique aids in the discovery of odd activity patterns. This makes it possible for the security team to handle any kind of possible compromise that might put the network in jeopardy [32].

• Intrusion prevention system (IPS): In order to detect and prevent possible dangers, this network security measure keeps an eye on every network activity. Regular updates to the rule sets allow control over the operating time cycles [33].

FIREWALLS AND NETWORK SECURITY

A firewall controls a device's safe data inflow and outflow. It serves as a barrier between the trusted and untrusted networks and monitors network traffic. Based on pre-established rules, a firewall is a security system that guards an internal network against unauthorized servers and networks. It serves as a barrier, enabling data transmission and reception only within the secured network. Simply said, a firewall is the vital barrier that separates an internal private network from an external public internet connection. Allowing legitimate communications while preventing malicious ones is the main job of a firewall. As the frequency of cybercrimes continues to rise, it is imperative that individuals and organizations take precautions to protect their data.

Virtualization and other software-as-a-service (SaaS) models, as well as public and private clouds, are all viable options for running firewalls [34]. Prior to firewalls, access control lists (ACLs) stored on rooters handled network security. ACLs are rules that specify whether to allow or prohibit a particular IP address from accessing the network. However, ACLs are unable to identify the kind of network that they are blocking. Furthermore, ACL is unable to prevent threats from entering the network. Thus, the firewall was put into place. Internet connectivity is now required for all organizations. Nonetheless, using the Internet to access information benefits the organization; it also makes it possible for external parties to communicate with the internal network of the company. This puts the organization in danger.

INTRUSION DETECTION AND PREVENTION SYSTEMS (IDPS)

When discussing application security methods aimed at reducing attacks and halting developing risks, two broad phrases come to mind: intrusion detection and prevention. The proactive method aims to detect and halt ongoing attacks by the use of an intrusion detection system. It can detect social engineering attempts that attempt to deceive users into divulging personal information and filter out harmful software like Trojan horses, backdoors, and rootkits.

Intrusion Detection System (IDS)

Intruder detection systems (IDS) keep an eye on data transfers across networks for suspicious activity and alert users immediately if they find anything suspicious [35]. Software that checks a computer system or network for malware or policy breaches is known as intrusion detection software. It is a common practice to notify upper management of any unlawful action or infraction or to keep track of it all in a centralized SIEM database. The objective of the learning problem for intrusion detectors is to develop a classifier or predictive model that can distinguish between "good (normal) connections" and "bad connections," which refer to intrusions or attacks.

Intrusion Prevention System (IPS)

The intrusion prevention system is sometimes known as an "intrusion detection and prevention system [36]." It is a tool for network security that monitors systems and networks for any signs of malicious behavior. The primary functions of an intrusion prevention system are to detect intrusions, collect relevant data about them, report them, and then take action to prevent or block them.

Network traffic is constantly monitored by an IPS, which then compares it to known attack patterns and signatures. This continues indefinitely. Upon detection, the system blocks any potentially harmful traffic from reaching the network.

Variety of IPS

IPS comes in two primary varieties:

- Network-The term "intrusion prevention system" (IPS) refers to a system that is located at the network perimeter and monitors all network traffic, both incoming and outgoing [37].
- Host-Based IPS: There is the possibility of installing a Host-Based Intrusion Prevention System (IPS) on a single host, which monitors all traffic coming into and going out of the host.

Network Security Best Practices

Network security includes defense against intrusions on networks and network hardware. However, endpoint security handles the security of devices that use the network, so it may not always cover that. The procedure for safeguarding your network varies based on how big your business is and what industry you work in. Firewalls and routers are only one part of network security; other methods include activity monitoring, authentication, and encryption.

Typical Types of Attacks on Networks

- Virus: A virus needs human interaction to function; the most basic kind is an email with a malicious linker attachment [38]. By activating the attachment or link, a rogue code is introduced into the system, rendering all security measures ineffective.
- Malware: One of the quickest methods for distributing harmful attacks is through malware. It was made with the intention of destroying the target and breaking into a system without authorization. Malware spreads primarily by self-replication and can access any networked computer because it travels over the Internet. Targeting network-connected external devices is another possibility.
- Worm: A worm can be used to attack a weak network application without involving the user. All an attacker needs to do is to send malware to the application, execute it, and share the user's internet connection [39]. As a result, a worm that attacks the network is created.
- Phishing: It is common to associate network intrusions with phishing. Sending emails that seem to be from famous or trustworthy organizations is one example of a phishing attack. The network becomes susceptible to potential data loss in the event that a malicious link or attachment is clicked.
- Botnet: In this scenario, malicious software is being downloaded onto a networked collection of personal computers. The attacker has total control over the computers, which have been transformed into zombies [40]. It is possible to do this without the owner's awareness. The attacker then makes use of this control to damage or infect additional devices.
- Denial of service (DoS) and distributed denial of service (DDoS): A denial of service (DoS) prevents any authenticated user access by forcing a network or even an entire infrastructure to crash, either totally or partially [41].
- Man-in-the-middle: This type of attack involves listening to and intercepting network conversations between two users. This gives the intermediary some degree of information capture, monitoring, and even control.
- Packet sniffer: When passive receivers are near a wireless transmitter, they duplicate each packet that is sent out. Sensitive and confidential data are contained in each of these packets. Subsequently, packet receivers transform into packet sniffers, extracting all transmitted packets within their proximity [42].
- DNS and IP spoofing: Hackers engage in DNS spoofing when they insert their own cache and modify DNS data. Consequently, while conducting a search, the name server inputs the wrong IP address. In contrast, IP spoofing enables the use of fictitious internet addresses to transmit packets in the name of another user.

DATA BACKUP STRATEGIES

- External hard drives:- To store data similarly to a USB drive, external hard drives can usually be connected through USB ports on a computer [43]. The amount of storage space that separates USB drives and external hard drives is the primary distinction. For instance, USB devices usually cannot store more than a terabyte of data, but some external hard drives might be able to.
- Backup software: When backing up data, backup software gives users more functionality. For example, it lets users choose which types of data to backup and where to store the data.
- Determine Vital Information: In order to be informed of any backup failures or anomalies, set up monitoring alerts. Review these alerts frequently in order to quickly address any issues
- Frequency of Backup: Based on the importance and rate of change of your data, create a regular backup schedule [44]. Less important data can have fewer backups, but critical data may need daily or even real-time backups.
- Automation: To reduce the possibility of human error and guarantee consistency, the backup procedure is automated. Automatic backups that are scheduled are more dependable and effective.
- Versioning: Use versioning to maintain several copies of your files over time. In the event of data corruption or unintentional modifications, this enables you to restore to a specific point in time, which can be vital [45].
- Frequent Testing: The integrity of your backups and the restoration procedure on a regular basis are checked. This guarantees that you can recover data when needed and that your backup system is dependable [46].
- Documentation: It keeps track of all the steps involved in your backup plan, including data restoration procedures. In addition to facilitating the onboarding of new employees, this documentation guarantees a seamless emergency recovery procedure [47].

CLOUD BACKUP SOLUTIONS

It is critical that you comprehend cloud computing and its benefits before you feel at ease putting your company's data on it. Businesses can save data securely online thanks to the cloud. The shared data is accessible to anyone with authorization at any time, from any location, and on any device.

DATA MASKING AND ANONYMIZATION

Data Anonymization

Data anonymization eliminates personally identifiable information from datasets, lowering the danger of both deliberate and unintentional disclosure of sensitive data [48]. Data anonymization technologies allow businesses to do this without breaking any data privacy laws and to use their data for more diverse reasons. Data anonymization techniques are used by almost any organization that has to gather, store, manipulate, or transport sensitive data. Data anonymization systems are typically customizable, allowing the degree and kind of anonymization to be changed to suit specific business needs, data types, and legal requirements.

Data Masking

Data masking is the process of removing private, confidential, or sensitive information from a dataset and substituting it with random numbers, pseudo-information, or other fictitious data [49]. In essence, this preserves the dataset's structural properties while producing an inauthentic version of the data. Data masking technologies safeguard the actual sensitive data while providing a workable replacement for essential organizational usage, enabling data to be utilized for things like user training and software testing.

Key Techniques for Data Masking and Anonymization

The privacy protections provided by each method and the usefulness of the resulting data vary slightly [50]. Generally speaking, privacy and utility in DMA are inversely correlated. Complete Random Substitution, or CRS is also known as pseudonymization.

Values from a suitable list or generator are randomly substituted for data in one or more table columns.

- This maintains the appearance of highly private data.
- It might change how the data is distributed, which might impact its usefulness in some use cases.
- There is no fine-grained control over privacy *versus* utility using this technique.

Generalization (*e.g.*, k-anonymization):

- Data may be changed into a range of values;
- This technique results in stronger privacy due to lower data dimensions;
- Data utility is compromised;
- Some data is purposefully removed to make it less identifiable.

Differential Privacy:

- Proper selection of its control parameters yields a fair balance between privacy and utility.

- This technique adds "noise" to the data set while maintaining stat distribution.
- The availability of support for non-numeric data is limited.

Artificial Information.

- Using this method, data engineers create fresh synthetic data based on an actual dataset.
- Appropriate models guarantee that privacy and utility are balanced. This method is effective for all forms of data.
- However, it is difficult to apply and occasionally calls for the development of new models.
- It goes without saying that the aforementioned techniques might be used for a single data set and DMA solution.

CONCLUSION AND FUTURE OUTLOOK

As a conclusion, the field of data security technologies is one that is both dynamic and vital. It plays a pivotal role in the process of fortifying enterprises against an ever-expanding array of cyber threats. Encryption, access controls, data masking, and advanced technologies such as cloud security measures and threat detection systems are all examples of the complex aspect of data protection, which has been discussed in this chapter. The availability, integrity, and secrecy of essential information are guaranteed by the combination of these devices, which comprise a robust defense. Priority should be data protection, often known as information security. Network security is critical for two reasons: first, to stop unauthorized users from abusing server resources, and second, to stop data breaches. Only really costly equipment, such as massive supercomputers, should be concerned about safeguarding their processing power [51].

Data protection must be seen by enterprises as a continuous and developing activity due to the increasing sophistication of cyber threats and the rapid advancement of technology. It is an ongoing procedure that is subject to change and improvement, rather than a one-time installation. It is a demonstration of the industry's dedication to staying one step ahead of risks by detecting and reacting to abnormalities in real time that the incorporation of machine learning and artificial intelligence into security frameworks occurs.

Data security solutions, in essence, are not merely a defensive barrier against cyber threats; rather, they are a strategic need for enterprises to retain their resilience and reputation in a world that is increasingly linked. They are able to traverse the intricacies of the digital ecosystem with confidence, knowing that they have taken extensive precautions to secure the data that has been entrusted to them, thanks to the deployment of these technologies in a strategic manner.

Looking ahead, the data protection landscape will be further shaped by the interplay of technology, regulation, and human understanding; companies need to be proactive and nimble to keep up with these changes.

REFERENCES

[1]   I. Englander, and W. Wong, *The architecture of computer hardware, systems software, and networking: An information technology approach.* John Wiley & Sons, 2021.

[2]   A. Meier, and H. Stormer, *eBusiness & eCommerce: managing the digital value chain.* Springer Science & Business Media., 2009.

[3]   A. Babate, "State of cyber security: emerging threats landscape", *International Journal of Advanced Research in Computer Science & Technology,* vol. 3, no. 1, pp. 113-119, 2015.

[4]   T. Zhang, H. Antunes, and S. Aggarwal, "Defending connected vehicles against malware: Challenges and a solution framework", *IEEE Internet Things J.,* vol. 1, no. 1, pp. 10-21, 2014.
       [http://dx.doi.org/10.1109/JIOT.2014.2302386]

[5]   A. Althonayan, and A. Andronache, "Shifting from information security towards a cybersecurity paradigm", *Proceedings of the 2018 10th International Conference on Information Management and Engineering,* 2018.
       [http://dx.doi.org/10.1145/3285957.3285971]

[6]   R. Baskerville, P. Spagnoletti, and J. Kim, "Incident-centered information security: Managing a strategic balance between prevention and response", *Inf. Manage.,* vol. 51, no. 1, pp. 138-151, 2014.
       [http://dx.doi.org/10.1016/j.im.2013.11.004]

[7]   D.B. Parker, "Toward a new framework for information security?", In: *Computer Security Handbook*, 2012, p. 3.1-3.23.
       [http://dx.doi.org/10.1002/9781118851678.ch3]

[8]   H. Arshad, A.B. Jantan, and O.I. Abiodun, "Digital Forensics: Review of Issues in Scientific Validation of Digital Evidence", *J. Inf. Process. Syst.,* vol. 14, no. 2, 2018.

[9]   M. Javaid, *Towards insighting cybersecurity for healthcare domains: A comprehensive review of recent practices and trends.* Cyber Security and Applications, 2023, p. 100016.

[10]   S. Bera, B. Roy, and D. Pal, *Network Securityand Cryptography: A Review.*

[11]   C. Castelluccia, A.C-F. Chan, E. Mykletun, and G. Tsudik, "Efficient and provably secure aggregation of encrypted data in wireless sensor networks", *ACM Trans. Sens. Netw.,* vol. 5, no. 3, pp. 1-36, 2009. [TOSN].
       [http://dx.doi.org/10.1145/1525856.1525858]

[12]   R. Dingledine, M.J. Freedman, and D. Molnar, "The free haven project: Distributed anonymous storage service", *International Workshop on Design Issues in Anonymity and Unobservability Berkeley,* Springer., 2001.CA, USA
       [http://dx.doi.org/10.1007/3-540-44702-4_5]

[13]   A. Biryukov, and L. Perrin, "State of the art in lightweight symmetric cryptography", *Cryptology ePrint Archive,* 2017.

[14]   M. Blumenthal, "Encryption: Strengths and weaknesses of public-key cryptography", *CSRS,* vol. 2007, p. 1, 2007.

[15]   E. Thambiraja, G. Ramesh, and D.R. Umarani, "A survey on various most common encryption techniques", *Int. J. Adv. Res. Comput. Sci. Softw. Eng.,* vol. 2, no. 7, 2012.

[16]   O.N. Akande, "A dynamic round triple data encryption standard cryptographic technique for data security", *International Conference on Computational Science and Its Applications,* Springer., 2020.
       [http://dx.doi.org/10.1007/978-3-030-58817-5_36]

[17]   T.S. Obaid, "Study a public key in RSA algorithm", *European Journal of Engineering and Technology Research*, vol. 5, no. 4, pp. 395-398, 2020.

[18]   M.N.B. Anwar, "Comparative study of cryptography algorithms and its' applications", *International Journal of Computer Networks and Communications Security*, vol. 7, no. 5, pp. 96-103, 2019.

[19]   S.M. Kareem, and A.M.S. Rahma, "A novel approach for the development of the Twofish algorithm based on multi-level key space", *Journal of Information Security and Applications*, vol. 50, p. 102410, 2020.
[http://dx.doi.org/10.1016/j.jisa.2019.102410]

[20]   A. Singh, *Novel cryptographic approach for SCADA systems using AES algorithm with 256 bit key in FPGA*. UPES: Dehradun, 2019.

[21]   K.H. Mohammed, A. Hassan, and D. Yusuf Mohammed, *Identity and Access Management System: a Web-Based Approach for an Enterprise.*, 2018.

[22]   S.M. Furnell, P.S. Dowland, H.M. Illingworth, and P.L. Reynolds, "Authentication and supervision: A survey of user attitudes", *Comput. Secur.*, vol. 19, no. 6, pp. 529-539, 2000.
[http://dx.doi.org/10.1016/S0167-4048(00)06027-2]

[23]   D. Bhattacharyya, "Biometric authentication: A review. International Journal of u-and e-Service", *Science and Technology*, vol. 2, no. 3, pp. 13-28, 2009.

[24]   A. Czeskis, *Practical, usable, and secure authentication and authorization on the Web.*, 2013.

[25]   R.P. França, *The fundamentals and potential for cybersecurity of big data in the modern world.* Machine Intelligence and Big Data Analytics for Cybersecurity Applications, 2021, pp. 51-73.
[http://dx.doi.org/10.1007/978-3-030-57024-8_3]

[26]   N.A. Sharma, A. Pillay, and M. Farik, "A Review Of Recent Cyber-Attacks In Fiji", *International Journal of Scientific & Technology Research*, vol. 5, no. 11, pp. 110-115, 2016.

[27]   M.S. Ackerman, L.F. Cranor, and J. Reagle, "Privacy in e-commerce: examining user scenarios and privacy preferences", *Proceedings of the 1st ACM Conference on Electronic Commerce*, 1999.
[http://dx.doi.org/10.1145/336992.336995]

[28]   A.D. Keromytis, and V. Prevelakis, "Designing firewalls: A survey", *Network Security: Current Status and Future Directions*, pp. 33-49, 2007.
[http://dx.doi.org/10.1002/9780470099742.ch3]

[29]   K. Ingham, and S. Forrest, *A history and survey of network firewalls.* University of New Mexico, Tech. Rep, 2002.

[30]   F. Martín Padilla, *Study of secure tunnels and VPNs applied to an educational practice.* Universitat Politècnica de Catalunya, 2022.

[31]   U.H. Rao, "Malicious software and anti-virus software", In: *The InfoSec Handbook: An Introduction to Information Security*, 2014, pp. 141-161.
[http://dx.doi.org/10.1007/978-1-4302-6383-8_7]

[32]   P. Sommer, "Intrusion detection systems as evidence", *Comput. Netw.*, vol. 31, no. 23-24, pp. 2477-2487, 1999.
[http://dx.doi.org/10.1016/S1389-1286(99)00113-9]

[33]   M. Felson, and R.L. Boba, *Crime and everyday life.* Sage, 2010.
[http://dx.doi.org/10.4135/9781483349299]

[34]   M. Vajaranta, *Security as a Service for Hybrid Clouds.*, 2014.

[35]   M. West, "Preventing system intrusions", In: *Network and System Security.* Elsevier, 2014, pp. 29-56.
[http://dx.doi.org/10.1016/B978-0-12-416689-9.00002-2]

[36]   N. Chakraborty, "Intrusion detection system and intrusion prevention system: A comparative study",

International Journal of Computing and Business Research, vol. 4, no. 2, pp. 1-8, 2013. [IJCBR].

[37]   "M.Y., K.A. Bakar, and A.H. Abdullah, Intrusion prevention system", *Survey (Lond.),* 2005.

[38]   P. Szor, *The art of computer virus research and defense: Art comp virus res defense.* Pearson Education, 2005, p. 1.

[39]   G.A. Abdalrahman, and H. Varol, "Defending against cyber-attacks on the internet of things", *in 2019 7th International Symposium on Digital Forensics and Security (ISDFS),* IEEE., 2019. [http://dx.doi.org/10.1109/ISDFS.2019.8757478]

[40]   F.T. Ngo, *Malicious software threats.* The Palgrave Handbook of International Cybercrime and Cyberdeviance, 2020, pp. 793-813.

[41]   B.B. Gupta, R.C. Joshi, and M. Misra, "Defending against distributed denial of service attacks: issues and challenges", *Information Security Journal: A Global Perspective,* vol. 18, no. 5, pp. 224-247, 2009. [http://dx.doi.org/10.1080/19393550903317070]

[42]   K.N. Choi, H. Kolamunna, A. Uyanwatta, K. Thilakarathna, S. Seneviratne, R. Holz, M. Hassan, and A.Y. Zomaya, "LoRadar", *Comput. Commun. Rev.,* vol. 50, no. 4, pp. 10-24, 2020. [http://dx.doi.org/10.1145/3431832.3431835]

[43]   A. Khurshudov, *The essential guide to computer data storage: from floppy to DVD.* Prentice Hall Professional, 2001, p. 356.

[44]   Æ. Frisch, "System Backup: Methodologies, Algorithms and Efficiency Models", In: *in Handbook of Network and System Administration* Elsevier, 2008, pp. 205-239.

[45]   N.R. Rao, and K.C. Sekharaiah, "A methodological review based version control system with evolutionary research for software processes", *Proceedings of the Second International Conference on Information and Communication Technology for Competitive Strategies,* 2016. [http://dx.doi.org/10.1145/2905055.2905072]

[46]   W.C. Preston, *Unix Backup and Recovery.* O'Reilly Media, Inc., 1999.

[47]   S.C. Ronolo, *Assuring Data Integrity towards Regulatory Compliance: A Study on Process Improvement in Data Integrity Compliance of Computerized Systems.,* 2023.

[48]   J. Czajka, *Minimizing disclosure risk in HHS open data initiatives.* Mathematica Policy Research, 2014.

[49]   D. Dhinakaran, and P. Joe Prathap, "A brief study of privacy-preserving practices (PPP) in data mining", *TEST Eng Manage,* vol. 82, pp. 7611-7622, 2020.

[50]   M. Yamac, M. Ahishali, N. Passalis, J. Raitoharju, B. Sankur, and M. Gabbouj, "Multi-level reversible data anonymization via compressive sensing and data hiding", *IEEE Trans. Inf. Forensics Security,* vol. 16, pp. 1014-1028, 2021. [http://dx.doi.org/10.1109/TIFS.2020.3026467]

[51]   A. Khang, K.C. Rath, B.K. Mishra, R.R. Rautrao, and L.P. Panda, "Future Directions and Challenges in Designing Workforce Management Systems for Industry 4", In: *Khang A., AI-Oriented Competency Framework for Talent Management in the Digital Economy: Models, Technologies, Applications, and Implementation.* 1st ed. CRC Press, 2024. [http://dx.doi.org/10.1201/9781003440901-1]

[52]   A. Khang, "Design and Modelling of AI-Oriented Competency Framework (AIoCF) for Information Technology Sector", In: *Khang A., AI-Oriented Competency Framework for Talent Management in the Digital Economy: Models, Technologies, Applications, and Implementation.* 1st ed. CRC Press, 2024. [http://dx.doi.org/10.1201/9781003440901-17]

CHAPTER 4

Elementary Knowledge of Hard Disk

Manni Rohilla[1,2]**, Anjali Garg**[1,3]**, Sachin Dhiman**[1]**, Heena Dhiman**[4]**, Rishabh Chaudhary**[5]**, Sanchit Dhankhar**[1]**, Nitika Garg**[1]**, Monika Saini**[5] **and Samrat Chauhan**[1,*]

[1] *Chitkara College of Pharmacy, Chitkara University, Rajpura, Punjab, India*

[2] *Swami Vivekanand College of Pharmacy, Ram Nagar, Banur, Punjab, India*

[3] *Swami Devi Dyal College of Pharmacy, Golpura Barwala, Panchkula, Haryana, India*

[4] *M.M. College of Engineering, Maharishi Markandeshwar (Deemed to be University), Mullana, Ambala, Haryana, India*

[5] *M.M. College of Pharmacy, Maharishi Markandeshwar (Deemed to be University), Mullana, Ambala, Haryana, India*

Abstract: A hard disk, also known as a hard drive or HDD (Hard Disk Drive), is an essential element of a computer system that offers extended storage for digital data. Hard disks serve as a storage medium for a diverse array of digital data, encompassing the computer's operating system, applications, documents, multimedia files, and other content. A hard disk is a durable storage device that has one or more magnetically coated platters, arranged in a stacked configuration. These platters are commonly composed of materials such as glass or aluminum. Information is stored on hard disks in the form of magnetically polarized regions on the platters. The platters rotate at high speeds, while a read/write head traverses them to retrieve and alter data. The storage capacities of hard disks can vary significantly, spanning from a few megabytes to many terabytes, and even exceeding that for drives designed for enterprise-level usage. Increased capabilities enable the storage of greater amounts of data. Hard disks have comparatively reduced data access and transfer speeds in comparison to other storage technologies such as Solid-State Drives (SSDs). The velocity of a hard drive is impacted by variables such as rotational speed (measured in RPM), data density, and interface type. Hard disks are mechanical devices, rendering them more vulnerable to physical impacts, which might result in data loss. It is crucial to handle and protect against physical damage in a correct and careful manner. Hard drives establish a connection with a computer through different interfaces, such as SATA (Serial Advanced Technology Attachment) and the more contemporary NVMe (Non-Volatile Memory Express). Over time, the data recorded on a hard disk can undergo fragmentation, which refers to the scattering of distinct parts of the same file across several physical locations on the drive. Performance can be impacted by this, and regular defragmentation can assist in alleviating this problem. To mitigate the potential

---

[*] **Corresponding author Samrat Chauhan:** Chitkara College of Pharmacy, Chitkara University, Rajpura, Punjab, India; E-mail: samrat.chauhan11@gmail.com

Alex Khang, Sanchit Dhankhar, Sandeep Bhardwaj, Avnesh Verma & Satish Kumar Sharma
(Eds.)

loss of data resulting from a drive failure or corruption, it is imperative to routinely create backups of critical data, either by utilizing an external hard drive or by utilizing cloud storage. The lifespan of hard disks is finite and can be affected by variables such as usage patterns, climatic conditions, and manufacturing quality. It is crucial to oversee the condition of a hard disk and contemplate replacing it whenever it begins to exhibit indications of deterioration or malfunction. SSDs are typically less cost-effective than hard disks in terms of storage capacity. Consequently, they are widely favored for extensive data storage requirements. To summarize, hard disks are mechanical storage systems that offer cost-effective long-term data storage, with a lower cost per gigabyte compared to SSDs. Desktop and laptop computers extensively utilize them for diverse functions, although consumers must acknowledge their constraints, such as reduced speed and susceptibility to bodily harm. Regular data backups are essential for safeguarding against data loss.

Keywords: HDD, Multimedia, Non-volatile memory express, SSD.

INTRODUCTION TO HARD DISK DRIVES

An HDD, or hard disk drive, is an essential component in contemporary computing, functioning as a key data storage option for many devices [1]. The system functions based on the concept of magnetic storage, employing high-speed rotating disks covered with a magnetic substance to store and retrieve digital data. Every platter is fitted with read/write heads that traverse its surface to retrieve and store data. The actuator arm, which is operated by an actuator motor, precisely sets these heads over the designated tracks on the platters. The entire assembly is driven by a spindle motor, which rotates the platters at different rates, measured as revolutions per minute (RPM).

Hard disk drives (HDDs) provide a cost-efficient option for storing large quantities of data, making them well-suited for applications that require significant storage capacity, such as desktop PCs, servers, and data storage systems. Although HDDs have a long history in the business and utilize mature technology, they encounter obstacles from SSDs because of their mechanical parts, slower speeds, and vulnerability to physical impacts. However, HDDs continue to be a dependable and extensively utilized storage option, effectively combining cost-effectiveness and large store capacities in the constantly changing field of data storage technology [2].

What is a Hard Disk Drive?

An HDD, or Hard Disk Drive, is a data storage device utilized in computers and other electronic devices for the purpose of storing and retrieving digital information. A non-volatile storage medium is capable of retaining data even in the absence of power. An HDD consists of magnetic platters, read/write heads, an actuator arm, an actuator motor, and a spindle motor.

The magnetic platters, commonly composed of aluminum or glass, are circular disks covered with a magnetic substance. The platters contain data in the form of magnetic patterns. Every platter is equipped with an individual read/write head that is positioned on an actuator arm. The actuator arm is responsible for displacing the read/write heads across the platter surfaces in order to access various tracks where data is stored [3].

A spindle motor is tasked with rotating the platters at high velocities, quantified in revolutions per minute (RPM). The velocity at which the platters rotate is a crucial determinant of the efficiency of a hard disk drive (HDD). The actuator motor governs the motion of the actuator arm, precisely positioning the read/write heads over the intended track to facilitate data reading or writing [4].

Hard disk drives (HDDs) are renowned for their substantial storage capabilities and comparatively economical cost per gigabyte in comparison to other storage technologies. For numerous years, they have served as an essential element of computer systems, offering a dependable and economical method for storing substantial quantities of data, such as operating systems, applications, and user files. Nevertheless, HDDs are comprised of mechanical components that are subject to physical deterioration, rendering them vulnerable to damage and potentially constraining their overall performance in comparison to more advanced storage technologies such as Solid-State Drives (SSDs). Notwithstanding these constraints, HDDs remain extensively utilized in diverse computing applications.

Historical Overview

The chronicle of hard disk drives (HDDs) extends over multiple decades and is characterized by notable progressions in technology, storage capacity, and operational efficiency. Below is a concise historical summary of the development of hard drives:

1950s-1960s: Early Concepts and Magnetic Drum Storage

The utilization of magnetic storage for data originated in the 1950s. Magnetic drum storage, although an early iteration of data storage, was characterized by its cumbersome size and restricted capacity [5].

1956: IBM Introduces the RAMAC

IBM unveiled RAMAC, the pioneering computer system equipped with a hard disk drive, marking its debut in the commercial market. The RAMAC employed 50 disks with a diameter of 24 inches, resulting in a cumulative storage capacity of 5 megabytes [6].

The 1970s: Advancements in Technology

During the 1970s, there were consistent advancements in hard drive technology, such as the implementation of lower physical sizes and higher storage capacities. Mainframes and minicomputers frequently utilized hard drives during this era [7].

1980s: Rise of Personal Computers

As personal computers became available in the 1980s, there was an increasing need for compact and cost-effective hard drives. As a result, the introduction of 5.25-inch and 3.5-inch form factors allowed for the compatibility of hard drives with desktop computers [8].

1983: IBM Introduces the PC/XT with a Built-in Hard Drive

IBM introduced the IBM PC/XT, which included an integrated 10 MB hard drive. This represented a notable advancement in establishing hard drives as a customary element in personal computers [9].

1990s: Increasing Capacities and IDE Standard

In the 1990s, there was a significant and swift growth in the storage capacity of hard drives, with sizes expanding to several gigabytes. The implementation of the Integrated Drive Electronics (IDE) standard streamlined the incorporation of hard drives into personal computers [10].

2000s: Introduction of Serial ATA (SATA)

SATA superseded Parallel ATA as the predominant interface for connecting hard drives to motherboards. This facilitated accelerated data transfer rates and enhanced performance.

2010s: Solid-State Drives (SSDs) Emerge

2010 witnessed the emergence of Solid-State Drives (SSDs), which provided enhanced performance in terms of faster data access and transfer rates, increased robustness, and reduced energy consumption in comparison to conventional Hard Disk Drives (HDDs).

Present: Coexistence of HDDs and SSDs

Presently, both Hard Disk Drives (HDDs) and Solid-State Drives (SSDs) exist simultaneously in the market. HDDs are still utilized for storing large amounts of data in data centers and mass storage applications, whilst SSDs are favored for tasks that require fast performance and as the main drives in many consumer devices.

The evolution of hard drives demonstrates a consistent advancement in technology, transitioning from bulky and costly initial versions to the current compact and high-capacity drives. The continuous advancement of storage technologies is actively influencing the domain of digital data storage.

Importance in Modern Computing

Hard drives play a crucial role in contemporary computing as they serve as the principal storage medium for a diverse array of digital devices. Hard drives are essential components in various computing devices such as personal computers, laptops, servers, and data centers [11]. They are responsible for the storage and retrieval of large volumes of data. Here are crucial factors that emphasize the significance of hard drives in contemporary computing. Their significance rests in their capacity to securely store and retrieve enormous quantities of digital data. Hard drives are essential components in a wide range of systems, including personal computers, servers, and data centers. They store operating systems, applications, and user data. The substantial storage capacities provided by hard drives render them essential for effectively handling the continuously expanding amount of digital content. Although Solid-State Drives (SSDs) have become popular due to their speed and durability, hard drives remain essential for cost-effective and high-capacity storage solutions. When it comes to situations where storing a large amount of data is crucial, such as for archiving or managing large-scale data collections, hard drives are still the favored option. Their extensive presence in the computing industry highlights their lasting importance, effectively combining affordability and dependable storage performance in the varied environment of contemporary computing.

Data Storage

Hard drives provide the bulk of storage capacity for operating systems, software applications, and user data. They are essential for storing everything from documents and images to videos and applications [12].

Affordability and High Capacity

Hard drives provide a cost-efficient option for storing large amounts of data. Hard drives often offer a higher storage capacity per unit of currency compared to alternatives such as Solid-State Drives (SSDs). This makes hard drives a suitable choice for users that require a large amount of storage space.

Mass Data Storage

When there is a requirement to economically store vast amounts of data, such as in data centers, hard drives are commonly chosen. Due to their substantial capacity, these devices are well-suited for archival applications, backups, and storing large amounts of data.

Versatility

Hard drives are available in several physical shapes and dimensions, which allows them to be employed in a wide variety of devices. They are capable of accommodating various computing requirements, ranging from small drives in laptops to larger drives in desktops and servers.

Long-standing Technology

Hard disk technology has seen significant development over several decades, developing a well-documented history of being dependable and trustworthy. The reliability of a system is especially crucial *in situ*ations when the accuracy and long-term preservation of data are of *utmost importance.*

Sequential and Random Access

Hard drives are highly effective *in situ*ations that require both sequential and random access to data. Due to their versatility, they are highly suitable for a range of tasks, such as booting operating systems, executing applications, and accessing extensive databases.

Complementary Role with SSDs

Although Solid-State Drives (SSDs) provide quicker access speeds, hard drives are frequently utilized in combination with SSDs to provide hybrid storage systems. This technology integrates the rapidity of solid-state drives (SSDs) with the cost-efficiency and extensive storage capacity of hard disk drives (HDDs).

Backup and Redundancy

Hard drives are frequently employed as backup solutions and for redundancy in RAID (Redundant Array of Independent Disks) setups. This guarantees the consistency and reliability of data, while also offering a safeguard against potential drive malfunctions.

COMPONENTS OF A HARD DISK

An HDD consists of multiple essential components that collaborate to store and retrieve digital data. The primary constituents of a hard disk drive are as follows:

Platters

Platters are disc-shaped objects that are usually composed of metal or glass. These are the tangible surfaces where data is magnetically stored. Contemporary hard drives are capable of accommodating numerous platters arranged in a stacked configuration on a spindle.

Read/Write Heads

The read/write heads are minuscule electromagnets positioned at the ends of the actuator arms. Their main purpose is to retrieve data from the platters and record fresh data onto them. They levitate slightly above the surface of the rotating disks.

Actuator Arm

The actuator arm is a mechanical element that provides support for the read/write heads. The actuator motor is attached to it, enabling the movement of the heads across the platter surfaces. The movement enables the read/write heads to reach various tracks and sectors on the platters [13].

Actuator Motor

The actuator motor is accountable for the movement of both the actuator arm and the read/write heads. It aligns the heads precisely with the designated track on the platter for the purpose of reading or writing data [14].

Spindle Motor

The spindle motor is linked to the spindle, which securely grips and rotates the platters. The spindle motor maintains a consistent rotational velocity of the platters, quantified in revolutions per minute (RPM). The rate of rotation directly impacts the time it takes to access data and the pace at which it is sent.

Controller Board (PCB)

The controller board, or PCB (Printed Circuit Board), oversees the general functioning of the hard drive. The drive's firmware encompasses the functions of regulating the read/write heads, managing data flow, and handling error correction [15].

Cache (Buffer)

The cache, also known as a buffer, is a limited quantity of fast and temporary volatile memory (RAM) located on the hard disk. It functions as a transient repository for frequently accessed or recently written data. This enhances the overall efficiency of data transmission [16].

Connectors and Interface

The hard drive is equipped with connectors that facilitate its connection to the computer's motherboard. The interface type, such as SATA (Serial ATA) or PATA (Parallel ATA), dictates the method by which the hard drive establishes a connection with the computer and impacts the speed at which data is transferred [17].

The integration of these components facilitates the smooth operation of storing and retrieving digital data on a hard disk drive. The accuracy and synchronization of these components enhance the overall efficiency and dependability of the hard disk.

Platters and Data Storage

Platters are essential elements in a hard disk drive (HDD) that are responsible for the physical storage of digital data. These platters are commonly composed of materials such as aluminum or glass and are covered with a thin coating of magnetic substance. The magnetic coating enables the platters to retain data by utilizing magnetic patterns that encode binary code, consisting of 0s and 1s [18].

The platters rotate rapidly on a spindle inside the hard drive case, usually measured in revolutions per minute (RPM). While the platters are in motion, the read/write heads, which are attached to an actuator arm, traverse the surfaces of the rotating platters. The read/write heads have the capability to retrieve data from or store data in certain positions on the platters [19].

The process of data storage entails encoding information onto the surface of the platter by modifying the magnetic orientation of the coating. The read/write heads generate magnetic fields, which alter the state of the magnetic particles on the platter. When data retrieval is necessary, the read/write heads identify the magnetic patterns on the rotating platter and turn them into usable digital information.

The quantity of platters within a hard drive and their storage density have a substantial impact on the total storage capacity of the hard drive. Technological advancements have facilitated the augmentation of platter density, resulting in enhanced storage capabilities in contemporary hard drives. Nevertheless, the fragility of the platters renders them vulnerable to harm, underscoring the significance of cautious manipulation and safeguarding against physical impacts to maintain the integrity of the stored data.

Read/Write Heads

Read/write heads are essential components in a hard disk drive (HDD) that are responsible for the retrieval and storage of data on the magnetic platters. The heads are affixed to the extremities of the actuator arms, and their exact motion is regulated by an actuator motor. The main functions of the read/write heads are to engage with the magnetic surface of the rotating platters, recover stored data, and write new data [20].

When data is stored on the hard drive, the read/write heads produce magnetic fields that modify the alignment of the minuscule magnetic particles on the platters' surface. The alteration in alignment signifies the binary encoding of the data being recorded. Precise positioning of the read/write heads on the platters is essential for the organization and retrieval of data [21].

While reading data, the read/write heads identify the magnetic patterns on the rotating platter. While the platters are in motion, the heads detect alterations in magnetic fields and transform them into electrical impulses then, these signals undergo processing and are then converted back into the digital data that was first stored.

The accuracy and precision of the read/write heads play a vital role in determining the overall performance and reliability of the hard disk. The heads must remain in close proximity to the platter surfaces, ensuring a minimal distance to avoid any physical contact that may result in harm or loss of data. Technological progress has resulted in the creation of thin-film heads and giant magneto resistive (GMR) heads, which have enabled higher data density and enhanced performance in contemporary hard drives [22].

Spindles and Motors

The spindle is a primary shaft that supports and holds the platters of a hard disk. The platters are affixed to the spindle and rotate rapidly around it. The platters' rotational speed is quantified in revolutions per minute (RPM), and it is a crucial determinant of the hard drive's overall performance. Typical spindle speeds are 5,400 RPM, 7,200 RPM, and 10,000 RPM. Increased spindle speeds typically lead to quicker data retrieval times and transfer rates, although they may also generate additional heat and need more power.

Spindle Motor: The spindle motor's primary function is to rotate the platters at the specified velocity. The motor must deliver a steady and regulated spin to guarantee precise access of data on the platters by the read/write heads. The motor's accuracy is essential for preserving the stability of the hard drive and averting problems such as vibration, which can impact performance and dependability [23].

The spindle and motor collaborate to maintain continuous movement of the platters, enabling the read/write heads to retrieve data from various tracks on the rotating disks. The motor and spindle system's efficiency plays a crucial role in determining the overall speed and dependability of the hard drive.

Contemporary hard drive manufacturers frequently prioritize the enhancement of energy efficiency, reduction of heat generation, and overall performance improvement by improving the design and materials of the spindle and motor components. The progress in motor and spindle technology has contributed to the enhancement of storage capacities and the acceleration of data retrieval in hard drives over time.

Controller and Cache

The controller and cache are integral components within a hard disk drive (HDD), which contribute to the overall efficiency, management, and performance of the storage system.

Controller (Printed Circuit Board - PCB)

The controller, typically found on the Printed Circuit Board (PCB), acts as the central processing unit of the hard drive. It oversees and organizes a range of operations, such as controlling the actuator arm, positioning the read/write heads, and communicating with the computer's operating system. The controller processes commands received from the computer, translating them into precise actions for the drive's components, and maintaining data integrity. In addition, the controller's firmware includes algorithms that handle error correction, bad sector management, and other important functions [24].

Cache (Buffer)

The cache, or buffer, is a small yet high-speed volatile memory (usually DRAM) situated on the hard drive. It acts as a temporary storage space for frequently accessed data or data that is awaiting read or write operations. Temporarily storing this data in the cache can significantly improve the overall performance of the hard drive. During read operations, data that is frequently accessed can be retrieved more efficiently from the cache compared to the spinning platters. During write operations, the cache enhances the drive's ability to quickly accept data and efficiently transfer it to the platters [25].

The cache size can differ between hard drives, and its significance becomes clear *in situ*ations where there are repetitive or predictable data access patterns. The cache collaborates with the controller to efficiently handle data flow, resulting in faster access times and enhanced responsiveness. The controller and cache work together to ensure smooth operation of the hard drive, facilitating fast data transfer, error correction, and coordination of different mechanical and electronic parts. Improvements in controller technology and cache management have significantly boosted the speed and reliability of hard disk drives in today's computing environments.

HOW HARD DISKS WORK

HDDs function through an intricate combination of mechanical and magnetic parts to facilitate the storing and accessing of digital data. The core of the HDD resides in its circular platters, which are covered in a magnetic material [26]. This is where data is stored as magnetic patterns. The platters rotate rapidly on a central spindle, powered by a spindle motor. Located directly above the rotating platters, the read/write heads, which are attached to an actuator arm, glide with accuracy across the surfaces of the platters. When data needs to be retrieved, the read heads detect the magnetic patterns and use them to generate electrical currents. These currents are then processed to reconstruct the stored information. On the other hand, while writing data, the write heads produce magnetic fields that change the alignment of magnetic particles on the platters to store fresh information. The entire process is managed by a controller on the Printed Circuit Board (PCB), which interprets commands from the computer's operating system and oversees the movement of the actuator arm. A cache is a small high-speed memory that serves as a buffer for frequently accessed or pending data, which helps to improve transfer speeds. The seamless combination of mechanical and electronic components highlights the complex inner workings of hard disk drives, solidifying their crucial role in data storage for contemporary computing. Continual advancements in technology are constantly enhancing these processes, resulting in faster, more efficient, and more dependable hard disks [27].

Data Storage and Magnetic Recording

Hard disk drives (HDDs) utilize the intricate principle of magnetic recording, a crucial process that allows for the encoding and retrieval of digital information. The magnetic platters, which form the core of this mechanism, consist of durable disks coated with a thin layer of ferromagnetic material. The platters rotate rapidly on a central spindle, with their surfaces divided into concentric tracks and sectors. When new data is written, the write heads, part of the read/write head assembly, generate precise magnetic fields that manipulate the orientation of the magnetic particles on the platter's surface, encoding the binary information. While retrieving data, the read heads carefully detect the magnetic patterns as the platters spin, generating electrical currents that are subsequently converted back into the original binary code by the controller. The arrangement of the platter into tracks and sectors enables the read/write heads to move across the surface accurately, accessing desired locations with great efficiency. With the ever-evolving demands of data storage in modern computing landscapes, hard drives are constantly improving their data density, reliability, and speed through innovative magnetic recording technology [28].

The data storage process can be broken down into several key steps

Magnetic Platters

The hard drive is composed of several magnetic platters, usually constructed from materials such as aluminum or glass. These platters are coated with a thin layer of magnetic material, typically a ferromagnetic alloy.

Magnetic Particles and Binary Code

The platters are coated with a multitude of minuscule magnetic particles. These particles symbolize the binary code of digital information, where the magnetic orientation of each particle can indicate a binary digit (bit) - either a 0 or a 1.

Writing Data

When data is written on the hard drive, the write heads, as part of the read/write head assembly, generate magnetic fields. The fields modify the magnetic orientation of the particles on the platter surface, encoding the desired binary information. This process is commonly known as magnetic flux reversal [29].

Reading Data

While retrieving data, the read heads detect the magnetic patterns on the rotating platter. As the platters spin, alterations in the magnetic fields generate electrical currents in the read heads. The controller processes the electrical signals and converts them back into the original binary data [30].

Tracks and Sectors

The surface of the platter is divided into concentric circles known as tracks, which are then further divided into sectors. The read/write heads traverse the tracks and sectors to reach specific locations where data is stored.

High Data Density

Recent technological advancements have enabled higher data density on platters. This allows for a greater amount of data to be stored in a given physical space, resulting in hard drives with larger storage capacities.

Magnetic recording continues to be a crucial and dependable technique for storing data in hard disk drives, with ongoing advancements focused on enhancing data density, access speeds, and overall storage performance. With the continuous advancement of technology, the magnetic recording process is constantly evolving to meet the growing demands for data storage in today's computing environments [31].

Data Access and Seek Times

The retrieval of information from the spinning platters in a hard disk drive (HDD) is influenced by various factors, such as seek times, which can affect the efficiency of the data access process. Seek times indicate the duration required for the read/write heads to align themselves with the intended track on the platters [32]. The access time, in turn, includes different elements of the overall data retrieval process:

Seek Time

The seek time is a crucial determinant that impacts the entire access time. The system is comprised of multiple elements, which include:

Seek Time (Mechanical): The duration required for the actuator arm to relocate the read/write heads to the appropriate track.

Rotational Latency refers to the duration required for the requested sector on the rotating platter to move beneath the read/write heads. This is determined by the rotating velocity of the platters.

Latency and Platter Speed

The latency is influenced by the rotational speed of the platters, which is measured in revolutions per minute (RPM). Increased RPM values typically decrease rotational delay, resulting in quicker data access. Typical RPM numbers include 5,400, 7,200, and 10,000 [33].

Transfer Time

Once the read/write heads are accurately aligned with the appropriate track, the data transfer process takes place. The duration of this data transmission is affected by variables such as the data density on the platters, the effectiveness of the read/write heads, and the velocity of the interface (*e.g.*, SATA).

Average Seek Time

The average seek time is a statistical metric that quantifies the average duration for the read/write heads to transition between tracks. Decreased mean seek times show enhanced efficiency in retrieving data.

Optimizing these access times is essential for improving the overall efficiency of a hard drive. The developments in HDD technology focus on reducing seek times by enhancing actuator arm designs, optimizing positioning algorithms, and improving platter and motor technologies. Although solid-state drives (SSDs) typically have faster access times than hard disk drives (HDDs) because they don't have moving parts, ongoing advancements are improving the efficiency of HDDs. This makes them useful for storing large amounts of data at a lower cost per gigabyte.

Understanding Sectors and Clusters

A comprehensive grasp of sectors and clusters is essential for the arrangement and storage of data on hard disk drives (HDDs) and file systems.

Sectors

A sector is the most basic unit of storage on a hard disk and is usually a constant size, often 512 bytes. A platter's surface is partitioned into concentric circles known as tracks, with each track being further divided into sectors. The read/write heads retrieve data by positioning themselves on the designated track and performing read or write operations within the sectors. The sector size plays a vital role in ensuring efficient data management and serves as a fundamental component in the storage architecture of hard drives [34].

Clusters

Clusters, referred to as allocation units, are utilized by the file system as logical units for storing files. Clusters, unlike sectors, are determined by the file system and can be composed of numerous adjacent sectors. When a file is saved on the hard drive, it is assigned to one or more clusters, which depends on its size. Clusters optimize file storage by minimizing space wastage when storing smaller files, as each file does not have to occupy a whole sector [35].

The interplay between sectors and clusters is crucial in file systems such as FAT (File Allocation Table) and NTFS (New Technology File System). Within these systems, the data in a file is partitioned into clusters, and the file system maintains a record of which clusters are associated with each file. This allocation strategy enables enhanced disk space use and more efficient storage.

HARD DISK INTERFACES

Hard disk drives (HDDs) employ different interfaces to make connections with computers and other devices, enabling communication between the storage device and the system. Over time, these interfaces have developed to adapt to higher data transfer speeds and technological progress. Parallel ATA (PATA), commonly referred to as IDE was widely used in previous computer systems for traditional hard drives. However, it has been mainly substituted by Serial ATA (SATA) in the present era. SATA has emerged as the prevailing interface for contemporary hard drives and solid-state drives (SSDs), providing enhanced data transmission speeds and utilizing slimmer, more pliable connections. High-performance computing environments make use of Small Computer System Interface (SCSI) and its contemporary version, Serial Attached SCSI (SAS). Fiber Channel is widely used in enterprise environments, particularly in Storage Area Networks (SANs), to provide rapid data transfers using optical fiber or copper cables. USB and Thunderbolt are widely used interfaces for connecting external storage devices. Thunderbolt, unlike USB, supports both data transport and video output. Non-Volatile Memory Express (NVMe) has become a dedicated interface for SSDs, utilizing the PCIe interface to provide considerably higher data transfer speeds compared to SATA. This makes it the preferred option for high-performance storage solutions. The selection of a hard disk interface is contingent upon elements such as compatibility, performance prerequisites, and the particular utilization scenario of the storage solution.

IDE, SATA, and SCSI

IDE (Integrated Drive Electronics)

IDE, short for Integrated Drive Electronics, was a widely used hard disk interface throughout the latter part of the 20th century. The IDE interface employed a parallel connection and served as the main means of connecting internal hard drives in desktop computers. IDE cables commonly came in two variations, one with 40 pins and the other with 80 pins. The 80-pin version offered enhanced capabilities such as quicker data transfer speeds and increased data integrity. Nevertheless, IDE has become outdated over time, as SATA has taken its place as the prevailing interface for contemporary internal hard drives [36].

SATA (Serial ATA)

SATA, short for Serial ATA, has replaced IDE as the prevailing interface for internal hard drives and SSDs. SATA utilizes a sequential connection, providing benefits such as enhanced data transfer speeds, slimmer and more adaptable cables, and enhanced air circulation within the computer enclosure. SATA ports are available in many versions, with SATA III being a highly prevalent one, capable of facilitating data transfer speeds of up to 6 gigabits per second (Gbps). SATA continues to be a prevalent interface for storage devices intended for consumer use.

SCSI (Small Computer System Interface)

The Small Computer System Interface, also known as SCSI, is a highly adaptable interface that has found extensive application in server environments and high-performance computing systems. Initially, SCSI used a parallel connection, but it later evolved to incorporate Serial Attached SCSI (SAS), which uses a serial connection. SCSI enables the connection of multiple devices on a single bus and provides capabilities such as command queuing and hot swapping. Although SAS has completely supplanted SCSI in enterprise environments, SCSI has had a significant influence on the evolution of storage interfaces, playing a role in the progress of high-performance storage solutions.

Solid-State Drives (SSD)

SSDs, also known as Solid-State Drives, signify a groundbreaking transformation in storage technology when compared to conventional Hard Disk Drives (HDDs). SSDs utilize NAND-based flash memory as opposed to spinning magnetic disks and read/write heads for data storage. Due to this fundamental distinction, SSDs offer significant benefits, leading to their growing popularity in diverse computing contexts.

Interfaces for SSDs

SATA SSDs

Early solid-state drives (SSDs) commonly employed the SATA interface, which is also found in conventional hard disk drives (HDDs). Although SATA SSDs offer a substantial boost in performance compared to HDDs, their data transfer rates are constrained by the maximum capacity of the SATA interface, which is up to 6 Gbps for SATA III [37].

NVMe SSDs (Non-Volatile Memory Express)

NVMe signifies a substantial advancement in the performance of solid-state drives (SSDs). The device employs the PCIe (Peripheral Component Interconnect Express) interface, initially developed for rapid communication with internal components such as graphics cards [38]. NVMe SSDs provide significantly higher data transfer speeds in comparison to SATA, rendering them well-suited for applications that require exceptional speed, such as gaming, content creation, and data-intensive workloads.

Advantages of SSDs

Speed

SSDs offer exceptional speed, which is one of their main advantages. They provide enhanced data read and write speeds, leading to speedier boot times, decreased program loading times, and greater overall system responsiveness.

Reliability

SSDs lack mechanical components, rendering them more robust and less susceptible to physical impact and vibration in comparison to HDDs. This attribute improves their dependability, especially in portable devices.

Energy Efficiency

SSDs often have lower power consumption compared to conventional HDDs, which enhances energy efficiency in laptops and other devices that rely on batteries. This is particularly crucial for prolonging the battery lifespan in portable devices.

Form Factor and Size

SSDs are available in different form factors, such as the conventional 2.5-inch size that can be inserted into regular HDD bays, as well as smaller M.2 and PCIe card form factors. Their ability to adapt to various sizes and forms makes them well-suited for a diverse array of devices, such as ultra-books and tiny desktop computers.

Silent Operation

SSDs function softly because of the absence of any moving components. This can be especially beneficial in settings where the reduction of noise is a top objective, such as home theaters or tranquil office areas.

Considerations

Although SSDs have some benefits, they often have a higher cost per gigabyte in comparison to HDDs. Consequently, users commonly employ a blend of SSDs for their core storage requirements, such as the operating system and frequently used apps, and HDDs for storing large amounts of data where capacity is the main concern. The decreasing cost of SSDs, driven by technological and manufacturing advancements, is expanding their accessibility to a wider user base.

Comparing Different Interfaces

The selection of an appropriate storage interface is contingent upon several criteria, such as performance prerequisites, compatibility, and the intended use of the storage system. Let us analyze multiple interfaces, taking into account their advantages, disadvantages, and common uses:

SATA (Serial ATA)

Advantages

1. Widely adopted and compatible with most motherboards.
2. Suitable for mainstream consumer applications.
3. Cost-effective for moderate performance requirements.

Considerations

1. Limited data transfer rates compared to some newer interfaces.
2. More suitable for traditional HDDs; SSDs may be constrained by the SATA III speed limit (6 Gbps).

NVMe (Non-Volatile Memory Express)

Advantages

1. Exceptional data transfer rates, significantly faster than SATA.
2. Ideal for high-performance computing, gaming, and content creation.
3. Commonly used for SSDs, providing low latency and high throughput.

Considerations

1. Requires a motherboard with NVMe support.
2. Typically, more expensive than SATA-based solutions.

SAS (Serial Attached SCSI)

Advantages

1. Commonly used in enterprise environments and server systems.
2. Supports higher data transfer rates compared to SATA.
3. Suitable for applications requiring reliability and scalability.

Considerations

1. More complex and expensive than SATA for consumer use.
2. Overkill for typical consumer applications.

USB (Universal Serial Bus)

Advantages

1. Universal compatibility; widely used for external storage.
2. Convenient for connecting external drives, thumb drives, and other peripherals.
3. USB 3.0 and later versions offer higher data transfer rates.

Considerations

1. Limited compared to internal interfaces for high-performance tasks.
2. May not be suitable for applications requiring constant, high-speed data access.

Thunderbolt

Advantages

1. High-speed data transfer and video output over a single cable.
2. Commonly used in professional and creative applications.
3. Daisy-chaining multiple devices is possible.

Considerations

- Limited adoption in mainstream consumer devices.
- Higher cost compared to some other interfaces.

Fiber Channel

Advantages

- High-speed data transfers over optical fiber or copper cables.
- Commonly used in enterprise environments, especially SANs.
- Suitable for large-scale storage systems.

Considerations

- Primarily designed for enterprise use; not common in consumer devices.
- Higher cost and complexity compared to SATA or SAS.

In summary, the choice of a storage interface depends on the individual demands of the user. For mainstream consumer applications and cost-effective solutions, SATA remains a popular choice. NVMe is particularly well-suited for individuals who demand the utmost level of performance, particularly in the realms of gaming and content creation. SAS and Fibre Channel are primarily designed for enterprise use, providing the capacity to grow and ensuring high dependability for storage systems on a big scale. USB and Thunderbolt offer easy options for external communication, with Thunderbolt specifically designed for professional and creative uses.

HARD DISK CAPACITY AND FORM FACTORS

Hard disk capacity refers to the amount of data that can be stored on a disk drive. Over the years, there has been a significant increase in storage capacity, driven by advancements in technology and manufacturing processes. Capacities are typically measured in bytes, with the following units commonly used:

- **Megabyte (MB):** 1 million bytes.
- **Gigabyte (GB):** 1 billion bytes.
- **Terabyte (TB):** 1 trillion bytes.
- **Petabyte (PB):** 1 quadrillion bytes.
- **Exabyte (EB):** 1 quintillion bytes.

Currently, hard drives typically have capacities in the terabyte range, but certain enterprise-level drives can reach capacities in the petabyte range. SSDs, or solid-state drives, exhibit a comparable pattern of progressively expanding storage capacities as time goes on. The selection of storage capacity is contingent upon the user's storage requirements, taking into account variables such as the quantity of data to be saved, the nature of the data (*e.g.*, documents, media files, apps), and financial limitations.

Hard Disk Form Factors

The form factor of a hard disk refers to its physical size, shape, and connector type. Different form factors are designed for specific applications, and they dictate how and where the drive can be installed [16]. Here are some common hard disk form factors:

2.5-inch Form Factor

- ***Common Use:*** Laptop and notebook drives.
- ***Connector:*** Typically, SATA or, in some cases, NVMe for SSDs.
- ***Advantages:*** Compact size, suitable for portable devices.

3.5-inch Form Factor

- ***Common Use:*** Desktop computer drives.
- ***Connector:*** Typically SATA for HDDs, but may also include SAS.
- ***Advantages:*** Larger size allows for higher capacities and additional features, often used in desktop systems.

5.25-inch Form Factor

- ***Common Use:*** Historically used for optical drives (CD/DVD), not common for hard disks.
- ***Connector:*** N/A for hard disks; primarily used for optical drives.

M.2 Form Factor

- ***Common Use:*** Ultra-books, tablets, and compact desktops.
- ***Connector:*** NVMe or SATA, depending on the drive.
- ***Advantages***: Small size, directly connects to the motherboard, often used for high-performance SSDs.

PCI Express (PCIe) Card Form Factor

- ***Common Use:*** High-performance SSDs.
- ***Connector:*** PCIe slot on the motherboard.
- ***Advantages:*** Direct connection to PCIe bus allows for high-speed data transfer.

External Form Factors

• ***Common Use:*** Portable and external drives.
• ***Connector:*** USB, Thunderbolt, or other external interfaces.
• ***Advantages:*** Portability and convenience, suitable for backup and data transfer.

Opting for the appropriate form factor necessitates deliberation on physical dimensions, compatibility with the device or system, and the desired level of performance. For example, M.2 and PCIe card form factors are frequently selected for high-performance SSDs in gaming systems or content production workstations, but 2.5-inch and 3.5-inch form factors are commonly found in laptops and desktops, respectively. External form factors offer versatility and portability for anyone in need of portable storage solutions.

Storage Capacity Measurements

Storage capacity is measured in bytes and its multiples, with each unit representing an order of magnitude increase in size. Here are the common storage capacity measurements:

Bit (b)

• The smallest unit of data.
• Either 0 or 1, representing binary code.

Byte (B)

• Consists of 8 bits.
• Basic unit used for measuring storage capacity.

Kilobyte (KB)

• 1 kilobyte = 1,024 bytes.
• Commonly used to measure small text documents and basic data.

Megabyte (MB)

• 1 megabyte = 1,024 kilobytes or 1,048,576 bytes.
• Often used to measure the size of media files, such as photos and MP3s.

Gigabyte (GB)

• 1 gigabyte = 1,024 megabytes or 1,073,741,824 bytes.
• Common unit for measuring storage in consumer devices like smartphones and personal computers.

Terabyte (TB)

- 1 terabyte = 1,024 gigabytes or 1,099,511,627,776 bytes.
- Frequently used to quantify the storage capacity of hard drives and SSDs.

Petabyte (PB)

- 1 petabyte = 1,024 terabytes or 1,125,899,906,842,624 bytes.
- Commonly used in enterprise storage systems and data centers.

Exabyte (EB)

- 1 exabyte = 1,024 petabyte or 1,152,921,504,606,846,976 bytes.
- Represents a massive amount of data, often used in discussions about global data storage.

Zettabyte (ZB)

- 1 zettabyte = 1,024 exabytes or 1,180,591,620,717,411,303,424 bytes.
- A unit of storage that is rarely encountered today but may become more relevant with the exponential growth of data.

Yottabyte (YB)

- 1 yottabyte = 1,024 zettabytes or 1,208,925,819,614,629,174,706,176 bytes.
- A theoretical unit often discussed in the context of vast amounts of global data.

These units adhere to the binary system, wherein each unit is a multiple of 2 raised to a power (1024), as opposed to the decimal method employed for metric prefixes. When examining storage capacity, it is crucial to take into account the circumstances and the particular unit employed, as capacities can significantly differ, particularly as technology progresses and storage devices continue to expand in magnitude [39].

Common Form Factors

Form factors pertain to the physical dimensions, configuration, and interface specification of hard disk drives (HDDs) and solid-state drives (SSDs). Specific applications necessitate the design of various form factors, which determine the installation method and location of the drive. Below are few prevalent shape factors:

2.5-inch Form Factor

- *Common Use:* Laptop and notebook drives.
- **Connector:** Typically, SATA or, in some cases, NVMe for SSDs.

- **Advantages:** Compact size, suitable for portable devices.

3.5-inch Form Factor

- **_Common Use:_** Desktop computer drives.
- **_Connector:_** Typically, SATA for HDDs, but may also include SAS.
- **_Advantages:_** Larger size allows for higher capacities and additional features, often used in desktop systems.

M.2 Form Factor

- **_Common Use:_** Ultra-books, tablets, and compact desktops.
- **_Connector:_** NVMe or SATA, depending on the drive.
- **_Advantages:_** Small size, directly connects to the motherboard, often used for high-performance SSDs.

PCI Express (PCIe) Card Form Factor

- **_Common Use:_** High-performance SSDs.
- **_Connector:_** PCIe slot on the motherboard.
- **_Advantages:_** Direct connection to PCIe bus allows for high-speed data transfer.

External Form Factors

- **_Common Use_:** Portable and external drives.
- **_Connector:_** USB, Thunderbolt, or other external interfaces.
- **_Advantages_:** Portability and convenience, suitable for backup and data transfer.

5.25-inch Form Factor

- **_Common Use_:** Historically used for optical drives (CD/DVD), not common for hard disks.
- **_Connector:_** N/A for hard disks; primarily used for optical drives.

These form factors accommodate a wide range of devices and applications, offering versatility in terms of physical installation and connectivity options. The selection of the form factor is contingent upon variables such as the device category (laptop, desktop, ultra-book), the intended performance level (conventional storage or high-speed SSD), and the particular demands of the application (internal or external storage). With the progression of technology, there is a possibility of new physical designs emerging that provide enhanced capabilities and better compatibility.

Factors Influencing Capacity

The storage capacity of hard disk drives (HDDs) and solid-state drives (SSDs) is determined by multiple factors, and comprehending these factors is essential for choosing the appropriate storage solution for specific requirements. The following are crucial determinants that impact storage capacity:

Technological Advancements

- Miniaturization: Advances in technology allow for the manufacturing of smaller components with higher storage densities, enabling increased capacities.
- New Materials: Innovations in materials used in storage media contribute to improved data density on platters for HDDs and smaller NAND cells for SSDs.

Storage Technology

- HDD *vs.* SSD: SSDs generally have higher storage capacities compared to HDDs at similar form factors. As SSD technology advances, manufacturers can pack more data into the same physical space.

Manufacturing Processes

- Nanotechnology: The use of nanoscale technologies in manufacturing allows for the creation of smaller, more densely packed storage elements, leading to increased capacity.
- Precision Manufacturing: Improved manufacturing precision contributes to higher areal density on HDD platters and more reliable production of smaller NAND flash cells on SSDs.

Areal Density

- HDDs: Higher areal density on platters means more data can be stored in the same physical space. This is achieved by placing data more closely together on the platter surface.
- SSDs: Areal density in SSDs refers to how tightly the memory cells are packed within the NAND flash chips.

Storage Form Factor

- Smaller Form Factors: Advancements in technology allow for the creation of smaller storage form factors like M.2 and PCIe, increasing storage capacity in limited space.
- Larger Form Factors: Traditional 3.5-inch HDDs and larger PCIe cards can accommodate more storage components, contributing to higher capacities.

Cost Considerations

- Economies of Scale: Larger capacity drives can benefit from economies of scale in production, potentially resulting in lower cost per unit of storage.
- Consumer Demand: Manufacturers may prioritize producing higher-capacity drives based on consumer demand and market trends.

Market Demand and Trends

- Consumer Needs: Manufacturers often respond to the increasing demand for higher-capacity drives driven by consumer needs, such as larger file sizes in media content, higher-resolution photos, and more significant data storage requirements.
- Industry Trends: Evolving industry trends, like the growing demand for high-capacity SSDs in data centers, can influence the development and production of storage devices.

Research and Development

- Investment in Innovation: Companies investing in research and development can push the boundaries of storage technology, introducing new materials, manufacturing processes, and architectures that contribute to increased capacities.

Gaining comprehension of these elements is crucial for consumers, system architects, and enterprises seeking to make well-informed choices regarding their storage solutions [40]. With the ongoing advancement of technology, it is probable that storage capacities will persistently expand, offering users a wider range of choices to fulfill their escalating data storage needs.

HARD DISK RELIABILITY AND LIFESPAN

When assessing the performance and durability of hard disk drives (HDDs) and solid-state drives (SSDs), it is crucial to evaluate their reliability and lifespan. Gaining knowledge about the variables that impact dependability and longevity will assist users in making well-informed choices regarding storage options and implementing efficient maintenance procedures.

Hard Disk Reliability Factors

MTBF (Mean Time Between Failures)

- Definition: MTBF is an indicator of a drive's reliability, representing the average time a drive is expected to operate before encountering a failure.

• Influence: Higher MTBF values suggest greater reliability. However, MTBF is a statistical measure, and individual drive lifespans can vary.

Error Rates

• Definition: The rate at which errors occur during data reads or writes.
• Influence: Lower error rates contribute to higher reliability. Modern drives use error correction mechanisms to enhance data integrity.

Vibration and Shock Resistance

• Definition: The ability of a drive to withstand physical shocks and vibrations during operation.
• Influence: Drives with better shock resistance are more reliable, especially in environments where physical stress is a concern (*e.g.*, laptops, portable devices).

Temperature and Environmental Considerations

• Definition: The operating temperature range and environmental conditions in which the drive can function reliably.
• Influence: Drives that can operate in a broader temperature range and varying environmental conditions are more versatile and resilient.

Load/Unload Cycles (for HDDs)

• Definition: The number of times the read/write heads are loaded onto and unloaded from the spinning platters.
• Influence: Frequent load/unload cycles can contribute to wear and tear. Drives with higher load/unload cycle ratings are generally more reliable.

Power-On Hours (POH)

• Definition: The total number of hours a drive has been powered on.
• Influence: Continuous operation over an extended period may contribute to wear. Monitoring power-on hours can help predict potential issues.

Bad Block Management (for SSDs)

• Definition: The effectiveness of a drive's mechanism in managing and isolating bad blocks.
• Influence: Efficient bad block management enhances the reliability of SSDs by minimizing data errors and preventing data loss.

Hard Disk Lifespan

Total Bytes Written (for SSDs)

- Definition: The total amount of data written to an SSD.
- Influence: SSDs have a finite number of program/erase (P/E) cycles. Monitoring total bytes written provides insights into the remaining lifespan of *an SSD*.

Wear Levelling (for SSDs)

- Definition: The process of distributing write and erase cycles evenly across the memory cells of an SSD.
- Influence: Effective wear leveling prolongs the lifespan of SSDs by preventing certain cells from wearing out prematurely.

Aging of Mechanical Parts (for HDDs)

- Definition: Over time, mechanical parts in HDDs, such as bearings and motors, can experience wear.
- Influence: Continuous use and mechanical wear contribute to the aging of HDDs, potentially affecting their lifespan.

Technology Obsolescence

- Definition: Advancements in storage technology may render older drives obsolete.
- Influence: As technology evolves, older drives may become less compatible with new systems and software, influencing their practical lifespan.

Manufacturer and Model Reputation

- Influence: Established manufacturers with a reputation for producing reliable drives may offer products with longer lifespans. Researching reviews and reliability studies can provide insights into specific models.

Maintenance Practices for Prolonged Reliability

Regular Backups

- Regularly back up important data to prevent data loss in the event of drive failure.

Temperature Monitoring

- Maintain a suitable operating temperature for the drive to prevent overheating, as high temperatures can reduce lifespan.

Firmware Updates

- Keep drive firmware up to date to benefit from performance improvements, bug fixes, and enhanced reliability features.

Monitoring Tools

- Use monitoring tools to keep track of drive health, temperature, and other vital parameters. This allows for proactive measures in response to potential issues.

Power Management

- Implement power management settings to reduce unnecessary power-on hours, especially for *devices with limited duty cycles.*

Avoid Physical Shocks

- Protect drives from physical shocks and vibrations, especially during operation, to prevent mechanical damage.

Secure Erasure (for SSDs)

- Follow recommended procedures for secure erasure before decommissioning SSDs to ensure data integrity and privacy.

DISK PARTITIONING AND FORMATTING

Gaining knowledge about the reliability aspects and lifetime concerns that are unique to HDDs and SSDs enables users to make well-informed choices, extend the longevity of their storage devices, and reduce the likelihood of data loss. Consistently monitoring, using correctly, and following established guidelines help ensure long-term performance and dependability.

Partitioning and Formatting

Partitioning

- Divide the hard disk into logical sections known as partitions.
- Allows for better organization and separation of data, operating systems, and applications.

Formatting

- The process of preparing a partition for data storage.
- Chooses a file system (*e.g.*, NTFS, exFAT, FAT32) and establishes a file structure.

File Organization

Folder Structure

- Organize data into a logical folder structure.
- Facilitates easy navigation and retrieval of files.

File Naming Conventions

- Adopt a consistent file naming convention.
- Helps in quickly identifying and locating specific files.

Categorization and Tagging

- Categorize files based on content and purpose.
- Utilize tagging for quick searches and filtering.

Backup and Redundancy

Regular Backups

- Schedule regular backups to external drives, cloud storage, or network-attached storage (NAS).
- Protects against data loss due to hardware failure, accidental deletion, or other issues.

Redundancy

- Implement redundancy strategies, such as RAID configurations.
- Ensures data availability and minimizes the risk of data loss.

Data Security

Encryption

- Encrypt sensitive data to protect it from unauthorized access.
- Utilize full-disk encryption for enhanced security.

User Access Controls

- Implement user access controls and permissions.
- Restricts access to files and directories based on user roles.

Antivirus and Malware Protection

- Install and regularly update antivirus and anti-malware software.
- Guards against threats that could compromise data integrity.

Performance Optimization

Defragmentation (for HDDs)

- Periodically defragment HDDs to optimize file placement.
- Enhances read and write performance by reducing seek times.

Trim (for SSDs)

- Enable the Trim command on SSDs.
- Helps maintain performance by marking blocks of data as no longer in use.

Storage Monitoring

- Use monitoring tools to track storage usage and health.
- Identifies potential issues before they impact performance.

Archiving and Cleanup

Archiving

- Archive infrequently accessed or older files to secondary storage.
- Frees up space on primary storage while preserving data.

Cleanup

- Regularly delete unnecessary files and folders.
- Prevents clutter and maximizes available storage.

Disk Maintenance

Firmware Updates

- Keep hard disk firmware up to date.
- Ensures compatibility, performance improvements, and security patches.

Temperature and Ventilation

- Maintain optimal operating temperatures for hard disks.
- Good ventilation prevents overheating and extends lifespan.

Cloud Storage Integration

Cloud Backups

• Utilize cloud storage for offsite backups.
• Provides an additional layer of data protection.

Sync and Collaboration

• Use cloud storage for file synchronization and collaboration.
• Facilitates access to files from multiple devices and collaboration with others.

Efficient data management on hard disks necessitates the implementation of organizational techniques, security protocols, and regular maintenance [41]. By applying these principles, users may guarantee that their data is efficiently arranged, protected, and easily retrievable, while also enhancing the performance and durability of their storage devices.

HARD DISK MAINTENANCE AND TROUBLESHOOTING

Performing regular maintenance and troubleshooting on hard disks is crucial for achieving peak performance, preventing data loss, and resolving any potential problems with storage systems. Implementing appropriate maintenance procedures can prolong the longevity of hard disks and improve the overall reliability of the system. Below are essential factors to consider when performing hard drive repair and troubleshooting.

Maintenance Practices

Regular Backups

• Schedule regular backups of important data.
• Use backup solutions that suit your needs, such as external drives, cloud storage, or network-attached storage (NAS).

Firmware Updates

• Check for and apply firmware updates for hard disks.
• Updated firmware may include performance improvements, bug fixes, and enhanced compatibility.

Disk Cleanup

- Regularly clean up unnecessary files and folders.
- Use built-in tools or third-party applications to remove temporary files and free up disk space.

Defragmentation (for HDDs)

- Periodically defragment hard disk drives (HDDs).
- Helps optimize file placement and improve read/write performance.

Trim (for SSDs)

- Enable the Trim command for solid-state drives (SSDs).
- Helps maintain SSD performance by marking blocks of data as no longer in use.

Temperature Monitoring

- Monitor the operating temperature of the hard disk.
- Ensure adequate ventilation and cooling to prevent overheating.

Disk Health Monitoring Tools

- Use disk health monitoring tools to track the overall health of the hard disk.
- Keep an eye on parameters such as SMART (Self-Monitoring, Analysis and Reporting Technology) data.

Troubleshooting

Check Physical Connections

- Ensure that cables connecting the hard disk are securely attached.
- Consider replacing cables if connectivity issues persist.

Power Supply Issues

- Verify that the hard disk is receiving proper power.
- Test the hard disk with a different power cable or power supply if needed.

Check for System Errors

- Examine system logs and error messages for indications of hard disk issues.
- Address any system errors or warnings related to disk operations.

Run Disk Check Utilities

• Use built-in disk checking utilities like CHKDSK (Check Disk) on Windows or fsck on Linux.
• These utilities can identify and repair file system and disk errors.

Bad Sectors Scanning

• Use tools to scan for and mark bad sectors on the hard disk.
• Avoid using or allocate those sectors for data storage.

Perform S.M.A.R.T. Tests

• Run S.M.A.R.T. tests to assess the health of the hard disk.
• S.M.A.R.T. data can provide insights into potential issues before they become critical.

Check for Firmware Updates

• Verify if there are any firmware updates available for the hard disk.
• Apply updates to address known issues and improve compatibility.

Data Recovery Tools

• In case of data loss or corruption, consider using data recovery tools.
• Ensure the tools are reputable and compatible with your storage device.

Consider Professional Assistance

• If troubleshooting efforts do not resolve issues, consult with professional data recovery services or seek assistance from hardware specialists.

Monitor Operating System Updates

• Keep the operating system up to date with the latest updates and patches
• Operating system updates may include fixes for disk-related issues.

Replace Faulty Components

• If hardware components, such as cables or power supplies, are identified as faulty, replace them promptly.
• Addressing hardware issues can prevent further damage to the hard disk.

Evaluate System and Software Changes

• Consider whether recent changes to the system or installed software coincide with the onset of disk issues.
• Roll back changes if necessary to isolate the cause.

Through proactive maintenance and troubleshooting, users may prevent potential data loss, assure system stability, and prolong the lifespan of their storage devices. Consistent surveillance and strict adherence to optimal methods enhance the dependability and effectiveness of the storage environment.

FUTURE TRENDS IN HARD DISK TECHNOLOGY

Hard disk technology is expected to undergo substantial changes in the future, fueled by the unwavering quest for greater capacities, improved speeds, and enhanced dependability. A significant current development is the investigation of holographic data storage, which entails storing three-dimensional data within crystals or polymers using laser beams. This technology has the potential to revolutionize data storage by providing unparalleled storage capacity and speedier retrieval speeds [42]. 3D magnetic recording is an important field of development that involves vertically stacking data layers to increase store density without requiring larger physical drives.

Heat-Assisted Magnetic Recording (HAMR) is becoming increasingly important since it utilizes laser-induced heat to provide more accurate magnetic writing, resulting in increased storage capacities and enhanced reliability [43]. Thermal fly-height control and multi-actuator technologies are designed to improve data accuracy and access rates by maintaining consistent head-to-disk spacing and allowing independent operation of numerous read/write heads. The utilization of Energy-Assisted Magnetic Recording (EAMR) and the incorporation of storage-class memory with hard drives are crucial in attaining enhanced storage densities and optimum performance.

Machine learning is being used to optimize drive performance, enhance smart storage controllers, and explore quantum storage solutions, indicating a promising future for intelligent and secure hard disk technology. The industry's dedication to prolonging drive lifespans and enhancing storage reliability is evident through developments in materials, coatings, and storage topologies. As these patterns develop, the future of hard disk technology assures to fulfil the escalating requirements of a progressively data-oriented world [46].

Shingled Magnetic Recording (SMR)

Shingled Magnetic Recording (SMR) is a technology employed in hard disk drives (HDDs) to get greater storage densities and enhanced capacity. The "shingled" method refers to the technique of stacking and overlapping tracks on the magnetic disk, similar to the way shingles are arranged on a roof [44]. This novel approach seeks to address the constraints of conventional perpendicular magnetic recording (PMR) technology, which has grown progressively difficult to expand for greater storage capacities.

Key Features of Shingled Magnetic Recording (SMR):

Overlapping Tracks

- In SMR, data tracks are partially overlapped, with each new track partially covering the previous one.
- This shingled arrangement allows for higher areal density, enabling more data to be stored in the same physical space.

Write Operation Challenges

- Writing data to an SMR drive involves not only writing the target track but also potentially modifying adjacent tracks due to the overlapping nature of the layout.
- This characteristic makes random write operations less straightforward and requires the drive to manage and optimize data placement.

Sequential Write Performance

- SMR drives excel in scenarios where sequential write operations dominate, such as in archival storage or backup applications.
- The sequential nature of writing aligns well with the shingled structure, allowing for efficient data storage.

Usage in Specific Applications

- SMR drives are often used in scenarios where write-intensive workloads are less common, and large-scale sequential writes are prevalent.
- Common applications include cold storage, backup solutions, and archival systems.

Host-Managed and Drive-Managed SMR

- There are two types of SMR implementations: host-managed and drive-managed.

- Host-managed SMR requires the host system to be aware of the SMR architecture and manage data placement accordingly. Drive-managed SMR handles data placement internally, with the drive managing the shingling process.

Advantages

Higher Storage Densities

- SMR enables higher areal densities, allowing for increased storage capacities without physically enlarging the hard disk.

Cost-Efficiency

- The use of SMR technology contributes to cost-efficiency in storage solutions, particularly in applications where sequential write performance is prioritized.

Archival and Backup Applications

- SMR drives are well-suited for use cases where data is primarily read sequentially, making them ideal for archival storage and backup solutions.

Challenges

Random Write Performance

- SMR drives face challenges in scenarios with a high frequency of random write operations, as modifying data in one track may impact adjacent tracks.

Host Awareness

- Host systems need to be aware of the SMR architecture to effectively manage data placement, especially in host-managed SMR implementations.

Write Management Complexity

- The complexity of managing write operations in SMR drives requires efficient algorithms and firmware to optimize data placement and maintain performance.

Heat-Assisted Magnetic Recording (HAMR)

Heat-Assisted Magnetic Recording (HAMR) is a cutting-edge technology developed to surpass the constraints of conventional magnetic recording techniques in hard disk drives (HDDs). The purpose of developing HAMR is to get greater data storage densities, hence enabling larger capacity on HDDs. The main breakthrough is the utilization of a laser to selectively raise the temperature of the magnetic recording medium while writing.

Key Components and Mechanism

Plasmonic Near-Field Transducer (NFT)

• A key component of HAMR is the plasmonic near-field transducer, which focuses a laser onto a tiny spot on the disk surface.
• The NFT generates a localized, intense electromagnetic field that heats the magnetic recording medium.

Magnetic Recording Medium

• The magnetic recording medium typically consists of a thin layer of magnetic material on the disk surface.
• HAMR relies on the ability to temporarily reduce the coercivity of this material with heat, allowing data to be written with greater precision.

Laser-Induced Heating

• During the writing process, a laser is focused on the specific area where data is to be written.
• The intense heat from the laser reduces the coercivity of the magnetic material, making it easier to change the magnetic state and write data.

Quick Cooling

• The cooling rate after heating is crucial in HAMR. The magnetic material needs to quickly return to its high-coercivity state after the data is written.
• Rapid cooling ensures that the written data remains stable and does not unintentionally change.

Advantages of HAMR

Higher Areal Densities

• HAMR enables higher areal densities, allowing for increased data storage capacities on HDDs.
• The ability to pack more bits into a smaller area is crucial for meeting the growing demand for larger storage capacities.

Capacity Scaling

• HAMR technology provides a pathway for scaling HDD capacities beyond the limitations of traditional magnetic recording methods.

- It addresses the challenge of achieving higher densities without sacrificing data stability.

Continued Relevance of HDDs

- By increasing HDD capacities, HAMR technology extends the relevance of HDDs in the storage market, especially for applications requiring cost-effective high-capacity storage.

Challenges and Considerations

Material Stability

- Ensuring the stability of the magnetic material under repeated heating and cooling cycles is a critical challenge in HAMR implementation.

Precision Control

- Achieving precise control over the laser and the heating process is essential for accurate and reliable data recording.

Reliability and Durability

- The long-term reliability and durability of HAMR-based HDDs require robust designs and materials that can withstand the stresses of repeated heating and cooling.

Manufacturing Challenges

- Implementing HAMR at scale presents manufacturing challenges, including maintaining consistency across numerous drives and ensuring cost-effectiveness.

The Role of Hard Disks in a Data-Driven World

In modern culture that is becoming more networked and focused on data, hard drives have a crucial function as fundamental components in the management, storage, and retrieval of large quantities of digital information [45]. The importance of hard disks in a data-centric environment is diverse, impacting multiple facets of contemporary computing and digital encounters.

Data Storage and Management

- Capacity: Hard disks provide the primary storage medium for data, offering a range of capacities to accommodate the ever-growing volume of information generated by individuals, businesses, and organizations.

• Organization: They facilitate the organization of diverse data types, from documents and images to videos and applications, enabling efficient data management and retrieval.

Information Accessibility

• Read and Write Operations: Hard disks enable rapid read and write operations, ensuring quick access to stored data. This is crucial for applications and processes that demand real-time access, such as operating systems, databases, and applications.

Data Backups and Redundancy

• Critical Backups: Hard disks serve as a reliable medium for backing up critical data. Regular backups on hard disks provide a safeguard against data loss due to hardware failures, human errors, or unforeseen events.
• Redundancy: In combination with backup strategies and RAID configurations, hard disks contribute to data redundancy, enhancing data resilience and availability.

Archiving and Long-Term Storage

• Archival Solutions: Hard disks are commonly used in archival storage solutions, preserving historical or infrequently accessed data. Their cost-effectiveness and reliability make them suitable for long-term storage needs.
• Data Retention: Hard disks play a role in maintaining data integrity over extended periods, making them instrumental in preserving valuable information.

Server and Data Center Infrastructure

• Data Processing: In server environments and data centers, hard disks form a fundamental part of the storage infrastructure, supporting data processing, applications, and services.
• Mass Storage: Large-capacity hard disks in data centers address the demand for mass storage, supporting cloud services, big data analytics, and other data-intensive applications.

Cost-Effective Storage Solutions

• Economies of Scale: Hard disks offer cost-effective solutions for mass storage, especially when considering large-scale storage requirements. This makes them practical for both personal and enterprise use.
• Affordability: Compared to certain high-speed storage technologies, hard disks provide a balance between affordability and ample storage space.

Hybrid and Tiered Storage Configurations

- Hybrid Storage: Hard disks are often integrated into hybrid storage solutions, combining the speed of solid-state drives (SSDs) with the high capacity of hard disks for optimal performance and storage balance.
- Tiered Storage: In tiered storage architectures, hard disks are strategically used alongside different storage tiers, aligning storage resources with the specific performance needs of applications.

Digital Transformation and Big Data

- Big Data Storage: As organizations embrace digital transformation and accumulate large datasets, hard disks are integral in addressing the storage requirements of big data analytics and processing.
- Scaling Infrastructure: Hard disks contribute to scalable infrastructure for managing and extracting insights from massive datasets, supporting innovations in artificial intelligence, machine learning, and data science.

Personal Computing and End-User Devices

- Personal Storage: Hard disks are fundamental in personal computing devices, providing ample storage for operating systems, applications, games, and personal files.
- Multimedia Content: They support the storage of multimedia content, facilitating the creation and consumption of digital media on a wide scale.

CONCLUSION

In conclusion, gaining basic comprehension of hard disks is an essential prerequisite for comprehending the foundation of digital storage systems. By comprehending the fundamental elements such as platters and read/write heads, as well as the complexities of various interfaces and advancing technologies like solid-state drives, customers gain the knowledge necessary to make well-informed choices regarding their storage requirements.

Understanding the importance of aspects such as storage capacity, physical size, and dependable data management techniques helps optimize the use and upkeep of hard disks. Looking ahead, the ongoing development of hard disk technology is seen in upcoming concepts such as HAMR and SMR, which aim to address the increasing requirements of a data-centric society. Hard disks are essential in creating our digital experiences, whether it be for personal computers, data backups, or large-scale server setups. Keeping up-to-date with progress and optimal methods is crucial for maintaining the dependability, effectiveness, and essential role of hard disks in our constantly evolving digital environment [47].

REFERENCES

[1]　R. Chaudhary, and A. Kansal, "A perspective on the future of the magnetic hard disk drive (HDD) technology", *International Journal of Technical Research and Applications,* vol. 3, no. 3, pp. 63-74, 2015.

[2]　A. Al Mamun, G. Guo, and C. Bi, *Hard disk drive: mechatronics and control.* CRC press, 2017. [http://dx.doi.org/10.1201/9781420004106]

[3]　Afridi, A., *Vibration analysis of the platter and the spindle assembly of hard disk drive: a thesis submitted to the faculty of Massey University in partial fulfilment of the requirements for the degree of Master of Engineering in Mechatronics.* 2011, Massey University.

[4]　S. Kalcher, *An erasure-resilient and compute-efficient coding scheme for storage applications.,* 2013.

[5]　P.E. Ceruzzi, *A history of modern computing.* MIT press, 2003.

[6]　K. Maney, S. Hamm, and J. O'Brien, *Making the world work better: the ideas that shaped a century and a company.* Pearson Education, 2011.

[7]　N. Zlatanov, "Hard Disk Drive and Disk Encryption", In: *in Conference of the Black Hat* Amsterdam, The Netherlands., 2015.

[8]　G. Zeytinci, *Evolution of the Major Computer Storage Devices.,* 2001.

[9]　C.H. Ferguson, and C.R. Morris, *Computer wars: how the West can win in a post-IBM world.* Beard Books, 2002.

[10]　Y.J. Yu, D.I. Shin, W. Shin, N.Y. Song, J.W. Choi, H.S. Kim, H. Eom, and H.Y. Yeom, "Optimizing the block I/O subsystem for fast storage devices", *ACM Trans. Comput. Syst.,* vol. 32, no. 2, pp. 1-48, 2014. [TOCS]. [http://dx.doi.org/10.1145/2619092]

[11]　V. Rajaraman, and N. Adabala, *Fundamentals of computers.* PHI Learning Pvt. Ltd., 2014.

[12]　I. Harris, *Application of hardware and software.* Bibliotex, 2022.

[13]　B.M. Chen, *Hard disk drive servo systems.* Springer Science & Business Media, 2006.

[14]　S. Roman, and S. Roman, "Hard Drives I: Physical Characteristics. Understanding Personal Computer Hardware", *Everything you need to know to be an informed.,* PC User· PC Buyer· PC Upgrader, pp. 231-249, 1998. [http://dx.doi.org/10.1007/978-1-4684-6419-1_15]

[15]　J.M. Hughes, *Arduino: a technical reference: a handbook for technicians, engineers, and makers.* O'Reilly Media, Inc., 2016.

[16]　A. Khang, V. Hahanov, V.A. Hajimahmud, L. Eugenia, R.N. Ali, and A.V. Alyar, "The Impact of the Cyber-Physical Environment and Digital Environment on the Socialization Environment", In: *Khang A., Dutta P. K., Aayedee N., Gupta S., Chatterjee S., Revolutionizing the AI-Digital Landscape: A Guide to Sustainable Emerging Technologies for Marketing Professionals.* 1st ed. CRC Press, 2024. [http://dx.doi.org/10.4324/9781032688305-22]

[17]　J. Casey, *Computer Hardware: Hardware Components and Internal PC Connections.,* 2015.

[18]　T. Skrzekut, M. Wędrychowicz, and A. Piotrowicz, "Recycling of Hard Disk Drive Platters via Plastic Consolidation", *Materials (Basel),* vol. 16, no. 20, p. 6745, 2023. [http://dx.doi.org/10.3390/ma16206745] [PMID: 37895729]

[19]　M. Lerttaveevit, *A Study of Magnetic Recording Head Defects and Auto Classification.* Asian Institute of Technology, 2015.

[20]　M. Taktak-Meziou, *Mechatronics of hard disk drives: RISE feedback track following control of a R/W head.* Nova Science Publishers, Inc., 2015.

[21]   J. Snehi, *Computer peripherals and interfacing.* Firewall Media, 2006.

[22]   S. Piramanayagam, and T.C. Chong, *Developments in data storage: materials perspective.* John Wiley & Sons, 2011.
[http://dx.doi.org/10.1002/9781118096833]

[23]   H. H. Khanh, and A. Khang, "The Role of Artificial Intelligence in Blockchain Applications", In: *Reinventing Manufacturing and Business Processes through Artificial Intelligence,* G. Rana, A. Khang, R. Sharma, A.K. Goel, A.K. Dubey, Eds., vol. 2. CRC Press., 2021, pp. 20-40.
[http://dx.doi.org/10.1201/9781003145011-2]

[24]   A. Khang, K.C. Rath, K. Madapana, N.V.J. Rao, L.P. Panda, and S. Das, "Quantum Computing and Portfolio Optimization in Finance Services and Digital Economy", In: In Khang PH, D.A. (Ed.), *Shaping Cutting-Edge Technologies and Applications for Digital Banking and Financial Services (1st Ed.).* Productivity Press, 2024.

[25]   Y. Deng, "What is the future of disk drives, death or rebirth?", *ACM Comput. Surv.,* vol. 43, no. 3, pp. 1-27, 2011. [CSUR].
[http://dx.doi.org/10.1145/1922649.1922660]

[26]   I.D. Mayergoyz, and C. Tse, *Spin-stand microscopy of hard disk data.* Elsevier, 2010.

[27]   R. Karedla, J.S. Love, and B.G. Wherry, "Caching strategies to improve disk system performance", *Computer,* vol. 27, no. 3, pp. 38-46, 1994.
[http://dx.doi.org/10.1109/2.268884]

[28]   K.H. Lee, *Computers in nuclear medicine: a practical approach.* Society of Nuclear Medicine, Incorporated, 2005.

[29]   R.E. Dessy, "Disks for the Laboratory Part I", *Anal. Chem.,* vol. 57, no. 6, pp. 692A-708A, 1985.
[http://dx.doi.org/10.1021/ac00283a774]

[30]   S.X. Wang, and A.M. Taratorin, *Magnetic Information Storage Technology: A Volume in the Electromagnetism Series.* Elsevier, 1999.

[31]   G.W. Qin, Y.P. Ren, N. Xiao, B. Yang, L. Zuo, and K. Oikawa, "Development of high density magnetic recording media for hard disk drives: materials science issues and challenges", *Int. Mater. Rev.,* vol. 54, no. 3, pp. 157-179, 2009.
[http://dx.doi.org/10.1179/174328009X411172]

[32]   P.T.N. Anh, "Vladimir Hahanov, Triwiyanto, Ragimova Nazila Ali, Rashad İsmibeyli, Hajimahmud V. A., Abuzarova Vusala Alyar. "AI Models for Disease Diagnosis and Prediction of Heart Disease with Artificial Neural Networks", In: *Khang, A., Abdullayev, V., Hrybiuk, O., & Shukla, A.K., Computer Vision and AI-integrated IoT Technologies in Medical Ecosystem.* 1st ed. CRC Press, 2024.
[http://dx.doi.org/10.1201/9781003429609-9]

[33]   W.W. Hsu, and A.J. Smith, "The performance impact of I/O optimizations and disk improvements", *IBM J. Res. Develop.,* vol. 48, no. 2, pp. 255-289, 2004.
[http://dx.doi.org/10.1147/rd.482.0255]

[34]   R. Stokes, *Focus on Computer Database Storage.* Bibliotex, 2022.

[35]   M.I. Seltzer, "File System Logging versus Clustering: A Performance Comparison", In: *in USENIX,* 1995.

[36]   D. Vadala, *Managing RAID on Linux: Fast, Scalable, Reliable Data Storage.* O'Reilly Media, Inc., 2002.

[37]   A. Skendžić, B. Kovačić, and E. Tijan, "Effectiveness analysis of using Solid State Disk technology", *in 2016 39th International Convention on Information and Communication Technology, Electronics and Microelectronics (MIPRO).,* IEEE., 2016.
[http://dx.doi.org/10.1109/MIPRO.2016.7522391]

[38]   D. Fakhry, *A review on computational storage devices and near memory computing for high performance applications.* Memories-Materials, Devices, Circuits and Systems, 2023, p. 100051.

[39]   L. Ratzan, *Understanding information systems: what they do and why we need them.* American Library Association, 2004.

[40]   C. Mele, and T. Russo-Spena, "The architecture of the phygital customer journey: a dynamic interplay between systems of insights and systems of engagement", *Eur. J. Mark.,* vol. 56, no. 1, pp. 72-91, 2022.
[http://dx.doi.org/10.1108/EJM-04-2019-0308]

[41]   A. Khang, V.A. Hajimahmud, R.N. Ali, V. Hahanov, and Z. Avramovic, "Triwiyanto, The Role of Machine Vision in Manufacturing and Industrial Revolution 4.0", In: *Machine Vision and Industrial Robotics in Manufacturing: Approaches, Technologies, and Applications.* 1st ed. Khang, A., Abdullayev, V., Misra, A., & Litvinova, E. CRC Press, 2024.
[http://dx.doi.org/10.1201/9781003438137-1]

[42]   K. Kelly, *The inevitable: Understanding the 12 technological forces that will shape our future.* Penguin, 2016.

[43]   G. Ju, *Heat-assisted magnetic recording.* Developments in Data Storage, 2011, pp. 193-222.

[44]   K. Gao, "Architecture for hard disk drives", *IEEE Magn. Lett.,* vol. 9, pp. 1-5, 2018.
[http://dx.doi.org/10.1109/LMAG.2018.2789888]

[45]   M. Chen, *Big data: related technologies, challenges and future prospects.* vol. Vol. 100. Springer, 2014.
[http://dx.doi.org/10.1007/978-3-319-06245-7]

[46]   A. Khang, K.C. Rath, S.K. Satapathy, A. Kumar, S.R. Das, and M.R. Panda, "Enabling the Future of Manufacturing: Integration of Robotics and IoT to Smart Factory Infrastructure in Industry 4.0", In: *Handbook of Research on AI-Based Technologies and Applications in the Era of the Metaverse.,* A. Khang, V. Shah, S. Rani, Eds., IGI Global, 2023, pp. 25-50.
[http://dx.doi.org/10.4018/978-1-6684-8851-5.ch002]

[47]   A. Khang, M. Muthmainnah, P.M. Seraj, A. Al Yakin, and A.J. Obaid, "AI-Aided Teaching Model in Education 5.0", In: *Handbook of Research on AI-Based Technologies and Applications in the Era of the Metaverse.,* A. Khang, V. Shah, S. Rani, Eds., IGI Global, 2023, pp. 83-104.
[http://dx.doi.org/10.4018/978-1-6684-8851-5.ch004]

CHAPTER 5

Hard Disk Data Organization

Sanchit Dhankhar[1,*], **Nitika Garg**[1] and **Himanshu Sharma**[1]

[1] *Chitkara College of Pharmacy, Chitkara University, Rajpura, Punjab, India*

Abstract: The ideas and sophisticated methods governing the storage and retrieval of digital information are explored in depth in this chapter as they pertain to the complex world of hard disc data organization. The path starts with a deep dive into hard disc drives (HDDs), exposing their inner workings, disc geometry, and storage basics. The research explores FAT32, NTFS, and exFAT, among others, to better understand their inner workings. The trade-offs involved in maximizing storage efficiency and performance are unpacked, including those involving sequential *versus* random access, fragmentation, and clustering schemes. Disk partitioning is also investigated in detail; topics covered include partitioning fundamentals, partition kinds, and the significance of the Master Boot Record (MBR) and GUID Partition Table (GPT). These frameworks provide the groundwork for learning how data is organized on storage devices, taking into account things like available space, compatibility, and redundancy. The last leg of the journey is an examination of developing tendencies, with a focus on the revolutionary effects of Solid State Drives (SSDs) and cloud storage. The trend toward quicker, more reliable, and scalable storage solutions is highlighted by comparisons between SSDs and conventional HDDs, insights into data organization on SSDs, and the incorporation of cloud storage and remote data organization. This section summarizes an exploration of the ever-changing world of data storage, with a focus on why it is crucial to be aware of current concepts and trends in data organizing on hard drives. These discoveries aid in the development of storage structures that meet the ever-changing needs of modern computing, allowing for the preservation of data accessibility, security, and efficiency in the face of shifting paradigms.

Keywords: Data, ExFAT, GPT, GUID, Hard disk, HDD, MBR FAT32, NTFS, Organization, SSD.

INTRODUCTION

The intricate tapestry of hard disc data organization emerges as a crucial facet shaping the functionality and efficiency of modern computing systems in today's ever-changing technological landscape, where the digital realm is pervasive and the demand for data storage has reached unprecedented heights [1]. Hard disc

* **Corresponding author Sanchit Dhankhar:** Chitkara College of Pharmacy, Chitkara University, Rajpura, Punjab, India; E-mail: sanchitdhankhar@gmail.com

Alex Khang, Sanchit Dhankhar, Sandeep Bhardwaj, Avnesh Verma & Satish Kumar Sharma (Eds.)

drives (HDDs) store an ever-increasing sea of digital information, and their pervasiveness highlights their everlasting significance as repositories [2]. This section begins an exhaustive investigation, a subtle voyage, into the complexities of hard disc data organization, peeling back the layers that govern how information is stored, retrieved, and administered within these magnetic archives [3].

One must become well-versed in the narrative that led us to the current technological juncture in order to fully grasp the relevance of hard disc data organizing [4]. The advent of the digital age did not happen all at once, but rather as a result of a cascade of technological breakthroughs [5]. The progression from the early days of computers, when information was saved on punch cards and magnetic tapes, to the modern era, when high-capacity hard disc drives are commonplace, has been nothing short of astonishing [6]. As we move forward through history, it becomes clear that the explosion of digital data has required a corresponding leap forward in data storage technology [7].

The introduction of hard disc drives changed everything by providing a more flexible and user-friendly option for archiving data [8]. Data storage, retrieval, and manipulation were no longer constrained by the slowness or inefficiency of physical media [9]. The sophisticated link of bits and bytes on hard discs serves a greater purpose than just archiving information [10]. The art and science of maximizing the terrain over which the digital storey is played out is at the heart of hard disc data organizing [11]. Data management is the art of making the retrieval, modification, and use of data flow like a well-orchestrated symphony of ones and zeros [12].

The effectiveness of hard disc data organization becomes the cornerstone upon which the stability and performance of computer systems swing, whether we're talking about desktop PCs, corporate servers, or massive data centers [13]. Now think about the personal computer, a tool that has become indispensable in today's world. Everything is deeply intertwined in the fabric of hard disc data management, from the operating system that controls its functionality to the countless applications and files that populate its storage. Not just technical jargon, measurements like access times, file fragmentation, and data integrity determine how easily and quickly information can be retrieved and used [14].

The stakes are considerably higher in the business world, where information is a commodity with enormous worth [15]. Enterprises rely on elaborate databases, complex file systems, and interconnected networks, all of which are grounded by the principles of hard disc data organization [16]. Effective data organization strategies are crucial to a company's success because they provide for easy access to relevant information, protection of sensitive data, and the capacity to adjust to changes in the company's digital footprint [17]. Data organization on hard drives is revealed to be more than just a technicality as we proceed through this investigation; it is the unseen conductor of today's computer symphony [18]. It determines whether or not a user has a quick, fluid interaction with a piece of technology or a slow, choppy one [19].

In a world where knowledge is encoded in the binary language of computers, it is the lynchpin that ensures the reliability of digital information [20]. Exploring the intricacies of data structure on hard drives is a complex adventure that spans the worlds of theory, practice, and a constantly shifting technological landscape [21]. This investigation is not a dry rundown of facts; rather, it is an open invitation to explore beneath the surface of this essential component of contemporary computing to discover its basic principles [22].

The storey will wind its way through the fundamental ideas that determine the very anatomy of hard disc drives as we move through the chapters. From platters and heads to the delicate dance of disc geometry, we will unpack the layers of complexity that make up these magnetic marvels. Deciphering the language in which the history of data storage is written requires an understanding of the fundamental parts. File systems, the underlying architecture that controls how information is stored and retrieved, will be investigated further. Each file system, from the common FAT32 to the powerful NTFS and the flexible exFAT, represents a different part of the wider storey of information management.

We will dissect file allocation tables, revealing their inner workings and exploring the benefits and drawbacks they bring to the table when it comes to arranging data. In addition, the route will take you through the many methods of data organization. Each thread in the tapestry of effective data retrieval and storage — the contrast between sequential and random access, the subtleties of fragmentation, and the strategic grouping of data — is essential. The methods behind digital information organization, including contiguous allocation, linked allocation, and indexed allocation, will be laid out in detail across the chapters.

BASIC CONCEPTS

Understanding Hard Disk Drives

Hard disc drives (HDDs) are the unsung heroes of today's ever-changing computer landscape, working in the background to make it possible to store and retrieve massive amounts of digital information. In order to really appreciate the ingenuity of a hard disc drive, one must take the time to explore its inner workings and become familiar with the complex interactions between its various parts.

Components of a Hard Disk

A hard disc drive's inner workings are comprised of a carefully crafted ensemble of parts, each of which plays an integral function in the device's otherwise faultless performance [23]. Usually made of aluminum or glass, the platters are the blank slate onto which information is magnetically engraved. These platters, which are stacked on top of a spindle, spin at high speeds, generating a symphony of motion that allows the read/write heads to reach all areas of the platter.

The read/write heads, which are only a few nanometers above the platter surface, look like a tiny needle moving slowly over the record's grooves [24]. They play a crucial part, reading information as it spins beneath them and adding new information as needed. Like a conductor's baton, the actuator arm guides the heads to the exact track where data is to be read or stored. This precise choreography is essential in the ever-changing world of data storage. Learning the intricate dance of these parts will help you appreciate the physical complexity that goes into making a hard disc drive so impressive. When platters, heads, and actuators work together, a hard drive becomes much more than a simple data repository; it can precisely orchestrate the recording and retrieval of information [25].

Disk Geometry

The magic of data storage lies not just in the hardware but also in the abstract location it occupies in the computer's memory [26]. Data on a hard drive is organized in accordance with a blueprint called disc geometry. Think of the platters like a record's grooves—concentric rings. The data lives along these arcs, which we call tracks. Data is further partitioned into sectors inside each track [27]. These sectors are the smallest individually addressable chunks of data, and they function similarly to the pages of a book. Finally, a cylinder, a key notion in disc geometry, is formed by the three-dimensional arrangement of tracks that align across many platters. Learning disc geometry is like absorbing the floor design for an arena. To effectively store, retrieve, and organize data, it offers the geographical context within which this delicate dance takes place.

Data Storage Principles

The fundamental concepts that govern the storage of digital information are where the true heart of data management for hard discs can be found [27]. The binary notes, also known as bits and bytes, create the alphabet that is used by computers to interact with one another and store information. These notes are at the center of this digital symphony.

Bits, Bytes, and File Sizes

Information is carried by bits, which are the binary digits 0 and 1 respectively. These bits cohere into bytes, where each of the eight bits stands for a discrete piece of digital data. Bits and bytes work together to provide the basis of all digital data and the language of computers [28]. Data is measured in larger and larger increments as its size increases, from kilobytes (KB) to megabytes (MB) to gigabytes (GB) and beyond. Each successive level in this structure indicates a more expansive realization of digital information, much like the crescendo in a symphony.

Sectors and Clusters

Data tells its storey in the granular space of markets and communities. The smallest logical unit of data storage on a hard drive is called a sector, and it corresponds to a chapter in a book. These regions are the fundamental units from which information can be read or written. On the other hand, "clusters" stand for the deliberate grouping of related industries. Clusters can be thought of as the structural elements that contain and manage the data. Disk space optimization and the efficacy of storage and retrieval activities are both affected by the cluster's total size.

The principles of sectors and clusters can be compared to an orchestra's strategic positioning of instruments [29]. It has an impact on the overall effectiveness of the ensemble by guaranteeing reliable and quick data storage and retrieval. By exploring the geography of these fundamental ideas, one can unveil the complexity of the data dance within the domains of hard disc drives. In order to delve more deeply into the realms of hard disc data organization, it is helpful to have a firm grasp on the fundamentals, which include everything from the material parts that make up the physical shape to the abstract laws that regulate the spatial symphony of data organization.

FILE SYSTEMS

File systems are the backbone of hard disc data structure, offering a logical foundation for storing and retrieving digital information [30]. Here we delve deeper into the workings of file systems, discussing their underlying concepts, typical implementations, and the dynamic nature of file allocation tables. A file system is the architecture that governs the coexistence of data on a storage medium; it is much more than just an organizational scheme. A file system plays a crucial role in designing the user experience and improving storage space utilization by specifying how files are named, structured, and accessed. Changes in file systems reflect the increasing importance of speed, safety, and portability from the early days of computers to the complex surroundings of today's technology.

Common File Systems

FAT32

The File Allocation Table 32 (FAT32) has been around for a long time and is still going strong today. FAT32 is a file system extension that aims to improve upon its predecessors by being both easy to use and widely compatible [31]. Because of its compatibility with Windows, macOS, and Linux, it has become the de facto standard for portable data storage. However, its shortcomings, especially in light of contemporary storage demands, are highlighted by its restrictions on file size and less efficient disc space consumption for little files.

NTFS

Microsoft Windows' New Technology File System (NTFS) has emerged as a more advanced and feature-rich alternative [32]. Access control lists (ACLs), encryption, and compression are just a few of the new features introduced by NTFS. Its journaling features improve data integrity by keeping track of modifications, facilitating speedy recovery after system crashes. Despite NTFS's superior performance and security, it is not without its limitations, especially when it comes to interoperability with operating systems other than Windows.

exFAT

In order to remedy FAT32's inadequacies, especially when it comes to managing files of extreme size, the Extended File Allocation Table (exFAT) was created [33]. Microsoft's exFAT file system was designed to accommodate files larger than 4 GB and to make better use of available storage space. External storage devices like USB drives and SD cards typically use exFAT due to its emphasis on cross-platform compatibility. Its adaptability makes it a great alternative for cases where cross-platform accessibility is crucial.

File Allocation Tables

Structure and Functionality

The File Allocation Table is the heart of FAT-based file systems [34]. The FAT's layout makes it easy to quickly find where files are stored on a device for the purpose of both reference and retrieval. The FAT automatically refreshes to reflect any changes to file allocations caused by the insertion, modification, or deletion of data.

Advantages and Limitations

FAT file systems have many benefits due to their simplicity and widespread support. Because of their cross-platform interoperability, exchanging and transferring information is much less of a hassle. These benefits, however, do not come without costs. Their unsuitability in settings where data security is critical is due to the absence of sophisticated features like access control and encryption [35]. The performance of bigger storage volumes is especially vulnerable to fragmentation over time.

Acquiring an appreciation for the subtle decisions made in the architecture of file systems requires more than just knowing their names. Each file system offers a different way of organizing data, from FAT32's universal accessibility to NTFS's focus on security and exFAT's balance between compatibility and performance [36]. As we delve deeper into the complexities of file allocation tables and their accompanying file systems, we get a more complete picture of the many moving parts involved in the world of hard disc data organization.

DATA ORGANIZATION TECHNIQUES

Sequential *vs.* Random Access

When it comes to the efficiency and effectiveness of a storage system, the means by which data is accessible play a crucial part in the complex terrain of data structure on hard discs [37]. Sequential access and random access are the two main methods, and they are very different from one another and have their own set of pros and downsides.

Sequential Access

The sequential access approach is a linear one, much like reading a book from beginning to end [38]. With this method, data is accessed sequentially, in a set order. There is no break in the action, and everything makes sense as it unfolds. Reading and writing data in the order it is physically recorded on a storage medium is what sequential access means in the context of hard disc data organization.

Advantages of Sequential Access

- Simplicity: Sequential access is defined by its simplicity, which is one of its defining characteristics. It is simple to create and understand thanks to the logical flow of accessing data pieces in the order that they are listed.
- Efficiency When Streaming Data: Sequential access has been shown to be highly efficient *in situ*ations where data is processed or retrieved in a continuous sequence, such as video streaming or batch processing [39]. This includes situations where data is processed or retrieved in a continuous series.
- Input/output operations: When data is accessed in the order that it is stored on the disc, sequential access can optimize disc input/output operations, contributing to enhanced performance. This is because sequential access accesses the data in the order that it is stored
- on the disc.

Disadvantages of Sequential Access

- Inefficiency for Random Access: When there is a need for direct access to particular data points, sequential access reveals its most significant flaw, which is its inability to provide that access [40]. When data is accessed out of sequence, it is necessary to navigate through all of the elements that came before it, which is inefficient.
- Limited Flexibility: Sequential access may lack flexibility in circumstances when the order of data retrieval is not predetermined or needs to be dynamic, which restricts its adaptability. This may be the case when the order of data retrieval is not predetermined or needs to be dynamic.

Random Access

On the other hand, random access enables immediate access to any data element regardless of where in the array that element is located [41]. This approach is analogous to being able to skip forward to any page in a book without having to read the pages that came before it. In the context of the arrangement of data stored on hard discs, random access eliminates the need for sequential traversal by providing direct and immediate access to particular spots on the storage medium.

Advantages of Random Access

- Flexibility: Random access offers flexibility since it enables users to gain immediate access to particular data points without having to first navigate through the pieces that came before them [42]. This is especially helpful in circumstances when particular data items must be retrieved in a manner that is independent of the physical order in which they are stored.

- Efficiency for Dynamic Access Patterns: Applications that have random access patterns or often get data from multiple locations stand to gain greatly from the effectiveness of random access.
- Reduced Seek Times: Direct access to particular areas cuts down on the amount of time spent seeking, which in turn speeds up the retrieval of data and boosts the efficiency of the system as a whole.

Disadvantages of Random Access

- Complexity: Implementing efficient random access can be more difficult than implementing sequential access, especially in cases with dynamic data structures or varied access patterns [43]. This is especially true when the access patterns fluctuate.
- Potentially Higher Overhead: Due to the necessity of indexing structures or other techniques to permit rapid access to certain data points, random access may result in a higher level of overhead being incurred.

Choosing Between Sequential and Random Access

The expected access patterns and type of data will determine whether sequential or random access methods should be used. Random access is preferred for applications with dynamic access patterns or a need for quick access to specific data points, while sequential access is best suited for cases where data is processed or retrieved in a linear fashion [44].

In practice, storage systems frequently combine multiple access methods, switching from sequential to random access seamlessly depending on the nature of the data being accessed. When developing storage systems to meet the needs of various data processing tasks, it is crucial to find a happy medium between these methods for maximum efficiency and flexibility.

Fragmentation

The efficiency, performance, and usage of storage space are all directly impacted by fragmentation, making it a crucial concern in the world of hard disc data organization [45]. Over time, fragmentation develops as a natural byproduct of file creation, modification, and deletion. It causes disc space to be allocated in pieces, which necessitates careful planning and administration.

Types of Fragmentation

External Fragmentation

When a disk's free space is broken up into independent pieces, it is said to be externally fragmented. Essentially, it causes empty spots to appear between the files that have been set aside [46].

Inefficiency in the use of available space is the main problem caused by external fragmentation. When files are generated or extended, they may need to be broken into pieces to fit into the available gaps. This can result in inefficient utilization of the limited space for storing things.

Internal Fragmentation

The allotment of storage space within files is related to internal fragmentation. This happens when the file's allocated space exceeds the size of the contents within the file. This occurs frequently in file systems that divide available space into discrete chunks of a certain size, known as "clusters." If a file size is not a perfect match for the cluster size, some of the allotted space may go unused.

Impact on Performance

The performance of a storage system may suffer for a number of reasons as a result of fragmentation [47].

Increased Seek Times

When files get fragmented, the read/write heads of the hard disc have to travel farther to reach the various pieces that make up the file [48]. Because of this heightened level of physical activity, search times have increased.

Slower data access speeds have a direct effect on the overall performance of the storage system, especially *in situ*ations where instantaneous data access is essential.

Degraded Sequential Access Performance

Particularly, external fragmentation can reduce the efficiency of sequential access operations. It is inefficient to read or write data sequentially when data is broken up into smaller, non-contiguous pieces.

The necessity to go across fragmented parts of files slows down sequential access, which is optimized for reading data in a linear fashion.

Efficiency Challenges for Large Files

Large files are particularly vulnerable to the problems caused by fragmentation [49]. When a large file is fragmented, it may require accessing several distributed fragments in order to retrieve or alter the file, which can reduce performance and cause more wear on the storage medium.

Mitigation Strategies

Defragmentation

By reorganizing files and free space on the disc to form contiguous blocks of data, defragmentation is a preventative method of managing fragmentation [50]. By consolidating files through routine defragmentation processes, seek times can be decreased and data access efficiency can be improved.

Dynamic Allocation Strategies

The effects of fragmentation can be reduced by the use of dynamic allocation mechanisms in place in modern file systems [51]. Space optimization can be achieved through the use of methods like dynamic cluster sizing and adaptive allocation.

Storage Tiering

Data access patterns and relative relevance can be used to create storage tiers. Data that is accessed frequently or is vital can be kept on fast, low-fragmentation levels, whereas data that is used less frequently can be stored on slower, higher-capacity tiers.

In sum, data fragmentation is a complex obstacle to overcome in the context of information architecture. Despite being an unavoidable byproduct of file system operations, fragmentation may be managed and its effects on hard disc storage systems mitigated with the help of dynamic allocation and defragmentation.

Clustering Strategies

The allocation and organization of files plays a crucial role in the complex web of hard disc data management, impacting storage efficiency, data retrieval speed, and overall system performance. Different ways to controlling the physical and logical organization of data on a storage media are represented by the many clustering algorithms, such as contiguous allocation, linked allocation, and indexed allocation.

Contiguous Allocation

Files using contiguous allocation are simply stored on the disc in one long chunk. In this method, each file is stored in a consecutive set of blocks without any gaps. It is the equivalent of setting aside a whole section of a book for one chapter.

Advantages of Contiguous Allocation

- Faster Access Times: Since the entire file is stored in a single, unbroken region, contiguous allocation can improve access times. This reduces the amount of time it takes for the read/write heads to access the entire file by limiting the distance they have to travel.
- Simplicity: Contiguous allocation's straightforward nature makes it simple to both implement and comprehend. The file system's logical structure is identical to the disk's physical structure.

Disadvantages of Contiguous Allocation

- External Fragmentation: The risk of external fragmentation is a major obstacle to contiguous allocation. If there are spaces between allocated files because of file creation, modification, or deletion, then that space is being wasted.
- Limited Flexibility: In cases when file sizes vary or when it is necessary to dynamically insert or enlarge files, contiguous allocation may present difficulties.

Linked Allocation

Linked allocation utilizes a linked list structure to join together file blocks that are not physically next to one another. Each block includes a reference to the following block in the chain. It is the equivalent of a book with pages that all lead to each other.

Advantages of Linked Allocation

- Adaptability to Dynamic File Sizes: Linked allocation is extremely responsive to variations in file size. Files can grow by linking together extra blocks, which does not require the added blocks to be physically next to each other.
- Efficient Space Utilization: Since files are not limited to contiguous blocks with linked allocation, the possibility of external fragmentation is decreased.

Disadvantages of Linked Allocation

- Traversal Overhead: Accessing data in a linked allocation structure may create overhead, as traversing the linked list to locate specific blocks can take additional time.

- Potential for Fragmentation within Blocks: Linked allocation reduces outward fragmentation but may cause internal fragmentation if any of the allocated blocks are not used in their whole.

Indexed Allocation

Indexed allocation creates and maintains a database of pointers to the real file blocks through the utilization of an index structure. The index functions as a map, allowing for expedited access to the specific location of the file on the disc. It is comparable to having a table of contents that is commented on in a book.

Advantages of Indexed Allocation

- Quick Access to Data: Utilizing the index as a point of reference, indexed allocation makes it possible to more quickly retrieve particular data points. Because of this, there is less of a need to travel through structures that are linked together or look for space that is continuous.
- Reduced Fragmentation: Since the index facilitates effective allocation and monitoring of file blocks, it can aid in minimizing both external and internal fragmentation.

Disadvantages of Indexed Allocation

- Overhead of Index Maintenance: The overhead of managing the index structure is considerable. When files are added, edited, or removed, the index must be refreshed, which uses up system resources.
- Potential for Wasted Space in Index Blocks: The disc space needed for the index may not be fully utilized in cases when only a few small files exist.

In the ever-changing world of data organization, considerations including the data's composition, expected access patterns, and system requirements all play a role in deciding which clustering strategy to use. To meet the wide range of processing, access, and management requirements for stored data, storage systems frequently adopt a hybrid of these approaches.

DISK PARTITIONING

Partition Basics

Disk partitioning is a cornerstone of storage management, since it is used to divide up and assign space on a hard drive or other physical storage medium [52]. This section delves into the fundamentals of disc partitioning, explaining its function, underlying principles, and effect on information architecture.

Purpose of Disk Partitioning

Disk partitioning is the process of logically separating data on a storage device by creating separate physical parts, or partitions [53]. Data, programs, and operating system files may all be managed in isolation thanks to partitions' own file systems.

Operating System Isolation: The installation of multiple operating systems on a single physical drive is made feasible through the process of partitioning the disc into multiple sections [54]. This is especially important in arrangements known as dual-boot or multi-boot, in which users can run numerous operating systems from a single computer.

Data Organization and Management: Users are able to organize their data in a manner that is more structured when the disc is partitioned. For instance, if you have a partition that is exclusively reserved for system files, another partition that is exclusively reserved for application data, and still another partition that is exclusively reserved for personal data, then you can manage data and backup methods more effectively.

Security and Stability: In the case that there are mistakes or failures in the system, partitions can serve as barriers to prevent problems in one partition from spreading to other partitions [55]. Because of this isolation, the system is more stable, and it is also much simpler to recover from specific categories of mistakes.

Optimizing Performance: Users may choose to partition their discs in order to get better performance [56]. For instance, improving data access times can be accomplished by putting files that are accessed frequently on a different partition or drive.

Principles of Disk Partitioning

Partition Table: The partition table is an essential feature of disc partitioning since it keeps track of how the disc is divided up. In addition to GUID Partition Table (GPT), Master Boot Record (MBR) is another popular partition table format.

Primary and Extended Partitions: The maximum number of primary partitions that can exist on a disc using MBR partitioning is four, or three primary partitions and one extended partition. It is therefore possible to further divide the expanded partition into other logical partitions. The number of main partitions can be increased without using extended partitions in GPT.

File Systems: On Windows, a partition may host the NTFS, FAT32, or exFAT file system; in Linux, ext4 and XFS are common. Compatibility, security, and the maximum file size are just some of the areas where your choice of file system makes a difference.

Partitioning Tools: Partitioning utilities, either built into the OS or made available as an add-on, are available. Windows has Disk Management, macOS has Disk Utility, and Linux has software like GParted.

Impact on Data Organization

Logical Organization: Users can better structure their storage space for certain purposes by partitioning their discs [57]. This separation of concerns helps keep things organized and makes backups easier to restore.

Efficient Resource Allocation: Users can ensure an equitable distribution of resources by assigning fixed sizes to individual partitions. A specific OS partition, for instance, can be sized so as to provide enough room for other software and user data.

Isolation for Data Protection: Partitions serve as secure storage compartments for sensitive information. It is less likely that data corruption or loss will occur if a problem occurs in one partition and not another.

Facilitating Upgrades and Maintenance: Upgrades and maintenance can be made easier by disc partitioning. For instance, you can reinstall the operating system or perform other maintenance on a single partition without affecting any other partitions that may contain data you need.

Disk partitioning is all about logically dividing up physical storage space, giving users more control over their storage setups and making it easier to maintain order and stability. Disk partitioning is an essential component of storage management, as it may be used to improve performance, accommodate various operating systems, and keep sensitive information separate.

Master Boot Record (MBR) and GUID Partition Table (GPT)

There are two independent partitioning systems used to organize and manage partitions on storage devices: Master Boot Record (MBR) and GUID Partition Table (GPT) [58]. The Master Boot Record (MBR) is an old mechanism that has seen extensive use, especially in the Windows ecosystem. It is possible to have up to four primary partitions or three primary partitions plus one extended partition. The Master Boot Record (MBR) is a vital part of the boot process and is optimized for discs up to 2 terabytes in size.

The GPT partitioning mechanism, on the other hand, was developed recently to address the shortcomings of MBR. This feature, included in the UEFI specification, is gradually replacing the older BIOS firmware. With GPT, you can have as many as 128 primary partitions without ever having to worry about extended or logical ones again. It is scalable, unlike MBR, which has a hard time dealing with disc capacities larger than 2 terabytes.

By including a backup partition table, GPT increases data integrity and recovery options through redundancy. The partition table's integrity can be checked with the use of built-in security mechanisms like CRC32 checksums. To ease the process of upgrading to new hardware, GPT is backwards-compatible with legacy BIOS systems.

There are a number of considerations while deciding between MBR and GPT. Some users favor MBR because it allows for smaller discs or works with older computer systems. However, GPT is the superior option when larger discs are to be used, contemporary systems that support UEFI are to be used, and increased data integrity and redundancy are required. The choice between MBR and GPT is determined by factors such as the disc size, the number of partitions, the system's compatibility with hardware and firmware standards, and the required level of data integrity. There is a wide variety of storage solutions available to meet the needs of various computer environments, each of which employs a unique partitioning method.

Partitioning Schemes

Organizing and allocating storage space on physical devices is governed by partitioning schemes, which are crucial frameworks. To guarantee effective data management, a variety of schemes are available to suit a wide range of requirements and architectural styles. To achieve optimal storage configurations, familiarity with these schemes is essential.

Primary, Extended, and Logical Partitions

Primary Partitions

- Most partitioning techniques begin with primary partitions. Up to four primary partitions can be created on a disc, and each partition can have its own set of files.
- Operating systems are often put on major partitions, and these partitions are typically bootable.

Extended Partitions

- With extended partitions, you can create more than the maximum of four partitions allowed by the standard Master Boot Record (MBR) scheme. They are used to hold logical partitions.
- An extended partition is not a storage space in and of itself, but rather a holding area for several logical partitions.

Logical Partitions

- The structure of an extended partition contains the logical partitions. The number of logical partitions is not limited in the same way that main partitions are.
- When more than four partitions are required on a disc, a logical partition can be a useful, flexible, and scalable method for data organization.

Dynamic Disk Partitioning

Introduction to Dynamic Disks

Windows operating systems pioneered a revolutionary method of managing data storage known as dynamic disc partitioning [59]. When compared to standard disc management, it offers more options.

Advanced data configurations are made possible by dynamic discs' support for advanced features including volume spanning, mirroring, and striping.

Dynamic Volumes

- Dynamic discs work with dynamic volumes instead of regular partitions. Simple volumes, spanned volumes, striped volumes, mirrored volumes, and RAID-5 volumes are all types of dynamic volumes.
- Similar to primary partitions, simple volumes are the most basic volume type, whereas spanned and striped volumes can be used to extend a volume's storage across many physical drives.

Flexibility and Resilience

- More options for organizing your data can be found with dynamic disc partitioning. Administrators, for instance, can grow volumes or add hard drives without having to reinstall everything.
- Data is more resilient against disc failures thanks to the fault tolerance provided by technologies like mirroring and RAID-5, which are only available on dynamic drives.

Compatibility Considerations

- While dynamic drives do offer some nice extras, it is important to remember that they only work under a Windows OS.
- Dynamic discs necessitate the more modern GUID Partition Table (GPT) partitioning strategy, which is incompatible with systems utilizing the older MBR partitioning scheme.

Choosing Between Partition Types

Basic vs. Dynamic

- Primary, extended, and logical partitions found on most basic hard drives are sufficient for general-purpose computing tasks. They are interoperable with many different architectures and OSes.
- Especially in Windows-centric settings, dynamic discs' sophisticated features shine *in situ*ations where dynamic volume management and fault tolerance are paramount.

Primary vs. Logical

- The needs of the system dictate which of primary and logical partitions should be used.
- Logical partitions provide scalability for data organization beyond the constraints of primary partitions, while primary partitions are appropriate for basic bootable partitions.

In conclusion, it is essential to grasp the differences between main, extended, and logical partitions, as well as dynamic disc partitioning, in order to customize storage configurations to match the needs of the system and its intended usage. There are many different types of partitions, each with its own unique function and differing degrees of scalability, robustness, and adaptability for managing data.

EMERGING TRENDS

Solid State Drives (SSDs)

Contrasts with HDDs

Multiple bits of information can be stored in a single memory cell because to SSDs' use of triple-level cell (TLC) and quad-level cell (QLC) technology. This enhances storage density, enabling bigger capacity SSDs without a commensurate increase in physical size.

DRAM Cache and SLC Caching

o DRAM Cache: Many SSDs feature a DRAM cache, a volatile memory that boosts data access speeds by caching frequently accessed data.

o SLC Caching: Write speeds can be increased with SLC caching because it treats a piece of the SSD as if it were Single-Level Cell (SLC) memory.

- NVMe (Non-Volatile Memory Express) Interface: Faster Interface: NVMe is the standard interface for SSDs since it allows for far faster data transfers than the previous-generation SATA standard. As a result, response times to requests for data are improved.
- Endurance and Lifespan: Endurance: Wear levelling algorithms are used in modern SSDs to ensure that all memory cells receive an equal number of write and erase cycles. This, together with developments in NAND flash technology, helps to boost durability and lifespan.
- Power Consumption: Low Power Consumption: SSDs have a lower power requirement than HDDs, which means they can help portable devices last longer between charges and help data centers save money on their utility bills.

Data Organization on SSDs

- Advanced Wear Leveling: Dynamic Wear Leveling: SSDs use wear levelling algorithms that dynamically adjust to usage patterns to guarantee consistent cell wear. This dynamic technique optimizes the overall efficiency of wear levelling.
- Garbage Collection Efficiency: Trim Command Optimization: By notifying the drive of any superfluous data blocks, the Trim command is essential for keeping SSD performance at peak levels. SSDs efficiently handle the Trim instruction, minimizing performance loss over time.
- Error Correction and ECC (Error-Correcting Code): Advanced Error Correction: Low-Density Parity-Check (LDPC) codes are just one example of the advanced error correction algorithms used by SSDs to identify and fix data corruption. This improves data reliability, especially in harsh operational settings.
- Over-Provisioning Management: Intelligent Over-Provisioning: In order to guarantee the highest levels of performance and dependability, SSDs skillfully manage over-provisioning, or the allocation of spare memory cells. To accomplish this, a happy medium must be found between over provided space and easily accessible storage.

Cloud Storage and Remote Data Organization

- Edge Computing Integration: Local Processing: Edge computing is being included by cloud storage providers, bringing data processing closer to the data's origin. For time-sensitive applications, this improves real-time processing and reduces latency.

- Smart Data Indexing and Metadata Management: AI-Driven Indexing: Smart data indexing using AI is at the heart of cloud storage platforms, allowing for quick and easy data retrieval. Patterns in data are analyzed by AI algorithms, which then tag and classify files automatically.
- Immutable Storage and Versioning: Immutable Storage Features: Immutable storage is available in some cloud services and safeguards data from being changed inadvertently or on purpose. File versioning improves data safety and restoration by letting users view and roll back to prior iterations of a file.
- Enhanced Security Measures: Zero-Knowledge Encryption: In order to ensure that only the user has access to their encryption keys, cloud storage companies are using zero-knowledge encryption. There will be less chance of theft or hacking because of this added safeguard.
- Blockchain-Based Data Integrity: Blockchain for Verification: Attempts are made to improve data security with blockchain technology. In order to provide a verifiable history of data exchanges, cloud services use blockchain to generate a transparent and immutable record of file modifications.
- Quantum-Safe Encryption: Preparation for Quantum Computing: In order to protect sensitive data from the potential risks posed by quantum computers, cloud storage companies are creating quantum-safe encryption solutions [60].

In conclusion, the development of solid-state drives (SSDs) and cloud storage has been defined by sophisticated technological developments and a commitment to enhancing performance, efficiency, and safety. These developments are helping to create a storage environment that is both flexible and responsive to the changing requirements of today's users and businesses.

CONCLUSION

In conclusion, learning about how information is stored and retrieved on hard drives gives a thorough grounding in the fundamental ideas and cutting-edge technology that support digital information management. Learning about HDDs, file systems, data organization methods, and disc partitioning exposes a complex environment where efficacy, performance, and dependability are of the utmost importance. Bits, bytes, and file sizes are the fundamental building blocks of data organization, together with the other components of a hard disc.

File systems like FAT32, NTFS, and exFAT have complex structures and features that regulate how data is saved, read, and managed on storage devices, and we'll learn about all of them in this lesson. Storage efficiency and performance tradeoffs are discussed in light of an analysis of data organization options ranging from sequential to random access, fragmentation, and clustering. We then move on to disc partitioning, where we cover the fundamentals, such as the different types of partitions and the importance of the Master Boot Record (MBR) and GUID Partition Table (GPT). When designing these structures, factors like as storage capacity, device compatibility, and data redundancy are taken into account.

Finally, we look at how new technologies, such as Solid State Drives (SSDs) and cloud storage, are expanding our horizons for how we can manage our data. Faster, more reliable, and scalable storage solutions can be seen in the comparisons between solid-state drives (SSDs) and hard disc drives (HDDs), the complexities of data organization on SSDs, and the incorporation of cloud storage and remote data organization.

Understanding the concepts and trends in hard disc data management is not only a technical study; it is fundamental to modern computing due to the ever-changing nature of the data storage landscape. To keep data available, protected, and efficiently structured despite shifting computer paradigms, these findings can be used as a road map for designing storage structures that meet the expanding needs of digital ecosystems [61].

REFERENCES

[1]   H. Allioui, and Y. Mourdi, "Exploring the Full Potentials of IoT for Better Financial Growth and Stability: A Comprehensive Survey", *Sensors (Basel)*, vol. 23, no. 19, p. 8015, 2023.
[http://dx.doi.org/10.3390/s23198015] [PMID: 37836845]

[2]   T. Sterling, M. Brodowicz, and M. Anderson, *High performance computing: modern systems and practices*. Morgan Kaufmann, 2017.

[3]   K.D. Bowers, "How to tell if your cloud files are vulnerable to drive crashes", *Proceedings of the 18th ACM conference on Computer and communications security*, 2011.
[http://dx.doi.org/10.1145/2046707.2046766]

[4]   J. Lapum, J.E. Angus, E. Peter, and J. Watt-Watson, "Patients' narrative accounts of open-heart surgery and recovery: Authorial voice of technology", *Soc. Sci. Med.*, vol. 70, no. 5, pp. 754-762, 2010.
[http://dx.doi.org/10.1016/j.socscimed.2009.11.021] [PMID: 20042262]

[5]   O. Henfridsson, L. Mathiassen, and F. Svahn, "Managing technological change in the digital age: the role of architectural frames", *J. Inf. Technol.*, vol. 29, no. 1, pp. 27-43, 2014.
[http://dx.doi.org/10.1057/jit.2013.30]

[6]   E. Paul, *A History of Modern Computing. Second edition*, 1998.

[7]   K.C. Clarke, and L.J. Gaydos, "Loose-coupling a cellular automaton model and GIS: long-term urban growth prediction for San Francisco and Washington/Baltimore", *Int. J. Geogr. Inf. Sci.*, vol. 12, no. 7, pp. 699-714, 1998.
[http://dx.doi.org/10.1080/136588198241617] [PMID: 12294536]

[8]   A.L. Moorthy, and C. Karisiddappa, "Mass storage technologies for libraries & information centres", *DESIDOC J. Libr. Inf. Technol.*, vol. 20, no. 5, pp. 3-20, 2000.

[9]   Khang, A. (2023). "AI and IoT-Based Technologies for Precision Medicine". (1st Ed.). *IGI Global.*
       [http://dx.doi.org/10.4018/979-8-3693-0876-9]

[10]   K-D. Lehmann, "Making the transitory permanent: the intellectual heritage in a digitized world of
       knowledge", In: *in Books, Bricks and Bytes.* Routledge., 2017, pp. 307-330.
       [http://dx.doi.org/10.4324/9781315082073-18]

[11]   A. Kerr, *The business and culture of digital games.* The Business and Culture of Digital Games, 2006,
       pp. 1-192.
       [http://dx.doi.org/10.4135/9781446211410]

[12]   K. Osenga, "Information may want to be free, but information products do not: protecting and
       facilitating transactions in information products", *Cardozo Law Rev.,* vol. 30, p. 2099, 2008.

[13]   S.J. Andriole, "The Management Conversation-It Still Needs to Make Sense", In: *in The 2nd Digital
       Revolution.* IGI Global., 2005, pp. 143-216.
       [http://dx.doi.org/10.4018/978-1-59140-801-7.ch006]

[14]   B. Seth, S. Dalal, V. Jaglan, D-N. Le, S. Mohan, and G. Srivastava, "Integrating encryption techniques
       for secure data storage in the cloud", *Trans. Emerg. Telecommun. Technol.,* vol. 33, no. 4, p. e4108,
       2022.
       [http://dx.doi.org/10.1002/ett.4108]

[15]   P.H. Bucy, "Information as a Commodity in the Regulatory World", *Houst. Law Rev.,* vol. 39, p. 905,
       2002.

[16]   A. Khang, K. Singh, M. Yadav, and R.K. Yadav, "Minimizing the Waste Management Effort by Using
       Machine Learning Applications", In: *Revolutionizing Automated Waste Treatment Systems: IoT and
       Bioelectronics.* In Khang A., Hajimahmud V. A., Litvinova E., Musrat G. L., Avramovic Z. (Ed.). IGI
       Global, 2024, pp. 42-59.
       [http://dx.doi.org/10.4018/979-8-3693-6016-3.ch004]

[17]   P. Malik, "Governing big data: principles and practices", *IBM Journal of Research and Development,*
       vol. 57, no. 3/4, pp. 1: 1-1: 13, 2013.
       [http://dx.doi.org/10.1147/JRD.2013.2241359]

[18]   M. Campbell-Kelly, *Computer: A history of the information machine.* Taylor & Francis, 2023.
       [http://dx.doi.org/10.4324/9781003263272]

[19]   D. Vogel, and P. Baudisch, "Shift: a technique for operating pen-based interfaces using touch",
       Proceedings of the SIGCHI conference on Human factors in computing systems, 2007.
       [http://dx.doi.org/10.1145/1240624.1240727]

[20]   M. Guzman, A.M. Hein, and C. Welch, "Extremely long-duration storage concepts for space", *Acta
       Astronaut.,* vol. 130, pp. 128-136, 2017.
       [http://dx.doi.org/10.1016/j.actaastro.2016.10.007]

[21]   A. Khang, A.V. Hajimahmud, T. Triwiyanto, V.A. Abuzarova, and R.N. Ali, "Cloud Platform and
       Data Storage Systems in the Healthcare Ecosystem", In: *Medical Robotics and AI-Assisted
       Diagnostics for a High-Tech Healthcare Industry.,* A. Khang, Ed., IGI Global, 2024, pp. 343-356.
       [http://dx.doi.org/10.4018/979-8-3693-2105-8.ch021]

[22]   D. Nolan, and D. Temple Lang, "Computing in the statistics curricula", *Am. Stat.,* vol. 64, no. 2, pp.
       97-107, 2010.
       [http://dx.doi.org/10.1198/tast.2010.09132]

[23]   J. Lutterbie, *Toward a general theory of acting: Cognitive science and performance.* Springer, 2011.
       [http://dx.doi.org/10.1057/9780230119468]

[24]   J. William Toigo, "Avoiding a data crunch", *Sci. Am.,* vol. 282, no. 5, pp. 58-74, 64-67, 70-74, 2000.
       [http://dx.doi.org/10.1038/scientificamerican0500-58] [PMID: 11056990]

[25]   D.J. Worden, *Storage networks.* Springer, 2004.

[http://dx.doi.org/10.1007/978-1-4302-0694-1]

[26]   A. Clements, *Principles of computer hardware.* Oxford University Press: USA, 2006.

[27]   A. Basu, J.S. Mitchell, and G.K. Sabhnani, "Geometric algorithms for optimal airspace design and air traffic controller workload balancing", *Journal of Experimental Algorithmics (JEA),* vol. 14, pp. 2.3-2.28, 2010.

[28]   M. Brain, *How bits and bytes work.* 2000, 1. Available from: howstuffworks.com

[29]   J. Gallagher, "Fell–Muir Lecture: Heparan sulphate and the art of cell regulation: a polymer chain conducts the protein orchestra", *Int. J. Exp. Pathol.,* vol. 96, no. 4, pp. 203-231, 2015.
[http://dx.doi.org/10.1111/iep.12135] [PMID: 26173450]

[30]   A. Doricchi, C.M. Platnich, A. Gimpel, F. Horn, M. Earle, G. Lanzavecchia, A.L. Cortajarena, L.M. Liz-Marzán, N. Liu, R. Heckel, R.N. Grass, R. Krahne, U.F. Keyser, and D. Garoli, "Emerging approaches to DNA data storage: Challenges and prospects", *ACS Nano,* vol. 16, no. 11, pp. 17552-17571, 2022.
[http://dx.doi.org/10.1021/acsnano.2c06748] [PMID: 36256971]

[31]   W.A. Bhat, and S. Quadri, "Io bound property: a system perspective evaluation and behavior trace of file system", *Glob J Comput Sci Technol,* vol. 11, no. 5, pp. 57-70, 2011.

[32]   D.T. Meyer, *Storage system tracing and analysis.* University of British Columbia, 2015.

[33]   P. Gupta, and R. Verma, *File System Simulation.,* 2015.

[34]   J. Nievergelt, H. Hinterberger, and K.C. Sevcik, "The grid file: An adaptable, symmetric multikey file structure", *ACM Trans. Database Syst.,* vol. 9, no. 1, pp. 38-71, 1984. [TODS].
[http://dx.doi.org/10.1145/348.318586]

[35]   S. Brands, *Rethinking public key infrastructures and digital certificates: building in privacy.* Mit Press, 2000.
[http://dx.doi.org/10.7551/mitpress/5931.001.0001]

[36]   SERIES, W.T., *Windows File System Troubleshooting.*

[37]   C.L. Philip Chen, and C.Y. Zhang, "Data-intensive applications, challenges, techniques and technologies: A survey on Big Data", *Inf. Sci.,* vol. 275, pp. 314-347, 2014.
[http://dx.doi.org/10.1016/j.ins.2014.01.015]

[38]   L. Manovich, "Database as symbolic form", *Convergence (London),* vol. 5, no. 2, pp. 80-99, 1999.
[http://dx.doi.org/10.1177/135485659900500206]

[39]   T. Kolajo, O. Daramola, and A. Adebiyi, "Big data stream analysis: a systematic literature review", *J. Big Data,* vol. 6, no. 1, p. 47, 2019.
[http://dx.doi.org/10.1186/s40537-019-0210-7]

[40]   D.H. Lawrie, "Access and alignment of data in an array processor", *IEEE Trans. Comput.,* vol. C-24, no. 12, pp. 1145-1155, 1975.
[http://dx.doi.org/10.1109/T-C.1975.224157]

[41]   S. Idreos, "The data calculator: Data structure design and cost synthesis from first principles and learned cost models", *Proceedings of the 2018 International Conference on Management of Data,* 2018.
[http://dx.doi.org/10.1145/3183713.3199671]

[42]   J.S. Meena, S.M. Sze, U. Chand, and T.Y. Tseng, "Overview of emerging nonvolatile memory technologies", *Nanoscale Res. Lett.,* vol. 9, no. 1, p. 526, 2014.
[http://dx.doi.org/10.1186/1556-276X-9-526] [PMID: 25278820]

[43]   D. Cash, "Dynamic searchable encryption in very-large databases: Data structures and implementation", *Cryptology ePrint Archive,* 2014.
[http://dx.doi.org/10.14722/ndss.2014.23264]

[44]   B. Salzberg, and V.J. Tsotras, "Comparison of access methods for time-evolving data", *ACM Comput. Surv.,* vol. 31, no. 2, pp. 158-221, 1999.
[http://dx.doi.org/10.1145/319806.319816]

[45]   T. Makatos, "ZBD: Using transparent compression at the block level to increase storage space efficiency", *2010 International Workshop on Storage Network Architecture and Parallel I/Os,* IEEE., 2010.
[http://dx.doi.org/10.1109/SNAPI.2010.15]

[46]   H. H. Khanh, and A. Khang, "The Role of Artificial Intelligence in Blockchain Applications", *Reinventing Manufacturing and Business Processes through Artificial Intelligence,* vol. 2, In Rana G, Khang A., Sharma R., Goel A. K., Dubey A. K. CRC Press, pp. 20-40, 2021.
[http://dx.doi.org/10.1201/9781003145011-2]

[47]   C. Ji, "An Empirical Study of {File-System} Fragmentation in Mobile Storage Systems", *8th USENIX Workshop on Hot Topics in Storage and File Systems (HotStorage 16),* 2016.

[48]   S. Dillon, "Hide and seek: concealing and recovering hard disk data", *James Madison University Infosec Techreport,* vol. 35, p. 17, 2006.

[49]   Ç.H. Şekercioğlu, P.R. Ehrlich, G.C. Daily, D. Aygen, D. Goehring, and R.F. Sandí, "Disappearance of insectivorous birds from tropical forest fragments", *Proc. Natl. Acad. Sci. USA,* vol. 99, no. 1, pp. 263-267, 2002.
[http://dx.doi.org/10.1073/pnas.012616199] [PMID: 11782549]

[50]   A. Khang, V. Abdullayev, A.V. Alyar, M. Khalilov, and B. Murad, "AI-Aided Data Analytics Tools and Applications for the Healthcare Sector", In: *AI and IoT-Based Technologies for Precision Medicine.,* A. Khang, Ed., IGI Global, 2023, pp. 295-313.
[http://dx.doi.org/10.4018/979-8-3693-0876-9.ch018]

[51]   J. Park, and Y.I. Eom, "Fragpicker: A new defragmentation tool for modern storage devices", *Proceedings of the ACM SIGOPS 28th Symposium on Operating Systems Principles,* 2021.
[http://dx.doi.org/10.1145/3477132.3483593]

[52]   W. Wang, *Storage management for large scale systems.,* 2004.

[53]   A. Thomson, "Calvin: fast distributed transactions for partitioned database systems", *Proceedings of the 2012 ACM SIGMOD international conference on management of data,* 2012.
[http://dx.doi.org/10.1145/2213836.2213838]

[54]   E. Bugnion, S. Devine, K. Govil, and M. Rosenblum, "Disco", *ACM Trans. Comput. Syst.,* vol. 15, no. 4, pp. 412-447, 1997. [TOCS].
[http://dx.doi.org/10.1145/265924.265930]

[55]   K. Birman, D. Freedman, Q. Huang, and P. Dowell, "Overcoming cap with consistent soft-state replication", *Computer,* vol. 45, no. 2, pp. 50-58, 2012.
[http://dx.doi.org/10.1109/MC.2011.387]

[56]   P. Scheuermann, G. Weikum, and P. Zabback, "Data partitioning and load balancing in parallel disk systems", *VLDB J.,* vol. 7, no. 1, pp. 48-66, 1998.
[http://dx.doi.org/10.1007/s007780050053]

[57]   W. De Jonge, M.F. Kaashoek, and W.C. Hsieh, "The logical disk: A new approach to improving file systems", *Proceedings of the fourteenth ACM symposium on Operating systems principles,* 1993.
[http://dx.doi.org/10.1145/168619.168621]

[58]   E. Akbal, Ö.F. Yakut, S. Dogan, T. Tuncer, and F. Ertam, "A Digital Forensics Approach for Lost Secondary Partition Analysis using Master Boot Record Structured Hard Disk Drives", *Sakarya University Journal of Computer and Information Sciences,* vol. 4, no. 3, pp. 326-346, 2021.
[http://dx.doi.org/10.35377/saucis...1022600]

[59]   P.T.N. Anh, "Vladimir Hahanov, Triwiyanto, Ragimova Nazila Ali, Rashad İsmibeyli, Hajimahmud

V. A., Abuzarova Vusala Alyar. "AI Models for Disease Diagnosis and Prediction of Heart Disease with Artificial Neural Networks", In: *Khang, A., Abdullayev, V., Hrybiuk, O., & Shukla, A.K., Computer Vision and AI-integrated IoT Technologies in Medical Ecosystem.* 1st ed. CRC Press, 2024. [http://dx.doi.org/10.1201/9781003429609-9]

[60]   V. Nagori, and V. Varadarajan, "Quantum Computing Posing a Challenge to the Businesses. International Journal of Research in Engineering", *Science and Management,* vol. 6, no. 1, pp. 52-55, 2023.

[61]   A. Khang, V. Hahanov, G.L. Abbas, and V.A. Hajimahmud, "Cyber-Physical-Social System and İncident Management", In: *AI-Centric Smart City Ecosystems: Technologies, Design and Implementation (1st Ed.)* vol. 2. CRC Press, 2022, p. 15. [http://dx.doi.org/10.1201/9781003252542-2]

CHAPTER 6

Common Cases of Partition Recovery

Heena Dhiman[1]**, Rajneesh Gujral**[1]**, Rajesh Khanna**[1]**, Neelam Oberoi**[1]**, Sachin Dhiman**[2]**, Rohini Tewatia**[3] **and Manni Rohilla**[2]

[1] *M.M. College of Engineering, Maharishi Markandeshwar (Deemed to be University), Mullana, Ambala, Haryana, India*

[2] *Chitkara College of Pharmacy, Chitkara University, Rajpura, Punjab, India*

[3] *Mahamaya Government Polytechnic of Information Technology, Hariharpur, Khajani, Gorakhpur, Uttar Pradesh, India*

Abstract: A number of automatic operations are carried out by partition recovery tools in an effort to repair damaged or erased partitions and/or recover data from them. A deleted partition results in the removal of its entry from the partition table. The data has not been erased from the disc, even if it looks intimidating that a whole information partition is no longer visible. In essence, eliminating the partition is like taking out a book's table of contents—all the material that is not on the table is still there; you simply need to use different techniques to locate it. Partition recovery tools can be useful in this situation. Partition table entry restoration is the process of looking across the disc space for a missing partition or a boot sector. It will contain all the data required to recreate the partition table entry by locating the partition boot sector. You can restore the boot sector to recover the volume because both FAT32 and NTFS drives keep backup boot sectors. Partition table entry reconstruction involves looking across the disc space for a partition boot sector or data from destroyed partition information. There are numerous tools for partition recovery that can be used to recover data that was accidentally erased or damaged to the partition. These tools have different features that can make the process of restoring data easier.

Keywords: Cyber Attacks, Corruption, Data Retrieval, Hardware, Malware, Partition, Recovery.

INTRODUCTION

Background

Within the domain of digital investigations, forensic examiners frequently face the significant obstacle of partition loss on storage systems. A partition is a crucial

---

* **Corresponding author Heena Dhiman:** M.M. College of Engineering, Maharishi Markandeshwar (Deemed to be University), Mullana, Ambala, Haryana, India; E-mail: dhimanheena001@gmail.com

element of any storage medium, functioning as a logical divide that arranges and stores data. Accidental deletion, corruption, or formatting of partitions can lead to the loss of important evidence that is crucial for forensic examinations. It is essential for forensic investigators to comprehend the complexities of partition loss and employ effective recovery methods in order to retrieve vital information from storage devices. Partition loss can result from a wide range of circumstances, including unintentional user actions and malicious interventions. Partition loss can occur due to several factors such as accidental deletion, disk formatting, partition table corruption, hardware malfunctions, software mistakes, and virus attacks [1]. Forensic examiners face distinct obstacles in recovering lost partitions and the crucial data they hold in each of these instances. The absence of partitions can greatly complicate forensic investigations, obstructing the recovery of crucial evidence and jeopardizing the integrity of the examination process. Lack of access to vital data contained in missing partitions might impede investigators in their efforts to recreate digital timelines, identify culprits, or establish the chronological order of events pertinent to the case at hand [2]. Furthermore, the incapacity to retrieve lost partitions could compromise the acceptability and reliability of evidence in court processes.

Purpose of Partition Recovery

Partition recovery in computer forensics serves multiple purposes and is crucial for effectively investigating digital occurrences. The main objectives of partition recovery in computer forensics are as follows:

1. Data Retrieval: The primary objective of partition recovery is to recover data that has been lost, erased, or is not accessible, and is contained within partitions on storage devices. Essential digital evidence for forensic investigations can be found in lost or destroyed partitions, encompassing many types of data such as documents, emails, photos, videos, system logs, and metadata. Forensic examiners can retrieve and extract significant evidence related to the inquiry by restoring lost partitions.
2. Evidence Preservation: Preserving the integrity of digital evidence is of utmost importance, and partition recovery is a vital component in achieving this goal. If partitions are lost or erased, there is a potential for data corruption or overwriting, particularly if the storage device is still being utilized. Forensic examiners reduce the possibility of data loss or modification and maintain the integrity and admissibility of evidence in judicial proceedings by rapidly retrieving lost partitions.
3. Reconstruction of Digital Timelines: The reconstruction of digital timelines involves recovering lost or deleted partitions that may include valuable historical data pertaining to the sequence of digital events being investigated.

Forensic investigators can develop timelines of user activity, system events, file updates, and conversations by reconstructing missing partitions and examining the data contained within them [3]. An accurate chronological reconstruction is crucial for comprehending the order of events and assigning actions to particular individuals or entities.

4. Identification of Malicious Activities: Malicious actions can be identified and analyzed through the use of partition recovery, which allows forensic investigators to detect and examine evidence of cyber assaults, data breaches, or insider threats. Restored partitions may contain traces of malicious software, unauthorized intrusion attempts, or data theft operations. Through the analysis of retrieved data, forensic examiners can ascertain the characteristics and extent of security events and identify the individuals or entities responsible for them.

5. Support for Legal Proceedings: Recovered partitions and their data are vital evidence in legal procedures, such as criminal investigations, civil litigation, and regulatory compliance problems. The retrieved data can be utilized to confirm or contradict assertions, determine responsibility, or exhibit adherence to legal obligations. Thoroughly established procedures for recovering partitions and conducting forensic examinations guarantee the acceptability and reliability of evidence in a court of law [4].

UNDERSTANDING PARTITION LOSS

Partition loss presents substantial obstacles to forensic investigations, requiring a sophisticated comprehension of its origins, consequences, and methods of recovery. This chapter seeks to provide forensic practitioners with the necessary knowledge and strategies to minimize the effects of partition loss and achieve favorable results in digital examinations. Partition loss in computer forensics can arise from various factors, each carrying its consequences for digital investigations [5].

Causes of Partition Loss

Partition loss in computer forensics can arise from diverse sources, each with its consequences for digital investigations. Below are a few prevalent factors that might lead to partition loss in computer forensic situations:

• Accidental Deletion: Human mistakes are frequently responsible for the loss of partitions. Novice users or system administrators may unintentionally erase partitions when attempting to carry out disk management operations.

• Disk Formatting: The process of formatting a storage device involves completely erasing all previous data, including any partition information. Although disk formatting is typically done purposefully to prepare a drive for usage or to address disk-related problems, it can also lead to partition loss if done accidentally or without sufficient backup precautions.

- Partition Table Corruption: The partition table, which is an important data structure that holds information about the arrangement and properties of partitions on a disk, can be damaged as a result of different events including software mistakes, disk failures, or malware attacks.
- Malware or Cyber Attacks: Malware or cyber-attacks have the ability to specifically target storage devices, resulting in the loss of partitions as a result of their harmful payload [6]. Ransomware can encrypt or rewrite partition data, making the partitions inaccessible.
- Hardware Failures: Hardware failures, such as physical damage or malfunction of storage devices, can result in the loss of partitions. Failures in hard disk drives, such as head crashes, motor failures, or platter damage, can result in partitions being unreadable or sectors carrying partition data becoming inaccessible.
- Software Errors and System Crashes: Software problems, defects, or system crashes have the potential to interrupt disk operations and result in the loss of partitions. Data corruption or partition structure damage may occur due to unforeseen system shutdowns or program conflicts, leading to the loss of partitions.
- User Mismanagement: Inadequate disk management techniques by users, such as inappropriate resizing of partitions, repartitioning, or altering disk structures without sufficient understanding or precautions, can result in the loss of partitions

Impact on Data

The consequences of partition loss on data in computer forensics can be substantial and diverse. The following are important consequences of partition loss on data within the context of forensic investigations:

- Data Accessibility: The main consequence of partition loss is the inability to access the data stored in the affected partitions. The data may contain crucial evidence pertinent to the investigation, such as papers, emails, photos, videos, system logs, and metadata.
- Data Integrity: Data integrity can be compromised when a partition loss occurs, potentially affecting the integrity of the data stored on the afflicted storage device. If partitions get lost or corrupted, there is a potential for data loss or overwriting, particularly if the storage device remains in operation.
- Evidence Preservation: The loss of partitions presents difficulties in maintaining the integrity of digital evidence. In the absence of timely recovery measures, there is a potential for data loss or modification, which could compromise the reliability and acceptability of evidence in legal proceedings.

- Timeline Reconstruction: In the case that partitions are lost or erased, they may include vital data that is important for the reconstruction of digital timelines pertaining to the investigation. Partition loss can impede the process of determining the chronological order of user activities, system events, file revisions, and communications.
- Attribution of Actions: The loss of partition might hinder the process of attributing activities to particular individuals or entities involved in the investigation. Lack of access to pertinent data stored on inaccessible partitions might pose challenges for forensic investigators in identifying culprits, establishing motives, or ascertaining culpability.
- Case Resolution: The consequences of partition loss on data can eventually impact the outcome of the forensic inquiry. The inability to recover lost partitions or retrieve crucial material may lead to partial or inconclusive findings, hence restricting the capacity to establish definitive conclusions [7].

The loss of a partition in computer forensics can have significant consequences for the accessibility, integrity, preservation of evidence, reconstruction of timelines, attribution of acts, and settlement of a case. Forensic examiners must acknowledge the importance of partition loss and utilize suitable recovery methods to minimize its effects and enable the effective conclusion of digital investigations [29].

Signs of Partition Loss

Identifying indications of partition loss is essential in the field of computer forensics as it helps to recognize any problems with storage devices and take suitable recovery actions. Below are a few typical indications of partition loss that forensic investigators may face during their examinations:

- An unmistakable indication of partition loss is the existence of unallocated space on a storage device.
- Forensic investigators may come across drives or partitions that seem to be inaccessible or absent from the file explorer of the operating system.
- Forensic examiners may observe that drives or partitions that were formerly reachable through particular drive letters are either no longer visible or have been assigned alternative letters.
- Encountering file system failures while performing disk activities, such as file system corruption or inconsistencies, can suggest the presence of underlying problems with partition structures [4].
- Examining disk management programs or forensic imaging tools can uncover irregularities that suggest the loss of a partition.
- If files and folders on a storage device disappear suddenly and without any

action from the user, it could indicate a possible loss of partition.

• Partition loss often manifests as a corruption of the partition table, a vital data structure responsible for storing information about disk partitions.

• Deviant disk performance, such as sluggish read/write speeds, atypical disk activity, or system failures during disk operations, could suggest fundamental problems with partition structures or integrity.

It is crucial for forensic examiners to identify these indications of partition loss in order to promptly commence partition recovery procedures and reduce the potential for data loss or corruption. Through early identification of potential issues during the investigative process, examiners can proactively take measures to maintain the integrity of evidence and enhance the likelihood of successful forensic exams [2].

TOOLS AND TECHNIQUES

Data recovery from storage devices in computer forensics involves the utilization of a range of tools and procedures. The utilization of these tools and procedures is imperative for the retrieval of data that has been destroyed, lost, or corrupted. This data may potentially contain vital evidence that is crucial for forensic investigations.

Overview of Recovery Tools

Tools and procedures are essential in data recovery endeavors during computer forensic investigations. Forensic examiners utilize these tools to retrieve erased files, reconstruct disk configurations, analyze disk images, and extract crucial evidence required for comprehensive forensic investigations. In the field of computer forensics, a range of tools and techniques are employed to recover data from storage devices. The utilization of these tools and approaches is imperative for the retrieval of deleted, lost, or corrupted data, which may encompass significant evidence for forensic investigations [8]. Below are many frequently utilized tools and methodologies for data recovery in the field of computer forensics:

Forensic Imaging Tools

• dd is a command-line tool found on Unix-like operating systems, which is used to generate forensic disk images. This software has the capability to generate exact replicas of storage devices, such as hard disks, SSDs, and portable media, by copying every single piece of data. dc3dd is an upgraded version of the dd program that offers further functionalities including hashing, error logging, and progress monitoring while performing disk imaging. FTK Imager is a software application created by AccessData that allows users to create exact copies of computer disks and analyze their contents using a graphical interface. Forensic examiners can utilize this tool to generate forensic images of storage devices and scrutinize disk architectures, partitions, and file systems.

Data Recovery Software

- EnCase Forensic is a popular software suite for forensic investigations, developed by Guidance Software (now OpenText). The software incorporates functionalities for collecting data, duplicating hard drives, extracting specific files, and examining digital evidence. Recuva is a data recovery application that was developed by Piriform, which is now a part of Avast. It is known for its user-friendly interface. This software has the ability to retrieve lost files from a wide range of storage media, including hard disks, SSDs, memory cards, and USB drives. PhotoRec is a data recovery program that is part of the TestDisk package and uses the command-line interface. Our expertise lies in the retrieval of lost files, encompassing various types such as documents, images, movies, and archives, from partitions that have been damaged or formatted [9].

File Carving Tools

- Foremost is a command-line tool specifically developed for file carving. Its purpose is to retrieve files by analyzing their file headers, footers, and internal data structures. This software has the capability to handle a diverse array of file formats and is capable of retrieving files that have been erased or fragmented from disk images. Scalpel is a command-line tool used for file recovery. It operates by identifying files using their signatures and metadata patterns. Forensic examiners can utilize this feature to establish personalized file carving guidelines and retrieve targeted file formats from storage devices.

Partition Recovery Tools

- TestDisk is a robust program used for recovering lost or deleted partitions and restoring corrupted partition tables. This software is capable of accommodating a diverse array of file systems and can be utilized to reconstruct partition configurations on storage devices. The EaseUS Data Recovery Wizard is a user-friendly software designed for data recovery. It offers several tools to recover lost partitions, formatted disks, and erased files. The software is compatible with a wide range of file systems and storage devices, such as hard disks, solid-state drives (SSDs), and external drives [7].

Memory Forensics Tools

- Volatility is a widely used open-source framework for studying volatile memory dumps, namely those from RAM. The software encompasses a diverse array of plugins that facilitate the extraction of process information, network connections, registry keys, and several other artifacts from memory pictures. Rekall is an open-source memory forensics framework that bears a resemblance to volatility. The software offers tools for examining memory dumps and extracting valuable forensic evidence, including processes, kernel modules, and user-level items.

Database Recovery Tools

- The SQL Server Recovery Manager is a software solution created by SysTools that specializes in retrieving data from SQL Server databases that have been corrupted or destroyed. It has the capability to restore database files, retrieve data, and export the recovered data in multiple formats. Stellar Repair for MySQL is a specialist program designed to fix faulty or unavailable MySQL database files. This software has the capability to restore tables, views, triggers, and other database objects from MySQL databases that have been corrupted.

Data Backup Strategies

Data backup solutions are crucial in computer forensics to guarantee the preservation and integrity of digital data. The purpose of these solutions is to generate dependable and confirmable replicas of data that can be utilized for forensic examination and inquiry [10]. Below are several primary data backup mechanisms frequently utilized in computer forensics:

- Full disk imaging is the process of generating a precise replica of the entire storage device, including all partitions, file systems, and unallocated space, by copying every single bit. This complete backup method guarantees the preservation of all data, including files that have been erased or concealed, for the purpose of forensic examination. Specialized forensic imaging programs, such as dd, FTK Imager, or EnCase Forensic, are commonly used for whole disk imaging.
- Incremental backups exclusively entail the preservation of alterations or revisions made to the initial data since the previous backup. This approach minimizes the duration and storage capacity needed for backups, as it solely duplicates newly added or altered data. Incremental backups in computer forensics are employed to record alterations made to evidence files or storage devices over a period of time. This enables forensic examiners to monitor adjustments and scrutinize digital artifacts.

- Verified hashing is the process of creating cryptographic hash values, such as MD5, SHA-1, and SHA-256, for both the original material and its backup copies. The hash values function as digital fingerprints that can be employed to authenticate and ensure the integrity of the backup data. Forensic examiners can verify the integrity of backup copies by comparing the hash values before and after backup processes, thus ensuring that the original data remains unaltered and free from corruption [7].
- Offsite backup storage refers to the practice of storing duplicate copies of data at locations that are physically far from the original data sources. This approach guarantees the presence of backup copies and the ability to recover from disasters, as the backups are shielded from physical harm, theft, or natural calamities that may impact the main data storage location. Offsite backup storage in computer forensics reduces the likelihood of data loss caused by unexpected incidents and strengthens the effectiveness of preserving forensic data.
- Chain of Custody recording: The recording of the chain of custody is crucial for preserving the integrity and acceptability of backup copies as forensic evidence. Forensic investigators are required to meticulously record every stage of backup activities, encompassing the procurement, retention, conveyance, and retrieval of backup data. Chain of custody documentation establishes a transparent record of individuals who have viewed the backup copies, together with the timing and reason for their access. This documentation guarantees accountability and dependability in forensic investigations.
- To safeguard backup data against illegal access, modification, or disclosure, it is essential to employ encryption and access controls. Forensic investigators ought to employ encryption methods and secure storage mechanisms to protect backup copies while they are being transported and stored. Access controls, such as role-based permissions and multi-factor authentication, serve to deter unauthorized personnel from tampering with or gaining access to critical forensic data.
- Consistent Testing and Validation: Consistent testing and validation of backup methods are imperative to guarantee the dependability and efficiency of data backup techniques. Forensic examiners should regularly conduct tests on backup restoration methods to confirm the successful restoration and accessibility of backup copies when required. Validation tests should encompass the verification of hash values, integrity checks, and the authentication of chain of custody documentation to guarantee adherence to forensic standards and optimal methodologies [11].

Importance of Regular Maintenance

Regular maintenance is vital in computer forensics to uphold the functionality of forensic tools and equipment, prevent data corruption or loss, comply with forensic standards, optimize forensic workflows, mitigate security risks, prevent equipment failure or downtime, promote professional development, and safeguard the integrity of forensic evidence. Regular maintenance is crucial for forensic teams to maintain the utmost professionalism, integrity, and excellence in their forensic examinations and investigations [12]. The significance of regular maintenance in computer forensics can be emphasized through the following reasons:

- Performing routine maintenance ensures the preservation of the functioning and dependability of forensic instruments, hardware, and equipment utilized in investigations.
- Forensic teams can optimize investigation procedures by identifying and resolving bottlenecks, inefficiencies, or outmoded practices.
- It ensures the authenticity and dependability of forensic evidence during the full process of forensic investigation.
- It promotes ongoing professional growth and the improvement of skills among forensic examiners.
- To mitigate the potential for data breaches, malware infections, or unauthorized access to sensitive forensic information, forensic examiners can minimize these risks by consistently updating software, firmware, and security patches.
- It aids in averting equipment malfunctions or interruptions during crucial phases of forensic investigations [7].

COMMON SCENARIOS

Partition recovery is a frequently used technique in computer forensics that focuses on recovering damaged or deleted partitions on storage devices in order to retrieve vital data for forensic examination. Partition recovery may be required in computer forensic investigations due to many circumstances. Presented below are a few typical situations:

Accidental Deletion of Partitions

Partitions can be inadvertently deleted by users or system administrators during disk management operations, such as partition formatting or resizing. Inadvertent deletion may result in the loss of vital data stored in the deleted partitions, necessitating forensic examiners to conduct partition recovery in order to restore the missing data.

Corrupted Partition Tables

Corruption of the partition table, a crucial data structure responsible for storing information about disk partitions, has the potential to make partitions inaccessible or undetectable by the operating system. Partition table corruption can arise from a range of sources, including software glitches, disk malfunctions, or malicious software assaults. Forensic examiners may be required to do partition recovery in order to recreate the partition table and retrieve lost partitions and data.

Formatting Errors

Mistakes made during disk formatting procedures, such as formatting the incorrect drive or choosing the inappropriate file system type, can lead to the inadvertent deletion of partitions and data. Forensic investigators may come across situations where partitions are unintentionally formatted or reformatted, requiring partition recovery to retrieve the lost data and restore the original partition structure [28].

Operating System Failures

Operating system failure frequently occurs in computer forensic investigations, presenting difficulties associated with data loss, corruption, system instability, and security breaches. Forensic examiners must possess the necessary skills to properly tackle these issues by utilizing specific procedures, tools, and methodologies for the retrieval, analysis, and preservation of data and evidence. To limit risks, maintain the integrity of forensic examinations, and assist successful resolution of digital investigations, forensic examiners should have a comprehensive awareness of common operating system failure scenarios [13].

STEP-BY-STEP RECOVERY PROCESS

The recovery procedure in computer forensics entails a methodical approach to collecting and safeguarding digital information from storage devices. Below is a systematic roadmap outlining the sequential steps involved in the recovery process of computer forensic investigations.

Assessment and Analysis

Evaluation and analysis are essential elements of the data recovery process in computer forensics. They encompass assessing the type of data loss or corruption, comprehending the root reasons, and devising a proficient data recovery plan.

- Commence with acquiring pertinent details on the data loss occurrence, encompassing the specific storage medium impacted, the surrounding circumstances of the loss, and any preliminary observations or suspicions.

- Evaluate the extent and gravity of the data loss, taking into account elements such as the amount of data impacted, the significance of the lost data for the inquiry, and any possible hazards or implications.
- Determine the storage device(s) or media that hold the lost or corrupted data, such as hard disk drives (HDDs), solid-state drives (SSDs), USB drives, or memory cards.
- Ascertain the magnitude of the data loss, encompassing the impacted partitions, file systems, or individual files, and ascertain whether any data remains accessible or undamaged.
- Examine the characteristics of the data loss or corruption, taking into account potential factors such as unintentional removal, file system impairment, partition table impairment, hardware malfunction, or malicious actions [14].

Choosing the Right Recovery Tool

When it comes to computer forensics, picking the appropriate recovery tool is of utmost importance in order to efficiently retrieve lost or corrupted data while maintaining the integrity of the evidence. Here are a few essential factors to consider when choosing a recovery program:

- Storage Device Compatibility: Verify that the recovery tool is capable of working with the specific storage devices used in the investigation, including hard disk drives (HDDs), solid-state drives (SSDs), USB drives, memory cards, and network-attached storage (NAS) devices.
- File System Compatibility: Ensure that the recovery tool is compatible with the file system(s) employed on the storage device(s), encompassing prevalent file systems like NTFS, FAT32, exFAT, HFS+, APFS, Ext4, and other similar systems. The program must possess the capability to effectively manage diverse file system structures and metadata in order to efficiently recover data.
- Data Recovery Capabilities: Evaluate the tool's data recovery capabilities, encompassing its proficiency in retrieving deleted files, recovering lost partitions, restoring formatted disks, and repairing corrupted data. Here, we search for functionalities such as file carving, partition recovery, raw data extraction, and sophisticated scanning techniques.
- Forensic Features: Select a recovery tool that possesses forensic capabilities specifically developed to safeguard the integrity of evidence and uphold the chain of custody. Search for features that include write-blocking capabilities, read-only modes, hash verification, metadata preservation, and compatibility with forensic imaging standards like Advanced Forensic Format (AFF) or Expert Witness Compression Format (EWF).

- User Interface and Usability Assessment: Assess the tool's user interface and simplicity of use, taking into account variables such as intuitive navigation, explicit instructions, and user-friendly functionalities. The tool should enable streamlined data retrieval processes, even for users with restricted technical proficiency [15].

Executing the Recovery

Executing the recovery procedure is a crucial step in computer forensics for extracting evidence from digital devices while preserving the integrity of the data. Below is a comprehensive overview of the recovery procedure:

- **File Carving:** File carving methodologies are used to extract files from unallocated space or fragmented disk sectors. This approach is beneficial in cases where the metadata of the file system is absent or damaged.
- **Real-time Analysis:** In certain situations, it may be imperative to do real-time analysis of operational systems in order to get ephemeral data such as active processes, network connections, and system logs.
- **Reconstruction:** Fractured or damaged files are restored to get viable evidence.
- **Password Recovery**: Password recovery tools and methodologies are utilized to gain entry into encrypted files or secured sections [6].

Verifying Recovered Data

Verification and Validation

The integrity of the retrieved data is authenticated by juxtaposing it with the original evidence to ascertain its unaltered and uncorrupted state post-recovery. The retrieved data is substantiated by cross-referencing it with alternative sources of evidence and supplementary analysis is conducted to corroborate its pertinence to the case.

Documentation and Reporting

We record in detail every action performed during the recovery procedure, encompassing the used tools, implemented methodologies, and achieved outcomes. An elaborated report isgenerated that outlines the results of the recovery procedure, encompassing all retrieved material, its relevance to the case, and any suggestions for additional investigation or analysis.

Legal Considerations

Comply with legal and ethical protocols during the recovery process, ensuring that all actions are carried out in a way that maintains the evidence's admissibility in court. Maintain a record of custody for all retrieved evidence, documenting its handling and storage to establish its integrity and dependability in legal proceedings.

PREVENTIVE MEASURES

Preserving data partition integrity is of utmost importance in computer forensics to safeguard critical evidence from being damaged or lost during investigations. Establish a resilient backup plan to consistently safeguard all essential data, including partitions, files, and system configurations. Backups must be securely kept and periodically verified to verify their integrity and efficacy in recovering data in the case of partition loss [3]. Prior to doing any analysis or investigation methods, it is imperative to generate forensic disk images of storage media. Disk imaging is the process of creating a precise duplicate of the complete disk, which includes all partitions, file systems, and unallocated space. These images function as a safe, non-modifiable duplicate of the original evidence and can be utilized for data retrieval in the event that the original partition becomes inaccessible or damaged. Adopt optimal strategies for partition management to reduce the likelihood of partition loss or corruption. This entails ensuring that partitions are correctly formatted, use dependable partitioning tools, and refraining from undertaking perilous actions like as resizing or relocating partitions without sufficient backups and safeguards in position.

Best Practices for Partition Management

Partition management is a critical aspect of computer forensics, as it directly impacts the organization and preservation of digital evidence. Here are some best practices for partition management in computer forensics:

- Record the initial arrangement of partitions, file systems, and disk structure prior to making any modifications. This documentation functions as a point of reference and guarantees that investigators possess a lucid comprehension of the original condition of the storage media.
- Whenever feasible, employ forensic disk images or write-protected duplicates of storage media to avert inadvertent modifications or contamination of partitions. This guarantees that the initial evidence remains unaltered and can be presented as valid in a court of law.
- Do not alter the original evidence unless it is absolutely essential. Any alterations made to the initial data have the potential to undermine its integrity and suitability as evidence in judicial proceedings.
- Reduce Write Operations on Storage Media: They decrease the frequency of write operations on storage media to mitigate the potential for data corruption or unintended alterations to partitions. To prevent illegal modifications to evidence

drives, it is advisable to employ write-blocking hardware or software.

- Employ forensically sound partitioning tools: Employ partitioning tools and software that are expressly created for use in forensic investigations, ensuring their adherence to established forensic standards. These technologies guarantee that partitioning activities are carried out in a way that safeguards the integrity of the evidence and adheres to legal norms.

- Generate Forensic Disk Images: Prior to engaging in any partitioning or analysis, generate forensic disk images encompassing the entirety of the storage media, encompassing all partitions and unallocated space. These photographs function as a reliable and verifiable duplicate of the initial evidence and can be utilized for examination without jeopardizing alterations to the original data.

- Validate the integrity of forensic disk images by employing checksums or hash values to ascertain that they have not undergone any modifications or corruption during the imaging procedure. The purpose of this verification phase is to uphold the dependability and acceptability of the evidence in a court of law.

- Record any alterations performed on partitions, such as resizing, deleting, or creating new partitions. Document the date, time, and objective of every alteration, along with the tools or software employed to carry out the partitioning tasks.

- Ensure a transparent chain of custody for all storage media and forensic photographs, meticulously documenting the handling, storage, and transfer of evidence throughout the investigation. This guarantees the responsibility and honesty of the evidence and confirms its eligibility for use in legal proceedings.

- Seek advice from seasoned forensic professionals or talk with colleagues to ensure that partition management actions are carried out in compliance with optimal procedures and legal obligations [5].

Regular Backups and Maintenance

Regular backups and maintenance are crucial components of computer forensic methods to guarantee the integrity, availability, and dependability of digital evidence. Below is an elaborate summary of each:

Regular Backups

- Preservation of Evidence: Consistently creating backups guarantees the safeguarding of digital evidence. To mitigate the risk of inadvertent loss, corruption, or tampering, investigators can create backup copies of forensic pictures or original data.

- Data loss protection: Backups alleviate the potential for data loss resulting from hardware malfunctions, software glitches, or criminal actions. Forensic examiners can retrieve data in the event of system crashes or other unexpected situations by keeping current backups [16].

- Redundancy and Fault Tolerance: By using redundant backup techniques, such as offsite storage or cloud-based backups, one can boost fault tolerance and guarantee data availability, even in the event of catastrophic occurrences like natural catastrophes or physical damage to storage media.
- Chain of Custody Documentation: Backup operations must be meticulously recorded, including precise information such as the date and time of backups, the specific contents of each backup, and the personnel accountable for executing the backups. This documentation verifies the sequence of possession and ensures the reliability of the evidence.
- Periodic testing and verification are essential to maintain the integrity of backups and their effective restoration when necessary. Regular testing facilitates the detection and resolution of any problems with the backup procedure, guaranteeing the dependability and comprehensiveness of backup copies.
- Compliance with Legal and Regulatory Requirements: Numerous jurisdictions and regulatory frameworks need enterprises to preserve backups of sensitive data to meet compliance obligations. Strict compliance with legal and regulatory obligations surrounding the preservation and retention of data is of utmost importance in forensic investigations.

Maintenance

- Disk Health Monitoring: Routine maintenance entails monitoring the condition and efficiency of storage devices utilized for keeping digital data. Utilizing disk health monitoring systems enables the detection of initial indications of disk failure or deterioration, empowering forensic examiners to proactively implement actions to reduce risks.
- File System Integrity Checks: Performing regular file system integrity checks is essential to maintain the coherence and dependability of stored data. File system analysis tools have the capability to detect and rectify faults in file systems, thereby averting the risk of data corruption or loss.
- Software Updates and Patch Management: Regularly upgrading forensic software tools and operating systems with the latest patches and security updates is crucial for preserving system integrity and safeguarding against potential vulnerabilities that may be exploited by attackers.
- Hardware Maintenance: It is important to frequently maintain hardware components used for forensic analysis, such as write-blocking devices, forensic workstations, and imaging hardware, in order to guarantee they perform at their best and are reliable [11].
- Documentation and Audit Trails: Thorough documentation and audit trails are crucial for maintaining a record of maintenance activities, such as software updates, hardware repairs, and system configurations. This documentation plays

a vital role in ensuring accountability and transparency during forensic investigations. Audit trails serve as a comprehensive documentation of modifications performed on forensic systems, aiding in the identification and resolution of issues, as well as ensuring the reliability and effectiveness of the system.

- Training and Skill Development: Continual training and skill improvement are essential for forensic examiners to remain up-to-date on the most recent tools, methodologies, and optimal practices in the field of computer forensics. Ongoing education guarantees that forensic experts have the necessary skills to address emerging dangers and difficulties in their sector [17].

Using Reliable Partitioning Tools

- Select Trusted Tools: We should choose partitioning tools that are generally acknowledged and verified by the forensic community. Forensic examiners typically rely on and have confidence in tools such as FTK Imager, EnCase, and X-Ways Forensics.
- Verify Tool Integrity: Before using a partitioning tool, verify its integrity and authenticity. Download tools from reputable sources and compare their hash values against official checksums provided by the software vendor to ensure they haven't been tampered with.
- Validate Tool Integrity: Prior to utilizing a partitioning tool, ensure its integrity and legitimacy. To secure the integrity of downloaded tools, obtain them from reliable sources and verify their hash values against the official checksums provided by the program vendor.
- Comprehend Tool Functionality: Acquaint yourself with the functionality and capabilities of the partitioning tool prior to executing any operations on storage media. Acquire the knowledge to safely and precisely perform tasks such as creating, resizing, deleting, or modifying partitions [18].
- Partitioning actions Documentation: Ensure comprehensive documentation of all partitioning actions. Document the date, time, and objective of every operation, along with the exact partitions involved. Keep comprehensive documentation of modifications performed on storage media to protect the integrity and admissibility of evidence in judicial processes.
- Utilize Write-Blocking techniques: When handling primary evidence, employ hardware or software techniques that prevent inadvertent writing to storage media. Write-blocking guarantees that partitioning tools are unable to alter the original material, hence maintaining its integrity for forensic investigation.
- Conduct Verification tests: Once the partitioning procedures are finished, carry out verification tests to confirm that the modifications have been implemented accurately and without any problems. Validate the integrity of partitions and file systems by utilizing the inherent verification capabilities or employing external

validation tools.

- Ensure Chain of Custody: Follow chain of custody protocols consistently during the partitioning phase. Record the management, preservation, and transmission of evidence to uphold responsibility and exhibit the trustworthiness of evidence management procedures.
- Utilize Read-Only Access: Whenever feasible, employ forensic disk images or write-protected duplicates of storage media to avert inadvertent modifications or contamination of partitions. This guarantees that the initial evidence remains unaltered and can be presented as valid in a court of law.
- Backup: Create backups of the original data before carrying out any partitioning actions. These backups function as a safeguard in the event of unintentional data loss or corruption during partitioning operations [11].

CASE STUDIES

Real-world Examples of Successful Recoveries

Computer forensic techniques have proven crucial in solving crimes, identifying offenders, and collecting vital evidence in a number of significant cases, despite the fact that the specifics of these cases are frequently kept hidden. Here are some instances from the actual world:

- BTK Killer (Dennis Rader): During the 1970s and 1980s, Dennis Rader, also referred to as the BTK (Bind, Torture, Kill) Killer, killed several people in Kansas. He teased the media and law enforcement with poems, letters, and information about the atrocities.
- Investigation: In 2004, Rader reappeared with a floppy disk that had information directing detectives to a certain printer manufacturer. The following involved forensic involvement. The hard drive had been examined by experts in forensics, who eventually connected it to the computer system at Rader's church and the crimes.
- Enron Scandal: Enron, one of the biggest energy corporations in the world at the time, went bankrupt as a result of accounting deficiencies and corporate fraud. Sarbanes-Oxley Act acceptance was one of the scandal's many long-term effects.
- The discovery of email correspondence and money transfers which indicated illicit transactions was made possible in large part by the use of computer forensics. For the purpose of gathering evidence against important players in the affair, investigators examined digital data.
- Sony Pictures Hack: Sensitive corporate information, employee data, and unpublished movies were made public by a major data breach that Sony Pictures suffered in 2014. North Korean intelligence was blamed for the attack as a

reaction to the movie "The Interview."

- The role of forensic science: For investigators to fully investigate the intrusion, digital forensic specialists were essential. They gave law enforcement and cybersecurity teams with important information, examined malware, and located the attack's source.

These actual cases highlight the vital role computer forensics plays in cracking investigations, from cybercrimes to cold cases. In order to assist in bringing offenders to justice, forensic specialists apply their expertise to evaluate digital evidence, identify trends, and support legal processes [19].

Lessons Learned from Failed Recovery Attempts

Failures in computer forensics recovery efforts can teach important insights that advance the field's techniques, resources, and standards. The integrity of digital evidence may occasionally be unintentionally compromised by efforts to retrieve data. The forensic inquiry may be hampered if files are removed, altered, or handled improperly while being recovered.

To prevent data from being altered or deleted during recovery efforts, forensic experts should place a high priority on evidence preservation. One way to preserve the integrity of the evidence is to make forensic copies and work on duplicates instead of originals. Subsequent analysis may be hampered by inadequate recovery procedure documentation and insufficient thorough logging. It could be difficult to verify and duplicate the outcomes if the procedures aren't well documented. All steps made throughout the recovery process should be meticulously documented by forensic analysts in logs. This covers the commands executed, the tools utilized, and any system modifications. Complete documentation promotes accountability and openness.

Forensic specialists need to be trained and educated continuously. More successful recovery attempts are a result of remaining up to date on advancements in file system technologies and knowledgeable about the nuances of various file systems. The information that has been encrypted could end up being recoverable if encryption and security precautions are disregarded [20].

CHALLENGES AND LIMITATIONS

Notwithstanding its use in examining cybercrime and digital incidents, computer forensics is not without its difficulties and constraints. Technological change, growing cyberthreats, complex legal systems, and the abundance and variety of digital data are all major contributors to these difficulties.

The growth of technology, cooperation, continuous education, and the creation of precise legislative structures are all essential elements of a complex strategy for tackling these issues. For investigations to be considered either ethical or successful, the field of computer forensics needs to continually adjust to the changing digital reality.

Technical Constraints

Numerous technical limitations that computer forensics faces can affect how well investigations turn out. Digital systems are complicated, technologies are evolving, and criminals constantly evolve to fight forensic procedures, resulting in the root of these restrictions.

Furthermore, when it involves forensic investigations, technology for encryption could render it difficult to get to and comprehend data. Sophisticated encryption techniques may render it hard for forensic experts to get important data. Decrypting data can be challenging for investigators, which makes it more difficult for them to find proof of criminal activity. Advances in encryption techniques could necessitate large computational resources. Anti-forensic techniques are used to purposefully delete or modify digital evidence. These methods may involve altering information, erasing data, and obfuscating files. Anti-forensic measures can be difficult to identify and defeat, which could result in the loss or tampering of evidence. Advanced techniques and instruments for countering forensic evidence could surpass forensic expertise [21].

Steganography

Steganography is the process of secretly encoding information into other files or media. It can be difficult for forensic analysts to find and retrieve concealed data.

Standard forensic methods might not be able to recognize steganographically buried content, which makes it harder to find hidden information and possibly leads to incomplete investigations. Data analysis and access from distant servers are becoming more difficult due to the widespread use of cloud computing. Research is made more difficult by jurisdictional concerns, access restrictions, and different cloud service providers. Furthermore, if not handled properly, digital evidence is brittle and easily lost or changed. The integrity of the evidence may be compromised by the seizure of a computer or storage device, which may alter its condition.

Interoperability

Interoperability problems may arise due to improper forensic tool standardization. For a thorough investigation, analysts may need to use various tools, as different techniques may yield varying conclusions. It can be difficult to guarantee the dependability and consistency of results across several instruments, which could result in inconsistent conclusions. The computer forensics profession needs to continue researching, working together, and remodeling in order to prevail over these obstacles to technology [5].

Incomplete Recovery

In computer forensics, the term "incomplete recovery" describes circumstances in which forensic investigators are not able to completely recover or recreate every relevant data or evidence from a digital device. Forensic investigations may face obstacles in their quest for success when this happens for an assortment of reasons. The following are some typical causes of insufficient recovery in computer forensics:

Data Overwriting

New data is written to a storage device, replacing older data, an action known as data overwriting. This may occur as an outcome of regular system operations, application utilization, or deliberate attempts to eliminate data.

Impact: Data that was recently overwritten may become unrecoverable, leaving gaps in the forensic investigation. Researchers who change parts of the original data might miss crucial details [22].

Data Fragmentation

When files are kept in non-contiguous clusters on a storage medium, file fragmentation happens. Certain pieces of a file might not be recovered if forensic technologies are not able to handle fragmentation well.

Impact: The accuracy and completeness of the forensic examination may be affected by the incomplete reconstruction of fragmented files that could result in the loss of contents or data.

File System Corruption

Data loss or unavailability may result from file system corruption brought on by computer malfunctions, malware, or software defects. The correct understanding of file structures may be impeded by corruption.

Impact: Researchers might discover it difficult to get to and examine relevant files and directories if they have been unable to retrieve information as a result of the file system damage.

Disk Errors and Bad Sectors

Physical errors on a storage medium, such as bad sectors on a hard disk, can result in the loss of data. Forensic tools may encounter difficulties recovering data from damaged areas.

Impact: Unrecoverable data in areas affected by disk errors may limit the scope of the investigation, particularly if critical evidence is located in those damaged sectors.

Unallocated Space

On a storage medium, unallocated space can hold data that has been erased or is no longer required. Incomplete conclusions may result from the inability to get data from unallocated space.

Impact: Leftover files from deleted files or traces of user activity may be found in space that was not allocated. Should the information be unrecoverable, the comprehension of the user's activities may be restricted [8].

In computer forensics, partial recovery calls for a mix of advanced instruments, techniques, ongoing training, and adherence to best standards in evidence analysis and preservation. For the purpose of reducing the likelihood of an incomplete recovery during an investigation, forensic accountants need to be aware of the possible obstacles and take steps to overcome them.

Data Integrity Concerns

Since the quality and dependability of digital evidence are vital to investigations and court cases, data integrity issues are of utmost importance in computer forensics. Maintaining digital evidence's consistency, validity, and dependability across the whole forensic procedure is necessary to ensure data integrity. To ensure that forensic investigations are credible and that the inferences drawn from them are legally valid, electronic proof must be properly preserved [23].

FUTURE TRENDS IN PARTITION RECOVERY

While it is difficult to forecast trends for the future with absolute confidence, developments in technology and modifications to the digital environment could have an impact on the partition recovery area of computer forensics. These are a few possible directions for partition recovery going forward.

- Solid-state drive (SSD) use is on the rise.
- Artificial intelligence (AI) and machine learning (ML) are being integrated.
- File system variations are better supported.
- Cloud-based partition recovery is offered.
- Blockchain technology is integrated.
- Privacy and legal considerations are taken into account.
- Open source tool development is underway.
- Advanced visualization techniques are prioritized.
- User-friendly interfaces are the focus.
- Integration with incident response platforms is integrated.
- Advances in Recovery Technologies

The dynamic nature of digital technology, storage mediums, and complex cyber-attacks have propelled the development of recovery remedies in computer forensics. The objective of these developments is to improve the effectiveness, precision, and range of data recovery in forensic inquiries.

Specialized forensics tools have been developed in response to the particular issues that SSDs present as they become more widely used. To efficiently recover data, these methods take into account wear leveling algorithms, trim operations, and the quirks of NAND flash memory. Investigators are able to retrieve data from hard drives using enhanced SSD forensics, taking into account the intricate details of the drive's design in order to guarantee an accurate assessment [24].

Proprietary and unusual file formats belong to a number of systems of files that forensic programs right now provide improved support for. Data from various file system structures can be recognized and retrieved using sophisticated algorithms. Enhanced file system support helps to prevent data loss from unsupported file systems by enabling forensic investigators to work with a wider range of storage mediums.

Forensic instruments are becoming more and more integrated with machine learning algorithms and methods for recognizing patterns. These tools can help retrieve pertinent data, find interesting patterns in massive datasets, and automate the investigation of those patterns. Through the automated execution of some processes, reduction of manual labor, and possible discovery of hidden patterns or abnormalities, machine learning speeds up the data recovery process [30].

The forensic tools that help with data recovery from cloud-based storage platforms have grown in tandem with the growing usage of cloud services.

Several user access points, cloud provider designs, and external storage provide issues that these remedies help with. A comprehensive approach to digital investigations in contemporary computer systems is ensured by advances in cloud forensics, which enable investigators to retrieve and examine evidence stored in the cloud.

The efficiency, breadth, and flexibility of recovery solutions in computer forensics are all enhanced by these combined developments. To successfully negotiate the difficulties presented through the creation of storage architectures and data protection techniques, experts in forensics need to stay up to date on the latest developments in technology [25].

EMERGING CHALLENGES AND SOLUTIONS

Computer forensics faces ongoing challenges due to the dynamic nature of technology, the evolving threat landscape, and the increasing complexity of digital systems.

Here are some emerging challenges in computer forensics along with potential solutions:

Encryption and Privacy Concerns

Challenge: Gaining access to and decrypting data during forensic investigations is difficult due to the frequent application of powerful encryption techniques, which raises privacy issues.

Solution: The key to finding a balance between privacy and the requirements of forensic investigations is cooperation between law enforcement, business interests, and technology vendors. It is essential to do research and build forensic techniques that can handle encrypted data under appropriate legal supervision.

Cloud Computing and Remote Storage

Challenge: It may be difficult to access and evaluate data kept on distant servers and in cloud environments. Investigations get more complex due to jurisdictional concerns and the diversity of cloud service providers.

Solution: To facilitate the recovery of data across different cloud platforms, methods must be updated and forensic specialists must gain proficiency in cloud forensics. The resolution of jurisdictional issues might be aided by international collaboration and legal frameworks [26].

Internet of Things (IoT) Devices

Challenge: Finding and evaluating information collected by an extensive variety of networked, sometimes resource-constrained devices becomes increasingly challenging as Internet of Things (IoT) gadgets proliferate.

Solution: IoT devices necessitate the development of forensic methods and instruments. It is of the utmost importance that we collaborate with IoT manufacturers to incorporate forensic-friendly features and to build specialized tools for IoT forensics.

Anti-Forensic Techniques

Challenge: Anti-forensic tactics, such as file obfuscation, encryption, and data wiping, are used by criminals to avoid detection and make it challenging to find and examine evidence.

Solution: It is imperative to conduct ongoing research and development of counter-anti-forensic tools and approaches. Maintaining the efficacy of investigations requires forensic specialists to be trained to recognize and conquer these strategies.

Data Fragmentation

Challenge: The retrieval process is complicated by the dispersion of data across storage media, necessitating sophisticated approaches to rebuild fractured information.

Solution: It is imperative to enhance data carving techniques and software for piecing together fragmented data. In order to guarantee the wholeness of recovered files, forensic technologies ought to be more skilled at handling data fragmentation.

Privacy Regulations and Legal Compliance

Challenge: Respecting privacy laws, such as the GDPR, and making sure that digital investigations comply with the law can be difficult and differ amongst legal systems.

Solution: Forensic professionals must stay informed about and comply with relevant privacy and legal frameworks. Collaboration with legal experts and adherence to ethical standards are crucial to maintaining the admissibility of evidence.

Addressing these emerging challenges in computer forensics requires a collaborative and adaptive approach involving professionals, law enforcement agencies, legal experts, and technology providers. As the digital landscape evolves, staying ahead of emerging threats and implementing effective solutions is essential for the success of forensic investigations [27].

CONCLUSION

Professionals in forensics need to be aware of and abide by pertinent privacy and regulatory frameworks. The preservation of evidence admissibility depends on cooperation with legal professionals and observance of ethical guidelines. Professionals, law enforcement organizations, legal experts, and technology suppliers must work together to develop a flexible and cooperative strategy to tackle these new computer forensics difficulties. The effectiveness of forensic investigations depends on keeping up with new dangers and putting practical solutions in place as the digital landscape changes.

KEY THOUGHTS

It is essential for practitioners to honor ethical principles, place a high value on data integrity, and adopt a proactive and adaptable approach when navigating the complicated field of computer forensics. Computer forensics will continue to be essential to the defense of digital evidence, cybersecurity, and the pursuit of justice as long as technology continues to advance. The accomplishment of successful forensic investigations is contingent upon the joint endeavors of experts, law enforcement organizations, and governmental bodies, as well as the ongoing development of instruments and procedures to address new problems.

REFERENCES

[1]   D.G. Revathi Jagarlamudi, "A Novel tool for Data Recovery in cyber forensics", *Ann. Rom. Soc. Cell Biol.,* pp. 19600-19611, 2021.

[2]   J. Zdziarski, "iPhone forensics: recovering evidence, personal data, and corporate assets", In: *O'Reilly Media, Inc*, 2008.

[3]   K. Lasker, "A modular platform for engineering function of natural and synthetic biomolecular condensates", *BioRxiv,* p. 2021.02.
       [http://dx.doi.org/10.1101/2021.02.03.429226]

[4]   J. Namgung, I. Hong, J. Park, and S. Lee, "A research for partition recovery method in a forensic perspective", *Journal of the Korea Institute of Information Security and Cryptology,* vol. 23, no. 4, pp. 655-666, 2013.
       [http://dx.doi.org/10.13089/JKIISC.2013.23.4.655]

[5]   E. Akbal, Ö.F. Yakut, S. Dogan, T. Tuncer, and F. Ertam, "A Digital Forensics Approach for Lost Secondary Partition Analysis using Master Boot Record Structured Hard Disk Drives", *Sakarya University Journal of Computer and Information Sciences,* vol. 4, no. 3, pp. 326-346, 2021.
       [http://dx.doi.org/10.35377/saucis...1022600]

[6]   I.P.A.E. Pratama, "Computer forensic using photorec for secure data recovery between storage media: A proof of concept. International Journal of Science", *Technology & Management,* vol. 2, no. 4, pp. 1189-1196, 2021.

[7]   A. Khang, and V.A. Hajimahmud, "Introduction to the Gig Economy", In: *Khang A. Jadhav B., Hajimahmud V. A., Satpathy I., The Synergy of AI and Fintech in the Digital Gig Economy.* 1st ed. CRC Press, 2024.
        [http://dx.doi.org/10.1201/9781032720104-1]

[8]   Y. Guo, and J. Slay, "Data recovery function testing for digital forensic tools", *in Advances in Digital Forensics VI: Sixth IFIP WG 11.9 International Conference on Digital Forensics,* Hong Kong, China, January 4-6, 2010, Revised Selected Papers 6. Springer, 2010, .
        [http://dx.doi.org/10.1007/978-3-642-15506-2_21]

[9]   M. Lovanshi, and P. Bansal, "Comparative study of digital forensic tools. Data", *Engineering and Applications,* vol. 2, pp. 195-204, 2019.

[10]   K. Ghazinour, D.M. Vakharia, K.C. Kannaji, and R. Satyakumar, "A study on digital forensic tools", In: *A study on digital forensic tools.* IEEE., 2017.*in 2017 IEEE international conference on power, control, signals and instrumentation engineering (ICPCSI).* IEEE., 2017.
        [http://dx.doi.org/10.1109/ICPCSI.2017.8392304]

[11]   G. Grispos, T. Storer, and W.B. Glisson, "A comparison of forensic evidence recovery techniques for a windows mobile smart phone", *Digit. Invest.,* vol. 8, no. 1, pp. 23-36, 2011.
        [http://dx.doi.org/10.1016/j.diin.2011.05.016]

[12]   A. Khang, T. Dave, D. Katore, B. Jadhav, and D. Dave, "Leveraging Blockchain and Smart Contracts For Gig Payments", In: *The Synergy of AI and Fintech in the Digital Gig Economy. (1st Ed.).* In Khang A. Jadhav B., Hajimahmud V. A., Satpathy I., (1st Ed.). CRC Press., 2024.
        [http://dx.doi.org/10.1201/9781032720104-11]

[13]   J.R. Bhat, and S.A. Alqahtani, "6G ecosystem: Current status and future perspective", *IEEE Access,* vol. 9, pp. 43134-43167, 2021.
        [http://dx.doi.org/10.1109/ACCESS.2021.3054833]

[14]   S. Tomer, "Data recovery in Forensics", *2017 International Conference on Computing and Communication Technologies for Smart Nation (IC3TSN),* IEEE., 2017.
        [http://dx.doi.org/10.1109/IC3TSN.2017.8284474]

[15]   J. Liang, *Evaluating a selection of tools for extraction of forensic data: disk imaging.* Auckland University of Technology, 2010.

[16]   S. Alqahtany, N. Clarke, S. Furnell, and C. Reich, "A forensic acquisition and analysis system for IaaS", *Cluster Comput.,* vol. 19, no. 1, pp. 439-453, 2016.
        [http://dx.doi.org/10.1007/s10586-015-0509-x]

[17]   R. Al Mushcab, and P. Gladyshev, "The significance of different backup applications in retrieving social networking forensic artifacts from Android-based mobile devices", *2015 Second International Conference on Information Security and Cyber Forensics (InfoSec),* IEEE., 2015.
        [http://dx.doi.org/10.1109/InfoSec.2015.7435508]

[18]   K.K. Sindhu, and B.B. Meshram, "Digital forensic investigation tools and procedures", *International Journal of Computer Network and Information Security,* vol. 4, no. 4, pp. 39-48, 2012.
        [http://dx.doi.org/10.5815/ijcnis.2012.04.05]

[19]   O.O. Oyelami, *Case study research as a method for digital forensic evidence examinations.* University of Pretoria, 2018.

[20]   G. Drennan, and J. Wooldridge, "10. Making recovery a reality in forensic settings. Center for Mental Health & Mental Health Network NHS Confederation. Implementing Recovery trough organisational", *Change,* pp. 1-28, 2014.

[21]   S. Omeleze, and H.S. Venter, "Digital forensic application requirements specification process", *Aust. J. Forensic Sci.,* vol. 51, no. 4, pp. 371-394, 2019.
        [http://dx.doi.org/10.1080/00450618.2017.1374456]

[22]   Y. Yusoff, R. Ismail, and Z. Hassan, "Common phases of computer forensics investigation models", *Int. J. Comput. Sci. Inf. Technol.,* vol. 3, no. 3, pp. 17-31, 2011.
        [http://dx.doi.org/10.5121/ijcsit.2011.3302]

[23]   S. Hraiz, "Challenges of digital forensic investigation in cloud computing", *in 2017 8th international conference on information technology (ICIT).,* IEEE., 2017.
        [http://dx.doi.org/10.1109/ICITECH.2017.8080060]

[24]   V. Civie, and R. Civie, "Future technologies from trends in computer forensic science", In: *in 1998 IEEE Information Technology Conference, Information Environment for the Future (Cat. No. 98EX228).* IEEE., 1998.
        [http://dx.doi.org/10.1109/IT.1998.713392]

[25]   K. Barmpatsalou, T. Cruz, E. Monteiro, and P. Simoes, "Current and future trends in mobile device forensics: A survey", *ACM Comput. Surv.,* vol. 51, no. 3, pp. 1-31, 2019. [CSUR].
        [http://dx.doi.org/10.1145/3177847]

[26]   V. Fernando, "Cyber forensics tools: A review on mechanism and emerging challenges", *in 2021 11th IFIP International Conference on New Technologies, Mobility and Security (NTMS).,* IEEE., 2021.
        [http://dx.doi.org/10.1109/NTMS49979.2021.9432641]

[27]   A.R. Javed, W. Ahmed, M. Alazab, Z. Jalil, K. Kifayat, and T.R. Gadekallu, "A comprehensive survey on computer forensics: State-of-the-art, tools, techniques, challenges, and future directions", *IEEE Access,* vol. 10, pp. 11065-11089, 2022.
        [http://dx.doi.org/10.1109/ACCESS.2022.3142508]

[28]   A. Khang, T. Dave, B. Jadhav, D. Katore, and D. Dave, "Gig Financial Economy- Big Data and Analytics", In: *The Synergy of AI and Fintech in the Digital Gig Economy. (1st Ed.)* In Khang A. Jadhav B., Hajimahmud V. A., Satpathy I., (1st Ed.). CRC Press., 2024.
        [http://dx.doi.org/10.1201/9781032720104-16]

[29]   A. Khang, "An AI-Driven Self-Sustained Approach for Redefining Urban Waste Management", In: *Revolutionizing Automated Waste Treatment Systems: IoT and Bioelectronics.* In Khang A., Hajimahmud V. A., Litvinova E., Musrat G. L., Avramovic Z. (Ed.). IGI Global., 2024, pp. 77-89.
        [http://dx.doi.org/10.4018/979-8-3693-6016-3.ch006]

[30]   A. Khang, Y. Singh, and D. Barak, "Review of the Literature on Using Machine and Deep Learning Techniques to Improve IoT Security", In: *Revolutionizing Automated Waste Treatment Systems: IoT and Bioelectronics.* Khang A., Hajimahmud V. A., Litvinova E., Musrat G. L., Avramovic Z. (Ed.). IGI Global., 2024, pp. 273-300.
        [http://dx.doi.org/10.4018/979-8-3693-6016-3.ch018]

CHAPTER 7

FAT16 File System Disk

Vishnu Mittal[1,*], Abhinav Singhal[1] and **Shushank Mahajan[2]**

[1] *Guru Gobind Singh College of Pharmacy, Yamuna Nagar, Haryana, India*

[2] *Chitkara College of Pharmacy, Chitkara University, Rajpura, Punjab, India*

Abstract: Background: The historical development of the FAT16 file system highlights its inception, evolution, and key milestones. It explores the technological landscape that necessitated the creation of FAT16, shedding light on the challenges and requirements that shaped its design.

Objective: The primary objective is to conduct a detailed analysis of the FAT16 file system considering its architecture, functionality, and historical significance. By dissecting the internal workings of FAT16, we aim to provide readers with a deeper comprehension of its strengths, weaknesses, and enduring relevance.

Method: The methodological approach involved a meticulous examination of the FAT16 file system architecture, data organization principles, and operational mechanisms. We employed a combination of literature review, system analysis, and practical experimentation to unravel the intricacies of FAT16 and its role in data storage.

Results: The findings present a nuanced understanding of FAT16, elucidating its role in early computing, its file structure, and the constraints it imposes on modern storage solutions. This chapter explores how FAT16 influences disk space utilization, directory organization, and file access, providing valuable insights into its impact on data management.

Conclusion: While recognizing its historical importance, we explored the constraints that FAT16 poses in light of present-day storage requirements. This conclusion reflects the lasting impact of FAT16 and ponders its influence on the design and development of future file systems.

Keywords: Disk Drives, Data Management, FAT16, File System, Storage Solutions.

---

* **Corresponding author Vishnu Mittal:** Guru Gobind Singh College of Pharmacy, Yamuna Nagar, Haryana, India; E-mail: Vishnumittal720@gmail.com

Alex Khang, Sanchit Dhankhar, Sandeep Bhardwaj, Avnesh Verma & Satish Kumar Sharma (Eds.)

INTRODUCTION

Over the years, computers have gradually become the primary record keepers of human activity. The trend has been further amplified by the emergence of PCs, handheld devices such as mobile phones, the Internet, multimedia, and telecommunications. Data have become increasingly important in today's world as they can be lost either intentionally by users to free up storage space or accidentally [1]. In the future, if the user requires the same data, it will not be possible to retrieve it at that time; it can only be obtained if a backup copy is obtained. Data recovery, both for the general public and for forensic purposes (*i.e.*, digital forensics), is an evolving field in computer applications [2].

File systems are the most critical component of a computer, as they serve as a durable storage and retrieval mechanism for data. File systems enable users to organize data in a hierarchical structure comprising directories and files (Fig. **1** & Table **1**) [3].

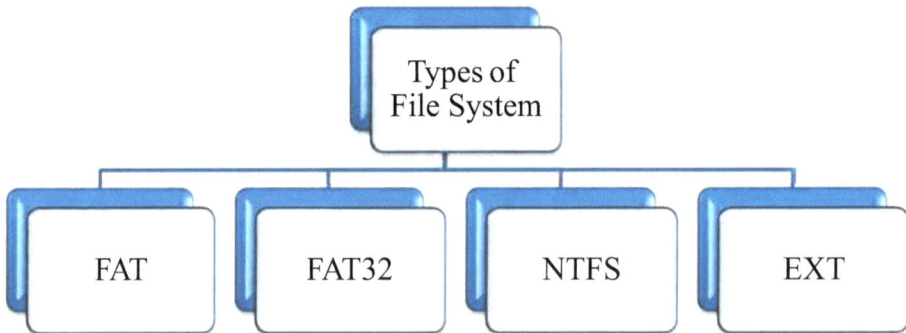

Fig. (1). Types of File System [5].

Table 1. Aspects of FAT16.

Aspects	Details
Definition	A file system is a structured method for organizing and managing data on storage devices, enabling the storage, retrieval, and modification of files.
Importance	File systems play a pivotal role in computer forensics, serving as the foundation for data storage and retrieval. Understanding them is essential for evidence extraction and data recovery.
FAT16 Overview	Definition: FAT16 (File Allocation Table 16-bit) is a file system commonly used in earlier Windows operating systems and on removable storage devices Structure: It consists of a boot sector, FAT, root directory, and data clusters.

(Table 1) cont.....

Aspects	Details
Key Concepts	Boot Sector: Contains critical information about the file system's layout and structure, crucial for forensic analysis. FAT Entries: Record the allocation status of data clusters, determining the file storage location. Root Directory: Initial directory structure containing file and folder information.
Data Storage and Retrieval	Allocation Methods: FAT16 employs cluster allocation for storing data files. Directory Entries: Information about files, including attributes, file names, and extensions. File Deletion: Deleted files leave traces in the FAT, posing challenges and opportunities for recovery.
Challenges in FAT16 Analysis	Fragmentation: Fragmented files impact data recovery and necessitate specialized handling. Deleted Files: Recovering deleted files involves understanding FAT entries and potential file carving.
Forensic Tools for FAT16	Disk Imaging: Essential for creating forensic copies, and preserving the integrity of the original disk. File Carving Tools: Aid in recovering files by searching for file signatures and structures.
Legal Considerations	Admissibility: Ensuring that forensic practices adhere to legal standards that is crucial for the acceptance of findings in court. Chain of Custody: Maintaining a secure chain of custody for forensic evidence is imperative for legal validity [4].

FAT16 BASICS

Basics and Historical Context

File systems typically possess a predetermined structure that is highly beneficial for storing a multitude of files within a storage array. Certain data require a fundamental structure and arrangement within their file hierarchy (Fig. **2**) [6].

Fig. (2). FAT16 Basics [7].

FAT is a file system that was designed for hard drives and uses 12 or 16 bits per cluster entry. The Operating System (OS) primarily uses FAT to manage and store files on hard drives and other computer systems [8]. FAT is designed to minimize seeking, which reduces wear and tear on hard disks and extends their lifespan. This file system is lightweight and compatible, making it a common choice for digital cameras, portable devices, and flash memory [9].

Key Components and Varieties of FAT

The key components and varieties of FAT are given in Figs. (**3 & 4**).

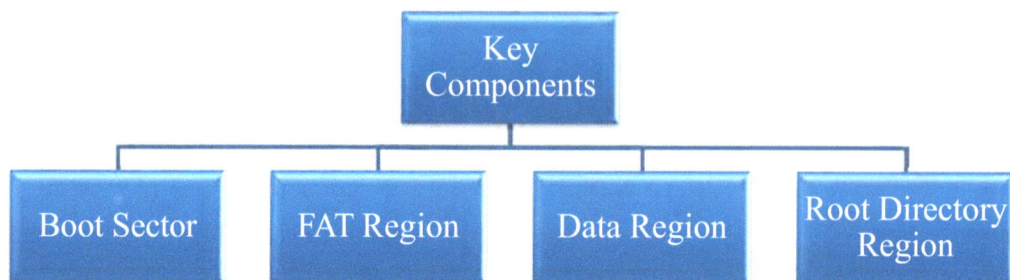

Fig. (3). Key Components [10].

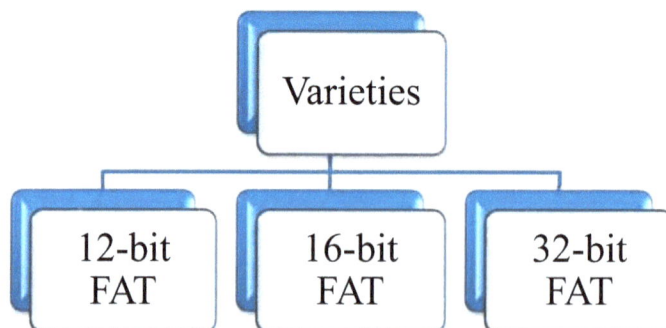

Fig. (4). Varieties of FAT [11].

Structure of FAT16 File System

Boot Block

The boot block serves as the initial point of contact for the disk and is responsible for loading the operating system into the memory. To achieve this, a special bootstrap program is required. The boot block typically measures 512 bytes in size; however, in FAT12 and FAT16, portions ranging from 62 to 509 bytes remain unused because they contain the boot code. Conversely, in FAT32, 90–509 bytes remain unused for the same reason [12]. The boot block also comprises critical areas that outline the file system configuration. The opening three bytes of the boot block are dedicated to a jump instruction that instructs the CPU to proceed with the execution of the boot code. The intricate details of the boot block are expounded below [13, 14].

Areas

The areas of FAT are given in Figs. (**5** & **6**).

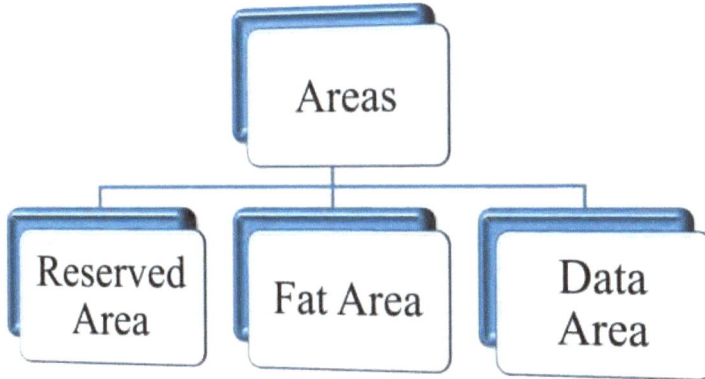

Fig. (5). Areas of FAT [15].

Reserved Area	FAT Area	Data Area

Fig. (6). Physical Layout of FAT [20].

Root Directory

The root directory is a vital element of the file system because it comprises an entry for every file positioned at the root of the file system. Each entry is 32 bytes in size and provides a synopsis of the attributes of the file. It is imperative to mention that the offset specified in the table is relative to the commencement of a particular entry rather than the inception of the block [16].

DATA STORAGE AND RETRIEVAL

Allocation Methods in FAT16

The FAT16 file system uses a static allocation method in which files are stored in fixed locations as clusters. Each cluster has a defined size, and the FAT contains information such as the address of each file's starting cluster and markers indicating the end of a file. This table also tracks the unused disk space or specially reserved areas on the disk for efficient data storage [17]. FAT16, introduced in 1984 as an upgrade to FAT12, increased the maximum partition size to 2GB and underwent several modifications such as supporting longer file names. The principal limitation of FAT16 is its fixed maximum number of clusters per partition, which leads to larger cluster sizes and more unusable space on larger hard disks. Despite this, FAT16 remains compatible with a wide range of operating systems, including Windows 95/98/Me, OS/2, and some versions of UNIX [18, 19].

Cluster Allocation

Cluster allocation refers to how data are stored on a disk. FAT16 uses a static allocation system in which files are stored in clusters of a fixed size. Each file is allocated one or more clusters depending on its size [20]. The File Allocation Table (FAT) tracks the location of these clusters. Each cluster has an entry in the FAT that points to the next cluster in the file or an end-of-file marker if it is the last cluster. This method allows the file system to efficiently manage both contiguous and fragmented files. The cluster size in FAT16 can vary, influencing the maximum partition size and efficiency of storage space utilization [21].

File Allocation Table Entries

In FAT16 file systems, the File Allocation Table (FAT) is crucial for managing file storage. Each file allocation is tracked through the entries in the FAT. These entries contain the address of the file's starting cluster and pointers to the subsequent clusters used by the file. FAT also includes an end-of-file marker to indicate the last cluster of a file. This structure allows the file system to manage file storage efficiently by handling both contiguous and fragmented files. Thus, the FAT entries play a key role in linking clusters to represent the entirety of a file's data on the disk [22].

Reading and Interpreting Directory Entries

Reading and interpreting directory entries in the FAT16 file system involves understanding how the file and directory metadata are stored and mapped. Each file and directory has a directory entry in FAT16, which is a 32-byte structure containing the necessary information. These directory entries are stored in clusters, similar to files, and the contents of a directory are represented by a set of these entries in a cluster or several clusters.

The layout of the FAT16 directory entry is as follows:

- Filename and Extension: The first 11 bytes (0×0) are dedicated to the filename and extension, following the 8.3 filename format (8 characters for the name and 3 for the extension). The first byte indicates the allocation status; 0x00 or 0xe5 means the entry is unallocated, with 0xe5 specifically indicating a deleted file. If the filename does not use all 8 characters, the unused bytes are filled with ASCII space (0x20) [25, 26].
- Attributes: A single byte (0xB) represents file attributes, which include read-only (0×01), hidden (0×02), system (0×04), volume label (0×08), directory (0×10), and archive (0×20) attributes. If the attributes are equal to $0 \times 0f$, it indicates a special "long file name" entry [25].
- Creation, Accessed, and Written Dates/Times: The entry also includes creation date/time (5 bytes at 0xD), accessed date (2 bytes at 0x12), and written date/time (4 bytes at 0x16), all in a specific FAT date/time format [23].
- Cluster Address and File Size: The high-order bytes of the first cluster address are at 0x14 (always 0 in FAT16, used only in FAT32), and the low-order bytes are at 0x1A. The file size is indicated in 4 bytes at $0 \times 1C$ (0 for directories).
- Allocation Status and Cluster Chain: The initial byte of a directory entry indicates its allocation status. If it has been allocated, the entry contains the first character of the file name. The FAT system maintains records of both the cluster allocation status and the clusters occupied by each file. Every cluster on the disk is assigned a corresponding entry in the FAT that specifies whether it is allocated or unallocated. In case of FAT16, each cluster entry in the FAT is represented by a two-byte value. The FAT Directory Entry specifies the initial cluster where the file is stored, and the FAT itself provides information on any additional clusters that the file may occupy [24].

FILE DELETION AND RECOVERY

Understanding the delete process in FAT16

The deletion process in the FAT16 file system involves several key steps and considerations.

- Marking Clusters as Available: When a file is deleted in the FAT16 system, the clusters that were used by the file are marked as available. However, the actual data in these clusters are not immediately erased.
- FAT Records Erasure: The File Allocation Table (FAT) records corresponding to the file are also erased. This means that while information about the file's initial address, attributes, and size can be retrieved, data on any subsequent clusters is lost.
- Recovery Approach: If a deleted file is sufficiently small to fit into a single cluster, it can be recovered by reading the first cluster. For larger files, an

algorithm is required to recover the rest of the file [25].

• Challenges in Recovery: The FAT system does not provide a straightforward way to identify which clusters belong to a deleted file. One method is to read the clusters following the initial one, regardless of whether they are occupied by other files. Another more sophisticated method reads only from clusters not occupied by other data, considering the file system's record of occupied clusters. The latter method tends to yield better results and can even recover fragmented files.

• Recovery Scenarios: Recovery can vary based on file fragmentation. In a non-fragmented file scenario, either recovery algorithm can correctly recover a file. However, in fragmented file scenarios, the simpler method may return a corrupted file, whereas the more sophisticated method can correctly recover the file, assuming that the clusters are not occupied by other files [26].

Techniques for Recovering Deleted Files in FAT16

The recovery techniques are given in Fig. **(7)**.

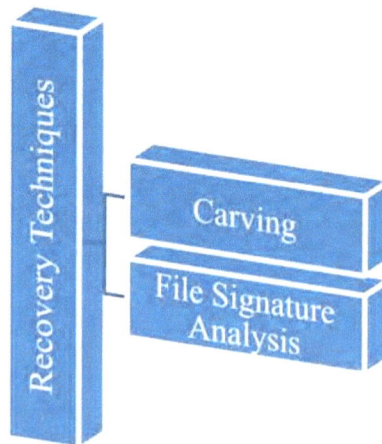

Fig. (7). Recovery Techniques.

Carving

Carving is a technique used in data recovery to extract files from a storage medium without relying on the metadata of the file system. This approach is particularly useful when the file system is damaged, incomplete, or non-existent. Carving involves scanning storage media for patterns or headers that match known file types. Once a potential file start is identified, the technique attempts to reconstruct the file by following the data stream until a footer or end of file marker is identified. This method is particularly effective for recovering files with distinct and consistent headers and footers, such as images or documents.

However, carving can be less effective with fragmented files or when file signatures are not well defined.

File Signature Analysis

File signature analysis is a data recovery technique that involves identifying files based on their unique signatures or headers, which are typically sequences of bytes at the beginning of a file. This method is employed when file system metadata are unavailable or corrupt. File signature analysis scans the storage medium for known patterns that correspond to specific file types, such as JPEG images or PDF documents. Once a matching signature is detected, the recovery process attempts to reconstruct the file. This technique is particularly effective for well-defined and non-fragmented files; however, it may struggle with files that have common or ambiguous signatures or those that are fragmented [27].

DISK IMAGING AND PRESERVATION

Importance of Creating a Forensic Disk Image

- Preservation of the Original State: The foremost principle in digital forensics is to avoid altering the original data. By creating a bit-for-bit copy of the storage media, forensic disk imaging preserves the original state of the data in the FAT16 file system, which is essential for analysis and evidence admissibility.
- Admissibility of Evidence: A forensic disk image is often required to ensure that any recovered data are admissible in legal contexts. This process follows standardized protocols to maintain the integrity of the data and establish a chain of custody.
- Hash Value Comparison: After imaging, a digital fingerprint or hash is generated for the acquired media. Comparing the hash values of the original and copied media verifies the authenticity of the copied data, which is crucial in legal and forensic investigations.
- Handling Complex Data Recovery: FAT16 file systems, like other file systems, can have complex data structures, especially when dealing with deleted or fragmented files. A forensic disk image allows for thorough analysis of these structures without risking the integrity of the original data.
- Expert Analysis: Ideally, the process of creating a forensic disk image should be performed by trained professionals using specialized software and hardware. This ensured the accuracy and reliability of the imaging process, which is vital for subsequent data recovery and analysis [28].

Tools and Techniques for Disk Imaging in FAT16

The techniques for disk imaging are given in Fig. (**8**).

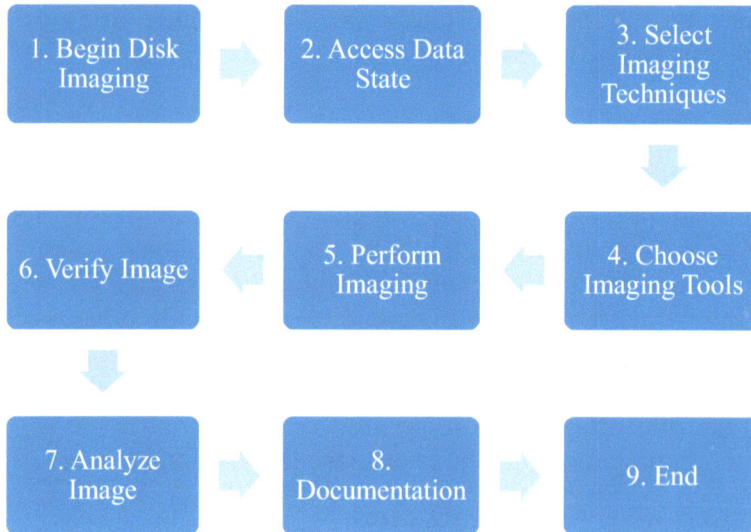

Fig. (8). Technique for Disk Imaging..

FORENSIC TOOLS FOR FAT16 ANALYSIS

Forensic analysis of the FAT16 file system involves a range of specialized tools designed to retrieve, analyze, and preserve data in a manner suitable for legal proceedings or detailed investigations. Here is an overview of the key tools and their functionalities in the context of FAT16 analysis:

Autopsy

- Overview: Autopsy is a widely used, open-source digital forensic platform.
- Functionality: This provides a graphical interface to analyze hard drives and smartphones efficiently. Autopsy can recover deleted files from the FAT16 file system and analyze the file system structures. It is particularly useful for timeline analysis and keyword searching [29].

FTK Imager

- Overview: The Forensic Toolkit (FTK) Imager is a data preview and imaging tool that allows for the acquisition of data in a forensically sound manner.
- Functionality: It can create exact replicas of data without making any changes, thus preserving the integrity of the data in FAT16 file systems. It is useful for imaging, examining, and exporting data from storage devices.

EnCase

- Overview: EnCase is a comprehensive forensic suite used by law enforcement and corporate investigators.
- Functionality: It can analyze data from various file systems, including FAT16. EnCase is known for its robust searching capabilities, reporting tools, and ability to recover deleted files and fragments.

The Sleuth Kit

- Overview: The Sleuth Kit is an open-source digital forensic toolkit.
- Functionality: This allows investigators to examine file systems in a non-intrusive fashion, making it suitable for FAT16 analysis. It includes tools for file system analysis and data recovery [30].

X-Ways Forensics

- Overview: X-way is an advanced work environment for forensic computer examiners.
- Functionality: It integrates disk cloning and imaging functionality and is capable of recovering lost or deleted files from FAT16 file systems. It is known for its efficiency and comprehensive feature set.

WinHex

- Overview: WinHex is a hexadecimal editor with advanced binary-data analysis capabilities.
- Functionality: This is useful for data recovery, low-level data processing, and IT security. An important feature is its ability to analyze and compare files, which is essential for FAT16 forensic analysis [31].

Cellebrite UFED

- Overview: Primarily used in mobile forensics, Cellebrite UFED also has applications for analyzing data storage devices.
- Functionality: This can be used to access and analyze data from devices using FAT16 file systems, particularly *in situ*ations involving mobile devices or smaller storage devices.

These tools play a crucial role in forensic investigations involving FAT16 file systems by enabling the recovery of deleted or corrupted data, analysis of file system structures, and secure preservation of evidence in a format that is admissible in legal contexts. Each tool has unique strengths, making it suitable for different aspects of the forensic analysis process [32].

Real-World Examples and Visual Aids

The FAT16 file system is widely utilized in various real-world applications, particularly in removable media and embedded systems. For instance, the design of a FAT16 file system on an MSP430 microcontroller interfacing with an SD card demonstrates its effectiveness in data collection, such as in electrocardiogram recording systems. Additionally, FAT16 is commonly used in RFID handheld readers, where it manages data storage efficiently despite limited memory capacity. Visual aids, such as diagrams illustrating the structure of FAT16 and its interaction with NAND-Flash storage, further enhance understanding of its implementation [33].

Real-World Applications

Electrocardiogram Systems: Utilizes FAT16 for data collection and storage, showcasing its reliability in medical devices.

RFID Handheld Readers: Employs FAT16 to manage data efficiently, even with small memory sizes [34].

Visual Aids

Diagrams: Illustrate the FAT16 structure and its integration with various storage media, aiding comprehension of its functionality.

Flow Displays: Show how file data is organized and accessed within the FAT16 system. While FAT16 is effective for many applications, its limitations in handling larger files and modern storage needs may prompt the exploration of more advanced file systems in future developments [35].

DISCUSSION

Recent advancements in the FAT16 file system highlight its adaptability and performance improvements, particularly in embedded systems and hybrid storage solutions. The integration of FAT16 with NAND-Flash technology has been explored, showcasing its structural compatibility and implementation methods. Additionally, research on optimizing memory usage in FAT16 for RFID handheld readers emphasizes the importance of preserving file system formats while maximizing storage capacity. Furthermore, reliability enhancements through methods like delayed sequential write have been proposed to mitigate issues during system crashes. Lastly, the hFAT design demonstrates significant performance gains by segregating data across hybrid storage systems, effectively reducing latency in file operations. These developments indicate a robust future for FAT16 in various applications, particularly in embedded and portable devices [36].

The most recent research on FAT16 file system recovery is included in a number of recent publications that look at advanced data recovery methods and useful applications. For instance, a 2023 study shows the continued importance of the FAT16 file system, especially in older devices and embedded systems where less complex systems and affordable storage are still essential [34]. These days, forensic tools like WinHex and X-Ways Forensics are used in recovery approaches to allow for complete analysis and file structure recovery even in cases of considerable damage or data loss. Since they have been updated to handle difficult cases like damaged or partly changed files, these tools show how FAT16 can still be managed with contemporary software solutions [37]. Moreover, hybrid techniques that combine traditional recovery tools and machine learning algorithms to estimate lost data sectors are a focus of efforts to build file sharing and recovery solutions for FAT16 and FAT32 [38]. This method is becoming increasingly popular as a better way to deal with damage to file systems caused by disk failures, malicious attacks, or inadvertent deletions. It was suggested in a scientific article from 2022. These studies show how antiquated systems, like FAT16, are being updated to satisfy contemporary recovery needs, indicating their continued importance in certain sectors, including embedded devices or backup storage [39].

CONCLUSION

In conclusion, the exploration of FAT16 file system disk recovery in this chapter sheds light on the intricate process of recovering lost or corrupted data within the FAT16 file structure. As we navigated through the complexities of this aging file system, it became clear that its limitations pose challenges; however, its historical significance requires understanding and recovery solutions. The chapter begins with an in-depth examination of the FAT16 architecture, highlighting its structural components and the significance of the File Allocation Table in data storage. Subsequently, we investigated the common causes of data loss in FAT16, ranging from accidental deletions to disk corruption. Understanding these factors is crucial for devising effective recovery strategies.

This chapter covers the FAT16 file system disk repair. It demonstrates not just how challenging it is to retrieve lost or damaged data in the FAT16 design, but also how this affects file system management and data recovery in more general ways. Even though FAT16 is an old file system, its historical relevance still affects current recovery methods. Basic ideas that underpin contemporary file systems are exposed via an analysis of its architecture and the vital function the File Allocation Table performs in data protection. Understanding the most common reasons of FAT16 data loss disk damage, system failures, and unintentional deletion is essential to improving recovery methods. Many methods of data recovery are covered in this chapter, including tool-based and manual methods. A document like this one, which shows how different types of data loss need different actions, is essential for staff to have. This in-depth understanding of FAT16 recovery is tremendously helpful to experts working with older systems, and it also helps shape future developments for newer file systems that still face same problems.

In addition to talking about technology, the conversation highlights how important proper data management is, especially when it comes to regular backups. Using the information gathered by saving files from FAT16, best practices for the presently in use file systems may be developed to enhance data protection approaches. Even when we go to more complex file systems, the information we acquired from FAT16 recovery serves as a useful reminder of how data storage is continually changing and how important it is to always have solid recovery choices. The research implications are clear: while FAT16 has been discontinued, studying these systems lays the groundwork for understanding data integrity and stability in more complicated systems. It is advised to do further study on data recovery from antiquated systems and to build new recovery solutions that work with both antiquated and contemporary technologies. By continuing to study the intricacies of file systems such as FAT16, experts may influence the future of data recovery and contribute to more sophisticated, reliable file management solutions. The recovery techniques covered, which ranged from hand methods to specialized equipment, provided practitioners and hobbyists with an extensive arsenal. Each method's advantages and disadvantages were carefully considered so that readers may choose the best strategy for their particular situation. This chapter also emphasizes the need of regular backups as a defense against data loss, stressing the proactive approach that people and institutions can take to protect their important data. The knowledge gained by comprehending and retrieving data inside the FAT16 framework is still useful in developing sound data management procedures, even as technology advances.

REFERENCES

[1]   R Madaan, R Kumar, and G. Gopal, *File Allocation and Recovery in FAT16 and FAT32.,* vol. 7, no. 12, pp. 343-8, 2016.

[2]   L. Simson, *Garfinkel, Digital forensics research: The next 10 years.* Elsevier, 2010, pp. 64-73.

[3]   "File System Implementation in Operating System (Internet)", 2023. Available from: https://www.geeksforgeeks.org/file-system-implementation-in-operating-system/

[4]   *Brian Carrier, File System Forensic Analysis.* Addison-Wesley, 2005.

[5]   X. Li H. Zhao, L. Chang, and X. Zang, "Fat File System Design and Research", *in International Conference on Network and Information Systems for Computers (ICNISC)*, 2015 pp. 568-571 Wuhan.

[6]   LI Chunwang Shen Yong, "FAT data recovery following the devastation of the table", In: *in Technical Education Journal*, 2003, pp. 26-31.

[7]   "Microsoft TechNet", Available from: https://technet.microsoft.com/en- us/library/cc938438.aspx

[8]   R. Kalal Soumya, "Logical Data Recovery Technique for USB Devices", *in International Conference on Emerging Trends in Communication, Control, Signal Processing & Computing Applications (C2SPCA)*, 2013 pp. 1-6 Bangalore.

[9]   "File System Implementation in Operating System (Internet)", Available from: https://www.geeksforgeeks.org/file-system-implementation-in-operating-system/

[10] "Chapter 41 - Cyber Forensics and Incidence Response", *Computer and Information Security Handbook (Third Edition)*, Editor(s): John R. Vacca, Morgan Kaufmann, pp. 603-628, 2017. ISBN 9780128038437.

[11] Khang A., Gupta S. K., Rani S., D. A. Karras, (1st Ed.) "Smart Cities: IoT Technologies, Big Data Solutions, Cloud Platforms, and Cybersecurity Techniques". *CRC Press*, 2023.
      [http://dx.doi.org/10.1201/9781003376064]

[12] J. De Bock, and P. De Smet, "JPGcarve: An Advanced Tool for Automated Recovery of Fragmented JPEG Files", *IEEE Trans. Inf. Forensics Security*, vol. 11, no. 1, pp. 19-34, 2016.
      [http://dx.doi.org/10.1109/TIFS.2015.2475238]

[13] E. Uzun, and H.T. Sencar, "Carving Orphaned JPEG File Fragments", *IEEE Trans. Inf. Forensics Security*, vol. 10, no. 8, pp. 1549-1563, 2015.
      [http://dx.doi.org/10.1109/TIFS.2015.2416685]

[14] A. Khang, Y. Singh, and D. Barak, "Review of the Literature on Using Machine and Deep Learning Techniques to Improve IoT Security", In: *Revolutionizing Automated Waste Treatment Systems: IoT and Bioelectronics*. In Khang A., Hajimahmud V. A., Litvinova E., Musrat G. L., Avramovic Z. (Ed.). IGI Global., 2024, pp. 273-300.
      [http://dx.doi.org/10.4018/979-8-3693-6016-3.ch018]

[15] Fontana John, "Microsoft expands exFAT multimedia file licensing", *Network World (online)*, 2009.

[16] M. Stewart, "Why SD cards refuse to flop", *PC Probe*, no. 269, p. 14, 2017.

[17] "In-vehicle infotainment gets boost from new Microsoft exFAT file system deals", *Internet Business News*, 2013.

[18] "Microsoft Signs exFAT Licensing Agreement with BMW", *PR Newswire*, 2014.

[19] Case Lenny, "e.Solutions Selects Tuxera exFAT for Audi and Volkswagen Infotainment Systems", *Automotive Industries*, 2012.

[20] M. Faheem, T. Kechadi, and N.A. Le-Khac, "The State of the Art Forensic Techniques in Mobile Cloud Environment", *Int. J. Digit. Crime Forensics*, vol. 7, no. 2, pp. 1-19, 2015.
      [http://dx.doi.org/10.4018/ijdcf.2015040101]

[21] C. Brian, "File System Forensic Analysis", In: *Pearson Education*, 2005.

[22] "FAT16 File System: Definition, Pros & Cons, and Applications (Internet)", 2023. Available from: https://recoverit.wondershare.com/file-system/fat16-file-system.html

[23] "File systems (FAT, FAT8, FAT16, FAT32, and NTFS) explained (Internet)", 2023. Available from: https://www.pctechguide.com/hard-disks/file-systems-fat-fat8-fat16-fat32-and-ntfs-explained

[24] "File Allocation Table (Internet)", 2023. Available from: https://en.wikipedia.org/wiki/File_Allocation_Table

[25] "FATs and Directory Entries (Internet)", Available from: https://people.cs.umass.edu/~liberato/

courses/2017-spring-compsci365/lecture-notes/11-fats-and-directory-entries/

[26]   Available from: https://flylib.com/books/en/2.48.1/directory_entries.html

[27]   "FAT and FAT Directory Entries (Internet)", 2009. Available from: https://www.sans.org/blog/fat-and-fat-directory-entries/

[28]   "What is Forensic Hard Drive Imaging? (Internet)", 2023. Available from: https://www.forensicon.com/resources/articles/what-is-forensic-hard-drive-imaging/

[29]   "Windows file systems showdown: FAT16, FAT32, NTFS and ReFS (Internet)", 2020. Available from: https://www.techtarget.com/searchwindowsserver/answer/Whats-the-difference-betwen-FAT32-FAT16-and-NTFS

[30]   "Distributed File Systems of the Future (Internet)", 2022. Available from: https://blog.huawei.com/2022/02/15/distributed-file-systems-future/

[31]   "The Evolution of File Systems (Internet)", 2019. Available from: https://learn.microsoft.com/en-us/windows/win32/stg/the-evolution-of-file-systems

[32]   Shullich Robert, "Reverse Engineering the Microsoft Extended FAT File System (exFAT)", *SANS Institute Reading Room,* 2009.

[33]   X. Luo. The design of FAT16 file system based on MSP430 and SD card. Application of Electronic Technique, 2008.

[34]   A., Noymai., U., Ketprom., C., Mitrpant. Increasing memory in FAT16 removable media of RFID handheld reader. 2008 5th International Conference on Electrical Engineering/Electronics, Computer, Telecommunications and Information Technology (ECTI-CON), 2008.

[35]   XL Pang. The Realization of FAT16 File System Base on NAND-Flash. Microcomputer Information, 2010.

[36]   Z. Maaku, F. Robaato. Method for storing of file data in disk, 1995.

[37]   XW Qio, M Lan. Method for storing data of file allocation table, 2013.

[38]   Z. Haoyu, L. Xiongfei, C. Liang, Chang, Z. Xuebai. Fat File System Design and Research. 2015, 568-71.
        [http://dx.doi.org/10.1109/ICNISC.2015.114]

[39]   Yang, Jirong. Embedded file system based on CF (compact flash). 2013.

CHAPTER 8

Management of FAT32 File System

Rohini Tewatia[1,*], Heena Dhiman[2], Rajneesh Gujral[2] and Sachin Dhiman[3]

[1] *Mahamaya Government Polytechnic of Information Technology, Hariharpur, Khajani, Gorakhpur, Uttar Pradesh, India*

[2] *M.M. College of Engineering, Maharishi Markandeshwar (Deemed to be University), Mullana, Ambala, Haryana, India*

[3] *Chitkara College of Pharmacy, Chitkara University, Rajpura, Punjab, India*

Abstract: File Allocation Table (FAT) is a file system that maintains track of where files are placed on a disk and how much storage space is available for new files. The FAT file system is divided into several sections that are arranged in a specific order. Initially, the boot sector holds the data that the file system requires in order to access the volume. The allocation table region includes a file index to the system. Small disks as well as basic folder structures were the original targets of the FAT file system's design. It is still utilized in drives that are meant to run multiple operating systems, like those found in shared environments for Linux, DOS, and Windows. The cluster number for the FAT file system needs to be a power of two and fit in 16 bits. FAT32 is so straightforward and has such a long history, nearly every operating system supports it. Moreover, Windows permits NFTS and FAT32 to live together on a system. ExFAT, the successor to FAT32, supports files and partitions up to 128 petabytes, or 128,000 terabytes, and comes with more options and more storage capacity than FAT32. There are some FAT security factors to consider such as hardening, passwords and several more will be covered in a later section.

Keywords: FAT32, Forensic, Linux, MacOS, Windows.

INTRODUCTION

Background

FAT32, an abbreviation for File Allocation Table 32, is a prevalent file system format employed in diverse storage devices, including USB drives, memory cards, and older hard drives. FAT32 was created by Microsoft as an expansion of the previous FAT file system. The introduction of the FAT32 file system in 1996 with Windows 95 OSR2 aimed to overcome the restrictions of the old FAT file system,

[*] **Corresponding author Rohini Tewatia:** Mahamaya Government Polytechnic of Information Technology, Hariharpur, Khajani, Gorakhpur, Uttar Pradesh, India; E-mail: er.heenacse@mmumullana.org

Alex Khang, Sanchit Dhankhar, Sandeep Bhardwaj, Avnesh Verma & Satish Kumar Sharma (Eds.)

such as the restricted maximum volume size and file size. FAT32 is capable of accommodating files up to 4 GB in size and volumes up to 2 terabytes, making it ideal for various storage devices. FAT32 enjoys extensive compatibility with many operating systems, such as Windows, macOS, Linux, and various embedded systems. It employs a hierarchical directory structure to efficiently arrange files and directories on the storage device. The system utilizes a File Allocation Table (FAT) to monitor the assignment of clusters to files. This cluster-based allocation method is used for storing data on the disk [1]. The cluster size is subject to variation based on the volume's size, with larger volumes often having greater cluster sizes. The size of the cluster directly impacts the effectiveness of utilizing disk space and storing files. FAT32 is widely utilized in portable storage devices such as USB flash drives, memory cards, and digital cameras due to its extensive interoperability and cross-platform support. Additionally, it finds applications in specific embedded systems and outdated external hard drives. Due to the emergence of more recent file systems like NTFS (New Technology File System) and exFAT (Extended File Allocation Table), which provide superior performance, increased file size support, and sophisticated functionalities, FAT32 has become less prevalent in contemporary computer settings [2]. Nevertheless, it continues to be favored in specific contexts where adherence to earlier systems is necessary.

Purpose of FAT32 File System

FAT32 is a crucial tool for forensic investigators, as it offers a standardized and easily accessible format for storing and examining digital evidence in different forensic investigations. The compatibility, simplicity, and well-documented structure of FAT32 make it a valuable tool for forensic examiners to conduct comprehensive and efficient examinations of storage media. FAT32 is widely supported by various operating systems such as Windows, macOS, Linux, and various embedded systems. Forensic examiners can conveniently access and analyze storage devices formatted with FAT32 on various platforms, enabling cross-platform forensic investigations.

The extensively documented structure of this file system simplifies the process for forensic investigators to recover deleted files and lost data from such storage devices. Examiners can reconstruct file systems and recover significant evidence that may have been erased or hidden by studying the File Allocation Table (FAT) and directory entries [3]. Forensic analysts have the ability to examine directory entries, timestamps, file attributes, and other metadata in order to reconstruct the structure of the file system and trace the usage and modification history of files and directories. By generating forensic disk images or logical backups of storage devices that are formatted with FAT32, analysts can ensure the preservation of the authenticity and admissibility of digital evidence in legal proceedings [1].

Scope of the Chapter

The scope of this chapter typically includes a comprehensive exploration of various aspects related to the FAT32 file system.

OVERVIEW OF FAT32

Introduction to FAT32

The progression and development of the file allocation table (FAT) system took place,specifically from the 16-bit version (FAT16) to the 32-bit version (FAT32). The transition from FAT16 to FAT32 in computer forensics signifies a notable progression in storage technology and the capabilities of file systems. Below is a summary of the change and its ramifications for forensic investigations:

- Enhanced Storage Capacity: The main motive behind the shift from FAT16 to FAT32 was the requirement for a greater storage capacity. The FAT16 file system imposed restrictions on both the capacity of volumes and files, which became more constricting as storage technology progressed.
- File System EfficiencyFAT32 resolved this constraint by enabling greater capacities for volumes and individual files, thus fitting the expanding storage demands of contemporary computer systems. FAT32 brought enhancements to file system efficiency when compared to FAT16.
- Compatibility and Interoperability: FAT32 improved storage efficiency by employing lower cluster sizes and optimized disk space allocation, resulting in enhanced storage use and reduced wastage on storage devices. The enhanced efficiency has ramifications for forensic investigations, as analysts were able to scrutinize storage media more efficiently and retrieve erased files with heightened precision.
- Forensic Analysis Challenges: FAT32 ensured compatibility with FAT16 while simultaneously enhancing interoperability with contemporary operating systems and devices. Due to its compatibility with various platforms, FAT32 became the favored option for portable storage devices like USB flash drives and memory cards. From a forensic standpoint, the compatibility and interoperability of FAT32 allowed investigators to examine storage media formatted with FAT32 using a diverse array of forensic instruments and software.
- Forensic Analysis Challenges: The shift from FAT16 to FAT32 posed difficulties and advantages for investigative purposes. Although FAT32 provided improved functionalities and compatibility, it also brought about intricacies in the process of recovering and analyzing data. Forensic examiners

have to modify their procedures and tools in order to successfully recover and evaluate digital evidence due to the implementation of lower cluster sizes and more complex data structures in FAT32.

• Data Recovery Techniques: Forensic investigators had to devise novel data recovery techniques and approaches to tackle the distinct characteristics and intricacies of the FAT32 file system. This encompassed methodologies for retrieving erased files, recreating hierarchical arrangements, examining file information, and detecting indications of user actions on storage media formatted with FAT32.

• Legal Implications: The shift from FAT16 to FAT32 also had legal ramifications for forensic investigations. With the advancement of storage technology, courts and legal authorities have to examine the effects of FAT32's capabilities and limits on the acceptance and reliability of digital evidence in legal processes. Forensic examiners had to follow established methods and standards to guarantee the dependability and acceptability of evidence acquired from storage media formatted with FAT32 [4].

In summary, the transition from FAT16 to FAT32 was a noteworthy achievement in storage technology and file system architecture, providing enhanced functionalities, efficiency, and compatibility for contemporary computing environments. From a forensic standpoint, the move necessitated the adjustment and advancement of forensic techniques and procedures to efficiently retrieve, examine, and safeguard digital evidence held on media formatted with the FAT32 file system.

Key Features and Characteristics

The utilization of the FAT32 file system is crucial for the efficient analysis of digital evidence. From a forensic standpoint, the following are notable characteristics of FAT32:

• The File Allocation Table (FAT) consists of entries that establish the correspondence between clusters and files or directories, hence easing the retrieval and arrangement of data in the context of forensic examination.

• Assigns storage capacity to individual files in a cluster-by-cluster manner. Every cluster has a predetermined size, and files are kept in one or several clusters.

• Arranges files and directories by employing a hierarchical directory framework. Directories consist of entries for both files and subdirectories, allowing forensic examiners to efficiently traverse and analyze the contents of the file system.

• The characteristics of FAT encompass read-only, hidden, system, archive, and directory features. Forensic analysts can examine file attributes to ascertain file

ownership, access permissions, and file formats [1].
- This program logs the timestamps of files and directories, capturing information about when they were created, modified, and last accessed.
- Preserve data regarding deleted files in the directory entries and FAT entries until they are replaced.

Characteristics

- File Allocation Table (FAT): The FAT32 file system employs a File Allocation Table (FAT) to monitor the allocation status of clusters on the disk. The File Allocation Table (FAT) consists of entries that establish the relationship between clusters and files/directories. This facilitates the process of reconstructing file allocation and storage patterns in forensic analysis.
- Cluster-Based Allocation: FAT32 utilizes cluster-based allocation to assign disk space to files. Each cluster represents a predetermined block of storage space. Comprehending the size of clusters is essential for forensic investigators, as it impacts the effectiveness of storing files, fragmentation, and the precision of data recovery endeavors.
- Directory Structure: The directory structure of FAT32 is organized hierarchically, with files and directories being arranged in a hierarchical manner. Directories store information on files and subdirectories, including details like file names, sizes, characteristics, and timestamps. By examining the directory structure, forensic investigators can effectively browse the file system and discover pertinent evidence.
- File Attributes: FAT32 has the capability to support multiple file attributes, including read-only, hidden, system, archive, and directory attributes. These properties include details regarding the features, permissions, and usage history of a file. Forensic investigators examine file properties to ascertain file ownership, access restrictions, and the probable importance of files in an investigation.
- Timestamps: FAT32 stores timestamps for files and directories, which include the timings of creation, modification, and last access. An essential aspect of forensic investigations is the examination of timestamps, which allows for the establishment of timelines, monitoring of file activity, and identification of correlations between occurrences.
- Deleted File Recovery: FAT32 preserves data regarding deleted files in the directory entries and FAT entries until they are replaced by new data. Forensic programs have the capability to retrieve deleted files by examining residual traces, enabling investigators to recover potentially valuable evidence that has been erased or deliberately concealed.
- Fragmentation: Fragmentation refers to the situation where the data of a file is spread out across numerous clusters on the disk that are not next to each other.

FAT32 file systems are prone to fragmentation, particularly on volumes with small cluster sizes or high file activity. Fragmentation analysis aids forensic examiners in comprehending the arrangement of stored data and enhancing their endeavors in data recovery.

- Data Carving: Data carving is a forensic method employed to retrieve fragmented or partially overwritten files from storage media. The structure of FAT32, which uses clusters of a predetermined size, allows for data carving by detecting file headers and footers within clusters. This process reconstructs files that may have been fragmented or destroyed.

- Cross-Platform Compatibility: FAT32 exhibits cross-platform compatibility, allowing it to function seamlessly across multiple operating systems and devices. Consequently, it has gained significant popularity as a preferred file system for detachable storage media, such as USB drives and memory cards. The cross-platform interoperability of the technology enables seamless data interchange and analysis between many systems, hence improving the accessibility of digital evidence for forensic investigators [5].

Advantages

There are several advantages of File Allocation Table (FAT):

- FAT is a highly compatible file system that may be used with several operating systems, such as Windows, Mac OS, and Linux. This facilitates the seamless transfer of files between various computers and devices.

- Simple to deploy: FAT is a comparatively uncomplicated file system that may be easily implemented on many storage systems. Consequently, this characteristic renders it highly favored for portable storage devices such as USB drives and SD cards.

- Enables storage of big disk sizes: The FAT file system allows for the storage of huge disk sizes, with the FAT32 version specifically capable of accommodating drives up to 2 terabytes in size. As a result, it is an appropriate file system for contemporary storage devices that have substantial storage capabilities.

- The FAT file system employs a journaling technique to mitigate the likelihood of data corruption resulting from power outages or system crashes. This measure serves to guarantee the integrity of stored data and mitigate the risk of data loss [1].

Limitation

- Fragmentation occurs when files are generated, removed, or updated, causing the clusters they occupy to be distributed over the disk. This can diminish the efficacy of the disk and decelerate file access times.

- Insufficient security measures: The FAT file system has limited capabilities when it comes to access control and file permissions, which increases its susceptibility to unwanted access and alteration.

- The initial iteration of FAT (FAT12) provides restricted compatibility for lengthy filenames, allowing only short filenames with a maximum of 8 characters and a 3-character extension. Although newer iterations of FAT, such as FAT16 and FAT32, allow for longer filenames, they still possess certain restrictions on the maximum length and character set of filenames.

STRUCTURE OF FAT32

The FAT32 file system has essential elements such as the Boot Sector, File Allocation Table (FAT), Root Directory, Cluster Chain, Directory Entries, File Attributes, and Long File Names (LFN). These components collaborate to arrange and oversee files and directories on a storage device. Below is a concise outline of the organization of FAT32:

Partition Table

The partition table of a storage device utilizing a FAT32 file system establishes the arrangement and configuration of the disk partitions. The partition table is usually found in either the Master Boot Record (MBR) or the GUID Partition Table (GPT), depending on the disk's partitioning strategy. In this explanation, I will outline the construction of the partition table specifically for an MBR-based disk, while GPT employs a distinct format. The MBR-based disk's partition table includes entries for a maximum of four primary partitions or three primary partitions and one extended partition. The partition table contains entries that define individual partitions on the disk. Each entry provides details such as the starting and ending sectors, partition type, and partition status [6]. Below is a concise description of the organization of the partition table in a disk that uses the Master Boot Record (MBR) format:

A Partition Table Entry (PTE)

PTE is a record within the partition table that represents either a primary partition or an extended partition. The partition table consists of four such entries. A Partition Table Entry (PTE) is the term used to refer to each individual entry. The format of the partition table entry is as follows:

Size

The size of each Partition Table Entry (PTE) is 16 bytes, and it follows the format described below:

- Byte 0: Boot Indicator (1 byte) - Indicates the bootable status of the partition.

Bytes 1-3: first CHS Address (3 bytes) - Indicates the first cylinder, head, and sector of the partition. Byte 4: Partition kind (1 byte) - Specifies the specific kind of the partition, such as FAT32 or NTFS. Bytes 5-7: Final CHS Address (3 bytes) - Indicates the concluding cylinder, head, and sector of the partition. Bytes 8-11: Starting LBA Address (4 bytes) - Indicates the first Logical Block Address (LBA) of the partition. Bytes 12-15: Partition Size in Sectors (4 bytes) - Indicates the size of the partition measured in sectors. Partition Type: The partition type field in each PTE specifies the specific file system employed in the partition. The partition type code for FAT32 partitions is usually 0x0B or 0x0C, depending on the shape of the disk.

- Boot Indicator: The boot indicator field in each Partition Table Entry (PTE) indicates whether the partition is capable of being booted or not. Only a single primary partition can be designated as active, and it houses the bootloader code utilized for booting the operating system.
- Extended partition: An extended partition can be defined using one of the four entries in the partition table, in addition to main partitions. An extended partition encompasses logical partitions, hence enabling the establishment of a greater number of partitions on the disk, surpassing the limit of four.

Boot Sector

The boot sector, referred to as the disk Boot Record (VBR), is the initial sector of a FAT32 disk. The file system includes vital information and is required for the volume to function correctly. The following is a concise summary of the organization and components of the boot sector within a FAT32 file system:

- Jump Instruction (3 bytes): The boot sector commonly commences with a concise jump instruction that redirects the system to the genuine boot code. The jump instruction facilitates the execution of the boot code stored in the boot sector by the system.
- OEM Name field: The OEM Name field, consisting of 8 bytes, contains a string that serves to identify the operating system or original equipment manufacturer (OEM) responsible for formatting the volume [7]. It usually consists of the file system's name, such as "MSDOS5.0" or "WINNT."
- BIOS Parameter Block (BPB): The BIOS Parameter Block (BPB) is a 53-byte structure that holds crucial details regarding the FAT32 disk. It encompasses specific information such as the byte count per sector, the sector count per cluster, and the count of reserved sectors.
- File Allocation Tables (FATs). The BPB additionally determines the dimensions of the File Allocation Table (FAT) and the overall quantity of sectors in the volume.
- Extended BIOS Parameter Block (EBPB): The Extended BIOS Parameter Block

(EBPB) is a 26-byte structure that contains more details regarding the FAT32 disk. The information provided encompasses specific specifics such as the version of the file system, the cluster number of the root directory, and the sector number of the backup boot sector. The presence of the EBPB in boot sectors is discretionary and may not be universal.

- Boot Code: The boot code, which is typically 420 bytes in size, consists of executable code responsible for performing initialization duties, such as configuring file system structures and loading the operating system kernel [8]. The amount of the boot code can vary, but it usually fills up the remaining space in the boot sector after the BPB and EBPB.

File Allocation Table (FAT)

The File Allocation Table (FAT) serves as a comprehensive record that monitors the allocation state of clusters on the disk. Every entry in the File Allocation Table (FAT) corresponds to a cluster, which is often referred to as an allocation unit, on the disk. Each element in the FAT stores a value that represents the status of the corresponding cluster. If the entry includes a distinct value (often 0x00 or 0xFF, depending on the version and state), it indicates that the cluster is presently unassigned to any file. From a forensic standpoint, this can be highly essential in ascertaining the amount of available space or pinpointing locations where deleted information might be located.

If the entry includes a value that signifies the subsequent cluster in a file's sequence, it signifies that the cluster is a component of a file and is now being utilized. The value is a linked list of clusters that constitute the content of the file. Occasionally, a value may indicate a faulty cluster, indicating that it is designated as unusable owing to flaws on the disk [9]. The FAT entry uses a specific value (usually 0xFFFFFFF or 0xFFFFFFFF) to signify the conclusion of a file. Examining the FAT32 File Allocation Table in forensic investigations entails various tasks:

- File Recovery: Analyzing the File Allocation Table (FAT) entries can assist in the retrieval of deleted files. Even if a file is destroyed, its clusters cannot be immediately rewritten, and their condition in the FAT can give information about the deleted files. Timeline Analysis: Monitoring the evolution of the File Allocation Table (FAT) over time enables the reconstruction of a chronological sequence of file-related actions, including the creation, modification, and deletion of files.
- Data Carving: Forensic investigators can analyze the File Allocation Table (FAT) to find fragmented files and then reconstruct them by tracing the cluster chains specified in the FAT entries.

• Corruption Detection: Unusual patterns or abnormalities in the File Allocation Table (FAT) entries may suggest filesystem corruption or tampering, which is crucial for assessing the data's integrity.

Cluster Size and Allocation

The cluster size is the allocation unit size, which denotes the smallest unit of allocation within a file system. The term refers to the smallest possible amount of storage capacity that can be assigned to accommodate a file. Increasing the size of clusters decreases fragmentation but might result in inefficient utilization of space for small files. Conversely, reducing the size of clusters minimizes wasted space for small files but may lead to higher fragmentation, when distinct parts of a file are dispersed across multiple clusters on the disk. Understanding the cluster size is essential in computer forensics as it allows for comprehension of file storage on the disk and estimation of file space usage. Allocation is the act of assigning clusters on the disk to store the contents of a file. The management of this process is overseen by the allocation mechanisms of the file system, such as the File Allocation Table (FAT) in file systems based on FAT or the Master File Table (MFT) in NTFS. When a file is created or expanded, the file system assigns an adequate number of clusters to accommodate the file's data. The clusters may not be adjacent to the disk, particularly if the file system is fragmented [10]. Forensic investigators examine allocation patterns to reconstruct file activity, ascertain file sizes, and evaluate the overall health of the file system. Unallocated clusters, which are clusters that are not currently assigned to any file, are of special significance in forensic investigations due to their potential to hold fragments of deleted files or other data. For a variety of tasks in computer forensics, it is crucial to have a comprehensive understanding of the cluster size and allocation patterns.

Cluster size: Understanding the cluster size is beneficial for determining possible locations of deleted files and retrieving their contents during the data recovery process.

File System Analysis: Examining allocation patterns can offer valuable information on file generation, alteration, and removal occurrences, facilitating the reconstruction of a timeline and the collection of evidence.

Fragmentation analysis: Fragmentation analysis involves evaluating the extent of fragmentation and comprehending the distribution of files among clusters. This process aids in enhancing data recovery endeavors and detecting any problems inside the file system [11].

Space Allocation Analysis: A thorough comprehension of the allocation unit size facilitates the estimation of disk space use and the detection of inefficiencies or anomalies in file storage.

MANAGEMENT OF FILES AND DIRECTORIES

File management in computer forensics encompasses the methodical manipulation, scrutiny, and interpretation of digital files to extract evidentiary material and reconstruct chronological occurrences. The following are essential components of file management in forensic investigations:

File Naming Convention

Forensic analysts begin by identifying relevant files on storage media, including documents, images, videos, databases, system files, logs, and application data. Various forensic tools are used to scan storage devices, analyze file system structures, and identify files based on file signatures, metadata, and content. File metadata contains information about each file, such as its name, size, timestamps (creation, modification, access), attributes (read-only, hidden, system), ownership, and permissions.

Forensic tools extract file metadata from file system structures (*e.g.*, MFT in NTFS, FAT in FAT32) to analyze file attributes, establish timelines of file-related activities, and identify anomalies or suspicious files.

Directory Structure

In computer forensics, the directory structure refers to the organization of files and directories (folders) within a file system. Analyzing the directory structure is crucial for understanding how data is organized, identifying relevant files, and reconstructing events [12]. Here are key aspects of directory structure in forensic investigations:

- Hierarchical Organization: Directories are organized in a hierarchical tree-like structure, with each directory containing files and/or subdirectories. The root directory is the top-level directory in the hierarchy, from which all other directories and files are organized.
- Directory Entries: Each directory contains entries for files and subdirectories, along with metadata such as names, sizes, timestamps, and attributes. Directory entries are stored in file system structures such as the Master File Table (MFT) in NTFS or the File Allocation Table (FAT) in FAT32.
- Pathnames: Pathnames uniquely identify the location of a file or directory within the directory structure. Absolute pathnames start from the root directory and

specify the full path to the file or directory (*e.g.*, /home/user/documents/file.txt).

- Relative pathnames specify the path to a file or directory relative to the current directory (*e.g.*, documents/file.txt).
- Navigation: Navigating the directory structure involves traversing directories to locate specific files or directories of interest. Forensic tools provide capabilities for browsing and searching directory structures, examining file metadata, and identifying relevant evidence.
- Timestamp Analysis: Timestamps associated with directory entries provide valuable information about when files and directories were created, modified, or accessed. Analyzing timestamps helps establish timelines of file-related activities and identify suspicious or anomalous behavior.
- Deleted Entries: Deleted files and directories may leave remnants in the directory structure, even after they have been removed from the file system's index. Forensic tools can recover deleted directory entries by analyzing unallocated disk space, file system journal entries, and metadata.
- File Association: Understanding the relationship between files and directories is essential for reconstructing events and identifying relevant evidence. File associations may be indicated by directory structure, file metadata, file content, or cross-referencing between files and directories.

File Attributes

In computer forensics, file attributes refer to the properties or characteristics associated with files that provide information about their state, permissions, and other relevant details [13]. Analyzing file attributes is crucial for understanding file behavior, identifying suspicious activity, and reconstructing events. Here are common file attributes examined in forensic investigations:

- File Name: The file name is a fundamental attribute that identifies a file within a file system. Analyzing file names can provide insights into file contents, purposes, and associations.
- File Size: File size indicates the amount of data stored within a file. Analyzing file sizes helps in identifying large files, detecting anomalies, and estimating storage requirements.
- File Type/Extension: File type or extension indicates the format or category of a file (*e.g.*, .docx for Microsoft Word documents, .jpg for JPEG images). Analyzing file types helps in identifying file contents, determining file compatibility, and detecting potentially malicious files.
- File Timestamps: File timestamps include creation, modification, and access times, indicating when a file was created, last modified, and last accessed. Analyzing timestamps helps establish timelines of file-related activities, identify suspicious behavior, and corroborate evidence.

- File Attributes: File attributes specify various properties or flags associated with a file, such as read-only, hidden, system, archive, compressed, encrypted, temporary, and offline. Analyzing file attributes provides insights into file permissions, visibility, and system status.
- File Ownership: File ownership indicates the user or entity that owns or has control over a file. Analyzing file ownership helps in identifying file creators, collaborators, and potential suspects.
- File Permissions: File permissions specify the level of access granted to users or groups for reading, writing, executing, or modifying a file. Analyzing file permissions helps in identifying authorized users, access restrictions, and security vulnerabilities.
- File Hashes: File hashes are cryptographic values computed from file contents using algorithms such as MD5, SHA-1, or SHA-256. Analyzing file hashes helps in verifying file integrity, detecting file tampering, and identifying duplicate files.
- File Attributes Changes: Changes to file attributes, timestamps, or metadata may indicate suspicious activity, such as file manipulation, tampering, or cover-up attempts. Analyzing attribute changes helps in detecting anomalies, establishing file provenance, and reconstructing events.
- Extended File Attributes (EAs): Some file systems support extended file attributes that provide additional metadata or custom properties for files. Analyzing EAs can reveal supplementary information about files, such as authorship, classification, or versioning [11].

Managing Files and Directories

Efficiently managing files and directories entails employing a methodical approach to handling digital evidence, structuring data, and performing investigations with effectiveness. Below is a comprehensive reference outlining the sequential process of managing files and directories in the field of computer forensics?

- Evidence Collection: Commence the process by gathering digital evidence from many sources, including PCs, storage devices, cloud services, and network shares. Utilize forensic methods and methodologies to obtain forensic pictures or duplicates of storage media, guaranteeing the integrity of data and the preservation of evidence.
- File Identification and Inventory: Generate a comprehensive inventory of all files and directories acquired throughout the process of collecting evidence. Employ forensic tools to analyze file system structures, retrieve metadata, and classify files according to their kind, extension, timestamps, and properties. Perform a preliminary inspection of files to discover potentially significant

material and determine the order of importance for further investigation. Employ keyword searches, regular expressions, and data carving techniques to detect files that contain certain information or patterns of interest [12].

- Directory Structure Analysis: Directory Structure Analysis involves examining the organization and storage of files within the file system. Perform directory navigation, inspect directory entries, and restore the hierarchical structure of files and directories. Metadata Analysis: Evaluate the metadata of a file, encompassing details such as names, sizes, timestamps, attributes, ownership, and rights. Detect any irregularities, contradictions, or strange trends in the file's metadata that could suggest tampering, modification, or unauthorized entry.

- Timestamp Analysis involves examining the timestamps of files (such as creation, modification, and access) in order to determine the sequence of file-related activities. By comparing these timestamps with other data, it is possible to reconstruct events, identify human behaviors, and establish the origin of the files.

- File Recovery and Reconstruction: Retrieve erased or impaired files through the use of forensic methodologies, including file carving, analysis of unallocated space, and parsing of journal entries. Perform file reconstruction on fragmented files, detect file associations, and retrieve data from files that have been corrupted or encrypted.

- File Integrity Verification: File Integrity Verification involves the computation of cryptographic hashes, such as MD5, SHA-1, and SHA-256, for the purpose of verifying the integrity of data and detecting any alterations or tampering. By comparing the hash values with known reference hashes, matches or discrepancies can be identified, ensuring the integrity of digital evidence.

- Documentation and Reporting: It is important to record any discoveries, the process of analysis, and the methods employed throughout the inquiry. Produce thorough reports that outline the outcomes of the forensic analysis, encompassing discoveries, deductions, and suggestions for subsequent actions or legal processes [14].

DISK FORMATTING AND MAINTENANCE

Disk formatting is the process of preparing a storage device for usage by establishing a file system, partition table, and appropriate data structures for storing files and directories. Prior to making any alterations, it is crucial to record the initial configuration of the storage medium in forensic inquiries. This encompasses the process of documenting partition configurations, file system categories, and any other pertinent metadata. Forensic tools can be employed, if needed, to generate forensic photographs of the original disk prior to any formatting or alteration, so guaranteeing the conservation of evidence [27].

Formatting a Disk to FAT32

To format a disk to the FAT32 file system, there are multiple techniques available, which vary based on your operating system. Below are guidelines for formatting a disk to the FAT32 file system on Windows, macOS, and Linux:

Windows

- Connect the disk to your Windows computer.
- Open File Explorer and locate the disk you want to format.
- Right-click on the disk and select "Format..."
- In the Format window, choose "FAT32" from the "File system" dropdown menu.
- Optionally, you can adjust the "Volume label" and allocation unit size.
- Click "Start" to begin the formatting process.
- Once the process is complete, click "OK" to finish.

macOS

- Connect the disk to your Mac.
- Open Disk Utility. You can find it by searching in Spotlight or navigating to Applications > Utilities > Disk Utility.
- In Disk Utility, select the disk you want to format from the list of drives on the left.
- Click on the "Erase" button at the top of the Disk Utility window.
- In the format dropdown menu, select "MS-DOS (FAT)".
- Optionally, you can enter a name for the disk in the "Name" field.
- Click the "Erase" button to start the formatting process.
- Once the process is complete, you can close Disk Utility.

Linux

- Connect the disk to your Linux computer.
- Open a terminal window.
- Use the fdisk command to identify the disk you want to format. For example:
  - Copy code
  - sudo fdisk -l
- Identify the disk you want to format from the list of disks.
- Use the mkfs.fat command to format the disk to FAT32. For example:
  - bashCopy code
  - sudo mkfs.fat -F 32 /dev/sdx1
  - Replace "/dev/sdx1" with the appropriate disk identifier for your system.

- Confirm the action by typing "y" and pressing Enter.
- Once the formatting process is complete, you can safely eject the disk [15].

Disk Checking and Repair

Disk checking and repair involve scrutinizing storage media for errors, inconsistencies, and corruption, and executing remedial measures to restore data integrity and retrieve lost or damaged information. Prior to initiating disk verification, undertake a first evaluation of the storage medium to ascertain the specific disk type (*e.g.*, hard disk drive, solid-state drive, USB drive), its storage capacity, and the file system employed (*e.g.*, NTFS, FAT32, exFAT).

- Disk Imaging: Utilize specialized imaging tools to generate a forensic disk image of the original storage medium. By utilizing write-blocking hardware or software, it is possible to maintain the integrity of evidence and conduct analysis without modifying the original data. This method guarantees that the original storage media remains unaltered throughout the imaging process.
- File System Analysis: File System Analysis involves employing forensic tools to examine the file system for errors, corruption, and inconsistencies. This process includes verifying the integrity of file system metadata, inspecting directory structures, examining file attributes, and assessing timestamps. Search for indications of file system impairment, such as files without a parent directory, files that are linked to several directories, and corruption of file system metadata [12].
- Error detection: Error detection can be achieved by utilizing disk checking applications that are specifically designed for the file system in question. For Windows operating systems, the CHKDSK (Check Disk) utility is recommended for scanning NTFS and FAT file systems. On Linux, the fsck (File System Check) tool is suitable for scanning EXT file systems. To verify and rectify disk permissions and file system issues on macOS, utilize the Disk Utility tool.
- Bad Sector Detection: Perform a thorough examination of the disk surface to identify any areas that may have been physically damaged or deteriorated. Employ disk diagnostic tools to conduct a thorough examination for faulty sectors and designate them as inoperable to avert the risk of data loss or damage. Determine any regions on the disk that are inaccessible or unreadable as a result of faulty sectors.
- Data Recovery: Employ data recovery tools and procedures to retrieve lost or deleted data. Retrieve erased files from unallocated clusters, fragmented disk regions, or file system journal entries. Perform file chain reconstruction and fix file system metadata in order to retrieve retrievable data.

- Verification and Validation: Assess the efficacy of disk checking methods by conducting a secondary scan of the storage media to identify faults and inconsistencies. Verify the integrity of retrieved data by cross-referencing it with established reference data or checksums. Verify that the disk inspection procedure has successfully corrected any faults or irregularities identified during the study.
- Documentation: Record all disk verification methods conducted during the forensic examination, encompassing the employed tools, acquired outcomes, and any remedial measures implemented.

Data Recovery and Backup

Managing defective sectors on storage media is essential for maintaining data integrity and guaranteeing the precision of forensic analysis. Bad sectors refer to regions on a disk that have suffered physical damage or are otherwise incapable of consistently storing data. Presented below is an all-inclusive manual on the management of faulty sectors in the field of computer forensics:

- Identification: Utilize disk imaging or diagnostic tools to accurately detect and pinpoint defective sectors on the storage medium. Bad sectors can be detected using disk imaging, file system analysis, or disk inspection processes. Maintain comprehensive documentation of the precise location and magnitude of identified faulty sectors, including their specific physical addresses on the disk.
- Documentation: Record all occurrences of faulty sectors identified during forensic investigations. Document the quantity, position, and intensity of defective sectors, together with any measures implemented to minimize their consequences. Ensure the meticulous documentation of the procedure for managing problematic sectors, which should include precise timestamps, detailed observations, and conclusive findings.
- Isolation: To prevent additional data loss or corruption, segregate the afflicted regions of the disk that contain faulty sectors. Utilize disk partitioning or file system functionalities to designate these problematic sectors as inoperable and exclude them from data storage.
- Data Recovery: Employ data recovery techniques to retrieve data from sectors neighboring the faulty sectors. Retrieve fragmented files or incomplete data from sections of the disk that are not impacted by faulty sectors. Utilize forensic techniques and software to retrieve recoverable data from impaired sectors and recreate files to the greatest extent feasible.
- Repair: Assess whether the defective sectors are a result of physical harm or logical flaws to decide whether repair or replacement is necessary. If the presence of bad sectors is a result of logical flaws, try to rectify the issue by utilizing disk repair utilities to fix the file system. If the defective sectors are a

result of physical damage, it is advisable to replace the damaged storage media with a new disk.

- Conservation of Authentic Evidence: It is crucial to maintain the original disk image and evidence in their unaltered condition, including any recorded occurrences of faulty sectors. Utilize write-blocking hardware or software to prevent any modifications or contamination of the original evidence [16].

Disk Optimization Strategies

Disk optimization solutions aim to enhance the efficiency of digital forensic investigations, bolster data recovery capabilities, and maintain the integrity of evidence. Here are many regularly used disk optimization methodologies in computer forensic investigations:

- Disk Imaging Optimization: Disk imaging optimization involves utilizing intelligent imaging technologies that have the capability to selectively target specific areas of interest on storage media. Utilize imaging techniques such as "live" imaging or "hot" imaging to collect data from operational systems without causing any interruptions. Employ compression and deduplication functionalities in imaging solutions to diminish the dimensions of forensic photographs and enhance storage efficiency [17].
- Write-Blocking and Read-Only Access: Utilize write-blocking hardware or software to guarantee the preservation of the original evidence during the process of data capture and analysis. Implement read-only access to storage media to prevent any unintentional modifications or contamination of the digital evidence.
- Hashing and Integrity Verification: Hashing and Integrity Verification: Utilize cryptographic algorithms such as MD5, SHA-1, and SHA-256 to calculate hash values of forensic photos and other digital evidence in order to ensure the integrity of the material. Verify the integrity of evidence by comparing hash values against established reference hashes to identify any modifications, manipulation, or corruption.
- Parallel Processing and Multithreading: Utilize the capabilities of parallel processing and multithreading in forensic tools to enhance the speed and efficiency of analysis. Utilize parallel processing by distributing computational work across numerous CPU cores or systems in order to expedite data processing and minimize the time required for research.
- Keyword Searching and Filtering: Employ sophisticated search functionalities in forensic analysis tools to swiftly identify pertinent files, keywords, or patterns throughout extensive datasets. Utilize filters and search parameters to refine search results and concentrate on particular areas of interest.

- Data Carving and File Recovery: Conduct live forensics investigation on active systems to capture volatile data and retrieve up-to-date information using volatility analysis. Utilize memory analysis tools to scrutinize the system's memory (RAM) for artifacts, processes, network connections, and other transient data.
- Live Forensics and Volatility Analysis: Create bespoke scripts or workflows to mechanize tedious operations and optimize forensic analysis procedures. Utilize scripting languages like Python, PowerShell, or Bash to automate the process of extracting, parsing, and generating reports for data activities [16].
- Automation and Scripting: Develop custom scripts or workflows to automate repetitive tasks and streamline forensic analysis processes. Use scripting languages such as Python, PowerShell, or Bash to automate data extraction, parsing, and reporting tasks.
- Documentation and Reporting Templates: Develop uniform documentation and reporting formats to guarantee uniformity and effectiveness in forensic reporting. Record all procedures, discoveries, and measures implemented during the inquiry to uphold a thorough record of activities and provide evidence for legal proceedings [11].

DATA RECOVERY AND BACKUP

Data recovery and backup are critical processes for preserving digital evidence integrity, ensuring data availability, and safeguarding against data loss.

Common Causes of Data Loss

Data loss can arise from a multitude of sources, spanning from inadvertent erasure to intentional manipulation. Comprehending the typical factors that lead to data loss is essential for forensic analysts to efficiently examine and alleviate such occurrences. Below are few prevalent factors that contribute to data loss in the field of computer forensics:

- Unintentional Erasure: Users inadvertently remove files or folders, either as a result of human fallibility or incorrectly perceiving them as dispensable.
- File System Corruption: File system corruption may arise from inadequate system shutdowns, hardware malfunctions, software glitches, or virus infiltrations, resulting in data loss or unavailability.
- Disk Formatting: Accidental disk formatting or reformatting of storage media can lead to the complete loss of all data saved on the disk.
- Hardware problems: such as malfunctions in hard disk drives (HDDs) or solid-state drives (SSDs), failures in controllers, or physical damage to storage media, can result in the loss of data.

- Software or operating system errors can result in data loss, such as crashes, freezes, or file or file system corruption [5, 7].
- Malware or cyber-attacks: such as viruses, ransomware, or malware infestations, have the potential to do harm by damaging files, encrypting data, or deleting important information.
- Physical damage refers to harm caused to storage media, such as scratches, water damage, or exposure to severe temperatures. This type of damage can make data inaccessible or impossible to retrieve.
- Data loss may arise when systems or storage media become old, unsupported, or approach the end of their lifecycle, rendering it arduous or unfeasible to access or retrieve data [18].

Tools and Techniques for Data Recovery

Data recovery employs a range of tools and procedures to retrieve data that has been lost, erased, or corrupted from digital storage medium. The following are often employed tools and methodologies in computer forensic investigations for the purpose of data retrieval:

- Forensic Imaging Tools: Forensic imaging tools, such as FTK Imager, EnCase, Access Data Forensic Toolkit (FTK), and X-Ways Forensics, are frequently employed to generate forensic disk images of storage media. These solutions guarantee the maintenance of evidence integrity by creating an exact replica of the original storage media, enabling analysis and data retrieval without modifying the original evidence.
- Data Recovery Software: Data recovery software, such as R-Studio, GetDataBack, Recuva, and Disk Drill, is employed for the retrieval of deleted or lost files from storage media. These programs utilize several methodologies like as file system scanning, file carving, and partition recovery to detect and recover data that has been lost or destroyed.
- File Carving Tools: File carving tools, such as Foremost, Scalpel, Photorec, and Bulk Extractor, are utilized for the purpose of retrieving files by identifying their unique file signatures or patterns. These tools analyze the unallocated disk space and detect file headers, footers, and other identifiable structures in order to restore deleted or damaged data.
- File System Analysis Tools: File system analysis tools, such as Autopsy, Sleuth Kit, and X-Ways Forensics, offer the ability to analyze file system structures, metadata, and directory entries. These tools aid in the identification of deleted, hidden, or damaged files, as well as in the reconstruction of file paths and metadata to facilitate data recovery.

Best Practices for Data Backup

Data backup is essential for mitigating the risk of data loss, guaranteeing data accessibility, and upholding business continuity. Below are few optimal strategies for data backup:

- Establish a consistent backup schedule that aligns with the frequency of data modifications and the importance of the data. The frequency of backups may differ based on the nature of the data, with crucial data necessitating more regular backups.
- Automatic Backup Processes: Establish automatic backup processes to guarantee consistency and dependability. Utilize backup software or the inherent tools within the operating system to establish a schedule and automate backup operations.
- Implementing several backup copies is essential for ensuring redundancy and resilience in the face of potential data loss. Ensure redundancy by storing backup copies on diverse storage media, at distinct physical locations, or on cloud-based storage platforms.
- Offsite backup storage involves storing backup copies in a location separate from the original data to safeguard against physical calamities like fires, floods, or theft. Employ cloud-based backup services for secure storage at a remote location and convenient retrieval.
- Encryption and Security: Safeguard sensitive information from unauthorized access or data breaches by encrypting backup data. Establish robust access controls and authentication systems to restrict access to backup data to only authorized individuals.
- Periodic Testing and Validation: Conduct regular assessments of backup processes and procedures to verify the successful execution of backups and the ability to restore data as required. Verify the integrity of backup data by conducting regular inspections and comparing backup copies with the original data.
- Implement versioning and retention procedures to effectively manage backup versions and maintain adherence to regulatory standards. Establish retention periods for backup data according to legal, regulatory, or business requirements.
- Documentation and Inventory: Ensure meticulous record-keeping of backup methods, encompassing schedules, protocols, and settings. Maintain a record of backup media, storage locations, and data sets to streamline the process of managing and monitoring them.
- Consistent Maintenance and Updates: Routinely perform maintenance and updates on backup systems, hardware, and software to guarantee dependability and compatibility. Perform software updates, install patches, and apply security fixes to address vulnerabilities and safeguard data security.

- Disaster Recovery Planning: Create and uphold a thorough disaster recovery plan that delineates protocols for data restoration, system recovery, and business continuity in the occurrence of a calamity. Regularly test and revise the disaster recovery strategy to accommodate evolving company needs and technological landscapes.
- Employee Training and Awareness: Implement training and awareness initiatives for employees to enhance their understanding of the significance of data backup, their specific duties and obligations in backup procedures, and optimal strategies for safeguarding data.

PERFORMANCE OPTIMIZATION

Performance optimization employs many methodologies and tactics to enhance the efficiency of analytics and data processing. Data transformation, indexing, caching, parallel processing, resource allocation, and data storage and retrieval are all important aspects of data management.

Cluster Size and Performance

Cluster size denotes the minimum amount of disk space that the file system can assign to store a file. It impacts both the effectiveness of disk space use and the efficiency of file operations. The impact of cluster size on performance is as follows:

- Disk Space Efficiency: Increasing the cluster size often reduces disk space wastage, as smaller files occupy less space on the disk. Nevertheless, opting for smaller cluster sizes might enhance efficiency in storing a substantial quantity of little files by minimizing space wastage.
- File Access Time: Decreasing cluster sizes can result in improved file access times for smaller files as the file system can allocate space with greater efficiency. When cluster sizes are increased, smaller files can use more disk space, resulting in slower access times caused by longer seek times.
- Fragmentation: Increased cluster sizes might result in greater fragmentation, particularly when storing little data. This phenomenon arises due to the file system's tendency to assign complete clusters, even if the file does not necessitate the entire cluster size. Consequently, this leads to inefficient utilization of space and a higher degree of fragmentation.

Fragmentation Issues

Fragmentation poses a challenge in computer forensics as it hampers the effectiveness of data recovery and analysis procedures. It complicates data recovery by dispersing file fragments across various parts of the disk. Fragmented files have their data stored in non-adjacent clusters, making it more difficult to reconstruct the entire file during data recovery. Forensic tools and techniques must consider fragmentation when retrieving deleted or lost files to ensure accurate identification and reconstruction of all pertinent fragments [4, 19].

Optimizing Read and Write Operations

- Employ specialist forensic imaging tools to execute read operations for the purpose of generating forensic disk images. Select tools that provide rapid and effective imaging of storage media, while guaranteeing the integrity of data through features such as write-blocking and verification.
- Utilize write-blocking hardware devices to impede any write activities on the original evidence while doing data acquisition. Write-blocking is a technique that safeguards the original evidence's integrity by permitting read operations to retrieve data for forensic analysis.
- Utilize rapid storage devices, such as Solid-State Drives (SSDs) or high-speed External Hard Drives (HDDs), for data acquisition and analysis. The use of fast storage media can greatly decrease the time it takes to read and write data, resulting in improved efficiency for forensic operations. Optimize read and write performance by adjusting file system parameters, such as cluster size and block size, according to the characteristics of the storage media and the type of data being processed. Select cluster sizes that strike a balance between efficiency and storage space utilization in order to minimize fragmentation and enhance performance.
- Implement parallelization of data acquisition procedures to concurrently execute numerous read operations on distinct storage devices or partitions. This approach can significantly decrease acquisition time and enhance overall efficiency, particularly when handling substantial data volumes.

SECURITY CONSIDERATIONS

The primary focus in computer forensics is to prioritize security concerns in order to guarantee the preservation, secrecy, and genuineness of digital evidence throughout the investigative procedure.

Access Control

Enforce stringent access controls to limit access to forensic equipment, storage of evidence, and case files. Employ robust password authentication, two-factor authentication, or biometric authentication techniques to deter illegal access by users.

- Restrict the physical entry to forensic workstations, evidence storage facilities, and storage media that hold digital evidence.
- Implement physical security measures, such as secured doors, access badges, and surveillance cameras, to deter unlawful entry into forensic facilities.
- Enforce logical access rules to limit access to forensic instruments, analysis software, and stores of evidence.
- Verify the identity of users before giving access to sensitive resources by implementing robust password authentication, biometric authentication, or two-factor authentication.
- Allocate roles and permissions to forensic analysts, investigators, and other staff according to their duties and level of jurisdiction.
- Establish role-based access controls that limit access to particular functions, data, or resources according on the user's role within the forensic team [13].

Encryption and Decryption

Encryption refers to the procedure of transforming data into an unreadable form that can only be deciphered with the appropriate decryption key or passphrase. It is frequently employed to safeguard confidential data stored on digital devices, such as hard drives, USB drives, and mobile devices. Prominent encryption algorithms encompass the Advanced Encryption Standard (AES), Rivest Cipher (RSA), and Triple Data Encryption Standard (3DES). Decryption refers to the procedure of transforming encrypted data back into its original, intelligible state by utilizing the decryption key or passphrase. To decrypt the data, one must have access to the encryption key or password that was used to encrypt it. Forensic analysts may endeavor to decipher encrypted data during investigations in order to gain access to pertinent information and evidence [20].

Security Best Practices

Computer forensics experts advise maintaining the integrity of encrypted data during investigations and adhering to legal and ethical guidelines when attempting decryption. It is important for forensic analysts to thoroughly document their decryption efforts and consult legal professionals if decryption might involve accessing protected information or infringing upon privacy rights.

- Preserve a reliable sequence of possession for all digital evidence to guarantee its integrity and acceptability in a legal proceeding.
- Maintain a comprehensive record of all instances in which evidence is handled, documenting the individuals who accessed it, the specific dates and times of access, and the purpose for which it was accessed. This will ensure the establishment of a transparent and traceable audit trail.

- Safeguard digital evidence by storing it in secure areas with restricted access to deter physical tampering or theft.
- Employ tamper-evident seals, locked cabinets, or safes to safeguard physical storage medium housing evidence.
- Implement robust security measures to safeguard forensic workstations and networks from unauthorized access or infiltration, thereby mitigating the risk of data breaches or compromise of forensic data.
- Implementing firewalls, intrusion detection systems, and network segmentation is essential to isolate forensic environments and safeguard sensitive data.

COMPATIBILITY AND INTEROPERABILITY

Compatibility pertains to the capacity of distinct components or systems to function together without any conflicts or complications. Compatibility in computer forensics refers to the process of ensuring that forensic tools, software, and hardware are able to operate effectively within the forensic environment. This encompasses the ability to function well with many operating systems such as Windows, macOS, and Linux, as well as diverse file systems like NTFS, FAT32, and HFS+. Additionally, it covers compatibility with a wide range of hardware configurations, including desktops, laptops, and mobile devices. In order to streamline data collection, processing, and preservation duties during investigations, it is essential for forensic tools and software to be interoperable with a diverse array of systems and configurations. Interoperability is the capacity of various systems, software, or devices to exchange and analyze data without any difficulty. Interoperability in computer forensics facilitates the seamless collaboration and efficient interchange of information among forensic tools, methodologies, and processes. Interoperability enables forensic analysts to employ a diverse array of tools and methodologies [26].

FAT32 and Operating Systems

FAT32 is a file system that is compatible with different operating systems, such as Windows, macOS, Linux, and certain embedded systems. This compatibility makes FAT32 widely utilized for external storage devices like USB drives, memory cards, and external hard drives, which are frequently encountered as evidence in forensic investigations. The fact that FAT32 can work with multiple operating systems makes it an important file system in the field of computer forensics. Forensic analysts require the expertise and resources to proficiently examine evidence stored in the FAT32 format. This ensures that digital evidence is appropriately managed, scrutinized, and presented in judicial processes [21].

Cross-Platform Considerations

Factors to consider while developing software that may run on multiple platforms: Diverse operating systems, file formats, and devices are discovered throughout investigations. Digital evidence might originate from a range of operating systems, including Windows, macOS, Linux, Android, iOS, and others. In order to evaluate evidence from any source, it is essential for forensic tools and procedures to be compatible with many operating systems. This is because different operating systems use different file systems, such as NTFS, FAT32, exFAT, HFS+, APFS, ext3/ext4, and others. Forensic tools must possess the capability to effectively examine evidence from various platforms by supporting a diverse array of file systems. It is imperative to utilize forensic tools that are compatible with different operating systems and file systems. The utilization of cross-platform forensic tools guarantees that evidence can be processed and analyzed on multiple platforms without encountering any restrictions.

Compatibility with External Devices

• It is necessary to employ forensic tools that are compatible with diverse operating systems and file systems. Cross-platform forensic tools ensure that evidence can be processed and evaluated on numerous systems without limits.
• Forensic equipment and software should be compatible with USB drives and external hard drives widely used to store digital evidence.
• Ensure that forensic imaging tools can acquire disk images from USB drives and external hard drives while preserving data integrity and metadata [18].

FUTURE TRENDS AND DEVELOPMENTS

Several developing trends and developments are impacting the future of computer forensics, including breakthroughs in technology, changes in the threat landscape, and shifting legal and regulatory frameworks. Here are some major trends to watch for in the world of computer forensics:

Emerging File System Technologies

Emerging file system technologies are always emerging in response to the changing landscape of digital storage and computing environments. While established file systems like NTFS, FAT32, and ext4 remain widespread, some innovative file system concepts are gaining traction in computer forensics. Here are some notable examples:

• ZFS (Zettabyte File System): ZFS is a next-generation file system developed by Sun Microsystems (now Oracle) and extensively used in Unix-based operating systems like FreeBSD, OpenSolaris, and Illumos. ZFS offers features such as data integrity checking, built-in RAID support, snapshots, and copy-on-write functionality, making it well-suited for data storage and archival purposes.

- Btrfs (B-tree File System): Btrfs is a modern file system for Linux-based operating systems that offers features such as copy-on-write snapshots, check summing, and built-in support for RAID and SSDs. Btrfs is designed to address the scalability and reliability limitations of traditional Linux file systems like ext4, offering improved data integrity and flexibility for storage management. Forensic analysts may encounter Btrfs file systems in Linux-based environments and need to leverage tools capable of parsing and analyzing Btrfs-specific metadata and data structures.

- APFS (Apple File System): APFS is a proprietary file system developed by Apple for use in macOS, iOS, tvOS, and watchOS devices. APFS includes capabilities such as copy-on-write cloning, space sharing, snapshots, and native encryption, increasing storage efficiency and enhancing data protection on Apple devices. Forensic tools and techniques have evolved to support APFS, enabling analysts to acquire, analyze, and interpret evidence from macOS and iOS devices using APFS file systems.

- ReFS (Resilient File System): ReFS is a file system introduced by Microsoft in Windows Server 2012 and later versions, designed to address the scalability, reliability, and data integrity requirements of modern storage environments. ReFS includes features such as integrity streams, data deduplication, and built-in resilience against data corruption and hardware failures, making it suitable for use in enterprise storage solutions.

- Forensic analysts may encounter ReFS file systems in Windows-based environments and need to adapt their tools and techniques to handle ReFS-specific metadata and data structures. F2FS (Flash-Friendly File System): F2FS is a file system optimized for flash-based storage devices such as SSDs, eMMC, and SD cards, developed by Samsung for Linux-based operating systems.F2FS incorporates features such as wear leveling, TRIM support, and log-based structures to maximize performance and longevity on flash media. Forensic analysts may encounter F2FS file systems in embedded systems, smartphones, and other devices utilizing flash storage, necessitating specialized tools for data acquisition and analysis [22].

Potential Improvements to FAT32

One of the primary limitations of FAT32 is its maximum file size limit of 4 GB. Increasing this limit would allow for the storage and handling of larger files, which is increasingly relevant as file sizes continue to grow with higher-resolution media and large datasets.

- FAT32 is susceptible to fragmentation, which can degrade performance and increase disk space usage.
- Implementing better fragmentation handling mechanisms could help minimize fragmentation and improve overall file system performance.
- FAT32 lacks support for certain metadata features found in modern file systems, such as extended file attributes, file system journaling, and file-level encryption.
- Adding support for these features would enhance data integrity, security, and compatibility with modern computing environments.
- Integrating data compression capabilities into FAT32 could help reduce storage space requirements and improve efficiency, especially for devices with limited storage capacity or bandwidth-constrained environments.
- Enhancing error detection and repair mechanisms in FAT32 would help mitigate data corruption and improve data integrity.
- Automated tools for detecting and repairing file system errors could help minimize the risk of data loss and improve overall reliability.
- FAT32 has limited support for Unicode filenames, which can cause compatibility issues when handling files with non-ASCII characters [23].

The Role of FAT32 in Modern Computing

FAT32 is highly compatible with various operating systems, including Windows, macOS, Linux, and embedded systems. Its widespread support makes it a common file system choice for external storage devices such as USB drives, memory cards, and external hard drives.

- In forensic investigations, FAT32 compatibility ensures that forensic analysts can access and analyze digital evidence stored on FAT32-formatted devices, regardless of the operating system used.
- Many legacy systems and devices still utilize FAT32 due to its long-standing presence and compatibility with older hardware and software.
- Forensic analysts often encounter FAT32-formatted storage devices in investigations involving older computers, digital cameras, GPS devices, and other electronic devices.
- FAT32 remains a popular choice for formatting removable media such as USB drives and memory cards due to its simplicity and broad compatibility.
- Forensic analysts frequently encounter FAT32-formatted removable media in cases involving data storage, file transfer, and digital evidence collection.
- Forensic tools and software often provide robust support for FAT32, enabling analysts to perform tasks such as disk imaging, file carving, metadata analysis, and timeline reconstruction with ease [24].

CONCLUSION

Effective FAT32 management is essential for maintaining the integrity, performance, and reliability of storage devices formatted with the FAT32 file system. By implementing proactive maintenance practices and adhering to best practices for disk management, organizations can optimize storage resources, minimize data loss risks, and ensure compliance with legal and regulatory requirements.

- Proper FAT32 management helps ensure the integrity of stored data by minimizing the risk of file system corruption, data loss, and file fragmentation.
- Regular maintenance tasks such as disk checking, error repair, and defragmentation help identify and resolve issues that could lead to data corruption or loss.
- Effective FAT32 management improves the performance of storage devices by reducing file fragmentation, optimizing file allocation, and minimizing disk access times.
- Defragmenting FAT32 volumes consolidates fragmented files, improves read/write speeds, and enhances overall system responsiveness, especially on older hardware or devices with limited resources.
- Proper FAT32 management maximizes storage efficiency by optimizing file allocation and minimizing wasted space on disk.
- Regular disk cleanup, file system optimization, and data compression techniques help reclaim disk space and ensure that storage resources are used effectively [23].
- Regular disk maintenance and error checking help prevent file system errors, disk corruption, and data inconsistencies that could compromise the integrity of stored data.
- Proactive monitoring and management of FAT32 volumes allow for early detection and resolution of potential issues before they escalate into more significant problems.
- Effective FAT32 management facilitates data recovery and forensic analysis by maintaining accurate file system structures, metadata, and allocation information.
- Well-managed FAT32 volumes are easier to analyze and recover in forensic investigations, reducing the time and effort required for data reconstruction and evidence preservation [25].

REFERENCES

[1] B. Chen, J. Guan, H. Wang, and G. Yao, "novel data recovery algorithm for fat32 file system", *in 2021 2nd International Conference on Information Science and Education (ICISE-IE).,* IEEE., 2021.
[http://dx.doi.org/10.1109/ICISE-IE53922.2021.00143]

[2] J.M. Rodríguez Justiniano, "Computer Forensics Tutorial Disk File Systems (FAT16, FAT32, NTFS)", *Comput. Sci.,* 2011.

[3] B. Carrier, *File system forensic analysis.* Addison-Wesley Professional, 2005.

[4] A. Bahjat, and J. Jones, "File Allocation Chronology and its Impact on Digital Forensics", *in 2023 IEEE 13th Annual Computing and Communication Workshop and Conference (CCWC).,* IEEE., 2023.
[http://dx.doi.org/10.1109/CCWC57344.2023.10099265]

[5] N. Zhang, Y. Jiang, and J. Wang, "The research of data recovery on Windows file systems", *2020 International Conference on Intelligent Transportation, Big Data & Smart City (ICITBS),* IEEE., 2020.
[http://dx.doi.org/10.1109/ICITBS49701.2020.00141]

[6] FAT16, F.B. and F. FATX, *File Allocation Table.*

[7] A. Khang, N.A. Ragimova, V.A. Hajimahmud, and V.A. Alyar, ""Advanced Technologies and Data Management in the Smart Healthcare System", In: *AI-Centric Smart City Ecosystems: Technologies, Design and Implementation (1st Ed.)* vol. 16. Khang A., Rani S., Sivaraman A. K. CRC Press., 2022, p. 10.
[http://dx.doi.org/10.1201/9781003252542-16]

[8] V.S. Keshava Munegowda, and G. Raju, *The Extended FAT file system.,* 2011.

[9] K.L. Rusbarsky, and K. City, *A forensic comparison of NTFS and FAT32 file systems.* Marshall Univ, 2012, p. 29.

[10] I. Jóźwiak, M. Kędziora, and A. Melińska, "Methods for detecting and analyzing hidden FAT32 volumes created with the use of cryptographic tools", *Proceedings of the 8th International Conference on Dependability and Complex Systems DepCoS-RELCOMEX.*Brunów, Poland

[11] K.S. Sondarva, "Forensics Analysis of NTFS File Systems", In: *in Advances in Cyberology and the Advent of the Next-Gen Information Revolution* IGI Global., 2023, pp. 138-165.
[http://dx.doi.org/10.4018/978-1-6684-8133-2.ch008]

[12] I.P.A.E. Pratama, "Computer forensic using photorec for secure data recovery between storage media: A proof of concept. International Journal of Science", *Technology & Management,* vol. 2, no. 4, pp. 1189-1196, 2021.

[13] H. Khan, M. Javed, S.A. Khayam, and F. Mirza, "Designing a cluster-based covert channel to evade disk investigation and forensics", *Comput. Secur.,* vol. 30, no. 1, pp. 35-49, 2011.
[http://dx.doi.org/10.1016/j.cose.2010.10.005]

[14] G. Horsman, "Digital tool marks (DTMs): a forensic analysis of file wiping software", *Aust. J. Forensic Sci.,* vol. 53, no. 1, pp. 96-111, 2021.
[http://dx.doi.org/10.1080/00450618.2019.1640793]

[15] N. Zlatanov, "Hard Disk Drive and Disk Encryption", In: *in Conference of the Black Hat* Amsterdam, The Netherlands., 2015.

[16] ÖZDEMİR, A. and Ş. GÜLCÜ, "cientific Data Recovery Methods and Solutions in Optics Discs and HDDs", *Current Studies in Basic Sciences, Engineering and Technology,* p. 224, .

[17] D. Elrick, *Forensic Examination of Windows-Supported File Systems,* 2019. Available from: lulu.com

[18] G. Liu, and J. Xu, "A Redundancy Approach to FAT File System", *Proceedings of ICCD 2017,* Springer., 2019.
[http://dx.doi.org/10.1007/978-981-10-8944-2_46]

[19]   A. Ravi, T.R. Kumar, and A.R. Mathew, "A method for carving fragmented document and image files", *2016 International Conference on Advances in Human Machine Interaction (HMI)*, IEEE., 2016.
[http://dx.doi.org/10.1109/HMI.2016.7449170]

[20]   P. Shabana Subair, C. Balan, S. Dija, and K. Thomas, "Forensic decryption of FAT BitLocker volumes", *in Digital Forensics and Cyber Crime: Fifth International Conference, ICDF2C 2013, Moscow, Russia, September 26-27, 2013, Revised Selected Papers 5*. 2014. Springer, 2013.

[21]   H. H. Khanh, and A. Khang, "The Role of Artificial Intelligence in Blockchain Applications", *Reinventing Manufacturing and Business Processes through Artificial Intelligence,* vol. 2, In Rana G, Khang A., Sharma R., Goel A. K., Dubey A. K. CRC Press., pp. 20-40, 2021.
[http://dx.doi.org/10.1201/9781003145011-2]

[22]   D. Quick, and K.K.R. Choo, "Impacts of increasing volume of digital forensic data: A survey and future research challenges", *Digit. Invest.,* vol. 11, no. 4, pp. 273-294, 2014.
[http://dx.doi.org/10.1016/j.diin.2014.09.002]

[23]   T.M. Maung, and M.M.S. Thwin, "Proposed effective solution for cybercrime investigation in Myanmar", *Int. J. Eng. Sci. (Ghaziabad),* vol. 6, no. 1, pp. 01-07, 2017. [IJES].
[http://dx.doi.org/10.9790/1813-0601030107]

[24]   "H. and M.S. KILIÇ, Importance of Operating Systems Type in Computer Forensics", *International Journal of Information Security & Cybercrime,* vol. 4, no. 2, 2015.

[25]   T. Newsham, C. Palmer, A. Stamos, and J. Burns, "Breaking forensics software: Weaknesses in critical evidence collection", *Proceedings of the 2007 Black Hat Conference,* 2007.

[26]   A. Khang, M. Muthmainnah, P.M. Seraj, A. Al Yakin, and A.J. Obaid, "AI-Aided Teaching Model in Education 5.0", In: *Handbook of Research on AI-Based Technologies and Applications in the Era of the Metaverse.,* A. Khang, V. Shah, S. Rani, Eds., IGI Global, 2023, pp. 83-104.
[http://dx.doi.org/10.4018/978-1-6684-8851-5.ch004]

CHAPTER 9

Management of NTFS File System

Neelam Oberoi[1,*], **Mani Goyal**[1], **Heena Dhiman**[1], **Sachin Dhiman**[2] and **Shushank Mahajan**[2]

[1] *M.M. College of Engineering, Maharishi Markandeshwar (Deemed to be University), Mullana, Ambala, Haryana, India*

[2] *Chitkara College of Pharmacy, Chitkara University, Rajpura, Punjab, India*

Abstract: A sector is the smallest physical storage unit on an NTFS disk. The size of the data, expressed in power of two bytes, is typically 512 bytes. The smallest file allocation unit in NTFS, on the other hand, is called a cluster and is independent of sectors. It may consist of one or more adjacent sectors. As of right now, NTFS supports files up to 248 bytes in size. A straightforward yet effective method is used by NTFS to arrange data on a drive volume. Each element on a volume is a file, and each file is made up of a set of properties. To help secure user data, NTFS makes use of user-level encryption and access control lists, or ACLs. Thus, this chapter's goal is to manage the NTFS file system.

Keywords: ACLS, Bytes, NTFS, Windows.

INTRODUCTION

The NTFS File System, a marvel of software innovation that forms the foundation of data structure and management, is hidden away in the background of a Windows-powered machine. The New Technology File System (NTFS), which replaced the File Allocation Table (FAT) system, is the ideal combination of performance, security, and dependability. It converts the abstract disk space into an organized, readable environment of files and directories, serving as an elegant example of the intricacy and sophistication that underlie contemporary computing.

NTFS is more elegant than just a data storage system. Many cutting-edge capabilities, like as journaling, encryption, and access control, are hidden within its design and are carefully crafted to meet the diverse requirements of Outdated

---

** **Corresponding author Neelam Oberoi:** M.M. College of Engineering, Maharishi Markandeshwar (Deemed to be University), Mullana, Ambala, Haryana, India; E-mail: neelamoberoi1030@mmumullana.org*

contemporary users. This article delves deeply into the NTFS File System's inner workings, revealing its architectural wonders, its place in the Windows environment, and its ongoing development. For anyone interested in learning more about NTFS, be they an IT expert, a computer enthusiast, or just a curious user, it looks like an insightful and exciting intellectual journey.

Overview of NTFS

Microsoft developed the proprietary New Technology File System or NTFS File System. It was first included in Windows NT 3.1 in 1993, and since then, Windows operating systems have used it as their primary file system. Instead of its FAT family forebears, NTFS included a number of advancements and improvements, offering a strong foundation for contemporary computing requirements [1]. NTFS is primarily used for managing and organizing data on storage devices, such as SSDs and hard disks. It accomplishes this by using a tree-like hierarchical structure made up of files, directories, and different metadata properties. However, NTFS goes beyond simple categorization; it incorporates sophisticated features like disk quotas for user space management, encryption for security, journaling for data integrity, and complex permission systems for access control. As a result, a file system that supports anything from complicated enterprise-level processes to personal computing can be used with flexibility and control.

Evolution and History

The New Technology File System (NTFS) has undergone significant evolution since its introduction alongside the Windows NT operating system in 1993 [2].

NTFS was "built from the ground up," as is frequently stated (and occasionally even by me, I must confess). Nonetheless, that is not exactly true. From the perspective of not being reliant on the outdated FAT file system, NTFS is unquestionably "new." Rather than designing it to remain compatible with something else, for example, Microsoft made the decision to build its system with an awareness of the needs of its upcoming operating system. But parts of NTFS's ideas were borrowed from HPFS, another file system that Microsoft helped develop, so it is not totally original.

Operating System/2 existed prior to Windows NT. When OS/2 was first being developed in the early 1990s, IBM and Microsoft collaborated on it together.

Microsoft, on the other hand, has not allowed NTFS to stagnate. The file system has been enhanced with new functionality throughout time. The most recent version of NTFS was released with Windows 2000. The NTFS used in Windows

NT is largely comparable to it, however, it has a few extra features and functionalities. Over time, Microsoft has also fixed issues with NTFS, which has increased its stability and its recognition as a "serious" file system. NTFS is currently the most often utilized file system for implementations of new, high-end PCs, workstations, and servers. In the realm of small to medium-sized corporate systems, NTFS competes with other UNIX file systems and is gaining traction with individual "power" users [3].

Microsoft has made available five NTFS versions (Table 1):

Table 1. Available five NTFS versions made by Microsoft.

NTFS Version Number	First Operating System	Release Date	New Features	Remarks
1.0	Windows NT 3.1	1993	Initial version	NTFS 1.0 is incompatible with 1.1 and newer: volumes written by Windows NT 3.5x cannot be read by Windows NT 3.1 until an update (available on the NT 3.5x installation media) is installed [18].
1.1	Windows NT 3.5	1994	Named streams and access control lists	NTFS compression support was added in Windows NT 3.51
1.2	Windows NT 4.0	1996	Security descriptors	Commonly called NTFS 4.0 after the OS release.
3.0	Windows 2000	2000	Disk quotas, file-level encryption in a form of Encrypting File System, sparse files, reparse points, update sequence number (USN) journaling, distributed link tracking, the $Extend folder and its files	Compatibility was also made available for Windows NT 4.0 with the Service Pack 4 update. Commonly called NTFS 5.0 after the OS release.
3.1	Windows XP	October 2001	Expanded the Master File Table (MFT) entries with redundant MFT record number (useful for recovering damaged MFT files)	Commonly called NTFS 5.1 after the OS release. LFS version 1.1 was replaced by version 2.0 as of Windows 8 to improve performance.

Subsequent versions included additional file system-related features but did not modify NTFS. For instance, Windows Vista featured partition shrinking, self-healing, NTFS symbolic links, and transactional NTFS. All other capabilities are new to the operating system and leverage pre-existing NTFS features; NTFS symbolic links are new to the file system.

NTFS (New Technology File System) remains critically important in modern computing environments for several reasons:

- Scalability: NTFS is capable of handling massive amounts of storage, allowing volumes up to 256 terabytes in size and individual files up to 16 exabytes. Its scalability makes it appropriate for large servers and high-capacity storage devices, among other contemporary storage needs.
- Reliability: One feature of NTFS that helps to maintain file system integrity is journaling, which keeps track of changes made to the system before they are committed to disk.
- In the event of unplanned system shutdowns or power outages, this lowers the possibility of data corruption and enhances the overall system reliability.
- Security: Advanced security features like encryption, auditing, and file and folder permissions are available with NTFS. To prevent unwanted access to sensitive material, administrators can restrict access to files and folders depending on user accounts and groups.
- Compatibility: All Windows operating systems come with NTFS as the default file system, guaranteeing wide compatibility with Windows-based PCs and servers. It also provides third-party drivers and utilities for compatibility with other operating systems.
- Performance: NTFS has performance enhancements such as enhanced data structures and cluster allocation that assist in lowering fragmentation and speeding up disk access. Better overall system responsiveness and performance are a result of these performance improvements.
- Advanced capabilities: File compression, sparse files, transactional transactions, and symbolic links are just a few of the many advanced capabilities that NTFS provides. These features facilitate complex data management scenarios and allow for more effective use of storage resources.
- Tight Integration with Windows Ecosystem: Active Directory, Group Policy, and Windows Management Instrumentation (WMI) are just a few of the Windows ecosystem components with which NTFS is closely integrated. In Windows-based environments, this smooth connection makes management and system administration chores easier.
- Legacy Support: NTFS is still extensively used and maintained across a wide range of hardware and software settings, despite the introduction of successor file systems by Microsoft, such as ReFS (Resilient File System). Many individuals and organizations trust it because of its long history and track record of success.

As a dependable, scalable, and feature-rich file system that satisfies the many demands of companies, organizations, and individual users operating in Windows-based environments, NTFS continues to play a critical role in modern computing.

UNDERSTANDING NTFS STRUCTURE

File Allocation Table (FAT) *vs.* NTFS

Two distinct file systems, NTFS and FAT, are mainly utilized in Microsoft Windows operating systems [3]. These are the main differences between them:

Background

- FAT: Originally introduced in the early days of DOS, the FAT file system has been a part of Windows from Windows 95, 98, and ME.
- NTFS: Originally released in 1993 with Windows NT, NTFS has remained the standard file system for all subsequent versions of Windows, which includes XP, Vista, 7, 8, and 10.

Maximum File Size and Volume

- FAT: File and volume sizes are constrained by the FAT file system. One of the most often used versions, FAT32, for instance, possesses a maximum volume capacity of 2 terabytes (TB) and a maximum file size of 4 GB.
- NTFS: NTFS allows for substantially higher volumes and file sizes. Individual files up to 16 exabytes (EB) and volumes up to 256 TB can be managed by it.

Security and Permissions

- FAT: This file system is not very secure. Compared to NTFS, it is less secure since it supports file and folder permissions less thoroughly.
- NTFS: NTFS provides extensive security features like auditing, encryption (via the Encrypting File System, or EFS), access control lists (ACLs), and file and folder permissions. More precise control over who can see, edit, and remove files and folders is possible with these features.

Reliability

- FAT: This file system has no inherent mechanisms to protect data integrity or repair disk failures. It is more vulnerable to corruption of the file system, particularly when there is an abrupt power outage or a system breakdown.

- NTFS: NTFS has features like journaling that log changes prior to their being committed to disk, helping to preserve the integrity of the file system. As a result, there is less chance of data loss or corruption, and reliability is increased.

Performance

- FAT: On smaller disks and with smaller files, FAT usually provides quicker read/write performance in comparison to NTFS. However, if the drive fills up or file sizes grow because of fragmentation, performance could suffer.
- NTFS: NTFS has performance enhancements like enhanced data structures and cluster allocation that lessen fragmentation and speed up disk access. Larger drives and larger data yield better performance.

Compatibility

- FAT: A large variety of hardware and operating systems, including previous versions of Windows, macOS, Linux, and consumer gadgets like gaming consoles and cameras, are generally compatible with this file system.
- NTFS: NTFS is typically utilized in Windows contexts, and in order to fully support read/write on non-Windows operating systems, it might be necessary to install third-party drivers or utilities.

It can be summarized as follows: NTFS is the recommended option for modern Windows-based systems, especially for large-capacity storage and enterprise contexts, notwithstanding FAT's simplicity and compatibility.

Components of NTFS

The NTFS represents a highly advanced structure with numerous interlocking components that provide a wide range of capabilities beyond simple file storage. It is more than just a way to store files on a drive. As one looks more closely at NTFS's architecture, layers of complexity become apparent. It is a complex fusion of technical skill and design insight. This chapter delves into the architecture and structure of NTFS, revealing its inner workings and design and investigating the creative methods that give it the strength and adaptability of a multipurpose file system.

Master File Table

Every directory and file within the NTFS drive has its information stored in a central database called the Master File Table. Each item in the MFT represents a file or directory and contains details about the file, such as security descriptors, file attributes, and pointers to its data clusters. The MFT is an essential part of NTFS and is necessary for it to function [4].

Quick access to the data required to recover a file is made possible by the MFT, which serves as an index to all of the files and directories on the drive. Every file and directory on an NTFS drive has an MFT (Master File Table) entry, which is a unique record. The file name, timestamps, permissions, and a link to the file's contents are among the details included in the MFT entry. Every time a file is created or altered, the matching MFT entry is updated.

Structure of NTFS Volume

Even when a file is deleted, the actual data remains on the disk until it is replaced by new data, the accompanying MFT entry is designated as free. Since the data in the erased file can still be recoverable, this can be helpful in data recovery situations. The disk regions where the erased data was stored must not be overwritten in order for data recovery to be successful.

MFT Record Structure

A file or directory on the NTFS disk is represented by one of the many records that make up the complex NTFS file system's Master File Table (MFT) structure [5]. Because every MFT record is 1024 bytes, it is very easy to parse MFT data. An MFT record is generally structured as follows:

File Record Header: This part includes details about the record itself, such as its size, the update sequence offset, and the flags that represent the file or directory's current status.

Attributes of the File: File Attribute List: The name, size, data, and timestamps of the file or directory are listed here, along with other properties that describe it. Every attribute has its own format and is saved as a distinct structure.

Data Runs: This section details the disk location of the particular file or directory's data. The starting cluster and the length of each consecutive data block are described by a sequence of extents that are recorded with the data runs.

Depending on the file system version being used, the MFT in NTFS may have a different exact format and structure. The primary components of each MFT entry are the File Record Header, File Attribute List, and Data Runs, but the overall structure is still the same.

Attributes in MFT Records

- Standard Information: Basic information like timestamps and permissions.
- File Name: The file or directory name that is readable by humans.
- Data Attribute: The actual content that the file contains, or pointers if the data is

large.

• Index Root and Index Allocation: Used for directories to reference other files.

Attribute Types

Every piece of data connected to a file on an NTFS volume—file attributes: like its name, owner, contents, timestamp, and so on are implemented. Data is an attribute of a file; it's the "Data Attribute" denoted by $DATA. There are several properties included on an NTFS drive. The table below lists the attribute names that NTFS uses that NTFS uses (Table **2**).

Table 2. Attribute names that NTFS uses.

Attribute Name	Description
$ATTRIBUTE_LIST	Provides a location list for every attribute record that doesn't fit inside an MFT record.
$BITMAP	Characteristic for Bitmaps
$DATA	Includes the default file information.
$EA	The attribute index was expanded.
$EA_INFORMATION	Additional attribute data
$FILE_NAME	Name of file
$INDEX_ALLOCATION	The Directory Stream type name. An attribute code string used for index allocation
$INDEX_ROOT	utilized in support of other indexes and directories
$LOGGED_UTILITY_STREAM	Utilization by the file system encrypting
$OBJECT_ID	Every MFT record has a unique a GUID
$PROPERTY_SET	Obsolete
$REPARSE_POINT	utilized as volume mounting points
$SECURITY_DESCRIPTOR	Security descriptor keeps SIDs and ACLs stored.
$STANDARD_INFORMATION	Standard data, including quota information and file times Outdated
$SYMBOLIC_LINK	Obsolete
$TXF_DATA	Transactional NTFS data; volume status and version
$VOLUME_INFORMATION	Version and state of the volume
$VOLUME_NAME	Name of the volume
$VOLUME_VERSION	Obsolete. Volume version

Numerous file attributes that offer more details about files and directories are supported by NTFS. These properties include more sophisticated features like compression, encryption, and sparse file flags in addition to more common ones like file size, creation and modification dates, and read-only status.

Clusters and Sectors

A cluster is the smallest logical unit of disk space that can be reserved for storing a file [6]. The smallest physical units on the disk are called sectors, into which clusters are arranged. This alignment reduces waste by enabling effective storage and retrieval.

In order to identify each disk sector, the manufacturing track-positioning data is used. Sector starting address is identified by sector identity data, it appears just before the sector contents in the area.

Contiguous series, or putting a stream's contents in just one line, end to end, is the best way to store a file on a disk. Since many files are larger than 512 bytes, the file system must reserve sectors to hold the file's data. For instance, two 512 k sectors are reserved for an 800 byte file.

A sector or sectors that come after one another can make up a cluster. There are always two exponents in the number of sectors. One sector (2^0) could make up a cluster, or more commonly, eight sectors (2^3). A cluster can only have one odd number of sectors. It can't be an even number that isn't an exponent of two or five sectors. Instead of ten sectors, there might be eight or sixteen.

Because the space is set aside for the contents of the data, they are known as clusters. This procedure keeps data that has already been stored from being overwritten. The addition of data causes the file to grow to 1600 bytes in size, and clusters are allocated to hold the entire file inside four distinct groups. If contiguous clusters—clusters that are adjacent to one another on the drive—are not available, the second two clusters can be written anywhere on the same disk, inside the same cylinder, on a separate cylinder, or anyplace else the file system finds two sectors accessible.

A file is referred to as fragmented when it is stored in this inconsistent way. When the file system has to send the drive heads to different addresses in order to find all the data in the file you wish to read, fragmentation may cause a slowdown in system performance. Before the complete file is obtained, there is a delay due to the heads' longer transit times to numerous destinations.

To maximize file storage, cluster size can be adjusted. Although there is a greater chance of fragmentation with bigger cluster sizes, there is also a greater chance of empty space within the clusters. By using clusters bigger than a single sector, fragmentation is lessened and less disk space is required to hold data about the disk's used and empty portions.

Today's home (personal) computers typically use disks that revolve maintaining a steady angular velocity. In contrast to the tracks in the middle of the disk, the tracks on the disk's periphery are less densely loaded with data. Because of this, even though the disk surface moves more quickly on the tracks that are farthest from the disk's center, one can read a certain amount of material in a predictable length of time.

During disk assembly at the manufacturer, track location information is written to one side of a platter on modern disks.

NTFS FEATURES AND BENEFITS

Because of its many features and advantages, NTFS is a recommended option for contemporary computing environments. Here are a few of its salient characteristics and benefits:

Security and Permissions

Security and permissions provided by the New Technology File System (NTFS) offer a strong foundation for managing access to files and directories, guaranteeing the security and integrity of data.

Access Control Lists (ACLs)

ACLs are exercised by NTFS for specifying file and directory permissions. A set of Access Control Entries (ACEs) known as an ACL identifies which individuals or groups are authorized to carry out particular operations on a file or directory, including reading, writing, executing, and editing. NTFS (New Technology File System) and other file systems rely heavily on Access Control Lists (ACLs) to control file and directory permissions.

An ACL is a list of Access Control Entries (ACEs) associated with a file or directory [8]. Each ACE defines a specific permission (such as read, write, execute) for a particular user or group. Typically, an ACE is made up of the following elements:

- The Security ID (SID): It serves to identify the specific person or group to whom the authorization is granted. SIDs are special numbers that are allocated to every group and user within the system.
- Access Mask: It indicates which rights, such as read, write, execute, delete, *etc.*, are allowed or denied to the user or group.

- Access Control Type: It denotes whether the given permissions are granted or denied by the ACE.
- Inheritance flags: Find out how child objects, such as files or subdirectories, inherit the ACE.

Types of ACEs

There are two main types of ACEs:

- Explicit ACEs: ACEs that are specifically set on a file or directory, either programmatically or manually by an administrator, are known as explicit ACEs.
- Inherited ACEs: ACEs that are inherited from a parent object, such as a parent directory, are known as inherited ACEs. Unless inheritance is specifically prohibited, inherited ACEs can be applied to child objects automatically.

Permissions

Administrators can specify a variety of permissions for individuals and groups using ACLs, such as:

- Read: Gives you access to the contents of a file or directory.
- Write: Allows the contents of a file or directory to be changed.
- Execute: Permits the execution of scripts or executable files.
- Delete: Permits the removal of files or folders.
- Full Control: Gives the user or group access to all permissions.

Evaluation of ACEs

The ACL linked to that item is examined whenever a process or user attempts to access a directory or file to ascertain whether the requested rights are granted or refused. The access permissions for the user or group are determined by matching the first ACE found when traversing the ACL in a sequential manner.

Modification and Management

The operating system offers a number of tools and utilities for managing and modifying ACLs, including the Windows Security dialog and command-line tools like icacls. When it comes to granting or limiting access to files and directories, administrators have the ability to add, remove, or alter ACEs.

ACLs offer a versatile and detailed method of managing access to files and directories on NTFS and other file systems. By enabling administrators to set rights for individuals and groups, they guarantee that sensitive data may only be accessed and modified by authorized users.

Encryption and Decryption

One part of the New Technology File System (NTFS) is the Encrypting File System (EFS), which makes encryption and decryption easier. For the purpose of safeguarding sensitive data kept on NTFS volumes, EFS offers file-level encryption capabilities. In NTFS, encryption and decryption operate as follows:

Encryption

- A symmetric encryption algorithm, usually AES (Advanced Encryption Standard), and a randomly generated Data Encryption Key (DEK) are used to encrypt a file when a user uses EFS.
- The DEK is then encrypted using the public key of the individual who encrypted the file. This encrypted DEK is used to store the contents of the encrypted file.
- The encrypted data replaces the original information of the file.

Decryption

- The encrypted DEK is obtained from the file's metadata when a user with the required permissions tries to access an encrypted file.
- The DEK is then decrypted using the user's private key, which is linked to their encryption public key.
- The contents of the file can be decrypted using the symmetric encryption procedure once the DEK has been decrypted.

Compression and Decompression

Transparent file-based compression is supported by NTFS. To read or write compressed files, external software is not required for their (de)compression. When reading or storing a file, automatic decompression and compression are carried out at nearly no additional cost.

Compressed files require less storage space than their uncompressed equivalents. Compressed file types, like ZIP or JPEG files, might be compressed by 5% to 10%, while uncompressed files can be compressed by 40% to 60%.

TreeSize shows the actual disk space occupied by a file or folder in addition to its size. On the "Details" tab, an additional column may provide the compression ratio. Furthermore, compressed files and folders can be colored-tagged (this feature can be enabled in the "Options") box. The same holds true for the NTFS file system's other unique feature, sparse files.

TreeSize allows you to compress and decompress whole directory trees with just one click. Just select the appropriate function from the context menu.

Disk Quotas

Disk quotas work well with NTFS file systems because they let administrators limit how much data each user can keep on an NTFS file system volume. In order to stop users from using more disk space after they exceed their limit, administrators can configure the system to record an event when a user gets close to it. Furthermore, by utilizing the event monitor, administrators may keep an eye on quota issues and generate reports.

By examining the FILE_VOLUME_QUOTAS bit flag and utilizing the GetVolumeInformation function, you may find out if a file system supports disk quotas.

Windows users can manage how much storage space they have access to by using disk quotas. Disk quotas can be limited by an administrator to prevent any user account from going over. This implies that a user will be unable to add new data to the disk once their disk quota is exceeded. In addition, the administrator has the ability to configure warning levels, which alert users in advance when they are approaching their allotted amount.

A few more points related to disk quotas are:

• In Windows, disks or partitions formatted with the NTFS file system may have their disk quotas set up. You cannot utilize these file systems on a drive that is formatted with FAT32 or exFAT since they do not support this feature.
• The only way to define and enforce disk quotas and restrictions is to have a Windows account with administrator privileges. Regular users are unable to set disk quotas.
• Folders cannot have disk quotas set on them; disks or partitions can.

You have to set disk quota restrictions for each drive or partition that you have on your Windows machine. Disk quotas cannot be imposed concurrently for more than one disk or partition.

Journaling

Its goal is to monitor modifications that have not been committed to the file system. You may still access the most recent version of the file with a reduced chance of it getting corrupted, even after crashes or unplanned shutdowns [9]. The metaphor of keeping a diary is where the word "journal" originates. Changes you make in a journal entry are kept track of both by date and time. Similar to this, journaling enables the storage of all file updates in a single, continuous area of the disk.

Since the journal record items are dispersed around the disk, these revisions are not required to be physically close to one another. However, the entries are accessible in a diary-like order that is several thousand times quicker than if you were to access them at random. As contiguous memory allocations are used in journaling, file storage retrieval times are greatly reduced.

NTFS MANAGEMENT TOOLS

Permissions on the New Technology File System, or NTFS, control which shared resources end-user accounts can access. Administrators can increase security by limiting access to important or confidential data while enabling individual end users to share and exchange resources by customizing the user account, group member, and domain access rights applied to network drives, files, and folders.

All Windows operating systems use NTFS [11] as their file system formatting, which provides administrators with control over rights that are inherited and applied to specific files and folders. Both local and networked users can apply NTFS folder permissions and other shared resource permissions, so everyone who logs into any Windows workstation connected to the network or remotely will have the same set of NTFS file permissions.

Windows File Explorer

A graphical file management tool for the Windows operating system (OS) is called Windows File Explorer. After Windows 95 was originally released, Windows Explorer was rebranded as File Explorer. A computer user uses the Windows File Explorer program each time they access a drive or open a folder that contains files.

File management software is designed to make it easier for users to handle files and directories on any linked disk. Users can launch Windows File Explorer by clicking on the File Explorer icon in the taskbar or Start menu. Users can choose from a variety of context-aware actions, including renaming, moving, copying, publishing, emailing, printing, and deleting files, when a file is selected in the File Explorer interface.

You can open, browse, share, copy, cut, paste, move, and delete entire folders. Users can transfer folders into other folders and hard drives, search files, and drag & drop files between directories.

You can see files and folders in Windows File Explorer in a variety of formats, including lists, thumbnail image arrays, icons, and details with attributes like size, type, date, and time. The type of information being researched and the user's selections determine which display format is used. Document folders can be seen as an entire list, or a folder containing a massive library of image, video, or music file types can be shown in thumbnail format.

In Windows 10, the File Explorer is separated into three primary areas on a graphical toolbar that is further divided into the following three tabs:

- Home Tab: Windows 10 defaults to displaying the Home tab in the toolbar. It has universal icons for common operations like copy, paste, move to, rename, and properties.
- Share tab: Icons in the Share tab of Windows 10 File Explorer offer ways to share a chosen item with other users. Users can even burn an object to disk, print, fax, or email it.
- View Tab: The toolbar's View tab allows you to change the appearance of File Explorer. View options include extra-large icons, massive icons, medium icons, small icons, details, tiles, or content. The View tab allows you to reveal or hide filename extensions, item checkboxes, and hidden items. Its options allow you to reveal or hide the navigation, preview, and information windows on the fly.

The second of Windows 10 File Explorer's three parts is the navigation pane. It is shown along the left side of the interface in a tree-like format. The network drives display directories and libraries, including the desktop, documents, downloads music, image, and video libraries. The navigation pane may also have fast-access shortcuts to frequently used folders [8, 9].

The third section of the Windows File Explorer interface shows the files and folders at the location that is now selected. From now on, the user can browse the file system, open files with a double-click, and bring up a context-sensitive menu including sharing, open with, send to, and properties by right-clicking a file.

The object that is selected can affect how the File Explorer interface looks.

Disk Management Console

With the Windows system utility Disk Management, you can perform complex storage activities. The following are a few advantages of disk management:

- To learn how to start up a new drive, see 'Initializing a new drive'.
- To extend a sector onto a space on the same disk that is not being used by another volume, use the 'read expand a basic sector' command.
- View 'Reduce a fundamental volume' to shorten a segment, usually in order to extend a neighboring separation.

Disk Management is a Windows tool that can help you manage all of your disk-based equipment. It was initially available for Windows XP with the Microsoft Management Console plugin installed. It allows users to monitor and manage optical disc drives, flash drives, internal and external hard drives, and the accompanying partitions that are installed on their PCs or laptops. In addition to a number of other disc management operations, disk management can split hard floppy disks, convert drives, give discs different names, alter a drive letter, and more.

Partitioning the Windows server is necessary to protect the information we share and simplify data administration. Our hard drives only have one partition, thus that is the explanation. If the operating system is corrupted in one of your partitions, all of your data will be destroyed. However, if you have multiple partitions, you can save your data in any of them, regardless of whether the OS crashes or is damaged [10, 11].

Command-Line Tools

NTFS, or New Technology File System, is the file system that Windows operating systems use by default. Despite the fact that Windows provides a variety of command-line utilities for managing NTFS file systems, NTFS does not come with any command-line tools of its own. These are different tools commonly used such as diskpart, chkdsk, convert, compact, *etc*. Let us discuss the two tools in detail:

CHKDSK

A command-line utility is used for detecting logical and physical defects in a volume's file system and file system metadata. Errors found in it can also be fixed.

A Windows command-line tool called CHKDSK (Check Disk) is used to examine a volume's file system metadata and overall integrity for logical and physical problems. It can also try to correct any mistakes it discovers. Here are a few typical applications for CHKDSK:

- **Examining a Drive for** Errors: To check a drive for errors, use CHKDSK. As an illustration: This command looks for faults on the C: disk. CHKDSK will check the current drive if you leave out the drive letter.
- **Correcting Errors:** During the scan, CHKDSK discovers some errors that it can correct. When the /f parameter is added, CHKDSK is instructed to attempt automatic error correction. As an illustration: This command looks for faults on the C: drive and tries to correct them.

- **Examining and Fixing Startup faults:** CHKDSK will ask you to plan a scan for the next time the system restarts if it finds faults that necessitate locking or dismounting the volume. By adding the /r option, you can also make CHKDSK execute automatically during the subsequent restart. As an illustration: With the help of this command, CHKDSK is scheduled to launch and fix faults on the C: disk when the system restarts.
- **Displaying CHKDSK Log:** You can view the log to see the results of CHKDSK once it has finished. To locate the CHKDSK log entries, launch the Event Viewer by using the eventvwr.msc command. Then, go to Windows Logs > Application.
- **Checking for Bad Sectors on a Drive:** By adding the /r argument, CHKDSK is instructed to find corrupted sectors and retrieve legible data. As an illustration: This command looks for defects on the C: drive and tries to fix them, including corrupt sectors. Recall that it may take some time to perform CHKDSK on a disk, particularly if it is large or has a lot of mistakes. Before launching CHKDSK, it is advised to close any open files and applications. Once the software has begun, it is advised not to stop it.

DISKPART

It is a disk partitioning command-line utility that can be employed to format, add, remove, and manage hard drive partitions. Additionally, disks that have been formatted with NTFS can have their attributes set using this method.

Uses of DISKPART are:

- **Viewing Available Disks and Volumes**: To see a list of all the disks and volumes that are available on your system.
- **Selecting a Disk or Volume**: To carry out activities on a disk or volume, you can choose it.
- **Creating Partitions**: On a disk, you can make main or extended partitions using diskpart.
- **Deleting Partitions**: A disk's existing partitions can be removed:
- **Formatting Partitions**: Once a partition has been created, it can be formatted using an NTFS file system.
- **Assigning Drive Letters**: A volume's drive letter can be assigned or changed.
- **Extending and Shrinking Volumes**: Diskpart gives you the ability to resize volumes by stretching or contracting them.
- **Setting Attributes**: A volume can have several qualities set, like being marked as active.
- **Converting Disks**: Diskpart can change the format of disks, for example, from a basic to a dynamic disk.

- **Cleaning Disks**: With this process, a disk's volumes and partitions are eliminated.

When using Diskpart, keep in mind that improper use can result in data loss because it allows you to make low-level modifications to disk configurations. Prior to running any commands, always confirm that you are working on the correct disk or volume.

Third Party Utilities

Regarding third-party programs for NTFS file system management, a number of solutions give more features and functionalities than Windows comes with by default. A few of them are as follows:

- **EaseUS Partition Master:** With this tool, you can resize, move, merge, divide, format, and convert partitions in addition to providing a complete disk management solution. Moreover, it offers SSD/HDD optimization, partition recovery, and disk cloning capabilities.
- **MiniTool Partition Wizard**: Offering many of the same partition management functions as EaseUS Partition Master, MiniTool Partition Wizard allows you to resize, convert, clone, and recover data from your partitions. It supports several Windows versions and has an easy-to-use interface.
- **Acronis Disk Director**: It is a robust disk management application that makes it simple for users to make, resize, transfer, and merge partitions. Disk recovery, data migration, and disk cloning are among its other functions. It also supports GPT/UEFI systems and dynamic disks.
- **Paragon Partition Manager**: Advanced disk management and partitioning features, including partition resizing, splitting, merging, and alignment, are provided by Paragon Partition Manager. It also has functions for data deletion, recovery, and backup. It also comes with tools to migrate the operating system to SSDs and HDDs and supports virtual drives.
- **AOMEI Partition Assistant:** This is a flexible partition management application that lets you do a lot of different things, such as resizing, relocating, splitting, merging, and formatting partitions. Moreover, it provides partition recovery, OS migration, and disk conversion features. It also supports Windows To Go and dynamic drives.
- **Active@ Partition Manager:** You may create, erase, format, and resize partitions with this easy-to-use yet effective partition management utility. Moreover, it has partition recovery, disk wiping, and disk cloning capabilities. It also supports a number of file systems, such as exFAT, FAT, and NTFS.

For customers who need more sophisticated disk and partition management features than what the built-in Windows tools can offer, these third-party solutions may be helpful. It is crucial to do your homework, pick a tool that fits your needs, and make sure it works with the file system and operating system you're using. To avoid data loss or unstable systems, always proceed with caution when conducting disk operations.

BEST PRACTICES FOR NTFS MANAGEMENT

To effectively manage NTFS and guarantee the performance, security, and integrity of your file system, you must adhere to best practices. Let us now concentrate on the method for managing NTFS permissions. The key suggested methods for managing NTFS rights securely and effectively are asfollows.

Disk Optimization and Defragmentation

Disk optimization is the process of reorganizing files on a drive to improve read and write efficiency. While disk optimization in NTFS is sometimes referred to as "defragmentation," the phrase "optimize drives" is used instead in modern Windows operating systems. When we talk about disk optimization in relation to NTFS (New Technology File System), we mostly mean the defragmentation process [12]. Defragmentation: File access times are decreased by rearranging fragmented files on a drive so they are stored sequentially [12]. We call this process defragmentation. When data is stored on a disk in non-contiguous clusters, the disk head must traverse to multiple locations, which increases the read/write times for fragmented files.

The disk optimization tool that comes with Windows is called "Optimize Drives" (it was formerly called Disk Defragmenter). To locate this tool, type "Defragment and Optimize Drives" into the Windows search box or navigate to "Control Panel > System and Security > Administrative Tools > Defragment and Optimize Drives."

Windows automatically schedules automated drive optimization, often known as defragmentation, once a week. You have the option to alter the schedule or disable automated optimization. Start the Optimize Drives tool, choose the disk that needs to be changed, select "Change settings," and then adjust or turn off the schedule to do this [13].

Solid-state drives (SSDs), as opposed to conventional mechanical hard drives (HDDs), have a different optimizing process. Typical defragmentation is useless and may even shorten the SSD's lifespan by causing unnecessary write operations, as SSDs lack the mechanical seek times that HDDs have. Instead, Windows' Optimize Drives tool finds SSDs and performs TRIM operations to enhance performance.

If required, you may manually start optimization with the Optimize Drives tool, which also provides you with details on how fragmented each drive is. You can monitor the degree of disk fragmentation to determine whether further optimization is file [14].

Windows has built-in optimization tools, but some third-party defragmentation programs offer greater features and customization options. These tools may include more advanced scheduling options, real-time monitoring, and comprehensive fragmentation analysis.

Backup and Recovery Strategies

It is imperative to have strong backup and recovery plans in place to safeguard data kept on NTFS (New Technology File System) volumes. The following are essential elements and recommended procedures for NTFS backup and recovery:

1. **Identify Critical Data**: Ascertain which documents, subdirectories, programs, and system settings are essential to the day-to-day functioning of your company. Make data backup a top priority.
2. **Regular Backup Schedule**: Based on the requirements of your organization and the frequency of data changes, create a regular backup routine. Weekly or daily backups are typical, with mission-critical systems requiring more frequent backups.
3. **Full and Incremental Backups:** Periodically do full backups to ensure that all data is captured. You can then add incremental backups to these full backups to capture changes made since the last full backup. In doing so, data security and storage effectiveness are balanced.
4. **Use Reliable Backup Solutions:** Select backup software with scheduling, encryption, compression, and verification capabilities, and support for NTFS drives.
5. **Test Backup Integrity:** Do test restorations to ensure the integrity of backup files on a regular basis. This guarantees that backups are comprehensive, reachable, and ready to restore data when required.
6. **Disaster Recovery Plan:** Create a thorough disaster recovery strategy that describes how to restore data in the event of ransomware attacks, hardware failures, data corruption, and natural catastrophes.
7. **Backup Retention Policies:** Establish backup retention guidelines in accordance with business requirements, legal obligations, and storage capacity. Maintain backups for a predetermined amount of time in order to comply with regulations and aid with data recovery.

8. **Versioning and Archiving:** If your backup system has tools for versioning and archiving, turn them on. This lets you save various iterations of your files over time and recover data at particular moments in time.

Organizations can reduce the risk of data loss, preserve business continuity, and safeguard important assets kept on NTFS volumes by adhering to these backup and recovery procedures.

Monitoring Disk Usage

Monitoring disk usage in NTFS (New Technology File System) volumes is essential for ensuring optimal performance, preventing storage issues, and managing disk space efficiently [15]. Here are several methods and tools you can use to monitor disk usage in NTFS:

File Explorer

- To view disk use for specific folders and drives, use Windows' built-in File Explorer.
- To check disk utilization data, such as total size, used space, and free space, right-click on a folder or drive, select "Properties," and then go to the "General" or "Tools" tab.

Disk Management

- To check disk utilization and partition details for all connected disks, use Windows' Disk Management program.
- To access the Disk Management console, press Win + X and choose "Disk Management" from the menu.
- Use the "Properties" option when you right-click on a disk or volume to see information about disk usage.

Command Line

- To keep an eye on disk utilization, use command-line tools like Diskpart and Disk utilization (diskusage.exe).
- Diskpart: Type diskpart into Command Prompt after opening it as an administrator. Then, to inspect disk and volume information, use commands like list disk, list volume, and detail volume.
- Disk utilization: To create a report displaying disk utilization statistics for all directories and subdirectories, run diskusage.exe from the command line.

Performance Monitor

- To keep an eye on disk performance metrics such as disk read/write activity, queue length, and response time, use the Performance Monitor (perfmon.msc).
- Develop a fresh Data Collector for the Performance Monitor. To track disk performance over time, set and add counters associated with disk utilization (*e.g.*, % Free Space, Disk Read Bytes/sec, Disk Write Bytes/sec).

Third-Party Monitoring Tools

Third-party disk monitoring programs offer more sophisticated capabilities and visualization choices.

Disk Quota Management

Administrators have the ability to track and control how much storage space is used by individuals, groups, or directories by managing disk quotas in the NTFS (New Technology File System). The following are the techniques to handling disk quotas in NTFS:

Enable Quota Management

- The NTFS volume's quota management must be enabled before you may manage disk quotas. This can be accomplished by opening "File Explorer," performing a right-click on the NTFS disk, choosing "Properties," opening the "Quota" tab, and checking the box next to "Enable quota management."

Set Quota Limits

- You can establish quota limitations for certain users, groups, or directories after quota management is enabled. In order to establish quota restrictions, select "New Quota Entry" after selecting "Quota Entries" under the "Quota" tab of the volume properties window.
- Define the quota limit (in MB or GB), choose the user or group for whom you wish to set it, and set up additional parameters like logging settings and warning levels.

Edit Quota Limits

- To modify current quota limitations, navigate to the volume properties window's "Quota Entries" section, choose the quota entry you need to change, and then click "Properties." You can then modify the quota limit, warning threshold, and other settings as needed.

Delete Quota Entries

You can eliminate quota limits for a user, group, or directory by going to the volume properties window's "Quota Entries" section, choosing the quota item you wish to remove, and then clicking "Delete."

View Quota Usage

In the "Quota Entries" part of the volume properties pane, you may view quota consumption for certain users, groups, or directories. This displays for each quota entry the current disk space consumption, the quota limit, and the warning threshold.

Security Best Practices

The protection of sensitive data and the integrity of file systems depend on the implementation of strong security measures in NTFS (New Technology File System). The following are some recommended security practices for NTFS:

Use NTFS Permissions: To restrict access to certain files and directories, make use of NTFS permissions [7]. Give specific people or groups access permissions, and only allow access to those that need it. Follow the principle of least privilege and grant users the bare minimum of access necessary to finish their tasks.

Implement File Encryption: To encrypt important files and folders, use NTFS encryption capabilities like Encrypting File System (EFS). EFS shields data at rest against unwanted access by transparently encrypting and decrypting files.

Enable Auditing: To track and monitor access to important files and folders, enable file and folder auditing in NTFS. Set up audit policies to record actions like adding, deleting, and altering files. Examine audit logs on a regular basis to look for unusual or unauthorized activity.

Secure Remote Access: If users need remote access to files on NTFS disks, employ secure techniques like virtual private networks (VPNs) and secure file transfer protocol (SFTP). These methods encrypt data in transit and guard against sensitive information being intercepted or eavesdropped on.

Regularly Patch and Update: Update NTFS-based systems with the most recent Microsoft security patches and updates. Install security upgrades on a regular basis to address vulnerabilities and defend against known threats.

Use Antivirus and Antimalware software: On NTFS drives, install and keep up antivirus and antimalware software to find and get rid of dangerous programs like trojans, worms, and viruses. To successfully identify and mitigate emerging threats, keep your antivirus definitions up to date.

Disable Unnecessary Services and Features: On NTFS-based systems, disable superfluous services, protocols, and features to lower the attack surface and the chance of exploitation. Enable only those features and services that are necessary for the operation of the system

ADVANCED NTFS CONCEPTS

TxF (Transactional NTFS)

File actions on an NTFS file system volume can be carried out in a transaction thanks to transactional NTFS (TxF). TxF transactions simplify application development by drastically lowering the amount of error-handling code and boosting application reliability by safeguarding data integrity against failures.

TxF takes advantage of the Kernel Transaction Manager's (KTM) transaction framework. This makes it possible for TxF file operations to be integrated into transactions using other data sources, like Transacted Registry (TxR) and SQL Server.

Files and directories can be created, changed, renamed, and removed atomically using transactional NTFS.

This functionality is enhanced by Transactional NTFS to include: Operations atomic to a single file: Saving a file from an application is a typical example of this; if the program or computer crashed while writing the file, just a portion of it could be written, potentially leading to a corrupted file [16].

By separating your modifications from those of other users while they are being made, TxF enables an application to protect the integrity of data on a disk that has been damaged by unforeseen error conditions and assist in resolving concurrent file-system user scenarios.

Microsoft highly advises developers to use alternate methods in order to fulfill the requirements of your application. Many of the circumstances for which TxF was designed can be accomplished with easier-to-find methods. Moreover, TxF might not be accessible in upcoming Windows versions from Microsoft. Please refer to Alternatives to utilizing Transactional NTFS for more details and alternatives to TxF.

By integrating transactions into the NTFS file system, Transactional NTFS (TxF) makes it simpler for administrators and application developers to manage mistakes graciously and maintain data integrity.

TxF can be used for the following since it can take part in distributed transactions that are coordinated by the Distributed Transaction Coordinator (DTC):

• Transactions spanning several data stores, such as a single SQL and file operation transaction.
• Transactions involving several computers, such as one transaction for file updates across several computers.

Sparse Files

A file is considered to have a sparse data set if a sizable portion of its data is made up entirely of zeros [17]. Usually quite big files include things like matrices that must be handled and stored in a high-speed database. Files with sparse data sets have the drawback of being wasteful disk space users because the majority of the data in the file is meaningless.

One partial answer to the issue is the NTFS file system's file compression. Every piece of unwritten data in the file is set directly to zero. These zero ranges are compressed during file compression.

The NTFS file system adds incorporation of sparse files as an additional measure to improve the efficiency of disk space utilization. When a file has sparse file capabilities activated, the system only allocates hard drive space to it in the regions where the file has nonzero data. When a write operation is undertaken, most of the data in the buffer comprises zeros because the zeros are not written to the file. Rather, the file system generates an internal list that is retrieved during all read operations and contains the positions of all zeros in the file. The file system returns the precise number of zeros in the buffer designated for the read operation when a read operation is carried out in the sections of the file where zeros were found [18, 19].

For this specific circumstance, sparse file maintenance is more efficient than compression since it is invisible to all processes that access it.

A sparse file's data value can be set to any value except zero by default.

Such files can have several disadvantages:

1. They can lead to increased disk fragmentation and reduced disk performance, as the file system has to keep track of the non-contiguous blocks of the file.

2. They may not match the size of the file as reported by the file system, which can be confusing when attempting to ascertain the true size of the file.
3. They can cause unexpected behaviors in some programs, which may not be able to handle sparse files correctly.
4. When attempting to backup or transfer the files, they may not be detected by the backup software or transfer protocol, which can result in performance concerns that the file is sparse and will transfer all the "empty" blocks, resulting in a larger transfer.

Hard Links and Junction Points

Microsoft has included linking features from the latest versions of Windows NT and Windows 2000 as well into its NTFS operating file systems. The users can easily get their data by using these URLs.

Microsoft has made improvements to these features over time, so you may now link files and/or folders together using them. The most recent iteration of a file link was originally incorporated in Windows Vista and is still included in their most recent operating system. We'll examine these file links' definitions and variations in this essay.

Windows uses linking methods including junction points, symbolic links, and hard links to join particular files, folders, or volumes with other files or volumes. One method for creating file connections is to utilize the command line utility.

- Creating **file hard link**: *mklink /H linkName target*
- Creating directory **junction**: *mklink /J linkName target*
- Creating directory **symbolic link**: *mklink /D linkName target*
- Creating file symbolic link: *mklink linkName target*

Details on each kind of file link are provided in the ensuing sections.

Hard Links

A file that replicates the contents of another file on the same drive without doing so is known as a hard link. It is possible to construct many hard links that point to the same contents of the file. Hard links are unable to point to a file's contents on another drive, volume, or partition. Since hard links on directories would cause inconsistent parent directory entries, they are not supported.

Despite being effectively a mirrored copy of the target file it links to, a hard link file does not need to take up extra space on the hard drive. Instead of using 4GB of total storage, a partition with three hard links mirroring a 1GB file will only require 1GB.

Furthermore, even if the original file or files are deleted, the data will remain intact and accessible through the surviving links. Until all references to the file are eliminated, it won't be deleted. Any modifications made to the data contents *via* any of the hard links or the original will automatically propagate to the other items because all of the other items ultimately point to the same file data.

Only Microsoft Windows operating systems that support NTFS partitions (Windows NT 4.0 or later) can use hard links with the FAT and pre-ReFS file systems. ReFS implemented support for hard links in version 3.5.

If it is required, a user can keep a file in two distinct directories *via* hard links. He might make two copies of the identical file by copying it to the other folder. On the other hand, twice as much storage would be required. Additionally, unless the updated file is moved across to replace the old one, if the contents of one file change, the other file will become out of date. Hard links could be used to resolve both problems.

Junctions

A hard link connects to a single file, while a soft link, also known as a junction, points to a destination directory. Junctions may only be made locally on the same machine; they cannot be used to combine folders on different disks or partitions. It does this by making use of the reparse point NTFS feature. An absolute path in a junction defines redirected targets. A path that has every directory list and root element needed to find the destination is called an absolute path. \Main\Folder\report, for instance, is an absolute path. The path string contains all the information needed to find the target.

Directory junctions do not take up more space on the drive partition; they function similarly to hard links in that they point to the original files inside the original directory. Notably, if the target is moved, deleted, or renamed, all junctions pointing to it will break and keep referring to an empty directory. Any changes you make to the content on one of the targets or junction links will immediately update the others.

Consider the route "C:\Documents and Settings" on Windows Vista (and later), which points to C:\Users, as an illustration of how junctions are frequently utilized. Therefore, Vista and later versions will continue to function with older programs that require legacy file locations to be hard-coded.

Symbolic Links

Windows Vista and Windows Server 2008 brought symbolic links. An NTFS symbolic link is a file system object that points to another file system object. Stated differently, it is a more advanced form of shortcut. Symbolic links can point to any file or folder on the local computer or to distant targets over a network using an SMB path (the distant target system must have Windows Vista or later installed). There is no disk space used by them.

A symbolic link can point to its destination using either an absolute path or a relative path. To reach the destination file correctly, one path needs to be coupled with a relative path. Please see Microsoft's website for a thorough explanation of the distinctions between absolute and relative routes.

Users can see symbolic links as regular files or directories since they are transparent to them. Every program will be able to identify the target as well as the link. Symbolic linkages lose their validity if their target is changed, renamed, or removed, just like junctions. The target's existence is not verified by the operating system.

Junction points are a sort of reparse point that contains a link to a directory that serves as an alias for that directory. They are also known as Directory Junction or NTFS Junction. Similar to a symbolic link, but limited to directories, junction points function. Junction points are a Windows-only feature, despite being constructed similarly to a symlink. First available in NTFS 3.0, which came pre-installed with Windows 2000, was this capability. Although it functions similarly to a symlink, it is not the same. This article will examine the benefits, drawbacks, and applications of a junction point. Junction Points are a form of reparse point, hence in order to weigh its benefits and drawbacks, we would compare it to other reparse points. The benefits of Junction Points are as follows:

• Since Windows 2000 introduced Directory Junctions, they are compatible with all subsequent Windows versions (Windows Vista introduced symlinks). • Resolves more quickly. • Unlike symlinks, does not require administrator credentials for creation. • Since the target's absolute route is stored, issues pertaining to relative paths are eliminated.

Disadvantages of Junction Points

• Is unable to support UNC paths or remote SMB.
• Only directories for support.
• Only compatible with Windows OS, which results in decreased usage because it is not compatible with other operating systems.

Usage of Junction Points

- By referring Junction points to the more recent pathways, the operating system uses them to enable legacy Directory pathways on Windows.
- Junction points can be used for path redirection, which enables them to point to nonexistent paths on a disk because they are handled at the file system level.
- Prior to Windows Vista, this method of directory linking was known as the defector way.

NTFS Reparse Points

File system objects known as reparse points have properties that enable additional functionality. Where external data should be obtained from and which application is connected to it are indicated by a tag in the reparse point.

There could be several reparse points with various applications in a single file. When the system opens a file and reaches a reparse point, it finds the filter that matches the application specified in the tag. The data contained therein can subsequently be utilized to transparently finish any operation with the aid of the program that generated the reparse point.

Applications are the first step in using reparse points. Applications that want to use this feature store data into a reparse point that is special to their application, which could be any type of data. An application-specific identifier is used to identify the reparse point, which is preserved along with the file or directory. Reparse point tag type has an additional, unique application-specific filter—a kind of driver—connected to it. The same file or directory can be used by multiple applications to store reparse points, each with a unique tag. The Microsoffile System itself set aside a number of distinct tags for internal use.

Let us pretend for a second that the user chooses to open a file that has a reparse point associated with it. The reparse point linked to the file is located by the file system when it tries to open the file. It "reparses" the original file request after locating the relevant filter linked to the application that stored the reparse point and feeding the reparse point data into it. Depending on the reparse point capabilities provided by the application, the filter can then use the data in the reparse point to carry out the required action. The precise behavior of the reparse point is controlled by the application, allowing for great flexibility in the technology. One of the reparse points' greatest features is that they function in a transparent manner. The technology is very adaptable, with the application controlling the reparse point's precise operation. Reparse points function transparently to the user, which is a really nice feature. All you have to do is navigate to the reparse point; the rest is automatic. This makes it possible to seamlessly extend file system functions.

Apart from enabling reparse points to incorporate various customized functionalities, Microsoft used them to incorporate multiple features in Windows 2000, as mentioned below:

Symbolic Links

- **Symbolic linking:** Enables the creation of a pointer from one directory structure section to the actual file location located in a different section of the structure. The features of "true" symbolic file linking, which NTFS lacks but UNIX file systems implement, can be emulated *via* reparse points. A symbolic link is essentially a reparse point that directs file access between locations.
- **Junction points:** Comparable to a symbolic link, a junction point enables access to be moved between directories rather than between individual files.
- **Volume Mount Points:** Similar to a junction point or symbolic link, but more advanced because it allows dynamic access to full disk volumes, is the volume mount point. With this capability, you may even make many partitions (C:, D:, E:, and so on) appear to the user to be a single logical disk. For storage devices like detachable hard drives, for instance, you can establish volume mount points. Volume mount points allow Windows 2000 to access volumes without a drive letter, so getting around the standard 26 drive letter limit. Large CD-ROM servers can benefit from this as, in the absence of this; each disk would require its own letter, requiring the user to memorize every drive letter.
- **Remote Storage Server (RSS):** This Windows 2000 feature uses a set of rules to determine whether to move rarely used files from an NTFS drive to archive storage (such as CD-RW or tape). By doing this, RSS moves a file to "offline" or "near offline" storage while preserving reparse points, or future access points needed for the archived files.

These are but a handful of the uses for reparse points. It is clear that the functionality may be greatly adjusted. Since they allow you to increase the file system's capacity without having to change the file system itself, reparse points are a fantastic addition to NTFS.

An array of user-defined data stored in a file or directory is called a reparse point. The file system filter that you install to process and interpret the data, as well as the program that stores the data, both understand this format. A reparse tag, which uniquely identifies the data being stored, is also stored when an application provides a reparse location. When the file system opens a file with a reparse point, it searches for the file system filter associated with the data format specified by the reparse tag. If reparse data is found, the file system filter treats the file accordingly. Without a file system filter, the file cannot be opened.

For example, reparse points are used for implementing Microsoft Remote Storage Server (RSS) and NTFS file system connections. In compliance with administrator instructions, RSS moves infrequently used files to long-term storage, such as optical or tape. Data related to files is stored in reparse points within the file system. The stub file containing this information has a reparse point referring to the actual file's current location on the device. The file system filter can utilize this information to retrieve the file.

A directory must first be empty in order for reparse points to be generated for it. In all other cases, the NTFS file system is unable to build the reparse point. Moreover, folders having a reparse point and the directory bit set are the only ones where files and directories can be generated.

Extended attributes and reparse points are incompatible. The NTFS file system is unable to create a reparse point on a file that has extended attributes or to add extended attributes to a file that already has one.

The tag and optional GUID included in the reparse point data cannot be larger than 16 kilobytes. If more data needs to be added to the reparse point than can fit there, the reparse point cannot be set.

Every path has a maximum of 63 reparse locations.

TROUBLESHOOTING NTFS ISSUES

Common Error messages and solutions

Although there are numerous causes for the NTFS_FILE_SYSTEM, problems with your storage device or a corrupted file system are typically the main culprits. Malware may also be a problem, but this can be quickly fixed by upgrading your antivirus program and doing a thorough system scan. To fix the error, use the six troubleshooting procedures listed below.

1. Verify that your drive has enough space on it.
2. Update your SSD or HDD driver.
3. Examine and Fix Drive Errors
4. System File Checker Can Help You Repair Corrupted Files
5. Carry out a Windows 10 installation factory reset.
6. Manually reinstall Windows 10

Every time you attempt to use your computer, the NTFS_FILE_SYSTEM error—which occasionally appears as 0x00000024—causes a blue screen loop. Any version of Windows, even the most recent Windows 11 and Windows 7 through 10, may experience this problem. The NTFS_FILE_SYSTEM error can occur for a variety of causes.

There are several ways to fix the NTFS_FILE_SYSTEM problem. Some of the greatest ones are listed below. You might want to familiarize yourself with the process of booting into safe mode if you are not already, as some of the ways might require it. The following are the methods that can be used to resolve or fix the issues:

1. Clear Space on the System Disk
2. Update drivers for the system drive.
3. Try using Windows Startup Repair.
4. Scan the System Drive for Issues
5. Scan the System for Mistakes
6. Reset the installation of Windows

Data Recovery Techniques

In a nutshell, the file recovery procedure involves scanning a disk or folder for lost entries in the Master File Table (MFT), indicating which clusters chain needs to be restored for that particular deleted entry, and then moving those clusters' contents to the freshly created file

A recoverable file system called NTFS takes advantage of standard transaction logging and recovery methods to ensure the consistency of the volume [20]. In the event of a disk loss, NTFS has a recovery procedure that retrieves information from a log file to restore consistency.

The accuracy of the NTFS recovery method ensures that the volume is returned to a consistent state. There is very little overhead involved with transaction logging.

When an application accesses an NTFS volume for the first time after a computer restart, NTFS performs disk recovery procedures automatically to ensure the integrity of all NTFS volumes. Additionally, NTFS reduces the impact that a damaged sector can have on an NTFS drive by employing a method known as cluster remapping.

Every I/O operation that changes a system file on the NTFS drive is seen by NTFS as a transaction, and it is handled as a logical whole. After a transaction is started, it is either finished or, in the event of a disk failure, rolled back, which means the NTFS volume is restored to its initial state prior to the start of the transaction.

Before writing any suboperations to the disk, NTFS logs them all to make sure a transaction may be rolled back or finished [21]. NTFS completes a transaction's suboperations on the volume cache once the transaction has been fully documented in the log file. NTFS commits the transaction by indicating in the log file that the transaction has been completed in its entirety after updating the cache.

NTFS makes a guarantee that a transaction is visible on the volume even in the event of a disk failure once it has been committed. NTFS replays all committed transactions that are recorded in the log file during recovery operations. Next, NTFS reverses each transaction suboperation that was noted in the log file in order to find any transactions that were not completed during the system failure. Making minor volume adjustments is not allowed.

To log all redo and undo information for a transaction, NTFS makes use of the Log File service. NTFS replicates the transaction using the redo data. NTFS can undo transactions that are incomplete or include errors because of the undo information.

NTFS employs logging and transaction recovery to ensure that the volume structure is not changed. Because of this, even in the case of a system failure, all system files are still accessible. On the other hand, a bad sector or system failure could result in the loss of user data.

Cluster Remapping

Cluster remapping is a mechanism that NTFS employs to recover from bad-sector issues. NTFS dynamically remaps the cluster holding the problematic sector and forms a new cluster for the data when Windows 2000 detects a faulty sector. The data is lost and NTFS alerts the calling program to a read error if the issue arose during a read. Since NTFS writes the data to the new cluster, no data is lost if something goes wrong during writing.

To prevent the incorrect sector from being used again, NTFS keeps track of the address of the cluster that contains the faulty sector in its bad cluster file.

There is no fallback strategy offered by rearranging clusters. The disk should be regularly inspected once mistakes are found, and if the list of problems gets longer, it should be replaced. The Event Log has records of this kind of error.

Handling Disk Corruption

The only way your data can be totally lost is if it gets replaced by another file. Every Windows operating system uses NTFS. There are numerous built-in methods for recovering lost or corrupted data with this disk format. If the built-in techniques are unsuccessful, the NTFS file system can be repaired using Disk Internals' NTFS Recovery TM utility. However, let us first discuss the causes of data corruption before discussing the various approaches of NTFS restoration.

Reasons for File System Corruption

1. The erasure of unexpected system data can corrupt NTFS.
2. The NTFS partition table is also impacted by corruption of the NTFS file system.
3. To have any chance of restoring the partition and preserving the most of your data, you may require the Disk Internals NTFS Recovery utility if the boot sector of Windows 7, 8, or 10 becomes faulty.
4. In the case that MFT service data is corrupted, the Disk Internals Recovery tool will make it easier to repair the NTFS file system.

You may need to repair the disk by using the Disk Internals NTFS Recovery TM application to restore the most of your data if the NTFS file system partition is faulty.

Case Studies

NTFS management is essential for ensuring a secure, structured, and effective file system for Windows-based computers. Here are some practical instances of NTFS management:

User and Group Permissions

Setting: Within a corporate setting, a communal directory houses confidential financial records designated for exclusive access by the finance department. NTFS enables administrators to establish permissions for files and directories. Only the financial team members have been given read-and-write access in this situation, while other users have limited or no access. This guarantees the protection and privacy of data.

Storage Management Quotas

Scenario: Administrators aim to ensure equitable disk space allocation on a network device shared by multiple departments.

NTFS enables disk quotas for management purposes. Administrators have the ability to establish restrictions on the quantity of disk space that individual users or departments are allowed to utilize. This ensures that no single user or department dominates the storage capacity, encouraging equitable consumption and effective space allocation.

File Compression for Space Optimization: Scenario: A server is experiencing low disk space, prompting administrators to compress data to free up storage.

NTFS enables administrators to compress files and folders, decreasing their disk space usage. This is particularly beneficial for stored or infrequently accessed data. Compression may cause a small decrease in performance but is beneficial for optimizing storage efficiency.

Data encryption is essential for security. In this scenario, a laptop holds confidential customer data, and there is a potential threat of the device being lost or stolen.

NTFS incorporates the Encrypting File System (EFS) for encrypting individual files or directories. In this scenario, confidential files are encoded, ensuring that the data stays protected and incomprehensible to unauthorized individuals without the correct encryption key. The real-life instances demonstrate the various ways NTFS management capabilities can be utilized to meet specific requirements about security, storage efficiency, and data retrieval.

Lessons Learned and Optimal Strategies

Indeed, to effectively manage the NTFS file system, one must comprehend its capabilities, and potential concerns, and apply best practices. Below are key insights and optimal strategies for managing the NTFS file system.

Periodic Data Backups

Lesson Acquired: Data loss can occur due to accidental deletions, disk failures, or other unexpected circumstances.

Best Practice: Enforce consistent and thorough backup procedures. Utilize backup solutions that comprehensively record the complete file system to guarantee that essential data can be recovered in case of a failure or inadvertent data loss.

Security and Permissions: Lesson Acquired: Incorrectly set permissions can result in illegal entry or data leaks.

Best Practice: Consistently assess and examine file and folder permissions. Adhere to the principle of least privilege by assigning users and groups only the necessary permissions. Utilize security groups for simplified management and make use of inherited permissions when suitable.

Disk Quotas: Lesson Learned: Disk quotas are necessary to prevent users or applications from using too much disk space, which can cause performance problems.

Implementing and enforcing disk quotas is a recommended practice to prevent users or departments from dominating disk capacity. Consistently check disk utilization and modify quotas as necessary.

Regular disk maintenance is essential. Lesson learned: The buildup of temporary files, logs, and system caches can negatively affect performance and storage space.

Optimal Strategy: Establish a routine for performing disk cleanup tasks consistently. Utilize integrated features such as Disk Cleanup to eliminate redundant files. Regularly check disk space to anticipate and deal with potential problems in advance.

Data Encryption Lesson Learned: Unprotected sensitive data is vulnerable, particularly on portable devices.

Optimal Procedure: Use EFS to encrypt sensitive files and folders. Utilize BitLocker or an equivalent full-disk encryption system to enhance security on portable devices. Consistently refresh encryption keys and certificates.

Future trends in NTFS may prioritize improving resilience to hardware failures and enhancing data integrity. Checksums and error-correction algorithms can be enhanced to avoid and identify data corruption.

Performance Optimization: As storage technologies like NVMe SSDs advance and the need for quicker data access grows, file systems may adapt to enhance performance, minimize latency, and leverage new storage designs.

Integration with Cloud Services: As cloud storage becomes more common, file systems may connect more smoothly with cloud services. This may include improved assistance for cloud-based storage, synchronization, and collaboration functionalities.

Security enhancements in future file systems are expected to include advanced functionality to combat emerging cyber security threats. This could involve enhancements in encryption techniques, access controls, and stronger defense mechanisms against different types of malware.

Supporting higher storage volumes is essential as data storage needs increase, requiring file systems to properly accommodate these bigger volumes. This may include optimizations for handling extensive data, increased file sizes, and tackling scalability issues.

Enhanced metadata management could be prioritized to address the growing intricacy of file systems. This may involve improving indexing efficiency, search functionalities, and overall advancements in metadata management.

Enhancements and Refinements

As of my last knowledge update in January 2022, I lack particular details regarding any updates or enhancements to the NTFS (New Technology File System) that occurred after that date. Nevertheless, I can offer some broad perspectives on past patterns and future locations for enhancements and advancements in NTFS.

Security Improvements: Microsoft has traditionally concentrated on enhancing the security aspects of NTFS. Updates may involve improvements to encryption techniques, access control systems, and features aimed at safeguarding data integrity and confidentiality.

Performance enhancements may be made to NTFS to enhance performance on current hardware, such as providing support for faster storage devices like NVMe SSDs due to advancements in storage technologies.

NTFS updates are often designed to be compatible with new features and functionalities in Windows Operating Systems. Potential compatibility issues with technologies like Windows Defender, Windows Search upgrades, or other system-level improvements could be resolved.

Storage Efficiency: Efforts may be made to enhance storage efficiency by optimizing the processing of huge data quantities, minimizing fragmentation, and improving file compression techniques.

Enhancements to NTFS may be introduced by Microsoft to improve the file system's resilience to hardware failures, data corruption, and other difficulties. Advanced error correction mechanisms, such as checksums, could be implemented.

For the most precise and current information on upgrades and enhancements to NTFS, it is advised to consult the official Microsoft documentation, release notes, and announcements. Microsoft frequently issues updates for its operating systems, with enhancements to the file system commonly included in these upgrades.

Cloud Storage Integration

Cloud storage services are typically integrated at the operating system or application level. NTFS does not have built-in compatibility with certain cloud storage services, however, Microsoft's cloud platforms including Microsoft 365, OneDrive, and Azure are optimized to function smoothly with Windows OS.

OneDrive for Business

OneDrive for Business, a component of Microsoft 365, is intimately integrated with Windows and NTFS. It offers file synchronization, enabling users to access files from both local storage and cloud storage. OneDrive for Business files can be accessed through File Explorer using a navigation method similar to standard file and folder browsing.

Integration of Windows File Explorer

Cloud storage providers do not directly integrate with NTFS, but they typically enable connectivity with Windows File Explorer through client programs. Users can install synchronization programs for services such as Dropbox, Google Drive, or Box to access their cloud files together with local files in the same file-system view.

Third-party tools and apps can offer options for combining NTFS with particular cloud storage services. These programs may provide extra features like smooth syncing, encryption, or complex file management functions.

Azure File Sync allows organizations utilizing Azure cloud services to expand on-premises file servers into Azure. Although it does not directly integrate with NTFS, it enables enterprises to synchronize files across their on-premises systems and Azure File Shares.

Storage gateway solutions provided by cloud providers enable on-premises applications to effortlessly utilize cloud storage. The solutions may offer caching methods and file system interfaces that are compatible with NTFS.

Prospects

Future iterations of Windows or NTFS upgrades may incorporate advanced functionalities to integrate cloud storage more effectively as cloud computing advances. Monitor official Microsoft announcements and updates for the most recent information.

When examining cloud storage integration choices, it is crucial to examine aspects like security, data synchronization, access controls, and compatibility with particular cloud storage providers. Organizations frequently select solutions depending on their unique requirements and the cloud services they utilize. Consult the most recent documentation and authoritative sources for the latest information on integrations or features.

FUTURE FILE SYSTEM DEVELOPMENT IMPLICATIONS

The development of file systems like NTFS is influenced by user needs. Future file systems may need to adapt to new hardware capabilities as storage technologies progress. As SSDs, NVMe, and persistent memory become more common, file systems could be enhanced to provide quicker data access and better performance. Cloud computing is expected to impact the development of file systems. In the future, file systems could be more closely connected with cloud storage services, enabling features such as native synchronization, data tiering, and efficient data transfer between on-premises infrastructure and the cloud [22].

Security is a significant problem, and upcoming file systems can include improved encryption methods, access control mechanisms, and integrated security measures to defend against advancing cyber threats. The emphasis might also be on enhancing data integrity and offering solutions for secure data sharing. Enhancing metadata management and search functionalities in file systems has opportunities for growth. In the future, file systems could include sophisticated indexing and search capabilities, simplifying the process of finding and arranging data for users. Future file systems will probably have to tackle scalability difficulties due to the increasing amount of data. This involves enhancing performance to handle enormous directories, managing massive file sizes, and effectively expanding to meet the demands of contemporary applications and workloads.

File systems can utilize machine learning algorithms to examine user behavior, enhance data positioning, and offer insights about storage usage patterns. This integration has the potential to improve efficiency, performance, and resource use. Furthermore, as multi-platform environments grow more prevalent, file systems may develop to offer improved cross-platform compatibility. This involves enhancing compatibility among various operating systems and facilitating smooth data transfer across a variety of environments [23].

CONCLUSION

Efficient management of NTFS (New Technology File System) is essential for ensuring a secure, structured, and productive file system for Windows-based computers. NTFS enables administrators to establish precise permissions at both the file and folder levels. Efficient administration guarantees that sensitive data is only accessible to authorized users or groups, minimizing the chances of illegal access and data breaches. NTFS allows administrators to manage access permissions for specific files and directories, regulating reading, writing, executing, and modifying capabilities. Effective NTFS management enforces the concept of least privilege by granting users only the essential rights for their duties, reducing the likelihood of unintentional data alterations or removal [24].

NTFS offers disk quotas, enabling administrators to manage and oversee the disk space used by users or departments. Efficient management promotes equitable utilization, deters storage misuse, and aids in preserving optimal disk space availability. The Volume Shadow Copy Service (VSS) and the NTFS file system both include the Master File Table, which makes data recovery easier in the event of inadvertent deletions or alterations. Effective management involves performing routine backups and utilizing these functions for prompt data recovery. NTFS enables file compression and encryption, offering methods to improve storage efficiency and bolster data protection.

Efficient NTFS management requires making well-informed decisions about when to utilize these capabilities according to the type and confidentiality of the data. NTFS has technologies such as transactional NTFS (TxF) to ensure the consistency of the file system. Efficient management guarantees that file system operations are either fully executed or reverted in case of failure, reducing the likelihood of data corruption. Efficiently maintained NTFS file systems enhance the overall performance of the system. Performing routine maintenance tasks like disk cleanup, defragmentation (for mechanical hard drives), and organizing files can enhance data accuracy.

REFERENCES

[1]   R. Hermon, U. Singh, and B. Singh, "NTFS: Introduction and Analysis from Forensics Point of View", *2023 International Conference for Advancement in Technology (ICONAT),* IEEE., pp. 1-6, 2023.
[http://dx.doi.org/10.1109/ICONAT57137.2023.10080271]

[2]   Z. Kai, C. En, and G. Qinquan, "Analysis and implementation of NTFS file system based on computer forensics", *2010 Second International Workshop on Education Technology and Computer Science,* vol. 1, IEEE., pp. 325-328, 2010.
[http://dx.doi.org/10.1109/ETCS.2010.434]

[3]   A. Khang, K.C. Rath, S.K. Satapathy, A. Kumar, S.R. Das, and M.R. Panda, "Enabling the Future of Manufacturing: Integration of Robotics and IoT to Smart Factory Infrastructure in Industry 4.0", In: *Handbook of Research on AI-Based Technologies and Applications in the Era of the Metaverse.,* A. Khang, V. Shah, S. Rani, Eds., IGI Global, 2023, pp. 25-50. [http://dx.doi.org/10.4018/978-1-6684-8851-5.ch002]

[4]   N.M.M. Karresand, *Digital Forensic Usage of the Inherent Structures in NTFS.* MFT, 2023.

[5]   R. Russon, and Y. Fledel, "NTFS documentation", *Recuperado el,* p. 1, 2004.

[6]   M. Karresand, S. Axelsson, and G.O. Dyrkolbotn, "Using ntfs cluster allocation behavior to find the location of user data", *Digit. Invest.,* vol. 29, pp. S51-S60, 2019. [Cluster Allocation]. [http://dx.doi.org/10.1016/j.diin.2019.04.018]

[7]   A. Bettany, M. Halsey, M. Halsey, and A. Bettany, *Permissions, Ownership, and Auditing. Windows File System Troubleshooting.* Permission, 2015, pp. 31-54. [http://dx.doi.org/10.1007/978-1-4842-1016-1]

[8]   J.M. Cone, *ACACLS: A tool for examining and modifying file and directory security on NTFS volumes in a Windows NT environment.* California State University, Long Beach. (ACL), 2003.

[9]   V. Prabhakaran, A.C. Arpaci-Dusseau, and R.H. Arpaci-Dusseau, "Analysis and Evolution of Journaling File Systems", *USENIX Annual Technical Conference, General Track,* vol. 194, pp. 196-215, 2005.

[10]   V. H. Panchal, B. Panchal, and H. K. Desai, *Comparative study of two modern file systems: NTFS and HFS..*

[11]   C. K. Wee, "Analysis of hidden data in NTFS file system", In: *(Management Tools)* Edith Cowan University, 2006.

[12]   G.S. Cho, "Development of an anti-forensic tool for hiding message in a directory index of NTFS", *2015 World Congress on Internet Security (WorldCIS),* IEEE., pp. 144-145, 2015. [http://dx.doi.org/10.1109/WorldCIS.2015.7359431]

[13]   M. Danseglio, "The Shortcut Guide to Managing Disk Fragmentation", 2006. Available from: Realtimepublishers.com (disk fragmentation)

[14]   M. Danseglio, "The Shortcut Guide to Managing Disk Fragmentation", 2006. Available from: Realtimepublishers.com

[15]   M.S. Zareen, and B. Aslam, "LogFile of NTFS: A blueprint of activities", *17th IEEE International Multi Topic Conference 2014,* pp. 305-310, 2014. [http://dx.doi.org/10.1109/INMIC.2014.7097356]

[16]   J. Mankin, and D. Kaeli, "Dione: a flexible disk monitoring and analysis framework. In Research in Attacks, Intrusions, and Defenses: 15th International Symposium, RAID 2012, Amsterdam, The Netherlands, September 12-14, 2012", *Proceedings,* vol. 15, pp. 127-146, 2012. [Springer Berlin Heidelberg.].

[17]   H. H. Khanh, and A. Khang, "The Role of Artificial Intelligence in Blockchain Applications", In: *Reinventing Manufacturing and Business Processes through Artificial Intelligence.* vol. 2. Rana G, Khang A., Sharma R., Goel A. K., Dubey A. K. CRC Press, 2021, pp. 20-40. [http://dx.doi.org/10.1201/9781003145011-2]

[18]   V. van der Meer, H. Jonker, and J. van den Bos, "A contemporary investigation of NTFS file fragmentation", *Forensic Science International: Digital Investigation,* vol. 38, p. 301125, 2021.

[19]   A. Khang, M. Muthmainnah, P.M. Seraj, A. Al Yakin, and A.J. Obaid, "AI-Aided Teaching Model in Education 5.0", In: *Handbook of Research on AI-Based Technologies and Applications in the Era of the Metaverse.,* A. Khang, V. Shah, S. Rani, Eds., IGI Global, 2023, pp. 83-104. [http://dx.doi.org/10.4018/978-1-6684-8851-5.ch004]

[20]   D.G. Revathi Jagarlamudi, "A Novel tool for Data Recovery in cyber forensics", *Ann. Rom. Soc. Cell Biol.,* pp. 19600-19611, 2021. [Data Recovery].

[21]   S.G. Taskin, and E.U. Kucuksille, "Recovering Data Using MFT Records in NTFS File System", *Academic Perspective Procedia,* vol. 1, no. 1, pp. 448-457, 2018. [data recovery].
[http://dx.doi.org/10.33793/acperpro.01.01.88]

[22]   Khang A., Ali R. N., Bali S. Y., Hajimahmud V. A., Bahar A., Mehriban M., "Using Big Data to Solve Problems in the Field of Medicine," IN Khang, A., Abdullayev, V., Hrybiuk, O., & Shukla, A.K., Computer Vision and AI-integrated IoT Technologies in Medical Ecosystem. (1st Ed.) (2024). *CRC Press.*
[http://dx.doi.org/10.1201/9781003429609-21]

[23]   H.I. Sahib, N.H.A. Rahman, A.K. Al-Qaysi, and M.L. Attiah, "Comparison of data recovery techniques on master file table between Aho-Corasick and logical data recovery based on efficiency", *TELKOMNIKA (Telecommunication Computing Electronics and Control),* vol. 19, no. 1, pp. 73-78, 2021. [Telecommunication Computing Electronics and Control].
[http://dx.doi.org/10.12928/telkomnika.v19i1.16276]

[24]   P.T.N. Anh, "Precision Medicine Applications of AI-Integrated Biosensors", In: *Khang A. and Eswaran U., AI-Integrated Biosensors and Technologies for Automated Disease Detection and Drug Delivery.* 1st ed. CRC Press, 2025.

CHAPTER 10

Dynamic Disk

Himanshu Sharma[1], **Pooja Mittal**[1], **Ankit Kumar**[2], **Nitika Garg**[1], **Sanchit Dhankhar**[1], **Shushank Mahajan**[1,*] and **Samrat Chauhan**[1]

[1] *Chitkara College of Pharmacy, Chitkara University, Rajpura, Punjab, India*

[2] *Ganpati Institute of Pharmacy, Bilaspur, Haryana, Yamuna Nagar, India*

Abstract: The computer and consumer electronics sectors came together for the first time with the DVD (digital versatile disk) standard, but it also sparked an unprecedented discussion over copy protection and its ramifications. The DVD is much more than just an upgraded and redesigned CD. Many of the technological advancements that have transpired in the roughly fifteen years since the CD was invented are included in the new disc, including enhancements in disc manufacturing processes, optical storage, and signal processing. The music and film industries, however, have also benefited from the introduction of DVDs, which have prompted the new era of digital content delivery, preparing their intellectual property. Regarding the physical medium itself, there are four primary standards that apply: one for each of the DVD-ROM, DVD-R, DVD-RAM and DVD-RW. Then every application is supported by A STANDARD FILE SYSTEM definition at the logical layer. It was created by Santa Barbara, California Optical Storage Trade Association and is known as the universal disc format. An overlaying application set described by the DVD-Video, DVD-Audio, and DVD-professional standards are supported by the logical and physical layers working together.

Keywords: Basic disk, Dynamic disk, Disk spanning, Mirrored volumes, Mbr-master boot record, Raid.

INTRODUCTION

Full control over disk-based devices may be achieved with the Microsoft Windows application Disk Management [1]. The Microsoft Management Console was extended by it, and it was initially seen in Windows XP. Viewing and managing disk devices, including optical, flash, and internal and external hard drives as well as their corresponding partitions, is made possible for users of computers and laptops. Formatting drives, partitioning hard drives, renaming

---

[*] **Corresponding author Shushank Mahajan:** Chitkara College of Pharmacy, Chitkara University, Rajpura, Punjab, India; E-mail: shushank740@gmail.com

Alex Khang, Sanchit Dhankhar, Sandeep Bhardwaj, Avnesh Verma & Satish Kumar Sharma (Eds.)

drives, changing the drive letter, and performing numerous other disk-related operations are all done with the help of disk management.

Windows XP, Windows Vista, Windows 7, Windows 8, and Windows 10 now all have disk management accessible. Disk Management is included in every version of Windows, however there are some minor variations between them. Disk Management lacks a shortcut to open it straight from the Start Menu or Desktop, in contrast to other computer programs that have shortcuts to open them from the Taskbar, Desktop, or Start Menu alone [2]. This is because, unlike every other piece of software on a computer, it is not the same kind of program. It does not take long to open because there is not a shortcut accessible. Opening it takes relatively little time—a few minutes at most.

Evolution of Disk Structures

In the late 1980s and early 1990s, the first millimeter pictures (Beckwith *et al.* 1986, Sargent & Beckwith 1987, Rodriguez *et al.* 1992) and spectroscopy (*e.g.* Koerner *et al.* 1993) of these disks were obtained, indicating their presence and commonality as a by-product of star formation [3]. The double-peaked line profiles supported the regular Keplerian rotation pattern, and the mm dust emission showed that young stars were surrounded by extended structures.

The 1990 launch of the Hubble Space Telescope opened up a new field of research for protoplanetary disks. The Orion nebula, a star-forming area located 450 parsecs away, was able to be seen in detail thanks to the excellent spatial resolution obtained from space (O'Dell *et al.* 1992). The Wide Field Camera was used to capture these pictures using a variety of optical narrow band filters, including Hα, [Oiii], [Oi], and [Sii]. The data indicates the influence of disk irradiation and erosion by adjacent hot O and B stars, in addition to demonstrating the prevalence of such protoplanetary disks around recently formed stars (discard in 50% of stars) [4].

DIFFERENCE BETWEEN BASIC DISK AND DYNAMIC DISK

Basic Disk

One sort of hard drive configuration that comes with the Windows operating system is called a basic disk [5]. Regular partition tables or logical drives are used to handle all partitions and data on the hard disk. These are the kinds of storage that Windows users most frequently utilize. Either three primary partitions and an extended partition with several logical drives, or up to four primary partitions, can be found in it.

Tasks Must be Completed

- Main and extended partitions can be created and deleted.
- Inside an expanded partition, logical disks can be added and removed.
- Create a partition and designate it as active.

Dynamic Disk

A dynamic disk is a disk that has been configured for dynamic storage from the beginning. Not relying on a partition table to maintain track of every partition allows it to offer greater flexibility than a standard disk [5]. Using a dynamic disk setup, the partition may be expanded. In order to handle data, it employs dynamic volumes.

Tasks must be completed

- Simple, spanned, striped, mirrored, and RAID-5 volumes may be created and deleted.
- Stretch out a spread or basic volume.
- Maintenance on RAID-5 or mirrored volumes.
- Turn on an offline or missing disk again.

Let us see the difference between the basic disk and dynamic disk:

Characteristics of Basic Disks

Basic disks typically employ the Master Boot Record (MBR) partition format, but on systems that support it, they can also support the GUID Partition Table (GPT) partition style [6].

If the disk is MBR, it can handle four primary partitions or three primary partitions plus one extended partition, which can include up to 128 logical drives if an extended partition is made. Moreover, MBR disks are limited to 2 TB drives in capacity. A portion of the surplus capacity cannot be used if the basic disk space exceeds 2TB.

The following operating systems are compatible with MBR disks: Microsoft MS-DOS, Microsoft Windows 95, Microsoft Windows 98, Microsoft Windows, Millennium Edition, all NT versions, all XP versions, all Windows Server 2003 versions, and all versions for x86 and Itanium-based computers.

An extended partition is not necessary if the disk is GPT, as it can accommodate up to 128 main partitions. GPT disks are compatible with the following operating systems: Windows 10, Windows 8, Windows 7, Windows Vista, and so on. As you can see, MBR drives unquestionably support a wider range of Windows operating systems than GPT disks [7]. This explains why the most often observed disks are the simple MBR disks. You can pick the MBR partition style for a simple drive to address the compatibility issue, or, if your operating system supports GPT disks, you can use it for improved performance.

Advantages of Dynamic Disks

Modifiability is the primary advantage of a dynamic disk. Volumes and partitions can be created in addition. It permits the fusion of unallocated space across many disk volumes [8]. Performance on disks is improved by multi-disk volumes. Veritas Storage Foundation for Windows, which is included in disk upgrades, has dynamic volumes that hold volume management data and give you the following extra benefits:

• You can build and manage volumes using a dynamic disk, which also offers more sophisticated storage management features.
• It supports several RAID levels, which helps enhance speed and data availability.
• If you wish to provide a certain volume of more or less space, a dynamic disk allows you to effortlessly increase or decrease a volume.
• Various operating systems, including Windows, Linux, macOS, *etc.*, can be supported by a dynamic disk.
• Unlike with simple drives, it allows you to build volumes greater than 2 TB.
• Disk volumes may be transferred between systems without causing data loss.

What is Dynamic Disk? A dynamic disk is a disk that has been configured for dynamic storage from the beginning. In order to handle data, it employs dynamic volumes [9]. On dynamic disks, every volume is referred to as a dynamic volume, and the idea of volumes provides the foundation for dynamic disk configuration. Flawless and fault-tolerant volumes (mirrored and RAID-5 volumes) are among the capabilities that dynamic disks offer above basic drives. Other characteristics include the ability to build volumes that span several disks (spanned and striped volumes).

Because dynamic disks employ a database to monitor information about the disk's dynamic volumes and other dynamic disks in the computer, they provide more flexibility when it comes to volume management. Due to the fact that the dynamic disk database is replicated on each dynamic disk within the machine. Using the database on another dynamic disk, for instance, one corrupted dynamic disk can be repaired. The database's placement is determined by the disk's partition style. Within the final 1 megabyte (MB) of the disk on MBR partitions, the database is located. A reserved (hidden) partition of 1 MB holds the database on GPT partitions.

Different from other volume management techniques, dynamic disks enable volumes to have non-contiguous extents on one or more physical disks. Logical Disk Manager (LDM), Virtual Disk Service (VDS), and related functionalities are necessary for dynamic disks and volumes. You may construct fault-tolerant volumes and transform basic drives into dynamic disks with these characteristics. To promote dynamic disks, multi-partition volume functionality was dropped from basic disks and is now only available on dynamic drives [10]. Only dynamic disks are capable of carrying out the following operations:

- Make and destroy RAID-5, spanned, striped, mirrored, and basic volumes.
- Stretch a spread or basic volume.
- Take out the mirror from a mirrored volume or divide it into two volumes.
- RAID-5 or mirrored volume repair.
- Reactivate an offline or lost disc.

Key Differences between Basic Disk and Dynamic Disk

There are two main configurations for hard drives that are used to store data. Basic disks and dynamic disks are these setups. Both of these setups are effective at storing data, but they operate differently and have distinct features.

Basic Disk and Dynamic Disk are two different things. Basic Disk is a standard Windows-based hard disk data storage configuration that employs GPT and MBR partitions in cases when partition expansion is not available [11].

Below are some more important differences between basic disk and dynamic disk, such as (Table **1**):

DYNAMIC DISK CONCEPT

Volume Sets and Stripe Sets

- *Volume set:* A group of partitions that are handled as a single partition is called a volume set [12]. Two to thirty-two regions of unformatted free disk space can be combined to make one logical drive using this storage method.
- *Stripe set*: A stripe set creates one logical drive by combining unformatted free space from two to thirty-two physical drives. It functions similarly to a volume set. Over the disks, 64K blocks of data are written. Performance is accelerated and data is distributed uniformly across the drives thanks to this technique. Nevertheless, stripe sets do not come with built-in fault tolerance.

Table 1. Important differences between Basic Disk and Dynamic Disk.

Terms	Basic Disk	Dynamic Disk
Definition	The basic disk manages all of the hard drive's partitions using standard partition tables, which are included in both Windows and MS-DOS.	A hard drive is separated into dynamic volumes within a dynamic disk.
Partitions	When you establish partitions with a basic disk configuration or a predetermined size, the volumes within are called basic volumes and are not able to be altered. A single secondary partition from which logical drives can be created can house up to four partitions on each hard disk, or up to three partitions and one secondary partition.	Primary and extended partitions are not the only partition types that may be dynamic drives. Instead of being divided into partitions, the hard drive is divided into volumes, which might span one or more disks and be non-contiguous.
Volume type	Only the MBR and GPT partition types may be created on a basic drive. • The standard BIOS partition table is utilized in the Master Boot Record (MBR), a disk architecture that is often employed. • The Unified Extensible Firmware Interface (UEFI) is used by the GPT (GUID Partition Table) partition table. A hard drive with a GPT architecture may have up to 128 partitions.	Simple, spanned, striped, mirrored, and RAID-5 volumes are all found on a dynamic disk. Similar to the logical drive in a basic disk, a dynamic volume is a logical volume that is housed within a dynamic disk.
Conversion	Without erasing any data, converting a basic disk to a dynamic disk is simple. You do not need to restart the computer while the conversion is happening, and you may construct volumes that span numerous drives. However, you must make backups because of this.	Nevertheless, you have to remove all volumes from the dynamic disk in order to turn it into a simple disk. One reason to consider leaving 1 MB of space on the drive unpartitioned is because a dynamic disk needs that space for the disk management database. This way, if you ever need to convert a basic drive to a dynamic disk, you may utilize that space for that purpose.
Modifications	An existing partition on a basic drive cannot be altered.	Volumes can be expanded when they are in a dynamic disk.
Multi-boot configuration	The basic disk is capable of supporting several boot configurations. Simple disks enable multi-boot setups, which makes it simple to switch between several operating systems on a PC.	Boot loaders, which let users choose between several operating systems, are not used by dynamic disks. For this reason, in a multi-boot setup, this cannot be the sole drive utilized.

(Table 1) cont.....

Terms	Basic Disk	Dynamic Disk
Conversion	Without erasing any data, converting a basic disk to a dynamic disk is simple. You do not need to restart the computer while the conversion is happening, and you may construct volumes that span numerous drives. However, you must make backups because of this.	Nevertheless, you have to remove all volumes from the dynamic disk in order to turn it into a simple disk. One reason to consider leaving 1 MB of space on the drive unpartitioned is because a dynamic disk needs that space for the disk management database. This way, if you ever need to convert a basic drive to a dynamic disk, you may utilize that space for that purpose.
Modifications	An existing partition on a basic drive cannot be altered.	Volumes can be expanded when they are in a dynamic disk.
Multi-boot configuration	The basic disk is capable of supporting several boot configurations. Simple disks enable multi-boot setups, which makes it simple to switch between several operating systems on a PC.	Boot loaders, which let users choose between several operating systems, are not used by dynamic disks. For this reason, in a multi-boot setup, this cannot be the sole drive utilized.
Compatibility	Windows operating systems from the past also support a simple disk.	Only Windows 2000 and later provide functionality for dynamic disks.

Mirrored Volumes

- Mirror sets: These create two copies of a partition, one on one physical disk and one on the other. Put otherwise, two full copies of the partition are always maintained by a mirror set. Under these circumstances, data stored on one physical drive persists on the other.
- Creating Mirrored Volumes: With the help of the Windows 2000 fault-tolerance driver, FTDISK.SYS, a mirrored volume, also known as a mirror set, makes a full duplicate of one physical disk onto the second disk. The mirror is updated whenever changes occur on the disk, ensuring precise data redundancy at all times [13]. An efficient option is a mirror set, however, the requirement to have a separate disk set aside for the mirror will cut disk space by half. The system goes to the mirror disk to keep things running in case the primary disk dies.

Use these procedures to generate mirrored volume, Right-click on an unformatted free space region in Disk Management.

- Select "Create Volume."
- The wizard to create volumes opens.
- Hit the Next button.
- A window called Volume Types opens.
- Select Mirrored Volume.
- A second volume on a different disk of the same size on a different physical disk will be requested by the wizard. In addition, you will need to designate a drive

letter and format the volume. You see a summary after the wizard is done.
• For the mirrored volume to be created, click Finish.

RAID 5 Volumes

Block-level striping with distributed parity makes up RAID 5. The disks share parity information, in contrast to RAID 4 [14]. To function, all but one drive must be present. In the event that a single drive fails, it is possible to determine the succeeding reads from the distributed parity in order to prevent data loss. Three drives are required for RAID 5.

Depending on the order of writing across the disks, a RAID 5 disk drive array can have a variety of data and parity configurations, such as:

• The arrangement of data blocks stored on disks 0 through N in a left-to-right or right-to-left fashion.
• Whether the parity block is at the start or finish of the stripe.
• Where a stripe's initial block falls in relation to the preceding stripe's parity.

RAID 5's distributed parity distributes the load of a specialized parity disk among all RAID members, in contrast to RAID 4. Furthermore, because every RAID member takes part in fulfilling write requests, write speed is improved. This no longer acts as a bottleneck, even though it won't be as effective as a striping (RAID 0) configuration because parity needs to be written [15].

BENEFITS OF DYNAMIC DISKS

Windows operating systems come with a feature called dynamic disks, which has many advantages over basic drives. Dynamic disks have the following main benefits:

Management of Volume

Dynamic Volume Expansion

Dynamic disks enable volume (partition) resizing without requiring their deletion and reconstruction. This facilitates storage space management and allows for little downtime as you adjust to changing storage needs.

Spanned and Striped Volumes

Dynamic disks allow for the creation of striped volumes, which disperse data across several drives for better performance, and spanned volumes, which combine free space from numerous disks into a single logical volume. This has the potential to improve both capability and efficacy.

Fault Tolerance

- Mirrored Volumes: Dynamic disks are capable of supporting mirroring, which is the process of duplicating data between two drives. By guaranteeing that the data is still accessible on the mirrored drive in the event of a disk failure, this offers fault tolerance.
- RAID-5 Volumes: RAID-5 volumes, which spread parity information over many disks for fault tolerance, may be made using dynamic drives. The parity information can be used to rebuild the data in the event that one disk fails.
- Disk Spanning: With dynamic disks, volumes may be created that extend over several different physical drives. When a single disk cannot hold the necessary amount of data, this is especially helpful.
- Online Volume Management: Dynamic disks allow you to modify volumes online without having to restart your computer. In settings where constant availability is crucial, this is advantageous.
- Volume Stripe Size: Dynamic disks let you choose the stripe size when constructing striped volumes. Applications of particular kinds can benefit from this as they can be tailored to fit particular workloads.
- Centralized Storage Management: Logical Disk Manager (LDM) is used to centrally manage dynamic disks. Managing disk and volume duties is made easier with this single interface, which simplifies storage resource administration [16].

It is crucial to remember that even while dynamic disks provide these benefits, not all use cases require them. For less complex storage requirements, basic disks could be more than enough, whereas dynamic disks offer extra complexity that is not always necessary. Choosing between basic and dynamic disks requires careful analysis of the particular requirements and aims.

Enhanced Volume Management

The Disk Management interface is used to manage dynamic disk volumes. Additional details about the disk, including its layout, type, file system, status, capacity, and free space, are shown next to the volume label in the upper portion of the right pane [17].

Fault Tolerance and Redundancy6

In this Chapter, "redundancy" refers to the capacity to set up one or more backup components (or cards) to take over in the event of a malfunction. Redundancy helps ensure that the CSP processes call even in the event of a hardware or software failure by providing system-wide fault tolerance [18].

The CSP features two host connections and two bus structures. It can accommodate redundant Matrix Controller cards and be set up with two power supplies. For ISDN cards as well as line cards, the CSP enables N+1 configuration.

Redundant Matrix Controller Cards

Physically, the Matrix Controller cards in a redundant CSP are the same cards. The host's designation, *via* a procedure called "hardware arbitration," is the single factor that establishes which device is "active" and which is "standby." The "standby" Matrix Controller card is prepared to take over all of the responsibilities of the active Matrix Controller card in the following scenarios [19], while the "active" Matrix Controller card has complete access to all hardware resources:

• The presenter asks for a transition.
• The switch receives software downloads.
• Physically removing or restarting the Matrix Controller card in use.
• The Matrix Controller card that is in use is rearranged.
• Following the system's startup and stabilization, a hardware or software malfunction takes place.

Redundant Line Cards

If you set up one spare line card and its I/O card for every kind of card, you may give a CSP N+1 redundancy for its line cards [20]. One spare card acts as a backup in case of a hardware or software malfunction, and N is the total number of line cards of the same kind in the CSP. Though it can only support one kind of card, each redundant line card may support many cards.

In the event that one of the three T-ONE cards in your CSP fails, you can add a fourth T-ONE card to function as a backup. To obtain E1 redundancy, if your CSP also includes more than one E-ONE line card, you must have one E-ONE card in standby mode. In order to switch signals from the failing line card to the standby line card, the host sends the Matrix Controller a Line Card Switchover (0x0024) message after receiving notification from the Matrix Controller of a line card failure.

Performance Improvements

Under some conditions, dynamic disks in Windows operating systems provide various characteristics that may help with speed gains. The following are some ways that dynamic disks might improve performance:

1. ***Striped volumes (RAID-0):*** Striped volumes, or RAID-0, are made possible by dynamic disks. Data is written across many drives concurrently in a striped volume, which is composed of blocks [21]. Because many disks are used to service the I/O activities, this can result in enhanced read and write performance. Striped volumes do not offer fault tolerance; if one disk in the stripe fails, the entire volume is impacted. This is important to keep in mind even if they improve speed.

2. ***Mirrored Volumes (RAID-1):*** • Mirrored volumes, which are formed from dynamic disks, double data on two disks to provide fault tolerance. • Although the main goal of mirroring is to guarantee data availability and redundancy in the event of a disk failure, it can also help to improve read performance because reads can be handled from either of the mirrored copies, potentially increasing overall read throughput.

3. ***Disk spanning***: This feature enables you to build volumes over several physical drives. By spreading I/O over several drives and boosting storage capacity, this may help to enhance performance.

It is crucial to remember that although dynamic disks have these advantages, the real performance gains may differ depending on the workload and usage habits. Furthermore, there could be trade-offs between fault tolerance and administration due to the added complexity brought forth by dynamic disks, particularly in setups that use striping or mirroring [22].

DYNAMIC DISK IMPLEMENTATION

There are many processes involved in implementing dynamic drives in a Windows operating system. Features like spanning volumes, striping, mirroring, and more are offered by dynamic disks [23]. Using dynamic disks is explained in general in the following guide:

It is imperative that all critical data be backed up before implementing dynamic disk technology. If disk configuration changes are made carelessly, data loss may occur.

The Procedure for Using Dynamic Disks:

To access Disk Management, either right-click the "Start" button and select "Disk Management" or press Win + X.

To transform a Basic disk into a Dynamic disk, follow these steps: • Locate the disk you wish to convert in Disk Management.

If you perform a right-click on the disk itself, rather than a partition, select "Convert to Dynamic Disk."

To finish the conversion, adhere to the directions displayed on the screen.

Establish Dynamic Volumes: 1. After the disk is dynamic, you may establish dynamic volumes (partitions) in a variety of configurations.

• Simple Volume: One disk, one volume.
• Spanning volume: a logical volume that combines unallocated space from many drives.
• Stripped Volume: By dividing data over many drives, this optimizes performance (RAID-0).

By replicating data over two drives, Mirrored Volume (RAID-1) offers fault tolerance.

• RAID-5 Volume: For fault tolerance, parity data is distributed among many drives.

1. Select Volume Configuration and Size:

• During the construction process, specify the dynamic volume's dimensions and setup.

• Take into account your workload while selecting the stripe size for striped volumes.

First, format the volume. To do this, right-click on the dynamic volume and select "Format."

• Execute the format, set the file system, and allocate the unit size.

2. Assign a drive letter or mount point by doing the following:

• Right-click on the volume and select "Change Drive Letter and Paths."

• To make the disk accessible, assign a drive letter or mount point.

2. Carry out Extra Configuration (Optional): You may choose to adjust other options, such as volume labels, file permissions, or encryption, based on your needs.

3. Test and Monitor: After configuring the dynamic disk and volumes, examine how well they work. Keep an eye out for any unusual activity on the system and make sure the volumes are performing up to par.

4. Best Practices and Things to Think About:

Backup: Prior to making any changes to disk settings, always make a backup of your data.

5. Plan for Fault Tolerance: • Recognize the fault tolerance offered by various dynamic disk configurations and select the one that best suits your requirements.

6. The purpose of performance testing is to verify that dynamic volumes work as expected, particularly when features like striping are being used.

• Documentation: Keep track of all the configurations for the dynamic disks, including volume sizes, configurations, and any unique factors.

Supplementary Materials:

Dynamic Disks in Microsoft Documentation First, Microsoft TechNet Make a Dynamic Disk Out of a Basic Disk

For precise and current details on dynamic disk implementation in your particular Windows version, always consult the most recent official documentation.

Converting Basic Disks to Dynamic Disks

If you upgrade from Windows NT 4.0 to Windows 2000 Server, your disk will remain in its original configuration, meaning that it will be a basic disk [24]. To fully utilize the disk-management features of Windows 2000 Server, you can upgrade the basic disk to a dynamic disk. Naturally, "Should I upgrade?" is the next question. Whether or not to update your basic disk to a dynamic disk may be determined by following one simple guideline. Upgrades to your drive should be avoided if your machine also runs MS-DOS, Windows 98 or earlier, or Windows NT 4.0 or earlier. These operating systems are unable to access dynamic volumes. The basic drive should be upgraded to a dynamic disk if your machine only runs Windows 2000.

You may better manage your drive in Windows 2000 Server by doing this operation.

There must be at least 1MB of unformatted free space at the end of any drive before you may upgrade it to dynamic. The update will not work if there is not. It is possible that partitions or volumes created with Windows NT do not have this free space easily available. Drive management uses this free space when creating partitions or volumes on a drive. Your Windows NT partitions become dynamic volumes when the upgrade is complete, and you are unable to convert them back to partitions. On your drive, the update will convert any Windows NT volume sets, mirror sets, striped sets, or striped sets with parity to Windows 2000's spanned volumes, striped volumes, mirrored volumes, or RAID-5 volumes. After the update is finished, keep in mind that operating systems other than Windows 2000 cannot access the drive [25]. Additionally, the following concerns need to be considered prior to carrying out the upgrade:

- A basic disk with the boot partition can be upgraded to a dynamic disk. When the update is finished, the boot partition turns into a basic boot volume.
- A basic disk with the system partition on it can be upgraded to a dynamic disk. Upon completion of the update, the System partition is reduced to a basic system partition.
- Detachable media cannot be upgraded to dynamic volumes.
- You also need to upgrade the other disks that hold the partitions of the volume if a basic disk has any volumes that span several disks, such in a stripe set with parity.
- If the disc has a sector size of more than 512 bytes, you cannot convert it from a basic to a dynamic disk.
- Reverting a dynamic disk to a basic disk necessitates the deletion of all volumes. All of the disk's data is erased with this action. Right-click on the disk and select Revert to Basic Disk after the volumes have been removed.

Follow these procedures to convert a basic disk to a dynamic disk

1. Select Programs, Administrative Tools, and Computer Management from the Start menu. The window of the console opens.
2. Double-click Disk Management after expanding the Storage tree. Your disk(s) are displayed in the right pane of the Disk Management interface.
3. Use a right-click to update the disk. Make sure you are right-clicking the disk and not a disk partition. To switch to a dynamic disk, click Upgrade.
4. Your computer is requested to reboot when the upgrade completes. For the boot and system partition updates to be completed, you will need to restart your computer.

5. Disk Management will show the disk as dynamic when the update has finished.

Creating Dynamic Volumes

The primary goal of dynamic volume lines is to linearize three-dimensional volumes along a space-filling curve. Engineers are acquainted with the resultant line charts [26]. Numerous volumes may be compared using their line plots without occlusion. Using standard approaches proves to be challenging when comparing several volumes in their native 3D space that change just slightly from one another. For instance, there are significant issues with clutter and opacity in a direct volume representation of several datasets. As the number of volumes to compare rises, this impact is further strengthened.

Regarding 2D slice views, the same holds true [27]. It is possible to arrange two or four slice views of different volumes side by side, but finding locations where the volumes differ becomes practically difficult when there are more volumes to compare, for example, six. For instance, even for a specialist, it might be challenging to distinguish a brightness variation when individual voxels vary by 5000 intensities. In a line plot with a y-axis intensity range of 65000, this amplitude decrease would be 7%, making it simpler to identify as a positional difference. For indicating little changes, positional encoding works far better than color coding. Line graphs make it simpler to compare intensities than matching them in two or more 2D (or 3D) perspectives and then comparing their color encoding [28].

To identify a volume where the voxels contain the local ensemble variances, statistical aggregation might be used. However, occlusion and clutter still have an impact on rendering even with such decreased data. For instance, the opacity needs to be adjusted to a low value in order to make differences obvious inside the volume. Bigger changes, though, are only marginally apparent at that point. You'll lose little distinctions. Additionally, statistical aggregate volumes only offer an outline or summary; further in-depth visualizations would be necessary to compare individual members within a region of interest [26]. By comparing line plots, our technique makes it simple to examine the differences between the different members.

One disadvantage of linearizing volumes is that spatial coherency is lost. We selected a space-filling curve that offers the greatest spatial coherency preservation among the several options. In the straightened Hilbert line display, neighboring voxels in the 3D volumes are frequently transferred to adjacent positions because of the wavy nature of the Hilbert curve. We assess how well the Hilbert curve's spatial coherence compares to that of another straightforward volume linearization, or the scan line curve, which traverses the volume slice by slice and scan line by scan line inside successive slices. Significant spatial incoherences are introduced when scan lines or slices are switched. Hilbert curves also exhibit similar incoherencies, but far less so [26].

Resizing and Extending Volumes

Windows requires many procedures to resize and expand volumes on dynamic drives [29]. Here is a tutorial on using the Disk Management tool to accomplish these tasks:

Resizing the Volumes

1. To access Disk Management, either right-click on the "Start" button and select "Disk Management" or press Win + X.
2. Determine the Volume:

Choose the dynamic volume that you wish to resize under Disk Management.

Step 3: Shrink Volume: Right-click on the volume you wish to reduce and select "Shrink Volume."

- Type in the megabytes of space that has to be shrunk. Unallocated space is created on the disk as a result.

Volume Extension

First Choice: Utilize Adjacent Unallocated Space to Increase Volume:

1. Open Disk Management: To open Disk Management, follow the preceding instructions.
2. Find the Volume:
   ○ Decide which dynamic volume you wish to increase.
3. Extend Volume: Right-click on the volume you wish to increase and select "Extend Volume."
   ○ To increase the volume utilizing nearby unallocated space, according to the wizard's instructions.

Solution 2: Extend Volume to Non-adjacent Unallocated Space: You may use the diskpart command-line software to extend a volume if the unallocated space is not next to the volume you wish to expand.

1. Launch Command Prompt by pressing Win + X and choosing "PowerShell" (Admin) or "Command Prompt" (Expert).
2. Launch Disk part: • Input disk part and hit Return.

Listing of Volumes and Disks:

To view a list of available disks, type list disk and hit Enter.
   ○ To view a list of volumes, type list volume.

Select the Volume and Disk: Type select disk X, substituting the disk number for X, and hit Enter.

Enter the volume number Y and type "select volume" before hitting the Enter key.

Boost the Volume:

- Type expand size=Z, pressing Enter after substituting Z with the megabyte-worth of space.
     Leave-Ahead Disk part:
- Press Enter after typing "exit."

BEST PRACTICES AND CONSIDERATIONS

Compatibility Issues

Incompatibility issues

Windows Vista's Disk Management ignores earlier norms such as "drive geometry" or "CHS" and instead divides files based on a 1-MB alignment boundary. Put otherwise, Vista's Disk Management behaves as though it is utilizing a non-standard CHS geometry, with 2048 sectors per track/head and one track/head per cylinder.

Issues with compatibility when utilizing a 1-MB alignment border

Using Windows XP Disk Management to modify extended partition tables that have been modified using Vista Disk Management is not recommended [30]. These expanded partitions might be silently erased by XP Disk Management. Using just one partition editor on the disk and erasing every partition (rebooting or reconnecting the drive) are two methods to fix these jumbled partition tables.

- Partitions made with Vista Disk Management might not allow you to install Windows Server 2003 or XP.
- Previous CHS conventions, such as the regular intervals at which partitions start and finish and the separation between the expanded boot records and their logical drives, are disregarded by these 1 MB alignments.

Partitions that do not align according to a CHS may not be viewable or editable by other operating systems (such as boot loaders, partitioners, or DOS programs used by backup or recovery software) [31]. (Generally, if several partitioners are used on the same partition table without alignment checks using tools like Ranish Partition Manager, unexpected results may occur. For instance, if all partitions are not removed (and the machine is not reset) prior to installing the operating system, it could be crucial that the partition editor used by the operating system installer follows the same alignments as the ones used by earlier partition editors. Almost usually, the difference in CHS geometry is the number of heads per cylinder—240 instead of 255, for example. Partition editors, however, may appear to overlook this kind of geometry under some circumstances. In this context, "track" and "head" have the same meaning [32].

Backup and Recovery Strategies

Backup Plans

Make a decision on the database's protection against future media failures before creating an Oracle database [33]. If you do not plan for backups before building your database, you might not be able to restore the data files, control files, or online redo log files in the event of a disk failure.

The broad recommendations described in this section will assist you in determining which aspects of a database to back up and when to execute database backups. Naturally, the particulars of your approach rely on the limitations that you are facing. This section contains these topics:

• Adhering to the backup and recovery golden rule

Selecting the database archiving mode;

• Multiplexing control files, online redo logs, and Archived redo logs;
• Backing up frequently used tablespaces; performing backups after unrecoverable operations;
• Performing whole database backups after opening with the RESET LOGS option;
• Archiving older backups;
• Understanding the constraints for distributed database backups;
• Exporting data for greater protection and flexibility;
• Avoiding the backup of online redo logs;
• Maintaining records of the server's hardware and software configuration

Following the Golden Rule for Backup and Recovery

A data file, control file, or online redo log that is required to recover from the failure of any Oracle database file is referred to as the redundancy set [34].

• The most recent backups of all the data files and the control file are included in the redundancy set.
• A duplicate of the online redo log files produced by Oracle multiplexing, operating system mirroring, or both • All archived redo logs produced after the previous backup was made
• A duplicate of the current control file produced by Oracle multiplexing, operating system mirroring, or both
• Configuration files and the server parameter file

Datafiles, online redo logs, and control files should be stored on different drives from the set of disks or other media that contains the redundancy set [35]. This is the golden rule of backup and recovery. The use of this technique guarantees that the loss of backups or redo logs necessary for datafile recovery does not occur as a result of the failure of a disk housing the datafile. For this reason, a minimum production-level database needs at least two hard drives: one for storing the database files and another for storing the files in the redundancy set.

In any scenario, it is best to maintain the redundancy configured on different volumes, file systems, and RAID devices from the primary data. Though they are dependable, these systems can and do malfunction. You can recover from a failure without losing committed transactions if you keep the redundancy set apart.

There are other approaches you may take to put in place a golden rule-based system. Oracle advises heeding these recommendations:

• Instead of merely multiplying the online redo log files and current control files at the hardware or operating system level, do so at the Oracle level as well. One benefit of multiplexing at the Oracle level is that a lost write or I/O failure should only affect one copy.
• Since Oracle does not fully support control file multiplexing—if one multiplexed copy of the control file fails, the Oracle instance will terminate—use operating system or hardware mirroring for at least the control file.
• If at all feasible, use hardware or operating system mirroring for the main data files to prevent the need for media recovery in the event of straightforward disk failures.
• Maintain a minimum of one hard drive copy of the whole redundancy set, which includes the most current backup.

- Splitting a local mirror to make a redundancy copy depends on the mirroring subsystem for both the primary files and the redundancy set copy, therefore it is not as reliable as a backup made using RMAN or operating system commands. Redundancy set copy refers to the last file backup, including the last backup to tape. Keep the archived logs that are necessary to retrieve this copy, then.
- If a RAID device is used to store your database, then you should put the redundancy set on a different group of devices.
- Keep at least two copies of the data if you keep the redundancy set on cassettes, as tapes might malfunction. Additionally, think about preserving backups from various times if you have several copies of the same data. This allows you to have an older backup from before the corruption occurred if just one backup or split mirror was made when the database was affected.

Performance Optimization Tips

What is Disk Optimization?

On a Windows computer, files may be created and deleted. Windows attempts to fill the empty storage blocks left by erasing a file, which further writes commands to try to fill [36]. Should a file exceed the capacity of the blank blocks, some of the file will write to the blank blocks and the remaining portion will move to other empty storage blocks on the disk. A fragmented file is the outcome.

As a result of mechanical heads moving across a disk's surface to read and write data, disk fragmentation is an issue. Upon file fragmentation, the disk heads shift to many locations in order to read every block inside the file. The more head movements needed, the longer it takes to read or write a file. These bodily motions take time to complete.

CHALLENGES AND LIMITATIONS

Windows dynamic disks offer capabilities including spanning volumes, software-based RAID setups, and dynamic volume expansion. They do, however, have unique difficulties and restrictions. There are certain limitations with dynamic disks. Dynamic disks may not be completely recognized or supported by certain operating systems, including Linux, macOS, and earlier versions of Windows (such as Windows 9x and DOS).

Dynamic drives are linked to the particular Windows installation from which they originated. You can have trouble accessing the data if you try to reinstall Windows or move a dynamic drive to a different machine. Compared to basic drives, retrieving data from dynamic disks might be more difficult in the event of a system failure or corruption. Retrieving data from dynamic volumes may be difficult for standard data recovery software. Dynamic disk use is restricted in some Windows versions.

Dynamic drives, for instance, are not supported by Windows 10 Home Edition. To take full advantage of dynamic disk capabilities, you must have Windows 10 Professional, Enterprise, or Education versions. In contrast to simple disks, dynamic disks provide more complexity. Dynamic disk management is more difficult to manage and troubleshoot since it incorporates several components, including striped volumes, spanned volumes, and volume sets. Data loss is a possibility if a dynamic disk malfunctions.

A disk failure in the disk structure or several disk failures occurring at the same time might cause data loss even if dynamic disks enable fault tolerance capabilities like parity and mirroring. There are few alternatives for downsizing, even when dynamic drives provide capacity growth. A basic or spanning volume can only be shrunk down to the location of any used data. It is also difficult to enlarge the system or boot disk. There are hazards and restrictions when converting a basic disk to a dynamic disk and vice versa. It is important to have backups before making such conversions because the procedure is not always reversible without data loss.

Performance issues with dynamic drives may arise, particularly when specific RAID configurations are used. Performance can be improved with striped volumes, but if one of the disks fails, there is a higher chance of data loss. Compared to simple drives, creating trustworthy backups and recovering data on dynamic disks might be more complicated [37]. Dynamic volumes are not completely supported by every backup software; you might require specialist tools for this. When considering whether to employ dynamic disks, it is critical to comprehend these difficulties and constraints. It is also critical to have appropriate backup and recovery plans in place to reduce any possible hazards.

THE FUTURE OF DYNAMIC DISK TECHNOLOGY TRENDS

There may be more interaction between cloud services and dynamic disks, enabling cloud-based solutions to provide seamless redundancy and growth of storage [38]. Improved cross-platform compatibility might make dynamic drives easier for non-Windows operating systems to detect and use, enabling multi-boot setups and data sharing.

More sophisticated data protection techniques could be included in future dynamic disk technologies to lower the possibility of data loss in the case of disk failures. This might include using intelligent error-correcting technology or creating novel RAID setups. Since data recovery is crucial, developments in dynamic disk-specific data recovery solutions may occur, making data recovery after disk failures or corruption simpler and more dependable.

Potential avenues for progress in dynamic disk technologies might include caching or RAID setups, as well as general performance optimization with an emphasis on speed, data transfer rates, and overall efficiency. It may be possible to create more flexible dynamic disk management tools that can be used to resize, move, and manage dynamic volumes without the assistance of outside vendors. These tools would be more user-friendly and better.

To satisfy the increasing expectations for data security and privacy, future dynamic disk technologies may include stronger encryption choices and other security features. Dynamic disk technologies may be more suited to handle contemporary applications, such as those involving virtualization, large data processing, and high I/O needs, as computing workloads evolve. It is possible that integration with storage virtualization technologies may become more commonplace, enabling more scalable and adaptable storage solutions to meet evolving business requirements.

More automated and intelligent decision-making about data location, optimization, and fault tolerance might be achieved by integrating AI-driven technologies with dynamic disk management. To stay current with dynamic disk technology, one must monitor industry announcements, product releases, and technical improvements. Though there may be additional developments or changes in the landscape, these tendencies are theoretical as of my last update. To stay current with dynamic disk technology, one must monitor industry announcements, product releases, and technical improvements [39].

CONCLUSION

In summary, a thorough understanding of storage technologies may be gained from the investigation of disk management, which covers everything from the historical development of disk structures to the subtle distinctions between basic and dynamic disks. The ideas of dynamic disks, such as mirrored volumes, RAID 5 volumes, and volume sets, highlight the versatility and cutting-edge capabilities that dynamic disks provide. Improved performance, fault tolerance, and volume control are only a few advantages of dynamic disks that highlight their importance in contemporary computer settings.

To illustrate the flexibility and scalability these structures provide, dynamic disks must be implemented through crucial steps such as converting basic disks, generating dynamic volumes, and dynamically resizing or expanding volumes. When navigating dynamic disk environments, it is important to follow recommended procedures and take certain precautions, such as fixing compatibility problems, putting strong backup and recovery plans in place, and speed optimization.

Organizations exploring these technologies can get significant insights from real-world case studies and success stories, which illuminate the practical uses and lessons learned from dynamic disk installations. But there are obstacles and limits as well; they might range from typical problems with dynamic disks to particular limitations that need calculated solutions. It is essential to acknowledge these constraints in order to sustain a robust storage system. It is expected that new developments in technology and creative approaches will influence future directions in dynamic disk technology.

Notable developments to keep an eye on include the incorporation of artificial intelligence, improvements in compatibility, and performance optimization. Dynamic disk technology predictions and advancements are anticipated to solve existing issues and improve storage capacities in order to satisfy changing user and organizational demands. To fully take advantage of dynamic disk solutions, it will be necessary to keep up with the latest developments in new trends in storage technology.

REFERENCES

[1]   R.K. Wadhwa, and K. Sharma, "The commercial hard disk backup system for quick recovery operating system in cloud storage system", *2022 International Interdisciplinary Humanitarian Conference for Sustainability (IIHC),* IEEE., pp. 204-209, 2022.
[http://dx.doi.org/10.1109/IIHC55949.2022.10060397]

[2]   A. Khang, N.A. Ragimova, V.A. Hajimahmud, and V.A. Alyar, "Advanced Technologies and Data Management in the Smart Healthcare System", In: *AI-Centric Smart City Ecosystems: Technologies, Design and Implementation (1st Ed.)* vol. 16. Khang A., Rani S., Sivaraman A. K. CRC Press., 2022, p. 10.
[http://dx.doi.org/10.1201/9781003252542-16]

[3]   C. Dominik, "Disk formation and structure", *InEPJ Web of Conferences,* vol. 102, EDP Sciences., p. 00002, 2015.
[http://dx.doi.org/10.1051/epjconf/201510200002]

[4]   D.J. Hollenbach, H.W. Yorke, and D. Johnstone, "Disk dispersal around young stars", *Protostars and planets IV,* vol. 401, p. 12, 2000.

[5]   E. Bugnion, S. Devine, K. Govil, and M. Rosenblum, "Disco", *ACM Trans. Comput. Syst.,* vol. 15, no. 4, pp. 412-447, 1997. [TOCS].
[http://dx.doi.org/10.1145/265924.265930]

[6]   H. H. Khanh, and A. Khang, ""The Role of Artificial Intelligence in Blockchain Applications", *Reinventing Manufacturing and Business Processes through Artificial Intelligence.,* vol. 2, In Rana G, Khang A., Sharma R., Goel A. K., Dubey A. K. CRC Press., pp. 20-40, 2021.
[http://dx.doi.org/10.1201/9781003145011-2]

[7]   B.J. Nikkel, "Forensic analysis of GPT disks and GUID partition tables", *Digit. Invest.,* vol. 6, no. 1-2, pp. 39-47, 2009.
[http://dx.doi.org/10.1016/j.diin.2009.07.001]

[8]   A. Khang, K.C. Rath, S.K. Satapathy, A. Kumar, S.R. Das, and M.R. Panda, "Enabling the Future of Manufacturing: Integration of Robotics and IoT to Smart Factory Infrastructure in Industry 4.0", In: *Handbook of Research on AI-Based Technologies and Applications in the Era of the Metaverse.*, A. Khang, V. Shah, S. Rani, Eds., IGI Global, 2023, pp. 25-50.
[http://dx.doi.org/10.4018/978-1-6684-8851-5.ch002]

[9]   S. Nath, and A. Kansal, "FlashDB: Dynamic self-tuning database for NAND flash", *Proceedings of the 6th international conference on Information processing in sensor networks,* 2007.
[http://dx.doi.org/10.1145/1236360.1236412]

[10] A. Kankaanpää, *Query performance and optimization in cloud databases,* 2022.

[11] L. Wu, L-Y. Yuan, and J-H. You, "BASIC: An alternative to BASE for large-scale data management system", *2014 IEEE International Conference on Big Data (Big Data),* IEEE., 2014.
[http://dx.doi.org/10.1109/BigData.2014.7004206]

[12] B. Hendrickson, and T.G. Kolda, "Graph partitioning models for parallel computing", *Parallel Comput.,* vol. 26, no. 12, pp. 1519-1534, 2000.
[http://dx.doi.org/10.1016/S0167-8191(00)00048-X]

[13] G.A. Gibson, and D.A. Patterson, "Designing disk arrays for high data reliability", *J. Parallel Distrib. Comput.,* vol. 17, no. 1-2, pp. 4-27, 1993.
[http://dx.doi.org/10.1006/jpdc.1993.1002]

[14] J. Wan, "${\rm S}^{2}$-RAID: Parallel RAID Architecture for Fast Data Recovery", *IEEE Trans. Parallel Distrib. Syst.,* vol. 25, no. 6, pp. 1638-1647, 2013.
[http://dx.doi.org/10.1109/TPDS.2013.225]

[15] D. Vadala, *Managing RAID on Linux: Fast, Scalable, Reliable Data Storage.* O'Reilly Media, Inc., 2002.

[16] F. Nzanywayingoma, and Y. Yang, "Efficient resource management techniques in cloud computing environment: a review and discussion", *Int. J. Comput. Appl.,* vol. 41, no. 3, pp. 165-182, 2019.
[http://dx.doi.org/10.1080/1206212X.2017.1416558]

[17] Yun-Hee Choi, Y-H. Choi, and T.S. Choi, "Design and implementation of hard disk drive embedded digital satellite receiver with file management", *IEEE Trans. Consum. Electron.,* vol. 48, no. 1, pp. 125-130, 2002.
[http://dx.doi.org/10.1109/TCE.2002.1010100]

[18] J.H. Lala, and R.E. Harper, "Fault tolerance in embedded real-time systems: importance and treatment of common mode failures", *Workshop on Fault Tolerance,* Springer., 1993.

[19] Y. Wan, "The adaptive heartbeat design of high availability RAID dual-controller", *2008 International Conference on Multimedia and Ubiquitous Engineering (mue 2008),* IEEE., 2008.
[http://dx.doi.org/10.1109/MUE.2008.31]

[20] D.N.J. White, J.N. Ruddock, and P.R. Edgington, "Molecular design with transparallel supercomputers", *Mol. Simul.,* vol. 3, no. 1-3, pp. 71-100, 1989.
[http://dx.doi.org/10.1080/08927028908034620]

[21] B.K. Goja, and D. Padha, *RAID Dependent Performance on Storage & Retrieval of Digital Forensics Meta Data Files with Different File Systems.*

[22] E. Rozier, *Understanding the fault-tolerance properties of large-scale storage systems.* University of Illinois at Urbana-Champaign, 2012.

[23] R.W. Watson, "High performance storage system scalability: Architecture, implementation and experience", *in 22nd IEEE/13th NASA Goddard Conference on Mass Storage Systems and Technologies (MSST'05).,* IEEE., 2005.
[http://dx.doi.org/10.1109/MSST.2005.17]

[24] C. Panek, *Windows Server Administration Fundamentals.* John Wiley & Sons, 2019.

[http://dx.doi.org/10.1002/9781119650676]

[25]   S.T. Andrew, and B. Herbert, *Modern operating systems.* Pearson Education, 2015.

[26]   J. Weissenböck, B. Frohler, E. Groller, J. Kastner, and C. Heinzl, "Dynamic volume lines: Visual comparison of 3D volumes through space-filling curves", *IEEE Trans. Vis. Comput. Graph.,* vol. 25, no. 1, pp. 1040-1049, 2019.
[http://dx.doi.org/10.1109/TVCG.2018.2864510] [PMID: 30130203]

[27]   P.S. Calhoun, B.S. Kuszyk, D.G. Heath, J.C. Carley, and E.K. Fishman, "Three-dimensional volume rendering of spiral CT data: theory and method", *Radiographics,* vol. 19, no. 3, pp. 745-764, 1999.
[http://dx.doi.org/10.1148/radiographics.19.3.g99ma14745] [PMID: 10336201]

[28]   N. Kumar, and I. Benbasat, "The effect of relationship encoding, task type, and complexity on information representation: An empirical evaluation of 2D and 3D line graphs", *Manage. Inf. Syst. Q.,* vol. 28, no. 2, pp. 255-281, 2004.
[http://dx.doi.org/10.2307/25148635]

[29]   L. Benini, A. Bogliolo, and G. De Micheli, "A survey of design techniques for system-level dynamic power management", *IEEE transactions on very large scale integration (VLSI) systems,* vol. 8, no. 3, pp. 299-316, 2000.
[http://dx.doi.org/10.1109/92.845896]

[30]   G. Martinovic, J. Balen, and B. Cukic, "Performance Evaluation of Recent Windows Operating Systems", *J. Univers. Comput. Sci.,* vol. 18, no. 2, pp. 218-263, 2012.

[31]   A. Khang, R.N. Ali, V.A. Hajimahmud, and V.A. Abuzarova, "Green Technologies and Sustainable Development for the Green World", In: *Revolutionizing Automated Waste Treatment Systems: IoT and Bioelectronics.* In Khang A., Hajimahmud V. A., Litvinova E., Musrat G. L., Avramovic Z. (Ed.). IGI Global., 2024, pp. 1-15.
[http://dx.doi.org/10.4018/979-8-3693-6016-3.ch001]

[32]   L. Talmy, "How language structures space", In: *Spatial orientation: Theory, research, and application.* Springer, 1983, pp. 225-282.
[http://dx.doi.org/10.1007/978-1-4615-9325-6_11]

[33]   C. Mullins, *Database administration: the complete guide to practices and procedures.* Addison-Wesley Professional, 2002.

[34]   I.A. Chukwu, I.J. Sunday, and N.F. Nwebonyi, "The Impact of Data Backup and Recovery in Organizational Development: Oracle 11g", *Perspectives,* 2017.

[35]   D. Kuhn, "Backup and Recovery 101", *RMAN Recipes for Oracle Database 12c: A Problem-Solution Approach,* pp. 1-20, 2013.
[http://dx.doi.org/10.1007/978-1-4302-4837-8_1]

[36]   S.L. Garfinkel, and D.J. Malan, "One big file is not enough: A critical evaluation of the dominant free-space sanitization technique", *6th International Workshop, PET 2006.*Cambridge, UK.
[http://dx.doi.org/10.1007/11957454_8]

[37]   M. Kljun, J. Mariani, and A. Dix, "Toward understanding short-term personal information preservation: A study of backup strategies of end users", *J. Assoc. Inf. Sci. Technol.,* vol. 67, no. 12, pp. 2947-2963, 2016.
[http://dx.doi.org/10.1002/asi.23526]

[38]   A. Alzahrani, T. Alyas, K. Alissa, Q. Abbas, Y. Alsaawy, and N. Tabassum, "Hybrid approach for improving the performance of data reliability in cloud storage management", *Sensors (Basel),* vol. 22, no. 16, p. 5966, 2022.
[http://dx.doi.org/10.3390/s22165966] [PMID: 36015727]

[39]   C. Shapiro, and H.R. Varian, *Information rules: A strategic guide to the network economy.* Harvard Business Press, 1999.

CHAPTER 11

Introduction of Data Security Software

Nitika Garg[1,*,#]**, Himanshu Sharma**[1]**, Sanchit Dhankhar**[1,*,#]**, Samrat Chauhan**[1] **and Monika Saini**[2]

[1] *Chitkara College of Pharmacy, Chitkara University, Rajpura, Punjab, India*

[2] *M.M. College of Pharmacy, Maharishi Markandeshwar University, Mullana 133207, Ambala, Haryana, India*

Abstract: In this chapter, we will explore the complex world of data security software and examine its basic concepts, components, and several advantages. Data security software is becoming increasingly important in the modern digital world, as it helps to prevent data breaches and protect against new forms of cybercrime like quantum computing and the Internet of Things. This chapter explains what encryption, access control, and intrusion detection are, as well as the other fundamental principles of data security. The narrative elucidates the far-reaching benefits, which extend far beyond mere precautions and include trust-building, regulatory compliance, intellectual property protection, and risk minimization. A look into the future reveals a world where technology advancements like AI-driven threat detection, zero-trust architectures, and breakthroughs like homomorphic encryption and blockchain will shape the way we live today. The emergence of automation, user-centric security, and continuous monitoring as cornerstones is indicative of a proactive approach. This synthesis foresees a time when data security software and broader cybersecurity initiatives combine to deliver unified platforms for comprehensive protection. In short, in today's linked, data-driven society, data security is no longer a tactical afterthought; it is a strategic imperative that determines an organization's trustworthiness and stability.

Keywords: Access control, Anti-malware, Artificial Intelligence, Cybersecurity, Cryptography, Data, Data loss prevention, Encryption, Firewalls, Internet of Things, IDPS, Security, Software.

INTRODUCTION

Data security has risen to the forefront of worry for consumers, companies, and governments in today's linked digital society [1]. The need for stringent data security measures is more pressing than ever before as the amount of sensitive

---

* Corresponding authors Nitika Garg and Sanchit Dhankhar: Chitkara College of Pharmacy, Chitkara University, Rajpura, Punjab, India; E-mails: nitikagarg1609@gmail.com, sanchitdhankhar@gmail.com
# Both the authors contributed equally

Alex Khang, Sanchit Dhankhar, Sandeep Bhardwaj, Avnesh Verma & Satish Kumar Sharma (Eds.)

information stored and communicated online continues to increase. In a world rife with cyber threats, data security software stands as the last line of defense, protecting the privacy, accuracy, and accessibility of sensitive information. This diverse sector of software solutions comprises a spectrum of tools, methods, and methodologies, all intended with a unified purpose: to safeguard data against unauthorized access, breaches, and tampering. This chapter digs into the varied world of data security software, revealing its relevance, important elements, deployment options, problems, rewards, and the expanding role it plays in our daily lives.

Software designed for data security has one major goal: to protect private information from the ever-present dangers that are always evolving around it. Hackers, thieves, and even state-sponsored espionage are all part of this picture because they aim to exploit security flaws in digital systems for their own ends [2]. Data breaches involving the unauthorized disclosure or theft of sensitive information, including personal details, financial records, and intellectual property, can result from security flaws. These infringements not only have the ability to inflict significant monetary damage, but they may also break trust, ruin reputations, and even have legal repercussions. The first line of defense against these dangers is data security software, which may be thought of as a digital fortress.

Data security relies heavily on encryption methods. Encryption is the process of transforming data using complicated algorithms into a format that is unreadable to all but those who have access to the correct decryption keys. Data encryption protects information at rest on a storage device or in transit across a network from being read by an unauthorized party who does not have access to the decryption keys [3]. Another crucial part is the technique used to regulate who can access what data and under what conditions. Access can be limited based on user roles, permissions, and the principle of least privilege with the use of role-based access control (RBAC) and user authentication. The risk of insider attacks or unauthorized access is mitigated because of these procedures, which grant users varying degrees of access to data and allow them to view, edit, or delete it.

When it comes to protecting your data and your network, firewalls are an essential piece of software. These virtual walls inspect both incoming and outgoing data packets on a network and selectively discard those that are malicious or otherwise inappropriate while allowing valid communications through. Along with firewalls, intrusion detection and prevention systems (IDPS) keep an eye out for any suspicious activity on a network or computer [4]. By immediately reacting to threats when they are discovered, IDPS helps strengthen the safety of the network. The use of anti-malware and anti-virus software is also crucial in this fight. These programs protect against the most common forms of cyberattack by detecting and removing malware like viruses, Trojans, worms, and ransomware.

When it comes to protecting sensitive information from being leaked either inside or outside of a business, data loss prevention (DLP) software is indispensable. Data leakage and accidental disclosures can be prevented by using this software, as sensitive information can be isolated and prevented from moving around. For businesses, especially those operating in highly regulated sectors, compliance with data privacy legislation and sector-specific rules is of utmost importance [5]. The General Data Protection Regulation (GDPR), the Health Insurance Portability and Accountability Act (HIPAA), and the Payment Card Industry Data Security Standard all have criteria that must be met, and data security software is a big part of that (PCI DSS).

SIEM (Security Information and Event Management) software acts as the ears and eyes of a network's security system. They examine security alerts from numerous programs and network components in real-time. By collecting and correlating these warnings, SIEM solutions may provide a comprehensive overview of an organization's security status. This facilitates real-time detection of security issues and permits prompt action, which may lessen the severity of any resulting breaches or assaults.

A company's data security software deployment strategy can be tailored to its unique requirements and available resources [6]. For on-premises deployments, a company uses its own servers and IT staff to set up and run the data security software. This method allows for unfettered access to all of your data and programs, but it comes with a hefty price tag for setup and upkeep. On the other side, cloud-based data security solutions are scalable and adaptable. In contrast to on-premises hardware and upkeep, these solutions are hosted on remote servers and typically offered as a service. Smaller businesses or those interested in taking advantage of cloud computing benefits will find cloud-based deployments particularly attractive. Factors such as a company's size, budget, and desired level of security should be considered when deciding between on-premises and cloud-based solutions.

There are always new risks and obstacles to deal with, despite the improvements in data security technologies. Hackers and cybercriminals are always coming up with new ways to attack data security, thus the threat landscape is always changing. As a result, data security software needs regular upgrades and tweaks to stay up with evolving threats. The relevance of human elements in data security cannot be understated [7]. Human error, such as falling for a phishing attack or accidentally revealing sensitive information, can damage even the most sophisticated data protection tools. Therefore, data security plans must include measures to raise user awareness and education.

In addition, there is a labyrinth of rules and regulations that data security software must follow. Organizations must ensure that their data security procedures are in line with the various data protection standards that apply in various industries and geographical areas. Non-compliance can result in serious penalties and damage to an organization's reputation. It can be difficult for organizations to keep their data safe while also meeting the requirements of these standards.

However, data security software's numerous advantages make it an essential part of today's IT infrastructures. Most importantly, this helps keep sensitive information safe from prying eyes. When data protection software is properly set up, it creates a formidable barrier that discourages hackers and lessens the likelihood of data breaches [8]. This, in turn, aids in protecting the privacy of sensitive information and keeping the faith of stakeholders.

Organizations can better meet regulatory compliance needs if they consistently practice good data security hygiene. Organizations that show they care about their customers' personal information and data security and privacy are more likely to be successful in the marketplace. In addition to meeting regulatory requirements, data security software protects intangible assets including intellectual property and trade secrets [9]. Organizations can preserve their innovativeness and competitiveness by guarding against the loss of such assets. The financial and reputational dangers of data breaches can be greatly reduced with the help of data protection software. The cost of a data breach can be quite high, including remediation efforts, legal expenditures, regulatory fines, and lost revenue from dissatisfied customers. Software designed to protect sensitive information can lessen the frequency and severity of data breaches while providing a healthy return on investment.

The society we live in now is data-driven and networked, making data security software an essential and rapidly developing topic. As a protector, it keeps private data safe from both existing and potential dangers. Data security relies on cryptography, access control, firewalls, IDPS, anti-malware, data loss prevention, and security information and event management.

THE DATA SECURITY LANDSCAPE

One of the most precious resources for individuals, companies, and institutions in today's ever-expanding digital world is data [10]. To fully grasp the importance of data security, one must first get an understanding of the context in which this information resides. In this section, we will examine the many facets of data security, paying special attention to the importance of data itself, the dynamic nature of the risks it encounters, and the devastating effects of any breach.

Data as a Valuable Asset

Due to its revolutionary potential and economic importance, data has been called the "new oil" in the modern period. Through transactions, user interactions, and operational procedures, businesses gather and generate enormous volumes of data [11]. Personal details, bank records, inventions, and trade secrets are just a few examples of the many types of data that businesses collect and store. Its importance as a strategic asset that drives innovation, decision-making, and competitive advantages well exceeds its immediate practical application.

Companies cannot cater their products and services to individual customers or conduct effective targeted advertising without first collecting and analyzing data on their clientele. Patient data similarly helps with healthcare research, individualized treatment strategies, and the development of healthcare technologies. As data becomes increasingly important to the operations of many fields, ensuring its safety becomes a top priority. The vulnerability of this precious asset to unwanted access, modification, or theft mandates the deployment of effective data security measures.

Emerging Data Security Threats

The data security landscape is dynamic, with threat actors continuously upgrading their strategies to exploit weaknesses in digital systems. Staying ahead of the constant cat-and-mouse game between security measures and hostile actions requires an awareness of the evolving nature of the threats.

Cyber Attacks and Malware: Phishing, ransomware, and DDoS attacks, the "big three" of cybercrime, are still very much a problem today [12]. Phishing scams try to trick customers into giving away private information, while ransom encrypts files and then holds them hostage until a ransom is paid. Malware such as viruses, worms, and Trojan horses also presents ongoing threats to information privacy. Insider Dangers Data security can also be compromised by a company's own workers or other trusted third parties, either by accident or on purpose. The need for access controls and staff education cannot be overstated in light of the potential for damage from insiders brought about by carelessness, ignorance, or malice.

IoT Vulnerabilities: The growth of Internet of Things (IoT) devices presents new access points for potential security vulnerabilities. If Internet of Things (IoT) devices are not adequately protected, hackers can use them to break into networks and steal private information.

Advanced Persistent Threats (APTs): In APTs, hackers launch targeted, persistent attacks on a single organization in an effort to steal confidential data [13]. The need for constant monitoring and proactive security measures is highlighted by the fact that these attacks typically go undetected for long periods of time.

Supply Chain Attacks: Increasingly, supply chain vulnerabilities are being exploited by cybercriminals to get access to the networks and data of their major targets. The attacks like these highlight how intertwined the digital world really is.

The Consequences of Data Breaches

The implications of a data breach extend far beyond the immediate loss of sensitive information. Individuals, businesses, and society as a whole may all feel the repercussions.

- *Financial Losses:* When companies have their data stolen, they usually lose a lot of money. The expenses may include incident response, legal fees, regulatory fines, and compensation to affected parties. When consumers lose faith in a company, sales, and market share often follow suit [14].
- *Reputational Damage*: The damage to an organization's reputation following a data breach can be long-lasting. When a company's security is breached, customers, clients, and business partners may lose faith in the company's capacity to keep their personal information safe.
- *Legal and Regulatory Ramifications:* Legal repercussions and regulatory measures may result from a data leak. Data protection regulations, such as the General Data Protection Regulation (GDPR) and the California Consumer Privacy Act (CCPA), have been enacted in a number of countries to ensure the security of citizens' private information [15]. Failure to comply with these rules may result in severe financial and legal consequences.
- *Identity Theft and Fraud:* Data breaches expose users to the risk of fraud and identity theft. Theft of personal information is a prime target for cybercriminals because it may be used in a wide variety of fraudulent schemes.
- *Operational Disruptions:* Organizational activities may be interrupted as a result of a data breach's aftermath. The requirement to investigate, rectify, and deploy additional security measures can divert resources and attention from routine business activities.
- *Impact on National Security:* National security is jeopardized when private information about the government or essential infrastructure is leaked [16]. The security of a country may be compromised if hackers gain access to vital government databases or infrastructure.

The necessity of strong and preventative data security measures is emphasized by an appreciation of data's complex character as a valuable asset, the diversity of data security risks, and the gravity of breach effects. Keeping their most valuable asset, data, safe from the growing number and sophistication of cyber threats requires businesses to adjust to the ever-changing digital landscape.

CORE PRINCIPLES OF DATA SECURITY

There are a few fundamental principles of data security that, when taken together, guarantee the safety of data in the digital world. CIA, which stands for "Confidentiality, Integrity, and Availability," is an acronym that encapsulates these guiding principles. If you want to create data security plans that are both successful and thorough, you need to understand and apply these principles (Fig. 1).

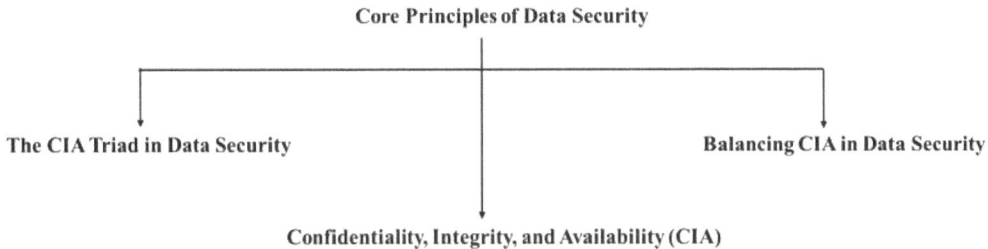

Core Principles of Data Security

The CIA Triad in Data Security   Balancing CIA in Data Security

Confidentiality, Integrity, and Availability (CIA)

Fig. (1). Core Principles of Data Security.

Confidentiality, Integrity, and Availability (CIA)

Confidentiality: In the context of data security, confidentiality is the prevention of unauthorized access to or exposure to private information [17]. As a result, sensitive information is protected from prying eyes and only authorized users and systems are able to access it. Personal information, confidential corporate information, and trade secrets all need to be guarded with strict secrecy.

Integrity: Informational precision and trustworthiness are at the heart of integrity. The integrity and veracity of data are protected in this way. Protections against accidental or malicious tampering with data ensure that it preserves its original form, accuracy, and meaning. In fields where the accuracy of data is crucial, such as banking, healthcare, and law, maintaining data integrity is crucial.

Availability: Accessibility guarantees that authorized users can always get to the resources they need, whenever they need them. System and network dependability is emphasized, with downtime kept to a minimum and information availability guaranteed at all times [18]. Particularly in fields where downtime can result in large financial losses or risk public safety, availability is crucial for continuing corporate operations.

The CIA Triad in Data Security

The CIA Triad is the foundation of data security frameworks since it offers a comprehensive strategy for the protection of information assets.

- Confidentiality in the CIA Triad: To protect private information, security measures such as passwords, encryption, and two-factor authentication must be put in place. Data confidentiality is maintained by the implementation of access controls, which limit access to only those who have been granted access. Encryption modifies information so that it cannot be read by an outside source, making it secure against eavesdropping. Authentication ensures that only authorized individuals have access to protected data by checking their identities.
- Integrity in the CIA Triad: Checksums, digital signatures, and version controls are only some of the methods used by businesses to guarantee data authenticity [19]. Digital signatures and checksums are used to ensure that no tampering has occurred with data during transmission or storage. Document or file alterations that shouldn't have been made can be found thanks to version controls. All of these safeguards ensure that the integrity and consistency of the data are maintained.
- Availability in the CIA Triad: To ensure accessibility, we employ strategies like redundancy, disaster recovery planning, and solid infrastructure. The goal of redundancy is to have a backup system or set of data ready to go in the event that something goes wrong with the primary system. Systems and data restoration techniques are outlined in disaster recovery plans. Robust infrastructure includes stable hardware, network architecture, and load balancing to minimize downtime and maintain continuous availability.

Balancing CIA in Data Security

Although the three pillars that make up the CIA Triad depend on one another, it is essential to strike a balance between them [20]. If one concept is emphasized more than the others, this could result in unforeseen effects. Finding the optimal compromise requires taking into account the particular needs of the business, the characteristics of the information that needs to be safeguarded, as well as the possible dangers.

- Balancing Confidentiality and Availability: Strict access controls and encryption are examples of techniques taken to increase privacy, but they may have unintended consequences for availability. Finding a happy medium requires both strong authentication techniques and access limits that do not stifle authorized users.

- Balancing Integrity and Confidentiality: Measures to ensure data integrity, such as digital signatures, may harm secrecy if they are extremely restrictive. Maintaining data confidentiality while keeping its integrity intact requires a careful application of access controls and encryption.
- Balancing Availability and Integrity: While dependable infrastructure and redundancy are necessary to guarantee availability, this should never come at the expense of data integrity [21]. Implementing measures such as data backups on a regular basis and testing disaster recovery plans helps ensure both the availability and integrity of the data.

Implementing the CIA triad successfully calls for a holistic and flexible strategy that takes into account each organization's specific requirements and risk profile. Finding this sweet spot will set the stage for a resilient and robust data security system by making sure data is not just secure but also accessible and dependable. Knowing and following these fundamental principles is essential for protecting data and keeping the confidence of stakeholders in a data-driven environment.

DATA SECURITY SOFTWARE

In today's ever-changing cyber threat landscape, data security software is crucial in protecting critical infrastructure [22]. This section provides a full introduction to data security software, addressing its definition, its role in preserving information assets, and the common features and functions that characterize these critical tools. The term "data security software" is used to describe a wide variety of programs and procedures that work together to keep sensitive data safe from prying eyes. It protects sensitive data from being stolen, altered, or otherwise compromised, and it acts as the first line of protection against any number of cyberattacks. The endpoints, networks, servers, and cloud environments are all places where data security software can be deployed and put into action. The primary goal is to reduce the likelihood of security incidents like data breaches and cyber assaults by locating, mitigating, and preventing them.

The Role of Data Security Software

The purpose of data security software is broad, addressing the diverse difficulties offered by an increasingly sophisticated threat landscape. One such challenge is the need to protect sensitive information. The following are important facets of its role:

- Risk Mitigation: When it comes to protecting sensitive information, data security software is indispensable [23]. It proactively closes security holes by monitoring them around the clock, identifying potential threats, and conducting vulnerability assessments, making the system more resistant to cyber-attacks.

- Data Encryption: When it comes to protecting sensitive information, encryption is a must. With encryption, sensitive information is converted into an unreadable format, making it impossible to read for anybody without the appropriate decryption keys. This is essential for the security of stored and transmitted information.

- Access Control: In order to manage and restrict user privileges, data security software implements access control techniques. The danger of insider threats and illegal access can be reduced with the use of role-based access control (RBAC), user authentication, and authorization methods.

- Threat Detection and Prevention: Mechanisms for detecting and avoiding threats are built into modern data security solutions, and these solutions frequently make use of machine learning and artificial intelligence. These systems perform real-time analysis of patterns, behaviors, and anomalies, allowing for rapid response to possible security incidents.

- Incident Response: Data security software allows for swift action to be taken in the case of a security incident or data breach [24]. It helps find the breach, keep it contained, eliminate the threats, retrieve the data, and put in place preventative measures so it doesn't happen again.

- Compliance Management: Compliance with laws and norms in one's sector is facilitated by data security software. With its log and report generation tools, it is easier for businesses to prove they are following data protection regulations like the General Data Protection Regulation (GDPR) and the Health Insurance Portability and Accountability Act (HIPAA).

Common Features and Functions

The term "data security software" refers to a category of applications that include a wide variety of features and functions, each of which is designed to handle a particular aspect of information security. Among the shared characteristics are:

- Firewalls: Firewalls, which control and monitor both incoming and outgoing network traffic, are used to increase network security [25]. Firewalls are barriers between an organization's trusted internal network and the internet, where malicious actors could potentially gain access and cause damage.

- Anti-Malware and Antivirus Protection: Strong anti-malware and antivirus components are included into data protection software to identify, isolate, and destroy threats like viruses, worms, Trojan horses, and ransomware. Signature databases are updated on a regular basis to guarantee that the software can detect new threats.

- Intrusion Detection and Prevention Systems (IDPS): IDPS keeps an eye out for attacks by analyzing network and system activity [26]. These systems improve the security posture by automatically responding to anomalies in order to prevent or lessen the impact of prospective threats.
- Encryption Tools: Encryption tools using cryptographic methods are part of the data security software toolkit. This involves encrypting communication routes (*e.g.*, SSL/TLS for web traffic) and encrypting files or databases to safeguard data at rest.
- Access Management: Features like RBAC in access control make that only authorized people can see sensitive information or use certain services. Protecting private data from being accessed by the wrong people is a top priority, which is why access management is so important.
- Data Loss Prevention (DLP): Data leakage prevention (DLP) functions track and manage the flow of private information throughout an organization. Data protection measures include blocking out-of-band transfers, keeping tabs on devices for leaks, and making sure everyone follows the rules [27].
- Security Information and Event Management (SIEM): Security information and event management (SIEM) technologies gather and examine information from a company's IT infrastructure's many logs. They help spot outliers and potential security incidents by providing real-time information into security occurrences.

Organizations that want to develop solid cybersecurity postures must have a thorough understanding of the nature of data security software. Businesses may safeguard their data assets, deal with security events, and stay in line with regulations in a dynamic online environment by making use of the aforementioned capabilities and solutions.

ELEMENTS OF DATA SECURITY SOFTWARE

Information security systems incorporate multiple safeguards to fend against hacking attempts. When taken together, these components strengthen an organization's security by preventing unauthorized access to private data. In-depth discussion of the fundamentals of data security programs follows (Fig. **2**).

Encryption

Encryption is a crucial part of any data security program, as it is what makes the data unreadable by anybody but the program itself [28]. During transmission over networks and storage on various devices, encrypted data is used to protect sensitive information from prying eyes. Encryption can be broken down into two categories:

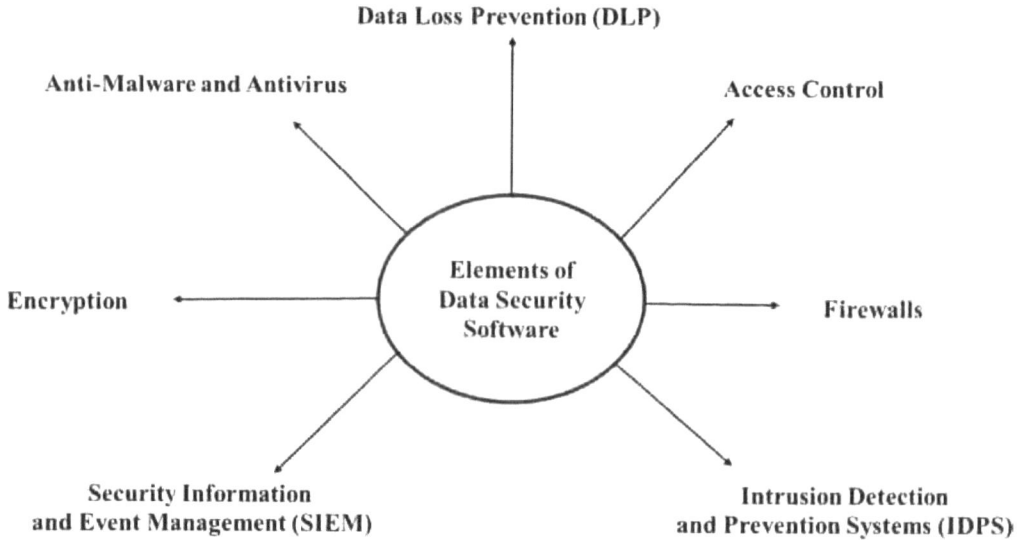

Fig. (2). Elements of Data Security Software.

- Data in Transit Encryption: Protects information while it is in transit between computers or networks. Secure Sockets Layer/Transport Layer Security (SSL/TLS) and Virtual Private Networks (VPNs) are two common protocols for encrypting data while it is in transit on the internet.
- Data at Rest Encryption: Safeguards information saved on computer components like hard drives, flash memory, and portable media. Data at rest can be protected in a variety of ways, the most prevalent of which are disc encryption, file-level encryption, and database encryption.

Encryption is essential for securing information against intrusion, whether the attacker has access to the data in transit or the storage media itself.

Access Control

In order to ensure that only authorized users or computers have access to sensitive information, access control is essential. Several parts make up an access control system:

- Authentication: Identifies and authenticates individuals or machines seeking to access information [29]. Passwords, biometric data, two-factor authentication (2FA), and multi-factor authentication (MFA) are all examples of popular authentication techniques (MFA).
- Authorization: Access privileges for logged-in users are calculated according to their assigned roles and permissions. RBAC is a method of controlling access to

resources by delegating privileges to users based on their specific roles within an organization.

In order to keep sensitive information safe from intruders and ensure that employees only have access to the information they need to do their jobs, strong access control is a must.

Firewalls

Firewalls are used to separate safe, internal networks from the wider Internet, where malicious attacks are more likely to occur. Firewalls are an essential part of any network's security infrastructure and can be set up on a number of different layers, such as:

- Network Firewalls: Function on the network layer by inspecting data packets and authorizing or blocking them based on a set of rules [30].
- Application Firewalls: Perform duties at the application layer, including traffic monitoring and management using the protocols used by applications. Attacks aimed at exploiting specific software flaws are thwarted as a result.

Firewalls are the first line of protection against cyber-attacks because they block bad traffic and stop unauthorized users from accessing sensitive data.

Intrusion Detection and Prevention Systems (IDPS)

Network and system administrators can use intrusion detection and prevention systems (IDPS) to keep an eye out for suspicious activity that could indicate a hack. When it comes to identifying and neutralizing danger, several systems are indispensable:

- Intrusion Detection Systems (IDS): Identify potential security incidents by analyzing network or system events and comparing them to attack signatures or aberrant patterns [31].
- Intrusion Prevention Systems (IPS): Take preventative action rather than merely reacting to threats that have already been discovered. This can be done in a number of ways, such as by isolating affected computers, blocking malicious IP addresses, or setting off alarms to prompt further inquiry.

IDPS improves security in general by monitoring potential security issues in real-time and automatically responding to them.

Anti-Malware and Antivirus

Software for detecting, preventing, and removing malware from your system is an integral part of any data protection suite. Threats to data security can come in many forms, but the most common are malware like viruses, worms, Trojans, and ransomware. Examples of salient traits include:

- Scanning and Detection: Performs routine checks of data and software for known malware signatures.
- Real-Time Protection: Keeps an eye on things in real-time to stop attacks before they can do any damage [32].
- Quarantine and Removal: Identifies malicious software and removes it to prevent it from doing any more harm.

Protecting data against harmful software and preventing it from being accessed or altered is the primary function of anti-malware and antivirus solutions.

Data Loss Prevention (DLP)

DLP stands for "data loss prevention," and it is a proactive feature of data security software that helps keep private information safe by identifying threats and blocking their access. Important features include:

- Content Discovery: Identifies confidential information, intellectual property, and other sensitive data within an organization.
- Policy Enforcement: Establishes and enforces guidelines for the safe collection, transfer, and storage of sensitive information.
- Monitoring and Incident Response: Protects sensitive information by keeping tabs on its whereabouts, looking for policy breaches, and reacting with notifications, blocking, or encryption.

DLP is essential for businesses that want to safeguard sensitive data and meet data protection standards.

Security Information and Event Management (SIEM)

Centralizing the collection, analysis, and management of security-related data from a wide variety of sources is made possible by Security Information and Event Management (SIEM), a crucial component. Examples of salient traits include:

- Log Collection: Log data is gathered from a variety of different systems, applications, and network devices.

- Correlation and Analysis: Analyzes the data for trends, abnormalities, and possible breaches of security by correlating the information.
- Incident Response: Provides insights into the happenings of security events and makes it possible to take immediate action, hence facilitating real-time incident response.

The visibility of a company's security landscape is improved by using SIEM, which helps with the detection of threats and the implementation of proactive responses to security issues [33].

In conclusion, data security software's components form an interdependent whole that offers a formidable barrier against an ever-evolving set of cyber threats. Encryption, access control, firewalls, IDPS, anti-malware, DLP, and SIEM jointly contribute to preserving sensitive information and assuring data confidentiality, integrity, and availability in an interconnected digital environment. If you want to build a comprehensive and durable data security plan, you need to make sure these pieces work together well.

DEPLOYMENT OPTIONS

On-Premises Data Security Software

On-premises data security software refers to solutions that are installed and operated within an organization's physical infrastructure rather than being hosted externally in the cloud [34]. This deployment architecture gives businesses extensive leeway in determining how they handle data security, but it also presents some unique difficulties.

- Control and Customization: When it comes to data protection, on-premises solutions give businesses unfettered authority. IT departments can tailor settings to meet the company's individual security and compliance regulations and operational demands.
- Data Residency and Compliance: Data residency and compliance standards can be quite stringent depending on the industry and geographical location. With an on-premises solution, businesses can manage exactly where their data is stored and processed, allowing them to stay in full regulatory compliance.
- Latency and Performance: For applications that need fast processing and low network latency, an on-premises deployment may be the best option [35]. For businesses that require constant access to data, this is crucial.
- Security Concerns: Companies that would rather not have their data stored remotely may find comfort in on-premises solutions. But this also means that the

company must ensure the data center is safe from the likes of theft, natural catastrophes, and other threats that could compromise the facility's infrastructure.

- Scalability and Upfront Costs: On-premises solutions might be more difficult to scale and can necessitate costly initial expenditures in hardware and software. In order to keep up with the ever-increasing demands for data protection, businesses must make plans for expansion.
- Maintenance and Updates: When it comes to software and technology, organizations that opt for on-premises solutions bear the burden of upkeep and upgrades. Protecting against new attacks necessitates implementing the latest patches, updates, and other security procedures.

Cloud-Based Data Security Solutions

Cloud-based data security solutions are provided as a service over the internet and run on remote servers [36]. The scalability, adaptability, and possibility for lower operational overhead of this deployment paradigm have contributed to its meteoric rise in popularity.

- Scalability and Flexibility: By storing their data on the cloud, businesses may quickly increase or decrease their data security infrastructure to meet fluctuating demand. This is helpful for any company, but especially those dealing with unpredictable workloads or experiencing rapid expansion.
- Cost-Efficiency: Subscription or pay-as-you-go pricing models are common for cloud-based solutions, eschewing the need for large initial outlays of capital. Since the business only has to pay for the resources it actually uses, this might be particularly beneficial for smaller enterprises.
- Automatic Updates and Maintenance: Cloud service providers handle the maintenance and upgrades of the underlying infrastructure, ensuring that enterprises benefit from the latest security features without having to manage these aspects themselves [37]. The IT department will have less work to do as a result of routine maintenance.
- Accessibility and Collaboration: Data security tools may be accessed and managed from anywhere with the help of cloud solutions, giving authorized users more freedom and flexibility. This facilitates cooperation and availability in today's international and remote workplaces.
- Global Reach and Redundancy: Since many cloud services run on servers located in data centers all over the world, businesses have the option of deploying data security measures in more than one geographic area. This not only provides redundancy and catastrophe recovery but also improves global accessibility.

- Security Measures of Cloud Providers: Trustworthy cloud service companies put forth significant resources to ensure their customers' data is secure, both online and off. Data is encrypted using strong algorithms, and top-tier security requirements are strictly adhered to.

Choosing the Right Deployment Model

Organizations often choose a hybrid architecture that combines components of both on-premises and cloud-based data security solutions. Important factors include:

- Security and Compliance Requirements: In order to keep full control of their infrastructure, companies with strict security and compliance needs, such as those with data residency concerns, may prefer on-premises solutions [38].
- Scalability and Flexibility: If a business anticipates rapid expansion, has changing workloads, or values the ability to scale resources on-demand, a cloud-based solution might be more suitable.
- Cost Considerations: In contrast to the pay-as-you-go model common to cloud-based solutions, on-premises options require initial investments. In order to select the most economical method, businesses must first consider their financial limitations and future cost forecasts.
- Operational Overhead: It is important to think about routine upkeep, new developments, and general operational duties. By shifting some of the burden of running an organization's infrastructure to the cloud provider, cloud-based solutions can significantly cut down on operating costs.
- Geographic Distribution: Cloud solutions that include data centers in several areas, allowing for low-latency access and redundancy, may be ideal for multinational corporations.
- Integration with Existing Infrastructure: When making a choice, it is important to consider how well a data security solution will work with your current network and software [39]. The solution's ability to interface with the organization's existing infrastructure is an important consideration.

An organization's demands, resources, and long-term goals should all factor into the decision between on-premise and cloud-based data security solutions. Organizations can improve their data security by selecting the best deployment type after carefully considering the aforementioned considerations.

CHALLENGES IN DATA SECURITY

Data security in the present digital landscape is fraught with difficulties due to the dynamic nature of cyber threats, the importance of human elements, and the severe standards of regulatory frameworks. The primary obstacles that businesses face while attempting to secure confidential information are explored in this section.

Evolving Threat Landscape

- Sophisticated Cyber Attacks: The increasing complexity of cyberattacks is defining this danger landscape [40]. It is difficult for businesses to stay one step ahead of cybercriminals since they're always coming up with new ways to overcome security protocols.
- Advanced Persistent Threats (APTs): APTs are sophisticated, long-term attacks launched by well-resourced and well-organized foes. The requirement for sophisticated threat detection and response mechanisms is highlighted by the fact that these attacks frequently go unreported for long stretches of time.
- Ransomware and Extortion: Data encryption and ransom demands by thieves have increased recently. Because of the monetary stakes involved, these attacks are prevalent and difficult to stop.
- Supply Chain Attacks: Cybercriminals increasingly target the supply chain to exploit weaknesses in third-party vendors [41]. Attackers can gain access to their primary targets' networks and data by compromising a trusted vendor.
- Zero-Day Exploits: As their name implies, zero-day exploits take advantage of undiscovered security holes. In order to prevent these flaws from being exploited, businesses should take preventative measures to discover them and fix them.

Human Factors and User Education

Phishing and Social Engineering: Phishing and social engineering are two common forms of human error that can compromise sensitive data. Cybercriminals frequently use social engineering techniques including phishing emails, texts, and phone calls to get access to sensitive information.

- Insider Threats: Whether on purpose or not, employees can be a major security risk. Sensitive data can be breached if employees within an organization either intentionally or accidentally violate security protocols.
- Weak Passwords and Authentication Practices: Weak passwords and sloppy authentication procedures are a major cause of data security issues. When workers make their passwords too simple to crack or when they reuse passwords across many accounts, hackers have an easier time breaking in.
- Lack of Security Awareness: There is a possibility of consumers engaging in unsafe practices due to a lack of education on the topic of cybersecurity [42]. It is critical to train staff to spot phishing attempts, report them, and adhere to security procedures that protect sensitive information.

- BYOD (Bring Your Own Device) Challenges: The growing number of people who bring their own gadgets to the office raises new concerns about data protection. Robust policies and enforcement mechanisms are needed to secure a wide variety of devices with various security postures.

Regulatory Compliance and Data Protection Laws

- Global Compliance Challenges: Organizations with a global reach face a maze of data protection policies and legislation that they must comply with. To be in compliance with regulations like GDPR, CCPA, HIPAA, and others, one must have a deep understanding of the relevant laws and regulations.
- Data Residency Requirements: Certain categories of data are required by law to be stored and processed exclusively within particular regions. It can be difficult for international corporations to balance compliance with these data residency laws with the need to keep operations running smoothly.
- Data Breach Notification: Notifying affected individuals, regulators, and sometimes the general public about data breaches promptly and openly is required by several statutes [43]. In order to comply with these notification requirements, businesses need to have solid incident response procedures in place.
- Changing Regulatory Landscape: There are always new laws being passed and old ones being revised. It is a constant battle for businesses to keep up with the ever-evolving regulatory landscape and maintain full compliance.
- Penalties and Fines: Serious fines and penalties may be imposed for violations of data protection legislation. Companies should spend money on safeguards to ensure data is secure, that compliance is evident, and that audit findings are addressed.

A comprehensive and preventative strategy for data security is required to meet these problems. Organizations need to invest in technology and training, change their approach to dealing with threats as they arise, and keep tabs on the ever-changing regulatory landscape. By doing so, they may strengthen their resilience against data security threats and negotiate the intricacies of the digital era.

BENEFITS OF DATA SECURITY SOFTWARE

Data security software is crucial in preserving sensitive information, minimizing risks, and ensuring the integrity and confidentiality of data. In this section, we will look at some of the most important gains a business can get by strengthening its data security protocols.

Protection against Data Breaches

- Prevention of Unauthorized Access: Data security programs create firewalls and other protections to keep out intruders and safeguard private data [44]. Encryption, authentication methods, and permission controls all fall under this category.
- Detection and Response: Intrusion detection and prevention systems (IDPS) are key components of modern data security solutions, as they proactively look for and stop intrusions. These technologies can issue warnings when a security risk is detected, quarantine compromised machines, and help authorities respond quickly and precisely.
- Data Encryption: If data is encrypted, then even if someone gains access to it without the right keys, they would not be able to read it. This is especially important for securing information while it is in motion and while it is stored.

Trust and Reputation

- Customer Trust: Customers and other stakeholders are more likely to have faith in a company that shows it values data security. People are more likely to stick with a company and recommend it to others if they feel their personal information is safe and secure.
- Brand Reputation: Reputational damage from data breaches can be substantial. On the other side, a strong data security posture helps build a positive company reputation by showing that the company cares about its clients' data protection [45].

Compliance with Regulations

- Adherence to Data Protection Laws: A wide variety of data protection laws and regulations exist, and data security software aids businesses in adhering to them [46]. Organizations can avoid trouble with the law and the accompanying costs of fines by taking the required security precautions.
- Audit Trails and Reporting: Features like logging, audit trails, and reporting are included in many data security solutions. Organizations can use these features to show auditors and regulators that they are following security procedures and standards.

Safeguarding Intellectual Property

- Protection of Sensitive Assets: Trade secrets, confidential information, and other forms of intellectual property are extremely valuable to many businesses. Software designed to protect sensitive information can prevent theft, illegal access, and even industrial espionage.

- Preventing Data Leakage: Software designed to protect sensitive data from accidental or intentional disclosure sometimes includes a data loss prevention (DLP) module. Organizations can protect their intellectual property through data mobility monitoring and management.

Early Threat Detection and Proactive Security Measures

- Proactive Threat Detection: Proactive threat detection features are common in data security software; these often make use of machine learning and behavioral analytics [47]. This allows businesses to spot early warning signs of security breaches.
- Incident Response Preparedness: Businesses can better respond to security incidents when they have robust data security controls in place. This requires swift threat management and mitigation, as well as incident response and stakeholder communication infrastructures.

THE FUTURE OF DATA SECURITY SOFTWARE

Evolving Technologies and Threats

- AI and Machine Learning in Threat Detection: Enhancing threat detection capabilities will be significantly aided by the combination of AI and ML. Cybercriminals will have a harder time evading discovery thanks to these technologies' ability to sift through massive volumes of data, recognize trends, and spot abnormalities that could point to vulnerabilities.
- Quantum Computing Challenges: Data security can benefit from and be threatened by the advent of quantum computing. The advent of quantum computers poses a threat to the security of currently used encryption algorithms, but it also necessitates the creation of quantum-resistant encryption techniques to keep private information safe.
- IoT Security Considerations: The security of Internet-connected devices is becoming increasingly important as IoT adoption rates keep rising [48]. To guarantee the safety of data generated and transferred by these interconnected systems, data security software will need to be developed to meet the specific problems given by the broad and varied landscape of IoT devices.

Trends and Innovations in Data Security

- Zero Trust Architecture: The Zero Trust security approach, which believes that no entity, whether inside or outside the organization, should be trusted by default, is gaining prominence. Data security software will increasingly follow Zero Trust concepts, including tight access controls, constant monitoring, and multi-factor authentication to boost overall security.

- Homomorphic Encryption: With homomorphic encryption, encrypted data can be processed in place of its unencrypted counterpart [49]. This new technology has the potential to facilitate private data processing in sectors like healthcare and banking.
- Blockchain for Data Integrity: The potential of blockchain technology, which is both decentralized and difficult to alter, is being investigated as a means of bolstering data security. Using blockchain for data security can give verifiable and unchangeable records, making it more difficult to falsify or alter information.
- Behavioral Analytics: Behavioral analytics, exploiting user behavior patterns to detect anomalies, will become more sophisticated. Data security software is able to detect outliers in user activity and take preventative measures against potential security breaches since it constantly monitors and analyses these activities.

The Ongoing Role of Data Security Software

- Integrated Security Platforms: Integrating several types of security features into unified platforms is the future of data security software [50]. Integrated security solutions will simplify management, improve interoperability, and offer a comprehensive strategy for dealing with the ever-changing nature of security threats.
- Automated Threat Response: Automation will be crucial in providing a rapid and effective response to security problems. Organizations can mitigate the effects of security events by using automated threat response methods in conjunction with AI-driven decision-making.
- User-Centric Security: Software designed to protect sensitive information will place a greater emphasis on protecting its end users as remote work and mobile device use become more commonplace [51]. Access controls, user behavior analysis, and adaptive security policies that keep up with the ever-changing nature of today's workplaces all fall under this category.
- Continuous Monitoring and Adaptive Security: Emerging threats must be identified and mitigated as soon as possible, therefore constant monitoring of networks, systems, and user behaviors is crucial. Maintaining a strong security posture will become more dependent on adaptive security systems that can dynamically adapt to the changing threat scenario.

In conclusion, the next generation of data security software will be characterized by proactive and adaptive security measures, the incorporation of cutting-edge technology to combat new threats, and other such developments. To remain ahead of the ever-evolving dangers in today's dynamic digital ecosystem, businesses must use cutting-edge technology and integrate them into all-encompassing data security policies.

CONCLUSION

To sum up, the data security software ecosystem is rapidly changing to match the requirements of an ever-evolving digital environment. The significance of strong data security procedures cannot be emphasized as firms continue to digitalize their operations and manage huge amounts of sensitive information. This investigation into data security software has shown the many ways in which it may prevent harm from happening, from traditional risks like hacking and data breaches to more recent ones like those posed by quantum computing and the Internet of Things.

Data security software components like encryption, access control, and intrusion detection are built upon the pillars of confidentiality, integrity, and availability. In addition to keeping sensitive information safe, businesses can gain trust and regulatory compliance, protect intellectual property, and reduce financial and reputational risks by employing data security measures. Data security software has a bright future that will be shaped by emerging technologies and novel approaches. The industry's dedication to staying ahead of future dangers is demonstrated by initiatives like integrating AI and ML for threat detection, adopting zero-trust architectures, and investigating homomorphic encryption and blockchain technologies.

Data security solutions that take a proactive and adaptable approach to cybersecurity should incorporate automated threat response, user-centric security, and continuous monitoring. Data security will eventually merge with larger cybersecurity activities as businesses attempt to adapt to an ever-changing environment. It is anticipated that unified security management systems, or integrated security platforms, will become the norm. When it comes to protecting sensitive information, data security software is now playing a more proactive role, one in which it anticipates and responds to new threats in order to keep businesses safe.

When it comes to the credibility, standing, and survival of businesses in today's linked and data-driven world, data security is more than just a technological requirement. Organizations may strengthen their defenses, construct more robust infrastructures, and win over the trust of their stakeholders if they take a comprehensive approach to cybersecurity and take advantage of the constant improvements in data security software.

REFERENCES

[1]   K.D. Martin, and P.E. Murphy, "The role of data privacy in marketing", *J. Acad. Mark. Sci.,* vol. 45, no. 2, pp. 135-155, 2017.
[http://dx.doi.org/10.1007/s11747-016-0495-4]

[2]   S. Rizvi, R.J. Orr, A. Cox, P. Ashokkumar, and M.R. Rizvi, "Identifying the attack surface for IoT network", *Internet of Things,* vol. 9, p. 100162, 2020.
[http://dx.doi.org/10.1016/j.iot.2020.100162]

[3]   G. Zyskind, and O. Nathan, *Decentralizing privacy: Using blockchain to protect personal data. in 2015 IEEE security and privacy workshops.* IEEE, 2015.

[4]   M. Mittal, A. Khan, and C. Agrawal, "A Study of Different Intrusion Detection and Prevension System", *Int. J. Sci. Eng. Res.,* vol. 4, no. 8, pp. 1526-1531, 2013.

[5]   R. Nyarko, *Security of Big Data: Focus on Data Leakage Prevention.* DLP, 2018.

[6]   S. Mittal, M.A. Khan, D. Romero, and T. Wuest, "A critical review of smart manufacturing & Industry 4.0 maturity models: Implications for small and medium-sized enterprises (SMEs)", *J. Manuf. Syst.,* vol. 49, pp. 194-214, 2018.
[http://dx.doi.org/10.1016/j.jmsy.2018.10.005]

[7]   C.P. Pfleeger, and S.L. Pfleeger, *Analyzing computer security: A threat/vulnerability/countermeasure approach.* Prentice Hall Professional, 2012.

[8]   A. McIlwraith, *Information security and employee behaviour: how to reduce risk through employee education, training and awareness.* Routledge, 2021.
[http://dx.doi.org/10.4324/9780429281785]

[9]   F. Banterle, *The interface between data protection and IP law: the case of trade secrets and the database sui generis right in marketing operations, and the ownership of raw data in big data analysis.* Springer, 2018.

[10]   M. Islam, and S. Reza, "The rise of big data and cloud computing", *Internet of Things and Cloud Computing,* vol. 7, no. 2, p. 45, 2019.
[http://dx.doi.org/10.11648/j.iotcc.20190702.12]

[11]   B. Brown, M. Chui, and J. Manyika, "Are you ready for the era of 'big data'", *McKinsey Q.,* vol. 4, no. 1, pp. 24-35, 2011.

[12]   P. Formosa, M. Wilson, and D. Richards, "A principlist framework for cybersecurity ethics", *Comput. Secur.,* vol. 109, p. 102382, 2021.
[http://dx.doi.org/10.1016/j.cose.2021.102382]

[13]   A. Alshamrani, S. Myneni, A. Chowdhary, and D. Huang, "A survey on advanced persistent threats: Techniques, solutions, challenges, and research opportunities", *IEEE Commun. Surv. Tutor.,* vol. 21, no. 2, pp. 1851-1877, 2019.
[http://dx.doi.org/10.1109/COMST.2019.2891891]

[14]   C.M. Gupta, and D. Kumar, "Identity theft: a small step towards big financial crimes", *J. Financ. Crime,* vol. 27, no. 3, pp. 897-910, 2020.
[http://dx.doi.org/10.1108/JFC-01-2020-0014]

[15]   G. Park, "The changing wind of data privacy law: A comparative study of the European Union's General Data Protection Regulation and the 2018 California Consumer Privacy Act", *UC Irvine L. Rev.,* vol. 10, p. 1455, 2019.

[16]   P. Cornish, *Cyber security and the UK's critical national infrastructure.* A Chatham House Report, 2011, pp. 11-50.

[17]   E. McCallister, *Guide to protecting the confidentiality of personally identifiable information.* vol. Vol. 800. Diane Publishing, 2010.
[http://dx.doi.org/10.6028/NIST.SP.800-122]

[18]   S. Pearson, and A. Benameur, "Privacy, security and trust issues arising from cloud computing", *2010 IEEE Second International Conference on Cloud Computing Technology and Science,* IEEE., 2010.
[http://dx.doi.org/10.1109/CloudCom.2010.66]

[19]   I. Kashukeev, S. Denchev, and I. Garvanov, *Data security model in cloud computing.,* vol. 5, Industry 4.0, no. 2, pp. 55-58, 2020.

[20]   S. Samonas, and D. Coss, "The CIA strikes back: Redefining confidentiality, integrity and availability in security", *Journal of Information System Security,* vol. 10, no. 3, 2014.

[21]   E. Bauer, and R. Adams, *Reliability and availability of cloud computing.* John Wiley & Sons, 2012.
[http://dx.doi.org/10.1002/9781118393994]

[22]   M. Lagana, *Information security in an ever-changing threat landscape, in The Routledge Companion to Risk, Crisis and Security in Business.* Routledge., 2018, pp. 255-271.
[http://dx.doi.org/10.4324/9781315629520-17]

[23]   D. Chen, and H. Zhao, *Data security and privacy protection issues in cloud computing. in 2012 international conference on computer science and electronics engineering.* IEEE, 2012.

[24]   G. Johansen, *Digital forensics and incident response: Incident response techniques and procedures to respond to modern cyber threats.* Packt Publishing Ltd., 2020.

[25]   J.M. Stewart, *Network Security, Firewalls and VPNs.* Jones & Bartlett Publishers, 2013.

[26]   D.P. Möller, *Intrusion detection and prevention, in Guide to Cybersecurity in Digital Transformation: Trends, Methods, Technologies, Applications and Best Practices.* Springer., 2023, pp. 131-179.
[http://dx.doi.org/10.1007/978-3-031-26845-8_3]

[27]   S. Alneyadi, E. Sithirasenan, and V. Muthukkumarasamy, "A survey on data leakage prevention systems", *J. Netw. Comput. Appl.,* vol. 62, pp. 137-152, 2016.
[http://dx.doi.org/10.1016/j.jnca.2016.01.008]

[28]   H. H. Khanh, and A. Khang, ""The Role of Artificial Intelligence in Blockchain Applications", *Reinventing Manufacturing and Business Processes through Artificial Intelligence,* vol. 2, In Rana G, Khang A., Sharma R., Goel A. K., Dubey A. K. CRC Press., pp. 20-40, 2021.
[http://dx.doi.org/10.1201/9781003145011-2]

[29]   S.P. Banerjee, and D.L. Woodard, "Biometric authentication and identification using keystroke dynamics: A survey", *Journal of Pattern recognition research,* vol. 7, no. 1, pp. 116-139, 2012.
[http://dx.doi.org/10.13176/11.427]

[30]   C. Sheth, and R. Thakker, "Performance evaluation and comparative analysis of network firewalls", *2011 International Conference on Devices and Communications (ICDeCom),* IEEE., 2011.
[http://dx.doi.org/10.1109/ICDECOM.2011.5738566]

[31]   D.A. Kumar, and S. Venugopalan, "Intrusion detection systems: a review", *International Journal of Advanced Research in Computer Science,* vol. 8, no. 8, pp. 356-370, 2017.
[http://dx.doi.org/10.26483/ijarcs.v8i8.4703]

[32]   M.K. Kagita, *A review on cyber crimes on the Internet of Things.* Deep Learning for Security and Privacy Preservation in IoT, 2022, pp. 83-98.

[33]   G. González-Granadillo, S. González-Zarzosa, and R. Diaz, "Security information and event management (SIEM): analysis, trends, and usage in critical infrastructures", *Sensors (Basel),* vol. 21, no. 14, p. 4759, 2021.
[http://dx.doi.org/10.3390/s21144759] [PMID: 34300500]

[34]   A. Khang, V. Hahanov, G.L. Abbas, and V.A. Hajimahmud, "Cyber-Physical-Social System and İncident Management", In: *AI-Centric Smart City Ecosystems: Technologies, Design and Implementation (1st Ed.)* vol. 2. CRC Press., 2022, p. 15.
[http://dx.doi.org/10.1201/9781003252542-2]

[35]   I. Pelle, F. Paolucci, B. Sonkoly, and F. Cugini, "Latency-sensitive edge/cloud serverless dynamic deployment over telemetry-based packet-optical network", *IEEE J. Sel. Areas Comm.,* vol. 39, no. 9, pp. 2849-2863, 2021.
[http://dx.doi.org/10.1109/JSAC.2021.3064655]

[36]   I. Zulifqar, S. Anayat, and I. Kharal, "A Review of Data Security Challenges and their Solutions in Cloud Computing", *International Journal of Information Engineering and Electronic Business,* vol. 13, no. 3, pp. 30-38, 2021.
[http://dx.doi.org/10.5815/ijieeb.2021.03.04]

[37]   R. Yeluri, and E. Castro-Leon, *Building the Infrastructure for Cloud Security: A Solutions View.* Springer Nature, 2014.
[http://dx.doi.org/10.1007/978-1-4302-6146-9]

[38]   Dhru N., "Innovate While Staying Compliant", In: *Office 365 for Healthcare Professionals. Apress, Berkeley, CA,* 2018, pp. 53-74.
[http://dx.doi.org/10.1007/978-1-4842-3549-2_3]

[39]   M.G. Avram, "Advantages and challenges of adopting cloud computing from an enterprise perspective", *Procedia Technol.,* vol. 12, pp. 529-534, 2014.
[http://dx.doi.org/10.1016/j.protcy.2013.12.525]

[40]   N. Kaloudi, and J. Li, "The ai-based cyber threat landscape: A survey", *ACM Comput. Surv.,* vol. 53, no. 1, pp. 1-34, 2021. [CSUR].
[http://dx.doi.org/10.1145/3372823]

[41]   B. Hammi, S. Zeadally, and J. Nebhen, "Security threats, countermeasures, and challenges of digital supply chains", *ACM Comput. Surv.,* vol. 55, no. 14s, pp. 1-40, 2023.
[http://dx.doi.org/10.1145/3588999]

[42]   M. Zwilling, G. Klien, D. Lesjak, Ł. Wiechetek, F. Cetin, and H.N. Basim, "Cyber security awareness, knowledge and behavior: A comparative study", *J. Comput. Inf. Syst.,* vol. 62, no. 1, pp. 82-97, 2022.
[http://dx.doi.org/10.1080/08874417.2020.1712269]

[43]   Y. Zou, "YouMight'Be Affected: An Empirical Analysis of Readability and Usability Issues in Data Breach Notifications", *in Proceedings of the 2019 CHI Conference on Human Factors in Computing Systems,* 2019.

[44]   M. Xiao, and M. Guo, "Computer network security and preventive measures in the age of big data", *Procedia Comput. Sci.,* vol. 166, pp. 438-442, 2020.
[http://dx.doi.org/10.1016/j.procs.2020.02.068]

[45]   I. Confente, G.G. Siciliano, B. Gaudenzi, and M. Eickhoff, "Effects of data breaches from user-generated content: A corporate reputation analysis", *Eur. Manage. J.,* vol. 37, no. 4, pp. 492-504, 2019.
[http://dx.doi.org/10.1016/j.emj.2019.01.007]

[46]   P.P. Swire, and R.E. Litan, *None of your business: world data flows, electronic commerce, and the European privacy directive.* Rowman & Littlefield, 2010.

[47]   A. Khang, K.C. Rath, S.K. Satapathy, A. Kumar, S.R. Das, and M.R. Panda, "Enabling the Future of Manufacturing: Integration of Robotics and IoT to Smart Factory Infrastructure in Industry 4.0", In: *Handbook of Research on AI-Based Technologies and Applications in the Era of the Metaverse.,* A. Khang, V. Shah, S. Rani, Eds., IGI Global, 2023, pp. 25-50.
[http://dx.doi.org/10.4018/978-1-6684-8851-5.ch002]

[48]   A.E. Omolara, A. Alabdulatif, O.I. Abiodun, M. Alawida, A. Alabdulatif, W.H. Alshoura, and H. Arshad, "The internet of things security: A survey encompassing unexplored areas and new insights", *Comput. Secur.,* vol. 112, p. 102494, 2022.
[http://dx.doi.org/10.1016/j.cose.2021.102494]

[49]   W. Ding, Z. Yan, and R.H. Deng, "Encrypted data processing with Homomorphic Re-Encryption", *Inf.*

Sci., vol. 409-410, pp. 35-55, 2017.
[http://dx.doi.org/10.1016/j.ins.2017.05.004]

[50]   Y.I. Alzoubi, A. Al-Ahmad, H. Kahtan, and A. Jaradat, "Internet of things and blockchain integration: security, privacy, technical, and design challenges", *Future Internet,* vol. 14, no. 7, p. 216, 2022.
[http://dx.doi.org/10.3390/fi14070216]

[51]   M. Grobler, R. Gaire, and S. Nepal, "User, usage and usability: Redefining human centric cyber security. Frontiers in big", *Frontiers in Big Data,* vol. 4, p. 583723, 2021.
[http://dx.doi.org/10.3389/fdata.2021.583723] [PMID: 33748750]

SUBJECT INDEX

A

Access 275, 279, 298, 299
  control techniques 298
  disk management 275, 279
  management 299
Activity monitoring 70
Address cyber threats 19
Advanced 158, 294, 306
  forensic format (AFF) 158
  persistent threats (APTs) 294, 306
Algorithms 65, 66, 88, 132, 141, 169, 182, 203, 208
  clustering 132
  cryptographic 208
Anti-forensic 19, 20, 166, 171
  methods 19, 20
  techniques 20, 166, 171
Anti-Malware 13, 298
  and antivirus protection 298
  technologies 13
Antivirus 13, 36, 37, 43, 46, 68, 298
  protection 298
  software 13, 36, 37, 43, 46, 68
Authentication 66, 67, 70, 155, 214, 296, 300
  biometric 67, 214
Authentication techniques 15, 213
  biometric 213
Automated threat 19, 310
  hunting technologies 19
  response methods 310
Automated tools 218

B

Bad sectors scanning 111
Balancing 296, 297
  availability and integrity 297
  CIA in data security 296
  integrity and confidentiality 297
Benefits of dynamic disks 271
Biometric data 300

Blockchain 19, 21, 57, 141, 169, 289, 310, 311
  -based data integrity 141
  -based systems 19
  forensics 21
  systems 19
  technology 19, 21, 141, 169, 310, 311

C

California consumer privacy act (CCPA) 294, 307
CHKDSK 238
  launching 238
  log 238
Chronological order 148, 151
CHS 280, 281
  conventions 280
  geometry 281
Cloud 17, 18, 22, 109, 141, 169, 170, 203, 257, 260, 284, 304
  backups 109
  computing and remote storage 170
  forensics 22, 170
  services 17, 18, 141, 169, 203, 257, 260, 284, 304
Cloud-based 22, 291
  deployments 291
  telemetry data 22
Cloud storage 20, 42, 50, 52, 107, 109, 122, 141, 142, 257, 259, 260
  integration 109, 259
  platforms 141
  services 20, 259, 260
Cluster-based allocation method 192
Coatings 85
  magnetic 85
  thin 85
Computer forensic 16, 17, 161, 164
  methods 161
  techniques 164
  procedures 16